Gallica

ISSN 1749–091X

General Editor: Sarah Kay

Gallica aims to provide a forum for the best current work in medieval and Renaissance French studies. Literary studies are particularly welcome and preference is given to works written in English, although publication in French is not excluded.

Proposals or queries should be sent in the first instance to the editor, or to the publisher, at the addresses given below; all submissions receive prompt and informed consideration.

Professor Sarah Kay, Department of French and Italian, Princeton University, 303 East Pyne, Princeton, NJ 08544, USA
The Managing Editor, Gallica, Boydell & Brewer Ltd, PO Box 9, Woodbridge, Suffolk IP12 3DF, UK

LETTERING THE SELF
IN MEDIEVAL AND EARLY MODERN FRANCE

Katherine Kong

D. S. BREWER

First published 2010
D. S. Brewer, Cambridge

ISBN 978–1–84384–231–6

D. S. Brewer is an imprint of Boydell & Brewer Ltd
PO Box 9, Woodbridge, Suffolk IP12 3DF, UK
and of Boydell & Brewer Inc.
668 Mt Hope Avenue, Rochester, NY 14620, USA
website: www.boydellandbrewer.com

A catalogue record for this title is available
from the British Library

The publisher has no responsibility for the continued existence or
accuracy of URLs for external or third-party internet websites
referred to in this book, and does not guarantee that any content
on such websites is, or will remain, accurate or appropriate

This publication is printed on acid-free paper

Printed in Great Britain by
CPI Antony Rowe, Chippenham and Eastbourne

Contents

Acknowledgements

It is a great pleasure to acknowledge the many debts I have incurred in writing this book. I am grateful to Catherine Brown, Frieda Ekotto, George Hoffmann, Peggy McCracken, and Charles Witke, who encouraged me from the earliest stages of this project. At the University of Michigan, many colleagues in Comparative Literature, Romance Languages and Literatures, and the medieval and early modern studies community provided useful feedback and stimulation, and I am grateful for financial support from the Program in Comparative Literature, the Rackham School of Graduate Studies and the Institute for Research on Women and Gender at various stages in my research. At the University of Tennessee, generous support from the Department of Modern Foreign Languages and Literatures, the Humanities Initiative, the Chancellor's Office, and the Exhibit, Performance, and Publication Expenses Fund have enabled me to complete the writing and preparation of my manuscript, and conversations and collaborations with my many colleagues in MFLL and the Marco Institute for Medieval and Renaissance Studies have enriched my thinking and research.

In particular I would like to thank Leah Chang, who has read the entire manuscript in its various stages and sustained the project with her sound judgment and good humor. Laura Howes, Rachel Golden, and members of the Renaissance Humanisms Faculty Research Seminar and the ongoing research and writing workshops organized by the Humanities Initiative have read portions of the manuscript and offered useful feedback. Sylvie Lefèvre provided invaluable advice and bibliography at the final stages. Last but certainly not least I wish to thank my family and above all my parents Tricia and Andrew Kong and my husband Aaron Nathan for their steadfast support of me and my work.

An expanded version of a portion of Chapter 3 appeared in "Rhetorical Teaching in the *Epistre au Dieu d'Amours*" in *Dalhousie French Studies* 78, Spring (2007): 3–15. I am grateful to *Dalhousie French Studies* and Heldref Publications for their permission to re-use portions of this material.

Introduction

The widely read allegorical and encyclopedic thirteenth-century *Roman de la rose* features a letter with an important role to play. This is not a love letter, as we might expect given the framing story of the *Rose*, but rather a letter of clemency. Nature wishes to offer terms to defectors to the army of the God of Love: they can gain absolution for their treachery in exchange for renewed loyalty to her. This is a matter of considerable importance, and Nature dictates her letter to Genius, who is also charged to deliver the message. Because this is an allegory, we can expect that certain elements in the story are not necessarily to be taken at face value. However, allegorical interpretation cannot resolve the discrepancy between Nature's message of more than two thousand lines and Genius's delivery of it, which is not at all a word-for-word account – in fact it is only about half as long. This episode also presents a problem of terminology: given the oral nature and content of Nature's missive, it is perhaps not surprising that it is called a "confession," and since it offers terms to defectors it is reasonably called a "sentence" and a "pardon"; however it is also a referred to as a "letre," "charte," and "sermon."[1] This multiplicity of function and terminology points to some of the fundamental questions of this study: what was a medieval letter? How do we read it? What can it tell us about its writer?

The episode of Nature's letter suggests that medieval letters differed in function and practice in dramatically different ways from letters today. The medieval letter was not a document that transparently made requests or reported news; it was a complicated composition that had distinct administrative, artistic, and communicative functions. It also offered a way to represent the self in relation to its various others: social superiors

---

[1] Guillaume de Lorris and Jean de Meun, lines 16730, 19496, 19408, 19501, 20668, respectively. Constable writes on synonyms for letters (*littera, epistola, libellus*) in *The Letters of Peter the Venerable* vol. 2, 3; Gerald Bond expands on the variety of terms to include *carta, cartula, opus, opusculum,* and *tabulae*, and pronounces: "the letter's variety was extreme," *The Loving Subject*, 47.

and subordinates; friends and lovers; teachers and students; allies and adversaries; patrons and supplicants; members of a spiritual community. These relationships were expressed both in the content and form of letters: the *ars dictaminis*, the highly rule-bound medieval discipline of letter writing, structured the expression of these relationships by prescribing epistolary elements that reflected the respective social status of correspondents.

However, letter writers did not simply follow established epistolary rules and conventions. They also actively navigated letter-writing rules to convey complicated and even coded personal and public messages, and to express contradictory and sometimes illicit relationships. By manipulating the positions codified by letter-writing rules, writers experimented with and challenged social roles, and in the process, I argue, defined concepts of personal identity and ways of thinking about the self. Thus, letters offer an invaluable window onto how premodern people conceived of the self, accepted and resisted socially determined positions, and, in some instances, tried to reshape them. Before examining some of these broader social functions of medieval letters, which is the primary focus of this book, I will first discuss their distinct forms, and the ways in which letter-writing norms were established.

The Influence of the *Ars Dictaminis*

The *ars dictaminis*, or art of composition, is critical for understanding the formal structures and conventions that governed the composition of letters. As a term it has come to apply to manuals that circulated letter-writing theory, letter-writing rules, and collections of sample letters, as well as the thriving discipline that taught letter writing in schools across Europe; all of these played an important role in the spread and standardization of letter-writing rules and conventions.[2] As scholars of epistolography point out, however, these manuals did not invent new rules and conventions for letter writing. Rather, they reflected what had probably been prevailing letter-writing practice for some time.[3] The first such

---

[2] Patt discusses the distinctions between the earliest texts in the dictaminal tradition and the varieties of letter writing manuals. Bibliography on the *ars dictaminis* is vast and complicated by generic overlap between letter writing, grammar, and rhetoric; for a useful introduction and bibliography see Murphy's "*Ars dictaminis*: The Art of Letter-Writing" in his *Rhetoric in the Middle Ages*; Murphy's *Medieval Rhetoric*; Camargo's *Ars Dictaminis Ars Dictandi*; and Poster and Utz's "A Bibliography of Medieval Latin Dictamen."

[3] Although this does not of course preclude continued development and refinement;

manuals were produced in Italy, and similar texts soon appeared in other areas of Europe.[4] What the manuals taught was largely the same: the *ars dictaminis* covered all forms of Latin composition and included a significant grammatical component, and its chief contribution was the teaching and practice of letter writing.[5]

The influence of the *ars dictaminis* is evidenced by the great number of letter-writing texts that were produced; the incorporation of letter writing into school and university instruction; and a widespread adherence to its rules, in particular the principal epistolary elements, in medieval correspondence.[6] As an administrative and communicative tool the letter was indispensable, and knowledge of letter writing was often a prerequisite for pursuing a career in administration; it could even be lucrative.[7] Intellectually, the cultivation of letter-writing practices and one of its dominant themes, friendship, was part of a classical inheritance that was particularly celebrated in the Middle Ages. Therefore, participation in epistolary culture could also constitute a learned, elite act, signaling erudition through the continuation of classical forms. Finally, for a number of reasons, there was a dramatic increase in the volume of letters and the variety of subject matter they treated in the eleventh and twelfth centuries.[8] All of these factors contribute to this period being called the "Golden Age of Medieval Epistolography."[9]

One the lasting teachings of the *ars dictaminis* concerned the varieties

---

the point is that the conventions were already in place, and the *dictatores* – teachers and practitioners of letter-writing theory, as distinguished from *notares*, professional letter writers – were not inventing letter-writing rules so much as working with developed, received epistolary traditions.

4 See Witt for an account of the spread of the *ars dictaminis* from Italy, 68–83; Murphy, "The Art of Letter-Writing;" and Richardson, 56–8.

5 Patt provides an account of the origins of the *ars dictaminis* and discusses the early transmission of these texts, as well as the development of the *ars dictaminis* in the context of the rise of other disciplines, such as law and rhetoric. See Faulhaber for a discussion of the *ars dictaminis* in Spain in *Latin Rhetorical Theory in Thirteenth and Fourteenth Century Castile* and "Rhetoric in Medieval Catalonia." Polak has compiled a census of dictaminal manuscripts in *Medieval and Renaissance Letter Treatises and Form Letters*.

6 Peter of Blois reveals some of the methods by which *dictamen* was learned: "[i]t was very valuable to me to be compelled in adolescence to learn by heart and repeat the urbane and elegant letters of Bishop Hildebert of Le Mans," cited by Southern, 117.

7 Patt, 134–5; Murphy, *Rhetoric in the Middle Ages*, 263–5; Richardson, 58.

8 See Patt, and Constable, *Letters and Letter-Collections*, on the social factors and intellectual and cultural traditions contributing to this development; and Camargo, *Ars Dictaminis Ars Dictandi*, especially 31–2.

9 Constable, *Letters and Letter-Collections*, 31.

and constituent parts of a letter. One anonymous letter-writing manual offers a definition of a letter:

> Est igitur epistola congrua sermonum ordinatio ad exprimendam intentionem delegantis institua. vel aliter epistola est oratio ex constitutis sibi partibus congrue ac distincte conposita delegantis affectum plene significans.[10]

> An epistle or letter, then, is a suitable arrangement of words set forth to express the intended meaning of its sender. Or in other words, a letter is a discourse composed of coherent yet distinct parts signifying fully the sentiments of its sender.[11]

While this seems a straightforward definition, this manual sets forth quite elaborate directions governing the composition of a letter, including a discussion of a letter's required parts, and instructions for rearranging the order of these parts and the shortening of a letter. It is noteworthy that these often quite numerous compositional prescriptions did not seem to hinder what a modern reader might consider the meaning of a letter; rather, the "suitable arrangement" of words and parts seems central to the success of "signifying the sentiments of the sender." One of the aims of this book is to examine this relationship between form and content, between the constituent parts of letters and the ways in which formal elements, far from constituting empty rhetorical gestures, could be employed to express complicated, at times contradictory, and often quite personal meanings.

In general, letters consisted of five principal elements: the *salutatio* or salutation, a particularly developed part of a letter that indicated the status of the sender and the recipient; the *captatio benevolentiae,* a securing of goodwill often consisting of a scriptural quotation or general saying to put the recipient into a favorable frame of mind for granting the request of the letter; the *narratio,* a narration of circumstances leading to the *petitio* or petition, articulating the specific request of the letter; and the *conclusio,* or conclusion.[12] Each of the requisite elements had a

---

10 *Rationes dictandi*, in *Briefsteller und Formelbücher,* ed. Rockinger, vol. 1, 10.

11 Anonymous of Bologna, *The Principles of Writing,* in *Three Medieval Rhetorical Arts,* trans. and ed. Murphy, 7.

12 Anonymous of Bologna, *The Principles of Writing,* 7. Murphy elaborates on this structure and its relation to the classical oration in *Rhetoric in The Middle Ages,* 224–5. There was as might be expected some variation in the number and naming of parts but the basic epistolary functions seem consistent; for example Hugh of Bologna does not treat the *captatio* as a separate element but rather a function of several parts of a letter; Murphy, *Rhetoric in The Middle Ages,* 220.

specific role to play in conveying the message as persuasively as possible. And, while the couching of the request was very important, equally significant was the situating of the addressee, with great care taken to acknowledge his or her position – which was of course not merely a question of accuracy but also an opportunity to apply flattery or exercise authority; letter writing was a highly refined rhetorical art. This five-part structure seems to have been one of the most enduring and observed of the precepts advanced by the *ars dictaminis*.

Despite this seemingly straightforward five-part structure, letter-writing prescriptions could be quite elaborate. This same manual details seventeen categories of salutation, varying in regard to the respective social positions of the writer and the addressee.[13] C. Julius Victor's *Ars rhetorica* articulates this concern with relative social status, setting forth general rules for respecting ranks of persons in letter writing:

> Epistola, si superiori scribas, ne iocularis sit; si pari, ne inhumana; si inferiori, ne superba ... Praefationes ac subscriptiones litterarum computandae sunt pro discrimine amicitiae aut dignitatis, habita ratione consuetidinis.[14]

> If you write to superiors, a letter ought not to be jocular; if to equals, not unpolished; if to inferiors, not haughty ... Prefaces and subscriptions to letters ought to be drawn up for the distinguishing of friendship or rank, with the rule of custom taken into account.

Although written in the fourth century, this account identifies a key element of letter writing that distinguishes epistolary theory and practice for centuries to come: status, and the role of the letter in communicating it. Formal elements of letters and their conventional use were not merely rhetorical gestures, but conveyed specific meaning and played a critical role in obtaining the request that was the ostensible purpose for writing the letter: tone, preface, and subscription, all reflected the relationship of

[13] LeBlanc cites another example: "The *Practica sive usus dictaminis* (c. 1300?) by Lawrence of Aquilegia represents an extreme example of this tendency to guide composition. With its charts of letter parts, linking words and sample clauses, this manual virtually eliminated the need for individual invention," 33.

[14] C. Julius Victor, *Ars rhetorica*, 448.16–7, 23–5, in *Rhetores Latini minores*, ed. Halm, 371–448, cited by Lanham, 89–90, my translation. Murphy observes that Victor's is the first discussion of *epistola* in the works of a Roman rhetorician, suggesting that there was no need for such a discussion in classical Rome, when "eloquent letters ... were expected to be the product of a broad rhetorical education," and implying that the appearance of this *ars* corresponded to a post-classical decline in rhetorical education; *Rhetoric in the Middle Ages*, 195.

the correspondents and their respective social rank.[15] This demonstrates the importance of social status in the composition of a letter; it also suggests that letters played an important role in creating this status.

In common with later *dictatores*, or teachers and practitioners of letter-writing theory, Victor's account of the positioning of the self in respect to its epistolary others insists on a hierarchical view of society: for letter writers, correspondents were superiors, equals, or inferiors, with differences among *dictatores* in the composition of these groups.[16] Giles Constable discusses how this tri-partite division was more than an organizational device for letter writers; he argues that the structure of medieval society can be deduced from letter-writing theory. This is one way in which letter writing can help us understand the contours of the medieval self: in the ways it articulates the larger groups within which these selves were situated.[17] I suggest that this view of the structure of society offers important insight into how medieval people viewed themselves – not only as members of a particular group, but also relationally, as inferior or superior to others. While I am not suggesting that the premodern self was first and foremost a hierarchized self, the evidence of the *ars dictaminis* shows how a particular group of writers and teachers theorized ways of thinking about society that describe the individual relationally and hierarchically. While their larger frame was status and the representation of individual in respect to others, their prescriptions and classifications provide a starting point for examining the constitution of a medieval self, which, as it is described in letters, resonates with how we continue to conceive of selfhood and identity today.

The Epistolary Situation

Medieval letters also represented medieval selves in other, more tangible ways, suggested by the very term *ars dictaminis*: *dictamen* derives from the intensive form of the verb *dico, dicere*, to speak, and *dictare* came to signify "to write" or "to compose": medieval letters had a distinctly oral

---

[15] Constable calls this epistolary observation of status one of the "most serious responsibilities of professional letter-writers in the Middle Ages," "The Structure of Medieval Society," 253.

[16] *Dictatores* did differ in some particulars, such as the descriptions of social classes and their members; Constable, "The Structure of Medieval Society," 253 and passim.

[17] While her focus is on spiritual and theological texts, Bynum also argues for the importance of the group in understanding the twelfth-century self in "Did the Twelfth Century Discover the Individual?"

component.[18] Practically speaking, this meant that letters were often dictated to scribes – as in the *Rose*, when Nature dictates her message to Genius. Scholars of the epistolary genre generally agree that letters originated as oral messages, necessitated by distance separating interlocutors. Termed the "epistolary situation," this distance was bridged by sending messengers entrusted with oral communications, assigning to the written letter an often secondary importance, consisting of reminders to the messenger.[19] Further underscoring the orality of medieval letters, messengers often read letters to their recipients, as literacy could not be assumed, even in aristocratic households, and the letter could well be read aloud to those present at the messenger's arrival.[20] Therefore, it seems safe to say that there was no guarantee of a private letter, at least in the way we think of it today.[21]

However, while it might well have had its origins as a placeholder for an oral message, the physical letter had an important representative function. Conrad of Mure, a thirteenth-century *dictator*, claims it as one of the three primary epistolary functions:

> Epistola tribus de causis precipue fuit inventa, scilicet ut secreta per ipsam celentur, occultentur, et ut imperitia seu rusticitas portitoris seu exhibitoris litterarum non noceat mittentis intentioni, et ut localis corporum sequestratio seu distantia non impediat comodum seu colloquium amicorum[22]

---

[18] Patt, 133 n. 2; Camargo, *Ars Dictaminis Ars Dictandi*, 16; and Clanchy, *From Memory to Written Record*, 125–6, 271. Symes discusses the oral and performative nature of medieval culture in *A Common Stage*. Scholars of medieval epistolography, or letter-writing practice, agree that classical rhetoric and oratory exerted an undeniable influence on medieval epistolary forms; on the influence of ancient rhetoric on the development of the *ars dictaminis*, especially Cicero's *De inventione* and pseudo-Ciceronian *Rhetorica ad Herennium*, see Patt, 152 and n. 78, and Camargo, *Ars Dictaminis Ars Dictandi*, 19–20.

[19] Constable, *Letters and Letter-Collections*, 13–14.

[20] Constable, *Letters and Letter-Collections*, 52–5; Camargo explains: "in many cases the bearer was expected to elaborate on the letter's contents, to respond to questions about them, or to supplement them with confidential information delivered (orally) in private," "Where's the Brief?," 4 and passim on the distinction between the written missive and the oral message.

[21] Contributing to this public nature of letters is the fact that some writers kept copies of incoming and outgoing correspondence, and letters received could be preserved as rhetorical exemplars or symbols of status; Constable, *Letters and Letter-Collections*, 56–62.

[22] *Die Summa de arte prosandi des Konrad von Mure*, ed. Kronbichler, 30–1, cit. and trans. Camargo, "Where's the Brief?," 2, 15 n. 5.

> The epistle was invented chiefly for three reasons, namely so that through it secrets might be concealed [or] hidden, and so that the ignorance or lack of sophistication of the bearer or presenter of the letter might not mar the intent of the sender, and so that spatial distance or separation of bodies might not hinder the profit or intercourse of friends.

Conrad notes the importance of letters in imparting or dissimulating confidential information, attesting to the tenuous privacy of written communications. Referring to medieval methods of epistolary expedition, he seems to imply that messengers entrusted with oral communications might lack the ability effectively or even accurately to communicate the intent of the sender. While Genius was neither ignorant nor uncouth, his departures from Nature's message underscore the problems involved with the oral expedition of messages, which, according to Conrad, necessitated the development of the letter as more than a prompt for its bearer. Most important, he describes the representative function of letters as missives that bridge physical distance by bringing to readers the discourse of absent friends. Conrad is not alone in valuing this function of letters; many classical and medieval writers refer to it, as do nearly all of the letter writers studied in this book.

Ambrose also writes about this distance-spanning capacity of letters, describing it as a revivifying function: "Epistolarum genus propterea repertum, ut quidam nobis cum absentibus sermo sit" (The genre of letters was invented for this, that a friend, through speech, might be present to us when absent).[23] This presence in absence is not exclusive to letters exchanged between friends. An anonymous nun writing in the twelfth century at the religious community of Admont in Bavaria provides a vivid example of presence mediated through letters. In a letter to the archbishop of Salzburg describing her distress at having abandoned her child for the cloister, she cites the story of the Canaanite woman in the gospels of Matthew and Mark:

> Carrying her in my arms, therefore, I have recourse to you, lord father, and, throwing myself down, I place her before the feet of your lordship, and I wail and cry out in the place of and in the voice of the Canaanite woman: *Lord, have mercy on my little daughter.*[24]

---

[23] Epistle 66, *Patrologia Latina* vol. 16, col. 1225A, cited in Constable, *Letters and Letter-Collections*, 113.

[24] Beach, 47.

The anonymous nun writes as if she were present before the archbishop. She vivifies her biblical citation by identifying with the Canaanite woman in her subjugation and plea, in which her body and voice are represented by her letter. She puts the representational function of letters to literal and figurative use, demonstrating the vivid ways in which letters bridged distance between people and showing how letters could be more than representatives of their writers; in the hands of skilled writers, they could exert vivifying, near-talismanic force.

The story of the Canaanite woman is well known for many reasons, not least among them that it is the story in which a woman talks back to Christ and wins her plea after having been initially refused.[25] The anonymous nun's letter indexes gendered relations of authority and power, and it shows how they could be exploited in epistolary entreaty. One early epistolary text describes the ten "accidents of persons" to be considered in letter writing: "birth, sex, age, training, character ('ars'), office, behaviour ('mores'), disposition, name, and dignity," and the nun's letter is written to someone occupying a higher rank in regard to these "accidents."[26] Yet she is able to make her plea powerfully, and her abject humility reinforces the position of supreme benefaction in which she casts her addressee. Her letter shows how distinctions of status could be deployed to powerful effect, contributing to the goal of obtaining the *petitio*, here a matter of heart-wrenching maternal regret.

In premodern letters, expressions of humility often take highly complicated forms, with implications for the relations of power and authority that structure correspondence. And, while letter writers might well have had to take into account accidents of persons in the composition of letters, social distinctions and their implied positions could in turn be manipulated in letters. Although seemingly determinative of so much in letter writing, these distinctions did not necessarily foreclose exercises of epistolary rhetoric that transcended the limits of classificatory schemes by voicing supplication poignantly and forcefully, even compellingly. Letter writers observed social classifications for positioning themselves

---

[25] The Canaanite woman asks Christ to heal her daughter, and he refuses because he came to save the Israelites only: "It is not fair to take the children's bread and cast it to the dogs." She answers famously, "Yes, lord; for even the dogs eat of the crumbs that fall from their masters' table," and wins from Christ the concession: "O woman, great is thy faith! Let it be done to thee as thou wilt," Matthew 15.22–8.

[26] Constable, "The Structure of Medieval Society," 253, from an anonymous paragraph on *De epistolis* found in an eight-century manuscript at Monte Cassino, Paris, Bibl. nat., MS lat. 7530, cited in *Rhetores latini minores*, ed. Halm, 448 and 589.

in relation to their correspondents, but they also transgressed them, complicating the humility and authority they were meant to confer, and producing in the process new, distinct ways of thinking about the self. Thus the anonymous nun of Admont shows us how seemingly "inferior" positions could lodge powerful requests, how humility could be more than supplicatory, it could also be compelling, and perhaps even commanding.

To return to the framing questions of this book: what was a medieval letter? How do we read it? What might it tell us about the medieval self? The *ars dictaminis* is critical for understanding the formal structures and conventions that governed the composition of letters. However, contrary to the evidence of the *ars dictaminis*, letters were more than schoolbook exercises and administrative tools. I argue that, despite its prescriptive nature, the *ars dictaminis* actually invited experimentation: it provided a structure and vocabulary that required positioning the self in relation to others, yet rules invite play and transgression, and they are also necessarily limited – selves and relations often resist easy positioning. I have briefly examined the *ars dictaminis* to explain how letter-writing rules constituted a kind of script for writers and imposed particular ways of representing the self. In each chapter that follows, I focus on a particular set of letters to identify the different ways writers represented their epistolary selves in specific cultural and intellectual contexts, in some instances in compliance with dictaminal convention, in others bending the rules. I show how writers were aware of the significance of their epistolary acts in their observation and manipulation of letter-writing conventions, and also in their direct discussion of what was at stake in breaching them.

This negotiation of epistolary convention is often best seen in the back-and-forth of epistolary exchange, and to this end, *Lettering the Self* examines sets of correspondence, for the most part exchanged between women and men. It thus brings women's writing into dialogue with men's writing, and shows how women and men were equally subject to dictaminal rules, despite their different access to and employment of epistolary rhetoric. With the exception of recent critical attention to the letters of Abelard and Heloise, studies of medieval and early modern letters have traditionally focused on the collected letters of single authors, who were almost always men, or on the formal development of the genre, specifically in regard to the *ars dictaminis*. In contrast, I argue for the crucial role women writers played in the development of the epistolary genre, and in bringing into dialogue the letters of women and men, I consider how gender emerges in epistolary practice as a central way of understanding the self and positioning it relation to others.

One of the arguments of my book is that medieval letter-writing conventions continued to structure epistolary composition in the sixteenth century. In this way my book reveals an important point of continuity between the Middle Ages and the Renaissance, and thus reconsiders a more traditional periodization of the two periods. In this focus on premodern France, *Lettering the Self* brings a perhaps occluded aspect of the French literary tradition to greater attention: while the *ars dictaminis* originated and flourished in Italy, it had a lasting impact on letters in France; moreover, there is evidence that dictaminal elements were in place in French epistolography before the arrival of the Italian *ars*.[27] French writers continued avidly to practice the epistolary arts and significantly shaped the development of the epistolary genre, and even influenced Italian *dictamen* in turn.[28] Letter-writing manuals continued to be written for several centuries, and the preoccupation with letters culminated in the seventeenth- and eighteenth-century "republic of letters" persuasively examined by scholars such as Janet Gurkin Altman, Dena Goodman, and Elizabeth Goldsmith, and the explosion of epistolary fiction in France and England in the eighteenth century.[29] *Lettering the Self* thus fills an important gap in the history of the letter, and also in the story of the self.

[27] Bond points out that the "constitutive elements" of the *ars dictaminis* had been developed in France much earlier than the mid-twelfth century, which is when Italian *dictamen* is thought to have reached France; *The Loving Subject*, 45–6, and 223 n. 15.

[28] In the late twelfth century, two Italian *dictatores* noted that French *dictamen* differed from its Italian forebear in some forms of the salutation, its preference for placing proverbs in the *exordium*, its *cursus* or prose rhythm patterns, and its considerable attention to composition, Witt, 73–4; Camargo adds to these the use of *auctores*, *Ars Dictaminis Ars Dictandi* 33–5.

[29] The influence of the *ars dictaminis* lasted well beyond the twelfth century but its innovation peaked in the thirteenth century; Murphy, *Rhetoric in The Middle Ages* 267; a special issue of *Rhetorica*, edited by Camargo, dedicated to "The Waning of the Medieval *Ars Dictaminis*" attests to dictaminal influence into the Renaissance; see in particular Vulliez, "L'*ars dictaminis*, survivances et déclin;" Ward, "Rhetorical Theory and the Rise and Decline of *Dictamen*;" and Henderson, "Valla's *Elegantiae* and the Humanist Attack on the *Ars dictaminis*." Poster and Mitchell's *Letter-Writing Manuals and Instruction* traces a history of letter-writing manuals into the twentieth century. For an account of how the production of letter-writing manuals continued beyond the eighteenth century and shaped correspondence beyond the confines of Western Europe, see Bannet's *Empire of Letters*.

In Chapter 1, I examine the amorous verse epistles of abbot Baudri of
Bourgueil and the nun Constance of Angers. Baudri wrote erotic letters to
Constance, she responded in kind, and both characterized their exchange
as play. Anticipating criticism of his impassioned missives, Baudri
explains: "Whatever I do is a game." Yet their play is also serious: it
places both writers on equal footing, making them epistolary, if not
social, partners. Constance's response offers admiration, claims neglect,
declares jealousy – all customary elements of the genre. However, she
also resists her teacher's playfulness and criticizes his ambiguity,
teaching him in turn and breaking with epistolary tone and convention. I
examine their exchange in the context of the period, commonly referred
to as the twelfth-century renaissance, and its "Ovidian age." I read this
exchange against other contemporary learned Latin verse epistles in
order to understand their originality: few letter-reply sets survive from
this period, even fewer between men and women, and within this group,
none of this length and complexity. In these letters, a male teacher and his
female student "play" with scripted roles, experimenting with what it
meant to deviate from accepted literary scripts, and interrogating the
possibility of sincerity in highly stylized literary letters.

Chapter 2 focuses on the well-known letters of Heloise and Abelard.
Their correspondence, often considered part of the tradition of spiritual
direction of women by men through letters, has been perhaps more
famously celebrated for its expression of impassioned love. As they
jockey for position, she claiming the bonds of lover and wife, he insisting
on those of friendship and spiritual companionship, they make letters a
space for enacting and contesting the highly charged terms of their relationship. I consider how letter writing might serve as a vehicle to bring
about spiritual and emotional change, offering a tangible way to carry out
the conversion that Abelard demands and Heloise, for a time, resists.
Through writing, Heloise can perform the obedience Abelard demands;
through the writing of her contrition, she might actually begin to feel it. I
examine these letters in the context of the "lost" love letters attributed to
them, and how the self produced in both sets of correspondence is a
profoundly textual and specifically epistolary construct, for which letter
writing is posited – whether successful or not – as a means to effect a
radical transformation of will, of unrepentant desire and deep suffering.

In Chapter 3, I investigate Christine de Pizan's participation in the
querelle du Roman de la rose, the first literary debate in France, which
takes place in letters. The debate letters, as well as Christine's other epis-

tolary interventions (her prelude to the debate, the "Epistre au Dieu d'Amours"; her various editions of the *querelle* letters addressed to prospective patrons; and her hortatory letter to the Queen), show that letter writing offered a way for women to challenge gender stereotypes and claim the male authority traditionally associated with the culture of learned letter writing. Her letters actively contest received misogynist views and rewrite contemporary perspectives on women in relation to learned discourse – a largely clerical, masculine field. Her writings also implicitly question the gendered nature of epistolary authority, and in revealing the constructed nature of epistolary positions, they also reveal the constructed nature of gender positions.

Lettering the Self shows how two of the most celebrated writers and humanists of the French Renaissance, Marguerite de Navarre and Michel de Montaigne, were steeped in medieval letter-writing traditions. Chapter 4 explores the correspondence of Marguerite de Navarre and Guillaume Briçonnet, who is often described as her spiritual director. I consider how each writer articulates a distinct approach to spirituality through letter writing, employing epistolary conventions to pursue different projects – favor-seeking, the practice of affective spirituality, the expression of spiritual inquietude and lack. Their letters exploit the dynamics of call and response, supplication and acquiescence or refusal, structured by epistolary exchange. Marguerite's repeated appeals for help after more than three years of correspondence suggest that the quietude she sought, and which Briçonnet provided in his fashion, remained elusive. While this implies the limits of letter writing for producing spiritual change, it suggests that their value lies in their convention-laden and even formulaic nature: their codified positions do more for their writers than what they denotatively "say." Letters in this instance are not so much vehicles for transformation or contestation as they are a respite for the spiritual self, and in these letters Marguerite develops rhetorical strategies that profoundly shaped her later writings.

In the last chapter, I examine the epistolary writings of Michel de Montaigne and Etienne de La Boétie, whose friendship is immortalized in Montaigne's famous essay "De L'Amitié." La Boétie also elaborates a nuanced idea of friendship in his Latin verse epistles "Ad Michaelem Montanum." Formally and topically, their writing reveals its medieval roots: both writers are skillful epistolarians, and their correspondence shares many of the concerns of the letters examined in the preceding chapters: friendship, sex, pedagogy, misogyny. I argue that this celebrated friendship is not only dependent on letters for its expression, it is itself a product of their letters. Moreover, Montaigne's pioneering development of the essay, while motivated by the biographical loss of his friend, imports many elements from his correspondence with La Boétie. This reveals the importance of the epistolary for his literary experimentation, even as he offers an unflinching portrait of himself, his tastes, his shortcomings and character. My analysis offers a new consideration of the literary genre he develops, and traces its medieval and specifically epistolary heritage. I show how, in Montaigne's hands, the medieval epistolary tradition not only shapes the legacy of letter writing into the early modern period, it also points the way to new ways of – and new genres for – writing about the self.

1

Love Letters in the Monastery:
Ambiguous Lessons and Epistolary Play in the Verses of
Baudri of Bourgueil and Constance of Angers

Some time toward the end of the eleventh century or the beginning of the twelfth, Abbot Baudri of Bourgueil wrote a letter in verse to Constance of the convent of Le Ronceray praising her beauty and eloquence, extolling the virtues of virginity, and celebrating their special love. However, lest she misunderstand the nature of their relationship, he is quick to assure that

> Nolo vir esse tibi neque tu sis femina nobis;
>   Os et cor nostram firmet amiciciam.
> Pectora iungantur, sed corpora semoveantur;
>   Sit pudor in facto, sit iocus in calamo.[1]

> I do not want to be your husband, nor you to be my wife:
>   Let mouth and heart confirm our friendship.
> Let our hearts be joined, but our bodies remain apart;
>   Let the shame be in the act, let the game be in the pen.

Baudri seems eager to establish the terms of their relationship by clarifying what it is *not*. Protestation begets suspicion, however, and this passage from his letter-poem to Constance invites a few questions: what is the nature of their friendship, and why would it require clarification? To what shameful act is Baudri alluding? And how, exactly, are their hearts to be joined? His verse-epistle references a host of letter-writing genres and the relationships they imply, and when his playfully contradictory verse enters into dialogue with Constance's resistant reply – which is contradictory in its own way – they show how epistolary positions can be deployed to productive effect, creating new and specifically epistolary ways of thinking about and expressing the self.

---

[1] "Baudri of Bourgueil to Lady Constance (of Le Ronceray?) probably 1096–1106," in Bond, *The Loving Subject*, 172–3, lines 43–6. All citations and translations of this verse epistle are from this edition and are identified parenthetically in the text.

Baudri, abbot of Bourgueil-en-Vallé by the early 1080s and archbishop of Dol in 1107, produced diverse writings, including religious and historical works and amorous letter-poems.[2] He is considered part of a group of ecclesiastics referred to as the Loire poets who composed varied secular writings, including poems of a seemingly personal nature, addressed to fellow religious and to young men and women.[3] Given this seeming convention of playful and often amorous verse composition among his contemporaries, Baudri's eagerness to profess the innocence of his relationship with Constance is conspicuous.[4] It also scripts a particular kind of addressee: whether one to whom he had made amorous advances or one who had made advances to him, his letter creates an addressee with expectations to be deflected.

Baudri's letter also claims an addressee who is highly learned; his letter to Constance and her reply mark their erudition in various ways.[5] Their letters are composed in verse, and reflect the influence of the dictaminally prescribed five-part letter.[6] In their choice of epistolary genre and their assumption of the positions of teacher and student in their letters, they situate themselves within the traditions of didactic exchange and learned humanist friendship. Their letter-reply set also actively evokes the amatory through thematic and textual reference and form: Baudri's letter consists of eighty-nine elegiac couplets, the classical meter of choice for amorous verse; Constance replies in eighty-nine

----

[2] In addition to dozens of verse-epistles, Baudri wrote a history of the crusades and was Robert of Arbrissel's first biographer. Tilliette discusses the range of Baudri's works in his introduction to *Baudri de Bourgueil: Poèmes*, vol. 1, x–xii.

[3] Baudri, Marbod of Rennes, and Hildebert of Lavardin are often referred to as members of the "Loire school" of poets. Raby observes that writing letter-poems constituted a sort of "fashion" among them; for an overview of Baudri's poetic milieu see Raby's *A History of Christian-Latin Poetry*, 257–87 and *A History of Secular Latin Poetry*, vol. 1, 307–65.

[4] Marbod, Baudri's contemporary, wrote an apology for verses penned in his youth, but from the vantage point of a mature writer reviewing and regretting his early works; poem 1 ("De apto genere scribendi"), *Liber decem capitulorum*, lines 1–15.

[5] Constance's reply is one of only two in the manuscript of Baudri's poetic works from non-mythological and non-historical figures, the other being from a certain Odo (Carmen 204, "Versus Odonis ad abbatem") that is twenty-four lines long and does not appear with the letter to which it replies; Constance's lengthy letter immediately follows Baudri's.

[6] Although the *ars dictaminis* principally discussed prose composition, it influenced the composition of verse epistles as well. For more on the relationship between poetry and prose as they relate to the *ars dictaminis*, see Curtius, 148–54. LeBlanc examines the distinction between prose and verse epistles in late medieval and early modern France, 9 and 33–44.

elegiac couplets in turn, in *Heroides*-inflected tone.[7] Baudri seems to anticipate the multiple and perhaps contradictory readings his text might generate – didactic, humanist, amical, amatory – and accordingly offers instruction for reading his missive. Yet, I argue, this instruction is as ambiguous as the contradictory messages it purports to explain.

Constance's reply both accepts and resists the epistolary role Baudri's letter scripts, meeting epistolary conventions and expectations by replying in kind, but also exceeding them. She does not provide answers to the questions suggested by his epistle, and she is complicit in withholding information regarding the "real" nature of their relationship. And while her reply echoes Baudri's literally and figuratively, it also departs from it in important ways that invite new interpretations of the literary manifestation of the teacher-student relationship, medieval uses of classical literature – specifically, Ovid's *Heroides* – and the ambiguity of amorous and erotic discourse.

In its navigation of various epistolary scripts, this letter-reply set reveals the flexibility of seemingly fixed literary forms and conventions during this period of immense intellectual and poetic creativity, and it demonstrates the important role letters play in this creativity. In my close reading of Baudri and Constance's letter-reply set, informed by Baudri's other writings and those of his contemporaries, I examine the contradictory subject positions and relationships taken in these letters – amorous abbot and jealous nun, playful teacher and accusatory student – and how they emerge through the manipulation of various epistolary scripts – that is, established letter-writing traditions and conventions. I argue that "playing" with these scripts constitutes experimentation with the boundaries of established subject positions, investing letter writing with creative, transformative possibility.

---

[7] The most well-known exemplar in the Middle Ages of the elegiac couplet, which came into vogue for writing of love and eros during the Augustan age, was Ovid's *Heroides*. The *Heroides*, among Ovid's more widely read works in the Middle Ages, consists of letters from spurned mythological women, a love letter from Sappho, and letter-reply sets from famous lovers. While the authorship of many of the letters and in particular of the last six paired letters has been at various points disputed and reclaimed, in the Middle Ages the *Heroides* was read as a collection of single and paired letters; for a discussion of the composition and authorship of the double and single letters, see Hexter, 138–41.

Addressing the Reader, Positioning the Writer: How Baudri Writes His Love

Baudri's letter to Constance scripts a particular kind of reader, and it also scripts a particular kind of writer. The versifying abbot writes from conflicting positions: he is at once pious and flirtatious, moralizing and playful, friend, teacher, and lover. He activates these contradictory roles by referencing several established epistolary genres and their attendant relationships. In positioning himself as Constance's guide, offering instruction on matters ranging from chastity to appropriate reading material, he participates in a spiritual tradition with a history of expression through epistolary exchange: that of male religious authority figures addressing letters of guidance to women.[8] Notably, however, he writes in verse, an unusual choice for letters of direction.[9] Verse composition and letter writing were actively cultivated as a result of increasing interest in classical and "humanist" learning in this period, and in his practice of both Baudri was very much a writer of his time.[10] By the eleventh century, letters had become a distinct part of the intersecting development of monasticism, humanism, and friendship, all vital to the flourishing of learning known as the twelfth-century renaissance.[11] The Loire poets can

---

[8] This is a well-established tradition in the Middle Ages. Jerome's letters of spiritual guidance to virgins and widows, notably, were well known in this period. See also the example of Fortunatus and Radegund, and, of course, the letters of Abelard and Heloise, examined in Chapter 2.

[9] Otter examines a near-contemporary counter-example in her study of Goscelin's prose letter to Eva in "Entrances and Exits." This too is a multi-valent work, at once an "anthology of texts and excerpts," a "guide to meditation" and also a "personal letter, a lament, a consolation, and self-consolation," 283. Despite this similarity in operating in multiple registers, it is strikingly different in tone and implication, throwing Baudri's epistolary play into sharp relief.

[10] Baudri's verse is perhaps best understood in light of the concurrent popularity of the letter and classical Latin poetry, an important part of the intellectual climate of the late eleventh century. His writings consist of those produced during his abbacy, about 1078–1107, collected in a single extant manuscript, Vaticanus Reginensis Latinus 1351, and others located in diverse sources. While the exact date of the manuscript is uncertain, critics agree that it appears to have been written in his lifetime; Bond puts the date at about 1096 and suggests that it was likely an autograph copy, *The Loving Subject*, 43 and 222 n. 5. Carmen 1, "Contra obtrectatores consolatur librum suum" supports this view, in which Baudri details directions to his scribes in the preparation of his "liber."

[11] The term "renaissance" has been variously disputed, but scholars seem in agreement that it was a period of important development and growth in many disciplines that saw in particular increased attention to classical works and thinking; see, among many others, Haskins, *The Renaissance of the Twelfth Century*; Knowles, "The Renaissance of

be considered forerunners of this renaissance in their cultivation of amatory writings and laudatory verse that privileged what Gerald Bond has convincingly argued to be the "loving subject."[12] Bond's study uncovers the various factors that went into producing this subject at the turn of the twelfth century in Romanesque France. My study extends his by examining the specifically epistolary way in which this poetry gives voice to the self.

Within this intellectual context, one of Baudri's most immediately recognizable roles is that of friend. Friendship is a central relationship in the literature of this period, with particular significance for the monastic tradition.[13] It is inspired by Ciceronian *amicitia*, governed by *leges amicitiae* that prescribe appropriate behavior in friendship: this is a relationship that must be tended carefully, motivated not by desire for gain or advantage, but rather inspired by virtue.[14] Friendship, like letter writing, required careful cultivation, mindful of standards for judging its practice. Baudri, an adept practitioner of this style of friendship, offers seemingly disinterested advice to his addressees to guard their chastity and cleave to

the Eleventh and Twelfth Centuries"; Nitze, "The So-Called Twelfth Century Renaissance"; Benson et al., eds., *Renaissance and Renewal in the Twelfth Century*; and Colish, "The Renaissance of the Twelfth Century," in her *Medieval Foundations of the Western Intellectual Tradition*.

[12] Loire circle writing includes genres such as satire, debate, elegy, epigram, epitaph, dream vision, and didactic poems. These writers have been described as part of a "humanistic movement" consisting of "a loose association of Latin writers who laid the formation during the final decades of the eleventh century for the poetic renaissance of the twelfth," Bond, *The Loving Subject*, 42; Tilliette observes the "coloration particulièrement 'humaniste' dans la prérenaissance angevine," "Introduction," *Baudri de Bourgueil: Poèmes*, 34. Jaeger describes them as "originators of a culture of female praise that was to find its highpoint in vernacular love lyric," *Ennobling Love*, 85. Bond's "loving self" emerged from elite French culture around the turn of the twelfth century and constituted a new secular identity attuned to the uses and effects of persona in literary production.

[13] Raby observes that Baudri and his contemporaries "revived the cult of friendship which had graced the Carolingian court, and like the Carolingians they wrote epigrams and poetical epistles," *History of Secular Latin Poetry*, 338; see 178–247 and 306–60 for a longer discussion of Carolingian humanism and its relationship to French Latin poetry in the eleventh century. Leclercq credits medieval monks with the "rediscovery of a type of friendship" that he describes as "pure" and "disinterested," and that "solicits no favors," *The Love of Learning and the Desire for God*, 181. He writes of the medieval notion of friendship developing on a trajectory from Augustine, beginning with friendship which is "la charité en acte," necessary for *societas amicalis*. This becomes, through the centuries, a "service mutuel," and recovers some of its classical affect in "un élément sentimental" in letters and prayers of the twelfth century; "L'Amitié dans les lettres au moyen âge," 401.

[14] Ciceronian friendship is a serious affair with a civic and even patriotic charge: without it, cities and nations cannot endure; *Laelius de Amicitia*, Chapter 7.

virtue. He explicitly identifies himself as a friend in the opening lines of his poem to Constance: he proclaims himself an "amicus," who not only "scripsit" (wrote) but also "dictavit" (dictated) and "composuit" (composed) "versus," drawing attention to the multiple roles involved in the production of an epistle, and hinting at the complexity in the construction of his epistolary voice.[15]

Baudri develops this advice-giving role in his letters to Constance and to other women, in which he offers praise and extols the value of virginity.[16] He also insists on their uniqueness as the sole female recipients of his letters. Despite his assurances to Constance that "Nullam preter te carmina nostra sciunt" (my verses know none but you) (line 168), he does, in fact, address verses to other women, including Adela of Blois. Baudri repeats similar claims of exclusivity to a certain Muriel, that "Nulla recepit adhuc nisi tu mea carmina, virgo/Nulli dixit adhuc cartula nostra 'vale' " (up to now no one received my songs except you, maiden/to no one did my letter bid farewell).[17] When these letters are read together, Baudri appears as something of a flirtatious scoundrel. His claims of singularity of address lose their force through repetition, and raise the question of what in these letters can be read as sincere and what is merely a repeated formula.[18] Sincerity is of course difficult to determine, particularly in this stylized genre, yet a repeated formula does not necessarily indicate lack of sincerity, nor is it necessarily devoid of meaning. By claiming singularity of address, whether or not he writes truthfully, Baudri positions himself as a writer who understands that ardent assurances of singularity carry a certain value with an addressee and are part of the repertoire of gestures performed in amatory discourse.

And Baudri's amatory missives can be ardent indeed, to a degree that

---

[15] "Baudri of Bourgueil to Lady Constance," lines 4–6.

[16] Of the more than eighty "direct or indirect participants" of the letter-poems in this collection, most are fellow religious; lay and anonymous friends comprise the next largest group of addressees. Of these dozens of addressees, twelve are women. Abrahams details the demographics of the letters in *Les Oeuvres poétiques de Baudri de Bourgueil*, lvii–lx. Bond disputes the accuracy of Abrahams's figures in "Iocus Amoris," 187 n. 121; as his figures are slightly more conservative I use his. The gender breakdown of Baudri's addressees is consistent with those of his colleagues; many Loire circle verse epistles are addressed to women, and several writers address missives to Adela of Blois, but the great majority of extant verse epistles are written by men and addressed to boys or men, and most are one-sided exchanges.

[17] Carmen 137, "Murieli," *Baudri de Bourgueil: Poèmes*, lines 37–8.

[18] Dronke suggests an alternative reading of this recurrence: "It is even possible that Baudri placed his fib deliberately, knowing he would be caught out in it, giving away the game of his 'exclusive' loves, his amatory poses," *Women Writers of the Middle Ages*, 87.

might seem to compromise his salutary role of advice-giving friend. He seems to acknowledge this potentially problematic ardor, assuring Constance that although "Quod sonat iste brevis, amor est et carmen amoris" (line 7) (what this letter speaks of is love and love poetry), it is safe for her to read. Yet the very terms in which he offers reassurance are suggestively erotic:

> Non timeas Ydram, noli dubitare Chymeram,
>> Dum tanget nudum nuda manus folium.
> Ipsa potes nostram secura revolvere cartam
>> Inque tuo gremio ponere tuta potes. (lines 11–14)

> Fear not the Hydra, waver not before the Chimaera
>> As (your) bare hand touches the bare page.
> You yourself can safely open this letter,
>> And you can safely put it in your lap.

The juxtaposed hydra and the chimera of line eleven, mythologically dangerous figures, are paralleled by another alarming pair in the following line, the suggestive and startling "nudum nuda manus folium." The hand and page, following hot on the heels of the adjectives that modify them, are both imaginatively bared by Baudri. This formulation at once imagines and commands Constance's hand touching his letter, a moment of tactility that describes her body in action, picturing her bare hand touching the bare page resting in her lap – a vellum page that is of course also skin.[19] This suggestiveness is all the more striking since Baudri's other writings show that he was not insensitive to the importance of avoiding suggestions of sexual impropriety; his biography of Robert of Arbrissel, whose mixed-sex monasteries drew censure, gives particular attention to the reformer's desire to avoid scandal and his plans to keep men and women safely separated.[20]

---

[19] Notice, too, this "folium," in contrast to the "tabellae" and "cerae" of Baudri's other verse epistles, vellum versus wood boards and wax. The range of his poetic vocabulary signals a close attention to the instruments of writing and their valences of meaning, which he deploys here to vividly evoke the image of skin touching skin, to erotic effect. Baudri also writes of a naked page to Countess Adela, with playfulness but not impropriety: he asks her for her patronage and support (and, specifically, a "cappam" and "tunicam") and beseeches: "cartula nuda venit, quia nudi cartuli vatis" (my letter arrived unadorned, because it is the letter of a plain poet) (Carmen 134, *Baudri de Bourgueil: Poèmes*, lines 1357–8). My translation follows Tilliette's suggestion that "nudus" is a modesty topos, an affected claim of unembellished rhetoric.

[20] Griffiths, "The Cross and the *Cura monialium*," 313. For a stark contrast in pedagogic tone, albeit in politically charged circumstances, see Robert's letter to Ermengarde of Anjou in Petigny's "Lettre Inédite de Robert d'Arbrissel à la comtesse Ermengarde."

This ardor, and this image of the hand, are both variously repeated in Baudri's poetry, calling into question the role of amatory gestures in his work. Their repetition suggests that what is of greater value in this poetry are the positions, and not necessarily the sentiments, claimed by this imagery and vocabulary, and that the primary role of these gestures is to signal poetic skill. Baudri's epistles craft a poetic subject who is a consummate poser: he strikes poses and claims positions with an aplomb that suggests that sentiment and sincerity are secondary to the skill with which he articulates these various epistolary positions: friend, advisor, lover, and above all eloquent and learned poet. Thus, when Baudri dispenses advice, he might or might not be developing a sound pedagogy, but he does claim a pedagogic, letter-writing position, in the pastoral tradition of Jerome writing to Paula and Eustochium, Fortunatus to Radegund. When he writes of his love, he might or might not be professing a love he feels, but he claims the poetic position of lover, in grand elegiac style. What purpose this might have served the historical Baudri is not clear, but their poetic effect is to create a subject that inhabits multiple positions playfully, attentive to the pleasures of epistolary composition.[21]

Despite this multiplicity, Baudri writes consistently of the pleasures of correspondence. Later in this letter, he again imagines Constance's bare hand, as it repeatedly handles ("revolvere") the letter in her lap.[22] The *manus* topos resurfaces in his other poems, including his letters to young men.[23] In "Cuidam Gauterio" ("To A Certain Walter") he writes

> Carmina Gauteri nuper mellita recepi,
> te scribente, tuam quae tetigere manum.[24]

> Lately I received a sweet poem from Walter
> Which, since you wrote it, has touched your hand.

Baudri's writing is particularly sensitive to the tactility of missives and

---

[21] Hugh of Saint Victor, writing about two decades later, notes the importance of *ludus* in Book 2 of the *Didascalicon* but specifically in regard to the theatrical arts. See also Huizinga's study *Homo Ludens*, especially "Play and Poetry," 119–35.

[22] Line 13. *Revolvere* can, of course, also mean to unroll, referencing again the material conditions of letter writing.

[23] Holsinger discusses Baudri's sensitivity to the fleshly in his poems about music and draws connections between Baudri's understanding of music and the eroticism of his verse, *Music, Body, and Desire in Medieval Culture*, 304–8.

[24] No. 56 "Cuidam Gauterio/To a Certain Walter," in *Medieval Latin Poems of Male Love and Friendship*, trans. Stehling, lines 5–6.

their ability to create a physical presence that substitutes for face-to-face contact.[25] These lines animate the verse epistle, referencing the voiced quality of both letters and poems by calling Walter's missive a "carmen," and endowing it with active force: the letter, presumably penned by Walter, is imagined as the agent that actively touched its writer's hand, not the other way around. The "te scribente" could also have temporal force, "when you wrote it," vivifying the scene of writing and again imagining the beloved's body in contact with an epistolary offering. Most striking, however, is the hold *manus* exerts on Baudri's poetic imagination: he commands Constance's hand to open his letter, and he fantasizes Walter's hand in the act of writing to him.

This oft-imagined hand is even a site of longing. Baudri writes to an anonymous addressee:

> O utinam legatus ego meus iste fuissem,
> vel quam palparet cartula vestra manus.[26]
>
> O would that I had been my own messenger
> Or been that letter which your hand softly touched.

Baudri reliably elaborates on the moments of physical contact with a letter, extending the material pleasures of exchange: his letter was "palparet," not just touched, but touched softly, stroked, caressed. Here, however, he does more than imagine a letter being touched by an addressee or a writer; he wishes that he *were* the letter, folding the rhetorical operation of metonymy onto itself. The recurrence of the *manus* trope shows that Baudri has favorite images for describing amatory love. It also suggests that love can be experienced in letters, in reading and writing missives – activities made newly tactile by Baudri's insistence on describing what bodies do with letters.

This epistolary love and amatory tone complicate his role as advising mentor in his verse-epistles addressed to women and also to young men, which share similar expressions of ardent admiration and suggestive vocabulary and images. He writes to a certain Walter:

---

[25] In the poem that opens the collection of his writing, Baudri muses over the future readers of his book, again employing the *manus* trope: he refers to the "manus multas" the book will pass through. Carmen 1, "Contra obtrectatores consolatur librum suum," *Baudri de Bourgueil: Poèmes*, line 1.

[26] No. 59 "Ad amicum cui cartam mittebat/To a Friend to Whom He Had Sent a Letter," *Medieval Latin Poems of Male Love and Friendship*, lines 1–2.

sique voles mecum stationem continuare,
    cor pectusque meum dimidiabo tibi;
dimidiabo tibi quod erit mihi dimidiandum;
    dimidiabo meam, si jubeas, animam,
tuque locandus eris nostro sub pectore totus
    proficiesque meae maxima pars animae.[27]

If you wish to take up lodging with me,
I will divide my heart and breast with you.
I will share with you anything of mine that can be divided;
If you command it, I will share my very soul.
You will be lodged completely within my breast
And will continue as the greatest part of my soul.

The affective tone takes on greater urgency with the inclusion of a more explicit corporality in his poem addressed to a certain Vitalis:

Vitali nostro dic nostrum carmen aveto,
    dic quod eum deceat, dic sibi quod placeat.
Me sibi gratifica, cupio sibi gratificari
    quem mihi complexum viscera nostra fovent.
Visceribus nostris prae cunctis solus inhaesit,
    solus prae cunctis me penitus tetigit[28]

O my song, send greetings to Vitalis.
Say to him what is appropriate and what will please him.
Endear me to him; I want to oblige him,
This boy my heart caresses and embraces.
More than all others, he alone has stayed in my heart;
More than all others, he alone has touched me deep inside.

Baudri repeats here gestures familiar from his verses addressed to women: assurance of the singularity of his addressee, and declarations of affection coupled with physically suggestive imagery. He expresses same-sex and opposite-sex love in the same terms, invoking eros in the same way, regardless of the sex of his addressee.

This is significant not so much for the licit or illicit nature of the desires expressed, but what it tells us about epistolary positions and how they are deployed. Baudri acknowledges that love is expressed in a conventional vocabulary, which he exercises with skill, indifferent to the sex of his addressee. For him, love is an epistolary relation, in which he can display his epistolary facility, mastery of verse forms, and familiarity

---

[27] Poem 56, "Cuidam Gauterio/To a Certain Walter," lines 11–16, ibid.
[28] No. 64, "Ad Vitalem/To Vitalis," lines 1–6, ibid.

with classical Latin poets.[29] This indifference to sex-specificity is most evident in "Ad juvenem nimis elatum" (To a youth too proud), which devotes fifteen lines of praise to the addressee's beauty, describing his cheeks, hair, mouth, voice, nose, eyes, and skin. Baudri rhapsodizes:

> Cor pectusque meum tua vitrea lumina tangunt
> sidus enim geminum cristallina lumina credo
> his bene respondet caro lactea, pectus eburnum.
> Alludit manibus niveo de corpore tactus.[30]

> Your bright, clear eyes touch my breast and heart,
> For I believe those crystalline lights truly are a double star.
> Your milky flesh and ivory chest match them;
> The touch of your snow-white body sports with my hands.

Cataloguing recurring tropes for beauty in Loire circle poetry, Thomas Stehling observes that both male and female beauty are described in terms of an idealized female beauty.[31] This shared vocabulary and criteria for beauty, like Baudri's *manus* passages addressed to both women and men, raises the question of how, if at all, the sex of the love object changes the nature and even the meaning of amatory discourse. Whether this vocabulary assimilates same-sex poetic love to opposite-sex expressions of love or vice versa, their coincidence suggests a structure of desire – the poet invoking in vivid terms the qualities of the distant beloved – that matters more than the sex, and perhaps even the identity, of the beloved. This distance is a notable feature of "courtly" love literature, in which the poignancy of the poet's love is sharpened by the unattainable quality of the beloved, marking another way in which Loire circle poetry

---

[29] I am not suggesting that gender does not matter in epistolary culture. However, what I examine here is how Baudri's amatory vocabulary does not necessarily profess specific love or desires, rather it crafts a particular poetic persona, one well versed in letter-writing traditions and fluid in the use of expressions of love. Likewise, this epistolary discourse crafts a position for the beloved as a placeholder, a witness to the poet's epistolary self-fashioning.

[30] No. 50, "Ad juvemen nimis elatum/To a Youth Too Proud," *Medieval Latin Poems of Male Love and Friendship*, lines 16–19.

[31] For Stehling, this gendered beauty "makes male beauty a category of female beauty," and both Baudri and Marbod "emphasize the femininity in male beauty by comparing their boys to girls"; "Hair is almost always golden, eyes almost always starlike; lips flaming or rosy; nose, chin, and mouth well proportioned; and everything else … like snow, ivory, or a mix of lilies and roses," "To Love a Medieval Boy," 156. I don't necessarily disagree, although the more pressing interpretive frame seems to be Ovidian rather than feminizing – Ovid regularly describes beauty, in both sexes, in terms that are decidedly youthful rather than exclusively feminine.

anticipates dominant themes in secular writing in the twelfth century.[32] This distance is also intrinsic to letter writing: letters reinforce the physical separation of writer and addressee while uniting them in a textual relationship. Baudri's verse epistles seem to revel in the constraints of this stylized love and of the epistolary situation, articulating an idea of love that depends on this structure of distance and desire. Whether writing to women or men, Baudri loves at a distance – through letters.

The recurrence of similar expressions of affect addressed to women and men reveals a significant overlap in the vocabularies employed by two epistolary traditions: love letters and letters of friendship. The tenor of these writings might seem to make the issue of intent rather urgent, since to read Baudri literally, that is, to take him as an ecclesiastic who entertained lustful thoughts about young men and women and carried on improper relations with them, would make him not only lascivious, but, more significantly, sinful.[33] Scholars have debated the nature of the love Baudri writes, and while the biographical question is an important one, for the purposes of literary analysis the question is not whether writing letters that merge these two traditions is evidence of sexual impropriety or transgression.[34] Rather, this shared vocabulary points to a generic intersection upon which Baudri's epistles seem to play. Given the interconnectedness of love and friendship and the difficulty of distinguishing

---

[32] "Amor de lonh" is, of course, an important motif in the lyric tradition, as well. Bond discusses the possibility of Loire circle influence on troubadour lyric in "Origins," in *A Handbook of the Troubadours*, 237–54.

[33] Abrahams notes that, after having been elected archbishop, "une cause mystérieuse l'avait forcé de quitter Bourgueil," and in 1120 "Baudri fut suspendu temporairement par le légat du pape … et c'est probablement à cette date qu'il quitta Dol pour se retirer à Saint-Samson-sur-Rille," xxi. Given these mysterious leavings of office, it is tempting to wonder whether poems of this tenor might have had a role to play in his censure. See Kuefler's "Male Friendship and the Suspicion of Sodomy" for a contextualization of homoerotic verse and the hostility it engendered in the context of social and political reforms, in his edited volume *The Boswell Thesis*. Holsinger and Townsend place Baudri at the beginning of a "watershed" in the history of sexuality in the pre-modern West, in which poets explored same-sex love with greater freedom than in the immediately preceding and following centuries.

[34] Scholars have interrogated the question of Baudri's sexuality; see Boswell's discussion of Baudri in "The Triumph of Ganymede," in *Christianity, Social Tolerance, and Homosexuality*; Holsinger writes of the "open and often courageous homoeroticism of several of Baudri's epistolary poems," 303. Tilliette doubts any connection between the content of the letter-poems and actual impropriety: "La frénésie auto-accusatrice qui manifeste son auteur vise-t-elle à dissimuler un crime de nature sexuelle, comme aimerait à le croire le trop naïf John Boswell? Rien ne l'indique avec certitude," "Hermès amoureux," 134.

them in this body of writing, my examination of this intersection aims not to separate out expressions of "friendship" or "romance," an often artificial distinction, or of same-sex versus opposite-sex expressions of affection.[35] Rather, my examination of Baudri's affective expression interrogates how the overlap between different epistolary vocabularies is manipulated to articulate a sometimes contradictory poetic subject who writes his love through layers of epistolary scripts. This expression suggests a love that consists in composition and exchange, and a self that loves, variously, through letters.

Baudri's Playful Reading Lesson

The polyvalence of Baudri's poetic voice accords with the ambiguous teaching he offers in his verse epistle addressed to Constance, which appears as Carmen 200 in the manuscript of his poems. Carmen 200 is distinct from Baudri's other letter-poems and those written by his contemporaries in several important ways. It includes the typical elements of praise of beauty and eloquence, expressions of regret at separation, and anticipation of meeting. And, as in his other verse epistles, his pedagogic voice is complicated by the suggestive overtones he cultivates. However, Carmen 200 is noticeably longer – Loire circle verse epistles are generally quite brief.[36] It is also the only one of his letter-poems to appear alongside its reply, Carmen 201 from Constance.[37] Baudri assumes a pedagogic role, Constance that of his student, and both employ the tropes of learned friendship so significant in the cultivation of medieval humanism. However, these letters are unusual for friendship and spiritual advice letters because they constitute a male-female letter-

---

[35] Bond writes, "because of the inherent ambiguity of the word *amor*, Baudri is able to flirt simultaneously with codes of friendship between monks and codes of desire between males," *The Loving Subject*, 50. And, as Boswell points out, to the extent that the difference between *amor* and *amicitia* is difficult to distinguish in this literature, attempts to distinguish between "homosexual" and "heterosexual" writings, interests, and behaviors in the Middle Ages are equally thorny, 47.

[36] Reading verse epistles from this period is often a project of sifting through tropes, as these letters are generally brief and highly stylized, and consistently include praise, instruction, and discussion of love as well as Ovidian descriptions and themes, considerable word-play, and the use of varied rhetorical figures.

[37] There are two other letter-reply sets in this collection, both fictional: the first is penned in the name of mythological characters, Paris and Helen; the second is an imagined exchange between Ovid and his friend Florus. See Bond's discussion of the relationship of Baudri's writing to an "Ovidian subculture" in "The Play of Desire," *The Loving Subject* 42–69.

reply pair in verse.[38] And, although Baudri advises Constance and praises her virginity as pleasing to God, their letters are secular and amorous in tone and reference. The poetic effect of this multiplicity of register invites interpretation to resolve these seemingly conflicting epistolary positions.

The resolution of these positions does not, however, depend on their authenticity of authorship. The authenticity of women's writing from premodern periods is often contested, and Constance's authorship has been both challenged and supported.[39] While it is not out of the question that Baudri might have authored the reply from Constance, given the medieval practice of collecting and compiling actual correspondence, and in the absence of evidence to the contrary, there is no compelling reason to question Constance's authorship of Carmen 201. Ultimately, however, I am not making an argument about how historical people "really felt," and for my analysis the actual authorship of these two verse epistles is less significant than the fact that tone-breaking comes from what is presented as a female voice, and that the exercise of epistolary agency issues from the position of a respondent who is a subordinate: a younger student, and a woman. This departure in register is all the more striking considering the playfully ambiguous letter to which it replies.

Given the complexities of Baudri's epistolary voice, it is perhaps not surprising that he himself seems to acknowledge the interpretive challenges his verses pose by stating openly what he wants:

> Nolo vir esse tibi neque tu sis femina nobis;
> Os et cor nostram firmet amiciciam.

---

[38] The Regensburg and Tegernsee love poems differ from these in a few respects: they are unattributed, much briefer, and do not constitute a continuous exchange between two writers, Mews, *The Lost Love Letters of Heloise and Abelard*, 102–3; in comparing these anonymous letters to the "lost" love letters of Abelard and Heloise, which I discuss in Chapter 2, Jaeger writes that the Tegernsee letters are "run-of-the-mill love letters," and the Regensburg songs have a "slightly stiff conventionality and wooden spontaneity," *Ennobling Love*, 161. There is an exchange in the Marbod dossier addressed to him, "Puella ad amicum munera promittentem," but the exchange is quite brief and its authorship is uncertain; see Dronke, *Women Writers*, 298 n. 10.

[39] See Tilliette's introduction for arguments in favor of Baudri's authorship of Carmen 201 (*Baudri de Bourgueil: Poèmes*, vol. 2, 294), and Dronke (*Women Writers*, 84–5) and Bond (*The Loving Subject*, 63 n. 71) for arguments in favor of Constance's authorship. I revisit the issue of authenticity of authorship in Chapter 2, in which questions of authorship are more complicated for a variety of reasons, including a greater number of letters and a greater quantity of biographical information and contemporary testimony available about the letter writers.

> Pectora iungantur, sed corpora semoveantur;
> Sit pudor in facto, sit iocus in calamo. (lines 43–6)

I do not want to be your husband, nor you to be my wife:
  Let mouth and heart confirm our friendship.
Let our hearts be joined, but our bodies remain apart;
  Let the shame be in the act, let the game be in the pen.

Offering clarification on the kind of relationship his writing might imply, Baudri excludes two roles for them – that of husband and wife – but invites a host of others. In addition to being Constance's teacher in this poem, he is the lover of her virginity, the friend who wrote, dictated, and composed verses addressed to her, a writer inspired by the figure of her as a Sibyl.[40] The various roles that Baudri scripts for himself and Constance reference established epistolary traditions and the relationships they imply, and this multiplicity suggests that fixed, exclusive subject positions are exactly what he resists in his writing.

Even as he clarifies that which he does and does not wish for their relationship, however, Baudri cannot resist muddying the waters. Declaring that he does not want to be Constance's "vir" might invite the question: why not? The obvious impediment of their monastic profession would seem to make this declaration unnecessary. Instead of explaining, he enjoins, "may our hearts be joined," accessing both the bodily, animal register of harnessing, and the connubial register he has just rejected with the verb *iungo*. *Iungo* carries distinct physical connotations, as in the yoking together of oxen; of persons, it has a more figurative charge, meaning to unite or to join, as in alliance, friendship, or marriage, or it can carry a quite literal meaning, to join in physical embrace or sexual intercourse.[41] As if acknowledging his wordplay, Baudri urges that they "let the shame be in the act, let the game be in the pen," drawing a distinction between the literal separation of bodies and the figurative joining of hearts. In his formulation, there is harm in doing, but not in writing: things that would be shameful to do are not shameful to write.

This distinction between saying and doing is humorously imagined by Jerome several centuries earlier, as he pictures Marcella attempting to

---

[40] Carmen 200, "Baudri of Bourgueil to Lady Constance," in Bond, lines 4–6, 81, 54, 124. Once again, this vocabulary resurfaces in another of Baudri's poems; in his letter to Emma, he writes that her language and sensibility remind him of the Sibyl: "Nobis, Emma, refers lingua sensuque Sibillam," Carmen 153, "Emme ut opus suum perlegat," line 13.

[41] And, as Bond points outs, "the common poetic use of *pectora* ('chests') for "hearts" also gains an ambiguous overtone in this context," *The Loving Subject*, 173 n. 4.

restrain him from "saying what others did not blush to do."[42] As with
Baudri, speech – whether spoken or addressed in a letter – is innocent, and
therefore has greater freedom than action. Baudri insists in particular on
the innocence of verse composition, and not just his own: in his poem in
the voice of Florus addressed to Ovid, Florus defends love as inherent in
human nature. As a result, Ovid's crime is not loving, but writing amorous
verses. If we cast Baudri into Ovid's position, as critics have done and
Baudri perhaps invites, a deft sleight of hand is accomplished: Baudri
shifts the scrutiny from amorous behavior to amorous writing, which he
exonerates in the letter-poem to Constance as not shameful, and therefore
not requiring defense.[43]

Given this distinction between shameful deeds and innocent writing,
Baudri is a remarkably defensive writer, repeatedly asserting his playfulness, harmlessness, and good intentions.[44] As Jerome's example demonstrated, the role of spiritual advisor to women incurred suspicion for men,

----

[42] "Jerome imagined how Marcella would want to put her finger to his mouth, were it
possible, to prevent him from *saying* what others did not blush to *do*," Shanzer, citing *Ep.*
27.2, "Some Treatments of Sexual Scandal in (Primarily) Later Latin Epistolography,"
397.

[43] Florus defends Ovid and, most likely, Baudri:
> Novit amare Venus versibus absque tuis.
> Naturam nostram plenam deus egit amoris
> Nos natura docet quod deus hanc docuit.
>
> …
>
> Quod sumus est crimen, si crimen sit quod amamus;
> Qui dedit esse, deus prestat amare michi
> (Carmen 97, "Florus Ovidio," *Baudri de Bourgueil, Poèmes*,
> vol. 1, lines 50–2, 55–6).

> Venus knew to love without your verses.
> God set forth our nature full of love
> Nature teaches us, that which God taught her.
>
> …
>
> What we are is a crime, if it be a crime that we love.
> God who gave being, meant for me to love.

While love is excused here, the capacity for which God placed in human nature, Boswell
writes that "Florus is obviously defending the author himself," *Christianity, Social Tolerance,
and Homosexuality*, 247; Bond corroborates, calling it a "syllogistic defense by Baudri of
both Ovid and – as every reader quickly realize – himself," *The Loving Subject*, 52.

[44] Defenses and apologies are of course also highly stylized elements in this discourse
and could even be considered among the stock elements explored in schoolbook exercises, but Baudri takes it to another level in his insistence on his innocence. Jaeger
observes that "[t]hings written were guaranteed the public and representative nature of the
subject and gave any statements the protection of discursive innocence," and continues in
a note that Baudri's stating this in a poem is "no doubt an indication that the innocence of
discourse is eroding," *Envy of Angels*, 312 and n. 53. See Obermeier for a discussion of
apology and humility in Marbod's writing, 80–3.

and he, too, defended his relationships with women, expressing outrage over accusations of illicit relations with his charges.[45] Baudri articulates his defenses in very different tenor. He anticipates that readers will criticize his book, either through error or envy, and he instructs his missive on what to say to detractors: "Hec, ut vitaret ocia, composuit" (he wrote these things in order to avoid idleness).[46] In another poem, he writes simply: "Nullus amor foedus michi quidlibet associavit" (no foul love whatsoever has been associated with me).[47] In "Ad Galonem" he exonerates himself of wrongdoing in terms that contradict his insistence on separating shameful deeds and shame-free writing:

> Nec iuvenilis amor nec me malus abstulit error
> Sed michi iocundo musa iocosa placet.
> Musa iocosa placet, quoniam michi vita iocosa;
> Vita iocosa tamen facta iocosa fugit.[48]

> Neither young love nor wicked love has carried me away
> But a playful muse amuses me, a playful person.
> A playful muse pleases me, because life is playful to me.
> And yet a playful life flees playful deeds.

This last passage performs the playfulness he claims and further develops a recurrent theme in his poetry: disavowing deeds in favor of cultivating his "Musa iocosa." In the work that opens the collection of his poems, he writes that "iocosa" words never harmed anyone.[49] However, in this passage deeds are also described as "iocosa." This shared adjective assimilates words and deeds, blurring the distinction between them that Baudi claims so insistently to Constance.

---

45 Most famously in "Ad Asellam," Ep. 45. Fortunatus, too, must profess that he loves Agnes as if she were his sister, *Venanti Honori Clementiani Fortunati presbyteri italici Opera poetica*, 260.

46 Carmen 1, "Contra obtrectatores consolatur librum suum," line 62, *Baudri de Bourgueil: Poèmes*. In one of his letters to Adela of Blois, Baudri writes that she will be his "testis" against the envy of calumnious others (Carmen 134, lines 1363–6). In enlisting the countess's aid in his defense, Baudri hints, however obliquely, at what must have been one of the motivations in writing to powerful personages: the procurement of patronage, protection, and status. He appears to be unusual in his claim and defense of playfulness; Olson observes that "justifications such as [Baudri's] are relatively rare before the rise of vernacular literature in the twelfth century and the incorporation of Aristotelian ideas into literary thinking in the thirteenth," "The Profits of Pleasure," *Cambridge History of Literary Criticism: The Middle Ages*, 282.

47 Carmen 85, "Qua intentione scripserit," line 40, *Baudri de Bourgueil: Poèmes*.

48 Carmen 193, "Ad Galonem," line 101–4, ibid.

49 Carmen 1, "Crede michi. Numquam nocuerunt verba iocosa," line 1, ibid.

This avowed playfulness is present throughout Baudri's corpus: he addresses letter-poems to his wax tablets, and writes a lament for a broken stylus.[50] His writing is notable for the degree of attention it gives to the material conditions of writing and correspondence – he even addresses a letter-poem to a messenger and two brief letter-poems to his scribes instructing them on the preparation of his verses.[51] In this way also, Baudri's verse resonates with Ovid's: in addition to his epistolary imper-sonations in the *Heroides*, Ovid has a great deal to say about letter writing. References to letter writing ranging from the material composition of letters (wax tablets, wet flax, invisible ink) to means of expedition (the importance of using trusted messengers, good hiding places for letters) and the importance of letters in courtship, all appear in the *Amores*, the *Ars amatoria,* and the *Remedia amoris*. In keeping with this playfulness, he addresses poems to young people and even identifies with them: in his poem to Constance he calls her his "iunior" and describes himself as "iuvenis" (line 41). Regardless of their actual age, this comparative asso-ciates them in their participation in epistolary exchange of a playful style associated with youthfulness.[52] This playfulness might well compromise Baudri's pedagogy, inviting a less than serious reading of his teaching, by undermining a pose he assumes frequently in his letters: that of authorita-tive teacher, counselor, advice-giver.

Baudri's playfulness is probably responsible for critical observations that he lacks the "*gravitas* of Hildebert," and that he is a *fantaisiste*, "un virtuose aussi superficiel que brillant."[53] In this regard Baudri is certainly a product of this "Ovidian age"; he, too, writes love poetry in suggestive terms, admirable for its wit and dexterity, if not always its propriety. Baudri identifies himself as a reader of Ovid in one of his more playful poems, and seems to invite identification with Ovid in a letter-reply pair between Florus and Ovid and his rewriting of two *Heroides* epistles.[54] In

---

[50] Carmina 12, 196, and 92, respectively; ibid.

[51] Carmina 84, 255, 9, respectively, ibid. See Rouse and Rouse, "The Vocabulary of Wax Tablets," on Baudri's usefulness in providing a range of writing vocabulary in this period. See also Bond's discussion of Baudri and the information he provides on the "material process of producing poetry," *The Loving Subject*, 53–4.

[52] Dronke discusses the question of Baudri's and Constance's relative ages and possible ages at the time of composition in *Women Writers*, 85.

[53] Raby, *A History of Secular Latin Poetry*, 337; and Tilliette, "Hermès amoureux," 122 and n. 7, respectively.

[54] Carmen 111, "Ad eum qui ab eo Ovidium extorsit"; Carmina 97 and 98, "Florus Ovidio" and "Ovidius Floro suo;" and Carmina 7 and 8, a rewriting of *Heroides* 16 and 17, between Paris and Helen. Holsinger describes him as "arguably the most avid reader

Carmen 200, he claims playfulness as more than a rhetorical topos. He uses it as an excuse, explaining that whatever he does, "iocus est" (it is a game):

> Quodsi nos aliquis dixisse iocosa remordet,
>   Non sum durus homo; quicquid ago, iocus est.
> Leta michi vitam fecit natura iocosam
>   Et mores hylares vena benigna dedit. (lines 143–6)

> But if someone should blame us for having said playful things,
>   I am not a solemn man: whatever I do is a game.
> A happy nature has made life playful for me,
>   And a congenial vein has given me a cheerful character.

Baudri blames the tenor of his writing on his nature – he is a playful man, and so too are his verses. This is a striking position: it claims amorous verse writing as an acceptable activity for an abbot, and, more serious, it refuses interpretation. Yet his repeated assurances that his words are harmless suggest exactly the opposite, that his words can cause harms that must be assuaged. And playful verse can have serious effects: a *iocus*, by nature, invokes fixed moral positions. When employed ambiguously, it reveals the limits of a discourse that scripts particular relationships between people. It can even blur the boundaries of this discourse and of these relationships, allowing bishops to be, as Bond writes, "loving subjects," teachers and directors as well as lovers of boys and girls, inhabiting a space of contradiction and inclusion.[55]

Baudri's letter-poem to Constance features the most striking and frequent declarations of the propriety of his intentions. As discussed earlier, he begins with an announcement of harmlessness: implying that love poetry customarily contains dangers, he claims that his love poem will be different. After proclaiming his trustworthiness and declaring his esteem for her, Baudri defends the nature of his love:

> Crede michi credasque volo credantque legentes:
>   In te me nunquam foedus adegit amor. (lines 37–8)

---

and inventive reviser of Ovid's love poetry before Petrarch," *Music, Body, and Desire in Medieval Culture*, 303.

[55] See Bond for a discussion of the idea of play in Baudri's verse in "The Play of Desire," *The Loving Subject*, 42–69. On contradiction and medieval culture and literature, see Bolduc's *The Medieval Poetics of Contraries*, Brown's *Contrary Things*, and Kay's *Courtly Contradictions*; on opposites, see Bouchard's *'Every Valley Shall be Exalted.'*

> Believe me (and I want both you and the readers to believe):
>> A filthy love has never driven me to you.

Several lines later, he repeats the same formula word for word:

> Crede michi credasque volo credantque legentes:
>> In te me nunquam foedus adegit amor
> Nec lascivus amor nec amor petulantis amoris
>> Pro te subvertit corque iecurque meum. (lines 47–50)

> Believe me (and I want both you and the readers to believe):
>> A filthy love has never driven me to you.
> Neither lascivious love nor a love of wanton love
>> Stirs up the depths of my heart on account of you.

These passages not only defend his innocence of "foedus amor," they are also reminders of the epistolary situation in this period: Baudri writes of "legentes," readers of his letter addressed to Constance other than Constance.[56] These "legentes" echo the "multas" to whom Baudri sends his book in the opening verse epistle; this opening epistle strongly suggests that Baudri oversaw the production of the manuscript of his verse writings, and the detailed instructions he gives his scribes in the preparation of his volume point to a keen awareness and anticipation of a reading public.[57] This first letter, the references to audience, and Baudri's insistent defensiveness, work together to reveal a carefully crafted poetic position, attentive to readership and interpretation regardless of the authenticity of his seemingly anxious defense.

Despite the care given to the preparation of the volume and his antici-pation of an audience for his work, however, Baudri paradoxically opens his letter to Constance with a gesture to privacy, commanding her to:

> Perlege, perlectam caute complectere cartam,
>> Ne noceat fame lingua maligna meae.
> Perlege sola meos versus indagine cauta (lines 1–3)

> Read through this letter, and carefully clasp it once read,
>> Lest malignant tongues harm my reputation.
> Read through my verse by yourself with careful hunting

Constance is to clasp his letter, and to read it "sola," alone. Of course,

---

56 This defense also appears in the above-cited "Qua intentione scripiserit."

57 "Vade, manus multas subiturus et atria multa" (Go, you who are going to pass into many hands and many homes) Carmen 1, "Contra obtrectatores consolatur librum suum" (Consolation for his book against detractors), line 1, *Baudri de Bourgueil: Poèmes.*

"complectere" also means "to embrace." She should embrace his letter, and also hide it, lest its meanings be misunderstood – or understood all too well – by enemies. Yet the penultimate lines of the verse epistle equivocate: "Si vis, ostendas, si vis, hec scripta recondas" (If you wish, display what I have written; hide it if you wish) (line 177). Baudri antici-pates the possibility of a plural audience and insists on the importance of secrecy from it.[58] Whether or not his defensiveness constitutes an admis-sion of impropriety, as protesting too much often does, it creates an awareness of audience: Constance and the *legentes*. It signals a concern to secure a proper reading from this plural audience and, with it, to preserve and further his reputation as a skilled writer and proper abbot. In their assured commands, these lines perform an intimacy with their addressee, assuming a shared concern for his reputation.[59] And, true to his playful word, Baudri insouciantly smooths it all over with the equivo-cating "si vis" – having laid out for her the potential dangers of exposure, she can do whatever she wishes with his letter.

Baudri's many equivocations resonate with the polysemous reading he teaches Constance. In his other letters-poems he issues brief, axiomatic commands, while in this one his pedagogy is more developed. He explains the value in reading the ancients for negative and positive exempla, and claims that Greek "trifles" teach, just as "every literature of the world" teaches.[60] He describes the acquisition of knowledge in distinctly martial terms:

[58] Jerome, too, urges secrecy, but again in very different manner: asked by a young man to write a letter to his wayward mother and sister, Jerome reluctantly assents, but cautions him to keep the letter "clam," secret, alluding to previous similar efforts that have been misinterpreted, "Ad matrem et filiam in Gallia commorantes," *Select Letters*, Ep. 117, 373.

[59] And, given Baudri's evocation of plural audience, it follows that his commands to Constance and the intimacy he performs with her implicate his "legentes" as eavesdrop-pers in this intimate discourse, or even partakers in this intimacy.

[60] "Ut sunt in veterum libris exempla malorum/[S]ic bona, que facias, sunt in eis posita" (Just as there are examples of old evils in books, So too are good deeds placed in them which you might do) (lines 105–6). He writes of Diana's virginity, the victory of Perseus, the might of Hercules, and explains his purpose in citing these pagan stories:

> Sed volui Grecas ideo pretendere nugas,
>   Ut quevis mundi littera nos doceat,
> Ut totus mundus velut unica lingua loquatur
>   Et nos erudiat omnis et omnis homo. (lines 121–4)

> But I wanted to put forward the Greek trifles as proof
>   That every literature of the world teaches us,
> That the whole world speaks as with one tongue
>   And that each and every man educates us.

> Hostili preda ditetur lingua Latina;
>   Grecus et Hebreus serviat edomitus.
> In nullis nobis desit doctrina legendi;
>   Lectio sit nobis et liber omne, quod est. (lines 131–4)

> Let the Latin tongue be enriched by enemy booty;
>   Let the vanquished Greek and Hebrew serve.
> Let us not miss reading's lesson in any (of them);
>   Let everything that is, be book and text for us.[61]

In letting everything be book and text, Baudri claims meaningfulness everywhere, including, implicitly, in his own writing.[62] However, while works by pagan authors were read in medieval France, they required proper interpretation through the *accessus ad auctores*.[63] As Baudri suggests by his various clarifications and equivocations, his writing requires interpretation as well, yet sifting through the various poetic tropes and epistolary relationships produces an inconclusive reading: is Baudri Constance's lover, admirer, friend, teacher? Could he be all at once? This need for interpretation assimilates Baudri to pagan authors whose writings were interpreted through allegorical reading, making of him an *auctor*, accessing *auctoritas*, whose writings must be interpreted to yield lessons.[64]

If indeed Baudri's letters contain both good and bad *exempla*, how exactly is this good teaching to be obtained? To read Carmen 200 literally would make Baudri an abbot who offers salutary teachings to a young nun while harboring and vividly expressing carnal thoughts about her.

----

[61] This vocabulary and sentiment anticipate Joachim du Bellay's sixteenth-century *Défense et illustration de la langue française*.

[62] Curtius credits Baudri with giving a "systematic basis" to the parallelism of biblical and antique *exempla*, 362. Swanson observes that the "integration of the pagan past into a Christian world was no novelty, being legitimated by no less an authority than St Augustine in the topos of taking the gold of the Egyptians," 47.

[63] See Minnis and Scott, eds., *Medieval Literary Theory and Criticism*, sections 1–2 on early scholastic *accessus ad auctores* and dialogue on authors; Minnis, *Medieval Theory of Authorship*; Hunt, "The Introductions to the '*Artes*' in the Twelfth Century;" Astell, "On the Usefulness and Use-Value of Books."

[64] As Carruthers explains, "[i]n considering medieval view of textual authority, *auctores* were, first of all, texts, not people" and "both 'authority' and 'author' were conceived of entirely in textual terms, for an 'auctor' is simply one whose writings are full of 'authorities,' " *The Book of Memory*, 190. Baudri thus marks himself as an "auctor" in several ways: through larding his verse with abundant references to classical texts, and by inhabiting the seemingly contradictory positions of ardent lover and well-meaning abbot and urging reconciliation of these positions through interpretation, placing himself on a level with pagan writings that also require interpretation.

This potential contradiction between tone and profession is seemingly resolved by his denial of seriousness in anything he does – and yet, playfulness as a catch-all defense dismisses the good as well as the harm in his verse.[65] He offers advice on resolving paradox in his instruction on reading Greek myth: "Just as there are examples of old evils in books/So too are good deeds placed in them which you might do." Picking through Greek myth for models for good behavior and discarding the more lascivious stories as negative exempla, he implies, is how Constance ought to read his letters, alert to his "good" as well as his "bad" teaching. He trusts her ability to interpret his playful verse into useful teaching, associating his flirtatious evocations of her body with "old evils," and taking his praise of virginity as an example of a salutary lesson to cleave to.[66]

Baudri thus seems to advise a literal reading of the passages of his verse epistle in which he declares his good intentions, and in which he "teaches" – that is, when he directs Constance to protect her chastity, to read his letter, to find meaning everywhere. When, then, are his epistolary expressions to be interpreted, read beyond their surface meaning? His defensiveness signals the presence of something in his letters that can be misunderstood, and insisting on his "iocosa" nature as an excuse for "iocosa" verses suggests that it is these passages that require interpretation: the passages imagining Constance's bare hand on the bare page, the letter in her lap, the very passages whose erotic undertones might cause a reader to read them again, carefully.[67] Baudri's inclusion of these elements inviting interpretation, complicating the more straightforward teaching he offers Constance, plays deliberately upon overlapping roles and registers, and relies on playfulness as a defense against wrongdoing. Constance's reply resists Baudri's ambiguity, exposes the insufficiency of playfulness as a defense, and seeks to establish a consistent interpretive frame, playful or not, grounded in her somatic experience of reading his letter.

---

[65] This would seem to constitute a softer version of the liar's paradox, to which Augustine refers in *Against the Academicians*, III.13.29.

[66] This conforms with Augustine's explanation of how to interpret obscurities in scripture: "… whatever appears in the divine Word that does not literally pertain to virtuous behavior or to the truth of faith you must take to be figurative," *On Christian Doctrine*, Book 3, Chapter 10, 88.

[67] This pleasure is double: the titillation provided by the suggestive imagery, and the fact that the imagery requires interpretation. As Augustine teaches, "… no one doubts that things are perceived more readily through similitudes and that what is sought with difficulty is discovered with more pleasure," *On Christian Doctrine*, Book 2, Chapter 6, 38.

Constance's Letter: Departing From The Heroidean Script

Baudri's writing demonstrates mastery of established epistolary genres, as does Constance's letter. Their exchange, celebrating love and expressing its anxieties in at times exaggerated fashion, situates it squarely in the *Heroides* tradition of lamenting and distanced lovers.[68] However, their exchange cannot simply be read as a calque of these fictional letters; it offers significant and distinctly medieval departures from the Ovidian literary script.[69] One of the most striking of these differences is the pedagogical dimension Baudri develops; the *Heroides* letters, single and paired, male- or female- authored, are written from the point of view of a frustrated lover. Baudri's letter to Constance teaches on a variety of subjects, the force of which is made clear largely through the imperative mood: "perlege," "complectere," "vive," "vale"; she is to read his letter carefully, and to hide it or show it as she sees fit; she is to find meaning everywhere. In addition to instructing her on the handling of his letter, he also urges the protection of her chastity, striking a distinctly different tone from his equivocating flirtation.[70]

An element that his pedagogy and courtship share is praise: Baudri applauds Constance's beauty and virginity, and also her writing. His compliments suggest that he has previously seen her *littera*, implying dialogue sustained through several epistolary exchanges:[71]

> In te sed nostrum movit tua littera sensum
> Et penitus iunxit me tua Musa tibi.
> Denique tanta tuae vivit facundia lingue,
> Vt possis credi sisque Sibilla michi. (lines 51–4)

---

[68] Dronke observes that Constance composes "an *Heroides* epistle" in "playfully feigned fashion," "Heloise's Problemata and Letters," 59, and "[s]he is consciously writing a modern *Heroides* epistle," *Women Writers*, 85.

[69] Dronke describes the letters of Fortunatus and Radegund as a "Christianized mode of *Heroides*," *Women Writers*, 85–6. Raby characterizes the exchange as "a kind of 'moralization' of the *Heroides*," 343. Cherewatuk also situates Radegund's correspondence in relation to the *Heroides*; see especially 31–3.

[70] "In te concivem volo vivere virginitatem,/In te confringi nolo pudiciciam" (lines 39–40) (I want virginity to live in you as a fellow citizen,/I do not want chastity to be shattered in you). As discussed earlier, praise of virginity is a common element in Loire circle poetry, and Baudri's writings to women are no exception. See also his letters to Cecile, Muriel, and "Agnes ut virginitatem suam conservet."

[71] Baudri writes another, much briefer letter to a Constance, Carmen 142 "Constantiae," which is admiring and unambiguous, and praises her pact with God. There is also an epitaph on the death of a Constance, "Carmen 213"; Tilliette claims that these are "sans doute" the same person.

> Your learned writing has moved my feeling for you,
>> And your Muse has joined me to you deep within.
> In short, so much eloquence lives in your tongue
>> That you could be believed to be, a Sibyl, and are to me.

He credits Constance with being a writer in her own right, and an eloquent one: the force of her *littera* moves him to respond.[72] This reference and the pairing of Carmina 200 and 201 emphasize a dialogic dynamic between the letters, and serve well the pedagogic relationship he claims: teachers expound lessons, students demonstrate mastery of material, and both participate in an exchange structured by lessons offered and learned – or not. Letters are an ideal structure for this kind of exchange, and the pairing of this letter-reply set underscores how correspondence mirrors the nature of dialogue and facilitates the dynamics of pedagogy. There are thus several layers of scriptedness in these letters, in which the rhetorical positions of call and response and the various dynamics they imply in amorous and pedagogical exchange are both encouraged and resisted.

Constance's letter responds dutifully to Baudri's teaching on virginity. However, unlike her teacher, she makes aggressive and specific extratextual demands. Formally responding in kind – he writes eighty-nine elegiac couplets, so does she – she declares her obedience to her teacher and his instruction:[73]

> Ipse iubes, dilecte meus, tu precipis, inquam,
>> Ut castis operam legibus attribuam.
> Attribuam; sic ipse iubes, sic ipsa preopto (lines 109–11)

> You yourself, my beloved, you order and, I say, instruct
>> me to apply my efforts to the laws of chastity.
> And I will: just as you order, so do I choose.

Having proclaimed her obedience to her teacher, she then gives her orders to him, seeking proof of his faithfulness:

> Si te Roma vocat, si te Magontia temptat,
>> Si meus es, retrahas mox ab utraque pedem. (lines 137–8)

> If Rome calls you, if Mayenne tempts you,
>> Quickly draw back your foot from each, if you are mine.

[72] "Littera" can mean "letter," suggesting at least one previous missive from Constance; Bond translates "littera" as "writing," which might hint at the circulation of other letters, as well as her reputation.

[73] See Fulkerson for a discussion of the *Heroides* heroines and the intertextuality of their letters, in *The Ovidian Heroine as Author: Reading, Writing, and Community in the* Heroides.

This desire for proof of faithfulness sounds a distinctly amatory and even proprietary note; Constance is perhaps all too apt a pupil at responding to Baudri's varied tones.

Constance expands on her desire for proof of Baudri's faithfulness. Not only is he to refrain from traveling too far away, he must also demonstrate his fidelity through paying her a visit:

> Ergo dico tibi: me pretermittere noli;
> > Nullam maioris invenies fidei.
> Si potes, et poteris, si tantum velle videris,
> > Fac, ut te videam, meque videre veni. (lines 151–4)

> Therefore I say to you: do not neglect me!
> > You will find no (girl) of greater faith.
> If you can and will be able, as you seem to want so much,
> > Arrange that I can see you, and come to see me.

Elaborating on repeated demands for a visit, she suggests that Baudri invent pretexts for visiting her:

> Maturato gradus et me visurus adesto;
> > Sumptus et comites sufficientur habes.
> Cur ad nos venias, occasio multa paratur:
> > "Ad quem sermo michi, presul in urbe manet;
> Clerus me mandat, abates, ille uel ille;
> > Me trahit ad comitem res facienda michi." (lines 161–6)

> Hasten your steps and be here to see me;
> > You have sufficient means and companions.
> Many an occasion is contrived why you might come to me:
> > "The bishop I must talk to is staying in the city;
> The clergy summons me, the abbots, or so-and-so and
> > > > > > what's-his-name;
> > Some affair I must take care of calls me to the count."

Having expressed her urgent desire to see him, reminded him of his ability to arrange a visit, and offered several ruses whereby he might do so, she reproaches: "Visere me debes" (you should visit me) (line 173). She closes her missive with a plaintive exhortation:

> Expectate, veni nolique diu remorari;
> > Sepe vocavi te; sepe vocate, veni. (lines 177–8)

> O long awaited one, come, and do not linger long;
> > Often have I called you: you who are called often, come!

Constance's letter transgresses the limits of the customary *narratio* and *petitio,* the central elements of a letter, by making a standard request for a visit and investing it with an almost immoderate urgency, and boldly fabricating pretenses that Baudri should use to justify a visit. These repeated demands exceed the self-proclaimed playful tone of Baudri's letter by demanding specific extra-textual action of dubious moral character – while not all convents were strictly enclosed, they were certainly not meant to harbor visits for which excuses had to be fabricated.[74]

Casting Constance's reply as a medieval extension of the *Heroides* tradition would account for its lamenting tone, yet its context suggests a different reading: Carmen 201 is not a standalone poem. It responds to a carefully crafted letter that is highly sensitive to tone and anxious to control its interpretation. Constance does not return a light-hearted reply to Carmen 200, a letter-poem insistent on its own playfulness. Rather, she engages in a more serious kind of play that makes specific demands, urgently requests action at the cost of dissimulation, and, as I will show, refuses the ambiguity seemingly excused by playfulness. Given Baudri's self-portrayal as at once loving and moralizing, and his pains to underwrite his various roles as above all playful, this refusal rejects his ambiguous teaching, making the love letter a space for mutual admiration and praise, but also resistance and competition.[75]

This letter-reply exchange shows how the epistolary positions of writer and addressee, and the dynamic of call and response they establish, shape literary and social relations and dynamics. It also reveals the unique opportunities for response for a woman writer in a predominantly male literary world.[76] In Jaeger's analysis of ennobling love, an important part of the climate in which this discourse was produced, medieval people responded to charismatic qualities in others and, as a result of their relationship with them, benefited by being "ennobled"; thus love was not solely an interior feeling but also a very public way of behaving.[77] As a

---

[74] Johnson discusses active and passive enclosure in *Equal in Monastic Profession,* 151–65.

[75] This anticipates the intellectual showmanship between Abelard and Heloise, which I examine in Chapter 2.

[76] *The Epistolae: Medieval Women's Latin Letters* project begun by Ferrante has begun the important task of collecting and translating letters written to and from women in the Middle Ages. However, of the more than 1000 letters currently catalogued (as of May 2010), fewer than 400 are attributed to women, and the large majority of these are letters of administrative and diplomatic nature.

[77] Ennobling love was a "form of aristocratic self-representation" whose "social function is to show forth virtue in lovers, to raise their inner worth, to increase their honor and enhance their reputation," Jaeger, *Ennobling Love,* 6.

way of augmenting praise and honor for lover and beloved, it afforded
medieval people a particular social performance of the self, whose stage
seems largely to have been writing and, particularly, letters. The
Baudri–Constance exchange perfectly demonstrates this dynamic in their
at times near-hyperbolic mutual praise and admiration. The laudatory
tone in their letters can be understood, in Jaeger's formulation, as a
seeking of social gain: the more the addressee is praised, the more the
writer is ennobled.

My analysis extends Jaeger's by considering how letters structured this
performance of love and self, and what this means for women. For Jaeger,
the inclusion of women in this poetic discourse necessitated a confronta-
tion of sexual love. In my reading, sex has different implications: it
changes how we understand the poetic self. Baudri wrote to men and
women in the same amatory vocabulary, which suggests an indifference
to the sex and perhaps even the identity of the addressee; the beloved is a
placeholder for the cultivation of his epistolary voice. However, the fact
that in this exchange his addressee is a woman, who writes back, has
significant implications for the idea of the poetic self. Put simply,
Baudri's learned letter and Constance's equally learned response reconfigure this literary field: it is no longer exclusively male-authored.

Of course, love letters had been written to and about women for centuries. What is important here is that the inscription of women into the
medieval literary and social discourse of mutual ennoblement implies
that women could possess qualities that motivated others to seek an ennobling relation with them; thus, women could confer nobility.[78] It further
implies that women could aspire to the same admirable qualities and
discursive positions as men. In short, once inscribed, or interpellated,
into this discourse, women were participants in ennobling love, seeking
and conferring nobility. Therefore, letters become a field of unexpected,
if limited, agency for women. While the Baudri-Constance exchange
might not permit definitive conclusions about the relative social status of
a historical Baudri and Constance, this is, as I have discussed, not central
to appreciating the significance of these poetic positions. This exchange
demonstrates something important about the subject positions available
to the Constance of Carmen 200 and 201: she has access to discursive
roles usually accessible only to men. When the poetic, loving subject

---

[78] Some have suggested the rise of the trope of the seigneurial lady in courtly love
from these beginnings. Brinkmann has argued that courtly love was a creation of learned
clerical poets writing to courtly women; cited in Jaeger, *Envy of Angels* 311 n. 47 and 317.

writes to a woman, she in turn can be a poetic, loving subject, and write back. In this space of admittedly limited subjectivity, women could exert a kind of agency and, as Constance shows us, resist the roles scripted for them by men.

Women's participation in this discourse also signals a tangible shift in the literary representation of women. It constitutes one sphere in which women have access, as do men, to writing and the performances it affords. This is not necessarily the same access – after all, Constance writes as a respondent, not an initiator – but it is nevertheless significant. The misogynist tenor of many literary works preceding, during, and following this period requires little attestation, and it overlaps with the caricatural nature of the *Heroides* women that similarly held sway for centuries, as well as the highly-troped figure of the lady in courtly litera-ture to come.[79] The intersection of varied epistolary genres upon which Baudri and Constance "play" perhaps unexpectedly affords women the possibility of participation and performance and, from within the space of reply, answering in ways unanticipated by the interpellating discourses to which they respond.[80]

The Position of Reply: A Response to Playful Teaching

Constance's reply does not just exceed the Heroidean script; it complies with, and departs from, the various epistolary scripts deployed in Baudri's letter. This is perhaps most immediately noticeable in her response to his pedagogy. As cited above, Baudri begins his verse epistle with instructions regarding his letter:

> Perlege, perlectam caute complectere cartam,
> Ne noceat fame lingua maligna meae. (lines 1–2)

> Read through this letter, and carefully clasp it once read,
> Lest malignant tongues harm my reputation.

To which instruction Constance replies, reproducing the language of his opening:

> Perlegi vestram studiosa indagine cartam
> Et tetigi nuda carmina vestra manu. (lines 1–2)

---

[79] There is compelling recent scholarship questioning how exactly this figure is to be read; see Griffiths's discussion of misogynist discourse and how it might be read positionally rather that at face value, "The Cross and the *Cura monialium*."

[80] On the representation of women's speech in medieval French literature, see Burns's *Bodytalk* and Solterer's *The Master and Minerva*.

> I have read through your letter with studious hunting,
> And I have touched your verses with my bare hand.

She demonstrates that she is a good student capable of responding in kind to her teacher's verse, continuing with a point-for-point reply to elements in Baudri's letter. He lauds her beauty, writing, and virginity,[81] and she returns the compliment, praising his beauty and intelligence. He writes of her muse and describes her as a Sibyl; she calls him a poet and a prophet, and fortifies her verse with references to figures from classical mythology.[82]

Constance does more than respond to Baudri's letter in kind. She acknowledges its teaching and returns its courtly gestures, but she also holds his letter close to her body:

> Composui gremio posuique sub ubere levo
> Scedam, quod cordi iunctius esse ferunt. (lines 9–10)

> I put together the sheet in my lap and put it beneath my left breast
> Which, as they say, is more closely joined to the heart.

Like Baudri, Constance invests the letter with a talismanic quality, treating it as a material representation of its writer. She clasps the letter to her body, and it, in turn, acts on her. Reading it kept her up late:

> Tandem fessa dedi nocturno membra sopori;
> Sed nescit noctem sollicitatus amor. (lines 13–14)

> At last I gave my weary limbs over to the night's sleep;
> But troubled love does not recognize the night.

Indeed, his letter kept her up all night:

> In somnis insomnis eram, quia pagina uestra
> Scilicet in gremio viscera torruerat (lines 17–18)

> In sleep I was sleepless, because your page
> In my lap had, of course, heated up my heart.

---

[81] "Forma," "littera," and "virginitas," lines 30, 51, and 81, respectively.

[82] "O quantus vates, quam preditus iste poeta" (Oh, how great a prophet, how gifted this poet), and "Si sermo fiat de forme compositura,/Impar est tante nostra Camena rei" (If talk should arise about the composition of his beauty,/My Muse is unequal to such a thing), "Lady Constance to Baudri of Bourgueil" line 21, and lines 51–2, in Bond, *The Loving Subject*. All citations of this verse epistle are to this edition and translation, and appear parenthetically in the text.

"Torruerat" can also convey a more charged state than "heated": her "viscera" were scorched by his "pagina," a word that means "page" but comes from *pangere*, to fasten. Baudri's page exerts a nearly feverish hold on the body. This physical vocabulary responds to the winking eroticism in Baudri's letter, but Constance goes a step further. She describes her response to his letter and paints the scene of her reading, inviting the reader into her room – a nun's room being a place to which outsiders do not normally have access.[83] He writes playfully, if suggestively, of her bare hand touching his bare page in her lap, and she responds with an excess of detail and imagery on the effects of his wordplay.

However playfully they might be intended, letters can produce perhaps unintended results, and Constance shows that Baudri's letter was not merely *iocosa* to its recipient. Her response, detailing her somatic distress, whether or not indicative of actual distress, creates for the diligent student a position unanticipated by her teacher's instruction. This exceeds the tone set by Baudri's letter, responding to his self-described playful verses with a reply that wrenches the poetic register from talk of praise and virtue, to invitations to forbidden places and recriminations and demands.

Of course, one could argue that Constance *is* being playful. As Baudri "plays" at being flirtatious, so could she be playing at being lovelorn. Within the logic of such a reading, Constance demonstrates that she is better – because more vivid and consistent – at role-playing than he is. In keeping with her teacher's literary game she answers back in a staged fashion, but it is a position of wretchedness, not delight, that she claims: he proclaims pleasure in his epistolary play, while she professes misery. What Constance "really felt" is inaccessible, as is the issue of whether she is "really" playing, but what is important is the range of tones and positions she claims in her response: obedient reader, diligent student, ardent admirer, aggrieved lover, bride of God, and, above all, capable writer. Both she and Baudri show how, through letters, men and women could write from a variety of positions and explore a complicated and

---

[83] Women's rooms are a different matter; in Carmen 134, Baudri invites us into Countess Adela's room – but for the purpose of describing the artwork it contains. This tapestry has been suggested to be the Bayeux tapestry, or one very like it, and Baudri's description of it suggests that he has seen it; Bloch, *A Needle in the Right Hand of God*, 39. Baudri writes more figuratively that his writing also fashions a "thalamum" worthy of the countess, lines 1351–3. The anonymous twelfth-century *chanson de toile* "Belle Doette" depicts the heroine weaving by her window when she receives the news that inspires her monasticism – but she is not yet a nun in this scene.

even contradictory range of interpersonal relations. And from the space
of reply, Constance crafts an answer that departs from her teacher's letter
in critical ways, breaking with scripts to craft a new, unanticipated epistolary position.

One of the most striking ways in which Constance's letter departs from
the tone set by Baudri's is in its near-insistence on somatic response.
Baudri's letter addresses corporeality in his description of Constance's
physical beauty; in his instructions on the reading of his letter; and when
he praises her virginity and the cleanness of her flesh.[84] Of his own body
and his somatic response, he writes:

> Nec lascivus amor nec amor petulantis amoris
> > Pro te subvertit corque iecurque meum (lines 49–50)

> Neither lascivious love nor a love of wanton love
> > Stirs up the depths of my heart on account of you.

Noticeably, these are negative descriptions: his feeling for Constance does
not provoke bodily responses. He repeats his assurances of singularity: "Te
solam nostris implico uisceribus" (you alone do I enfold within my heart)
(line 76), and claims an intimacy allowing no secrets between them: "Nulla
mei cordis potuit te vena latere" (no vein of my heart could lie hidden from
you) (line 161). All of these references are to his heart, his "cor" and
"viscera," and take place in fairly general language.

Constance writes variously and vividly throughout Carmen 201 of her
body. At first, she does so in response to Baudri's *manus* trope.[85] She
develops this theme, directing her reader's attention to the figurative and
literal loci of her reading:

> Si possem cordi mandare volumina vestra,
> > Cordi mandarem singula, non gremio. (lines 11–12)

> If I could send your volumes to my heart,
> > I would send each one to my heart, not to my lap.

She twice explicitly demands attention to her body with imperative
"ecce"s, first with specific reference to her lap and breasts:

---

[84] "Ipse tue semper sum virginitatis amator,/Ipse tue carnis diligo mundiciam./Nolo
vel ad modicum pro me tua mens violetur" (lines 81–3) (I myself am always the lover of
your virginity,/I love the cleanness of your flesh./I do not wish that your mind be violated
even a little bit on account of me) (line 55–70).

[85] This is the passage that opens this section: "... tetigi nuda carmina vestra manu"
(... I have touched your verses with my bare hand) (line 2).

> Hoc iacet in gremio dilecti scedula nostri;
>> Ecce locata meis subiacet uberibus. (lines 67–8)

> My beloved's little sheet lies in this lap;
>> Look, it lies placed beneath my breasts!

Repeating the commanding "ecce" at the start of the couplet, she directs attention to the image of her, sleepless:

> Ecce vigil vigilo, quia me liber evigilavit
>> Lectus multotiens, quem michi misit heri. (lines 77–8)

> Look, wakeful I lie awake, because the book which he sent me
>> Yesterday has been read many times and kept me awake.

Constance moves from describing parts of her body, to describing her body in its various states. The cause of this varied suffering is Baudri's letter, "iocosa" to him and a source of agitation for her.

The experience of reading his missive is not a pleasurable one, and afterward she is weakened and wakeful, tormented and suspicious.[86] Her descriptions of her anguished emotional state are, noticeably, also bodily descriptions:

> Nil est, quod rogito pectore sollicito. (line 80)
> What I beg for with troubled heart is nothing [to him].

> Pectore fluctivago deduxi tempora noctis; (line 99)
> With fluctuating heart I have passed the hours of the night …

> Virginis alterius sic nomen abominor, ut sim
>> Virginis ad nomen frigidior glacie. (lines 133–4)
> I hate the name of another girl so much, that
>> I am colder than ice at the name of (any) girl.

Constance invokes the jealousy expected of a jilted Heroidean lover, and perhaps hints at her knowledge of Baudri's many female addressees. In a gesture that figures prominently in troubadour lyric to come, she writes of desire as a sickness:

> Visere me debes; nescis, quo langueo morbo,
>> Quo desiderio scilicet affitior. (lines 173–4)

---

86 "Afficior desiderio precibusque diurnis" (I am weakened by desire and by day-long prayers) (line 61), and "Dum nova dat precepta michi, plus ipsa fatigor;/Nunquam non possum suspiciosa fore" (When he gives me new instructions, I am more tormented; I can never not be suspicious) (lines 89–90).

> You should visit me; you do not know what illness ails me.
> That is to say, what desire afflicts me.

Instead of lingering over a laudatory description of her addressee's body, she dwells on the suffering visited upon her own body. Baudri writes of his cheerful character; Constance, her misery.[87] In thus drawing attention to her condition, she disrupts the playful tone he claims in his letter, rendering her reply inescapably personal and demanding that her reader consider her wretched physical and emotional state. This is not an argument for a historical Constance's real misery, rather it is an attention to this letter's disruption of tone, and how this rhetorical gesture is unsolicited by the letter to which it replies.

Carmen 201 is in many ways a work elaborating upon impossibility and lack of action: Constance writes of what she cannot do, what she wishes she could do, what she longs for her correspondent to do, and which he has shown no signs of doing. Her letter is almost a caricature of powerlessness. And yet Constance's epistolary voice is quite powerful, in disrupting the light-hearted tone established by Baudri and in fashioning of the position of reply a space from which to express things not only unsolicited by, but even counter to, the tenor of the Baudri's letter. He is light-hearted, she dwells on her somatic suffering and exhorts him not to neglect her.[88] Her demands that he invent pretexts for visiting her, discussed earlier, are all the more striking since he does not ask for a visit or express desire for one, which he does in letters to other addressees; he does not even for ask a reply.[89] Again, it is not at all surprising that replies exceed the letters to which they respond, but highly stylized letters such as Baudri's not only script a particular relationship between writers, they also anticipate a certain tenor of response. Constance's letter exceeds this tone, insisting on her suffering, demanding dissimulating action, and most important, refusing Baudri's playful ambiguity.

Constance develops the jealousy topos, expounding on the subject of other girls to whom Baudri might send letters. Playing the role of neglected lover to the hilt, she deftly refuses Baudri the shelter of ambiguity:

> Quodsi preponis, quodsi pretenderis ullam,
> Scito, quod non est hic iocus in domino.

---

[87] Respectively, "mores hylares," line 146, and "miseram," line 60.

[88] Line 151, "me pretermittere noli."

[89] In contrast, he does ask another one of his female addressees for a reply; see Carmen 137, "Murieli."

Si fallis, malus es, si verum dicis, iniquus;
    Obsidet atque tenet crimen utrumque iocum.
Damnat falsiloquos Deus et prave facientes;
    Aut hoc aut illud vel simul ambo facis.
Sed Deus emendet, Deus in te corrigat ista;
    Hec me cura tui non sinit immemorem.
Virginis alterius sic nomen abominor, ut sim
    Virginis ad nomen frigidior glacie.
Sed, sicut tibi vis, credam credamque volenti,
    Credam dictanti; tu quoque crede michi. (lines 125–36)

But if you favor, if you prefer any other (girl),
    Know that this game is not in the Lord.
If you deceive, you are bad, if you tell the truth, wicked;
    Either crime besieges and emprisons the game.
God condemns liars and those acting perversely;
    You do one or the other, or both at the same time.
But let God emend, let God correct these things in you;
    This worry does not allow me to forget you.
I hate the name of another girl so much, that
    I am colder than ice at the name of (any) girl.
But I will trust you, as you wish, and I will trust your wanting
    and trust your writing; you, too, trust in me.

Constance offers here her own imperatives, laying claim to her teacher's preference and giving lie to his assurances of the exclusivity of his affection and the propriety of his conduct. She declares her obedience to Baudri, even as, ten lines later, she takes him to task for neglecting her. By claiming lack of faith in his assurances that she is the only recipient of his verses, she identifies the trope of exclusivity and calls attention to it as such. More than that, she accuses him of crime: in Constance's formulation, Baudri is guilty, either of deceiving her by claiming she is his only female correspondent when she is not, or of telling her the truth – that is, writing to her alone, but in a wicked, perverse fashion, as a lover and not as a teacher or guide. Her verses question Baudri's assurances that "Nullam preter te carmina nostra sciunt" (my verses know none but you). They also comment scathingly on the ambiguity of his letter, advising virginity in verses decidedly amorous in tone, insisting on the chaste nature of their relation, and equivocally declaring "let the game be in the pen." Yet despite her reproof, Constance is consistent in her devotion to Baudri: reminding him of God's punishment of criminals, she declares her affection for him regardless, and concludes with a promise of her trust and demand for his trust in return.

This is a curious display for an obedient student, pointing out her teacher's shortcomings, demanding proof of affection, and avowing unreasoned allegiance. Bond translates the primary verb of the final lines of this passage, "credo," as "trust"; Baudri's most defensive passages declaring his playful good intentions employ the same verb ("crede michi").[90] Baudri seeks the good opinion of his audience, Constance and others included; yet why would she need to ask the same?[91] Her echoing "crede michi"s acknowledge his instruction, but they also implicitly challenge his authority and insist on her own. Despite "proving" him untrustworthy, guilty of crime however he tries to spin his epistolary activities, she declares her continued affection and trust and demands his trust in exchange for hers, thus rhetorically maneuvering her teacher into a position of embarrassment and indebtedness, and gaining, at least rhetorically, the upper hand.

Just how good a pupil is Constance? Baudri instructs her to "let the shame be in the act"; she lays blame at his door, be he sincere or insincere, and regardless of his care to assert his playful good intentions. He teaches her to "let the game be in the pen"; as the cited passages demonstrate, her verses are anything but playful – or, if she does play, it is a very different game, returning gestures seemingly in kind but laced with judgment and insistent on the deleterious effects of this play. Baudri seems to find the verse epistle an ideal medium for conducting his ambiguous *iocos* to his addressees, since they "let the game be in the pen." Constance corroborates his preference for the letter, but for a different reason. For her, writing is a substitute for speech:

> Aggrediar ceram, quia nescit cera pudorem,
> > Que referat domino congrua verba meo.
> Multa quidem scribam, que nolim dicere presens;
> > Virgineos ausus sepe pudor reprimit. (lines 103–6)

> I shall turn to the wax, because wax knows no shame
> > And it can deliver words suitable to my Lord [or: lord].

---

90 Bond translates Baudri's "crede michi"s on lines 37 and 47 as "believe me."

91 While Constance does not mention "legentes" as Baudri does, it is likely that she was equally attuned to the possibility of plural audience. Baudri writes in the second person, commanding Constance in imperatives, addressing her in the second person singular "tu," while Constance writes in both the second and third persons, referring to Baudri as "tu" and "ille." This difference in address is another way in which Constance registers the difference and even the hierarchy in their relative status: "ille" could well be an apostrophe to herself, or it could function as an address to another reader; either way, it marks Baudri as a subject worthy of discussion and praise.

> Indeed, I will write many things which I do not want to say in person;
> Shame often curbs a girl's daring acts.

The words she would wish to speak are unsuitable, their utterance would constitute a shameful act. Therefore she turns to the wax for their expression – a metonym for wax writing tablets, so often referred to in Baudri's verses.[92] This privileging of word over deed has the effect of rendering letters, a substitute for presence, *preferable* to presence, presumably for their immunity from shame, suggesting one way in which their lovers' hearts might be joined in licit union.[93]

Constance represents writing as a space of possibility that permits expression of that which is impossible to express in person, either for shame, or perhaps lack of opportunity to meet: practically, letters can materially transport these expressions to her addressee. Baudri declares that actions can be shameful, but his writing is only play, and as such can never incur shame. Constance twists his formulation to claim that shame can curb actions but not writing. For her, a letter permits the expression of that which would be shameful to say in person, but not shameful to write. Thus, letters are not merely *iocos*, but also instrumental tools in the expression of licit and illicit desires. This is a distinct departure from Baudri's formulation, in which the polyvalence of written words is at once their danger and delight, upon which he plays to maintain a position of suspended ambiguity.

Carmen 201 has significant implications for the appearance of women's voice in this literature. In some ways, a reply will always exceed that to which it answers, but stepping outside of register and breaking tone represent subtle shifts in discursive relations that constitute, albeit to a limited degree, a form of agency. Attributing Carmen 201's tone-breaking to Constance's gender, thereby suggesting an essential and inevitably disruptive female voice in the Loire circle writings, would be as reductive and limited an interpretation as claiming that the verse-epistle's varied discursive gestures are determined by its status as a reply – after all, Constance could easily have penned a response fully in kind,

---

[92] See Rouse and Rouse. Another reason for which Constance might "turn to the wax" has to do with its ephemeral quality: because wax can be effaced, it might be a particularly desirable medium for illicit expressions; thanks to Andrea Tarnowski for this observation.

[93] This argument contrasts starkly with the debate over the relationship between words and deeds and their respective ability to cause harm and incur shame that increases in importance over the next few centuries, culminating in Christine de Pizan's heated quarrel with Parisian clergy in the fourteenth century; see Chapter 3.

light-hearted, without demands or challenges to Baudri's assured epistolary expressions of pedagogy, friendship and love. Her refusal to answer
in kind implicitly resists the force of generic scripting and expectation,
and amounts to an authoritative, if limited, exercise of voice. That this
takes place in an epistolary response from a woman claims space for the
articulation of women's voice in the literature of this period and its development to come, setting the stage for increasingly greater exercises of
authority.[94]

The Possibilities and Limits of Epistolary Play

In situating these letters in their various contexts – the tradition of spiritual guidance letters, the culture of ennobling love, the rise of humanist
letters and the practice of *amiticia* – my examination of the
Baudri–Constance exchange shows how it engages with contemporary
epistolary conventions to perform a contradictory relationship that is
particular to letters. In their letters, they inhabit a relationship between an
abbot and the younger nun he advises, in which they also perform the
rhetorical gestures of secular lovers – avowing fidelity, confessing jealousy, and expressing a longing desire to see one another. Their exchange
puts established letter-writing traditions to literally creative use: in their
letters, Baudri and Constance could simultaneously "be" abbot and nun,
teacher and student, as well as separated lovers, through writing from
these positions. In accessing these overlapping and at times seemingly
incompatible relationships, their exchange demonstrates how epistolary
genres offered a field for productive contradiction. Their easily recognized, established vocabularies and relationships were available for
deployment and manipulation, as Baudri and Constance show us, through
ambiguous play, simultaneity and contradiction, and departures from
recognized scripts. These varied epistolary gestures articulate a learned
self, steeped in generations of Latin letter-writing traditions, expressing
contradictory desires through inhabiting various positions scripted by
epistolary tradition.

Whether these epistolary expressions are real or "merely play," their
vividness and range attest to how letters, liminal to the fictional and

---

[94] As Solterer details in *The Master and Minerva*, medieval French literature
employed the figure of the female respondent in various ways to challenge claims of
masterly discourse and injurious language, and ultimately to counter slanderous representations of women.

non-fictional, provide men and women with possibilities for a particular, poetic exercise of agency. Appreciating the force of this exercise has less to do with determining sincerity or its lack, than with recognizing the staged quality of these poems. This quality is in part generically determined: verse epistles are often playful, often amatory, and replete with recognizable tropes. Baudri and Constance demonstrate their facility with epistolary genres, and they also aggressively situate themselves as learned readers and writers by referencing classical literature and activating the amatory dynamics typified by Ovidian verse, and as a result many passages might seem to parrot Ovidian sentiments and expressions. This staged quality is intensified by Baudri's insistence on his "iocosa" nature and writing. His refusal to play exclusively the role of virtuous abbot or ardent but perhaps rascally lover heightens this atmosphere in which there appear to be no genuine emotions or relationships, just staged positions.

While established epistolary traditions script these staged positions, they also structure another more fundamental layer of positioning: letters anticipate responses, and they set into motion dynamics of initiation, reception, and reaction. The recurrence of amatory vocabulary and imagery in Baudri's poems to young men and women reinforces the emphasis on scripted, anticipated positions and gestures, rather than biographical identity and desire. This helps us to think about love as an epistolary phenomenon not only structured but also facilitated by the exigencies of genre, and not by biography: love is a textual position.

From the space of reply, Constance crafts a response that catches ambiguity at its game. Whether she is playful or not, she identifies the indefensibility of Baudri's positions, cutting through the excuses for amorous verse-writing as light-hearted diversion. Her response expresses, from within a scripted position, refusal in an unanticipated tenor that shifts the parameters of this position and this exchange. Her reply is no less staged, but it shows how the position of response can be manipulated to articulate another contradictory position, acquiescence alongside pointed and skillful refusal. In Constance's hands, epistolary response is not merely reactive, but creative – a position of resistance, and authority. This letter-reply set reveals how stylized literary genres can be pushed beyond their customary spheres of meaning to create unexpected positions, and within this discourse, this very unexpectedness can be read as an exercise of agency. Thus Baudri's call to "let the game be in the pen," as answered by Constance, reveals that words can carry just as much force as deeds, and letter writing, itself a form of conduct, can be not only playful but also transgressive, and even transformative.

To claim that Constance's reply is representative of a feminism in medieval letters, or that she is an exemplary woman writer who sets the tone for future women writers, would bring too much weight to bear on one letter-poem. However, this letter-reply set does show how epistolary structures provided important resources for women and men in the articulation of a poetic, learned, loving self. That it is a woman's reply that most strikingly illuminates the agency available in letter writing does not necessarily suggest an inevitably gendered epistolary voice, but it is useful for what it reveals about epistolary structures: letters, in literal and figurative ways, script replies, and departures from highly stylized, scripted discourse can be read as evidence of an unexpected, if limited, form of agency. Verse epistles structure the performance of generically scripted roles, and, even if writers never quite break free of these roles, these structures invite the exploration of ways to exceed established social and literary boundaries.

Writing the Subjunctive into the Indicative:
Commanding Performances in the Letters of Abelard
and Heloise

[T]hroughout all Latinity, no phrase has yet been found that speaks clearly about how intent on you is my spirit, for God is my witness that I love you with a sublime and exceptional love.

[I]n omni latinitate non est sermo inventus qui aperte loquatur erga te quam sit animus meus intentus, quia deo teste cum sublimi et precipua dilectione te diligo.[1]

[M]ay it always be kept uncertain which of us loves the other more, since this way there will always be between us a most beautiful contest in which both of us will win.

[S]emper in dubio servetur, uter nostrum magis alterum diligat, quia ita semper pulcerrima inter nos erit concertacio ut uterque vincat.[2]

These anonymous verses, penned some time in the twelfth century and recopied in the early fifteenth century, have recently redirected an authenticity debate that has been called "one of the most controversial areas of medieval studies."[3] Argued – not undisputedly – to have been written by

---

[1] From Mulier 53, *Epistolae duorum amantium*, ed. Könsgen, 31. The anonymous letters are distinguished in the manuscript as written by "M" for "Mulier" and "V" for "Vir." Translations are from Mews and Chiavaroli, *The Lost Love Letters of Heloise and Abelard*, with modifications indicated.

[2] Vir, 85.

[3] McGuire, 303. Newman comments that the controversy over the authorship of the letters of Abelard and Heloise "has become a kind of institution in medieval studies," "Authority, Authenticity, and the Repression of Heloise," 54. The authenticity of these letters has been much contested; critics have weighed in on the irrelevance of the facts of authorship, as well as the vital necessity of taking a position on authorship. Through close analysis of the content and style of the letters, and in the absence of conclusive evidence to the contrary, scholarship in recent years has largely assumed authentic dual authorship of the letters. For an overview of the history of the debate, see Marenbon, and Clanchy's introduction in the revised translation of *The Letters of Abelard and Heloise*. Most recently Dalarun has presented compelling arguments for the authenticity of the correspondence, as well as an earlier dating of the sole manuscript containing the complete correspondence in "Nouveaux aperçus sur Abélard, Héloïse, et le Paraclet."

Abelard and Heloise in the early stages of their love affair, these "lost love letters" shed important light on the epistolary situation in early twelfth-century France.[4] They evidence the continued tradition of amatory Latin epistolary exchange in the twelfth century; a crossing over into prose of concerns more commonly addressed in verse, as examined in the previous chapter; and the exercise of the learned female voice in Latin. These two writers, identified only as "Mulier" (woman) and "Vir" (man), explore, among other topics, ineffability and contradiction in love. For them, language is insufficient to describe love, yet it is also the means by which they engage in continued enjoyment of it, demonstrated by the dozens of letters they wrote. This contradiction is mirrored in their "concertatio": love is a contest with no single winner, because both lovers win.[5] This epistolary competition and exploration of the nature of amatory relations resonates strikingly with some of the concerns in the correspondence of Abelard and Heloise, whose epistolary writings, I argue, extend our understanding of the parameters of medieval letters and their relationship to the medieval self. While the Baudri–Constance exchange illuminates some of the uses of literary and epistolary scripts, the Abelard–Heloise dossier aggressively mines letter-writing structures, vocabularies, and registers to voice contradictory desires and positions, and possibly, through shaping the expression of the self, even reshape the self.

The story of the historical Abelard and Heloise requires little rehearsing: the famous dialectician and his female student come to grief as a result of their love affair. The survival of their story in medieval French literature and beyond generally takes the form of a tragic tale of love, yet the story told by their letters reveals a much more complicated relationship that depends on the letter for its very existence.[6] Like Baudri

---

4 Newman provides an account of the reception of Könsgen's work on the *Epistolae duorum amantium* in her review of Mews's *The Lost Love Letters of Heloise and Abelard*, 6 January 2000. For differing views on the authenticity of these letters, see Jaeger, "*Epistolae duorum amantium* and the Ascription to Heloise and Abelard"; Constable, "The Authorship of the *Epistolae duorum amantium*: A Reconsideration"; Jaeger, "A Reply to Giles Constable;" and Ziolkowski, "Lost and Not Yet Found: Heloise." Piron provides a thorough overview of the authenticity debate and defends the attribution to Abelard and Heloise in his 2005 translation of the letters.

5 This suspension in desire offers a unique twist on the courtly love condition celebrated in troubadour lyric, in which the poetic subject similarly languishes, uncertain of whether his affections will be returned.

6 The portrayal of Heloise as a romantic heroine begins early. The best-known medieval account of their story appears in Jean de Meun's *Roman de la Rose*, discussed in the

and Constance, they were monastic writers, but at the time of their correspondence both occupied positions of authority: Abelard was an abbot,
Heloise an abbess. Composed during the 1130s, their missives comprise
a series of lengthy letters and replies in prose.[7] These letters are markedly
less playful than the Loire school epistles, and while Abelard and Heloise
both write of love and monasticism and express complicated desire, obligation, and reproach, the stakes are much higher in their extended epistolary exchange. In their letters, they wrestle with the very value of their
monastic vocation: the question of sincerity works not so much to expose
the infidelity of a lover as to question the value of a conversion, and
ambivalence seems not a playful subterfuge but part of a determined
effort to let writing effect its force.

The Loire school epistles were composed at the cusp of what is often
called the twelfth-century "renaissance." The correspondence of Abelard
and Heloise is situated squarely in this moment, and Abelard was
undisputedly one of its central figures.[8] Letters played an important part
in the vibrant intellectual landscape of the twelfth century, evidenced by a
marked increase in their volume and variety.[9] Scholars have noted the
tendency in this period toward writing letters in a more personal tone, and

next chapter; Dalarun calls this emphasis a "distorsion" that is, moreover, shared by
others, 29 and 55. For an account of history's insistence on a romantic reading of their
story, see the introduction to Kamuf's *Fictions of Feminine Desire: Disclosures of
Heloise*.

[7] The correspondence is generally held to consist of the *Historia calamitatum* and
seven ensuing letters: three letters from Heloise, and four from Abelard. The correspondence takes a marked turn in tone and subject matter in Heloise's third letter. This shift is
reflected in Radice's English translation, which divides the letters into two groups,
consisting of "Personal Letters" and "Letters of Direction," and the updated 2003 translation preserves this distinction; Charrier also divides the letters into two groups, "lettres
amoureuses" and "lettres de direction." While I agree that an important shift occurs in
Heloise's third letter, my study traces the evolution of Heloise and Abelard's epistolary
personae and argues for the consistency of certain dynamics throughout their letters.

[8] Ward and Chiavaroli describe Abelard as a defining figure of the early twelfth
century, which they suggest might be considered a "liminal" period between the Ovidian
humanism of the last half of the eleventh century and the "scholastic, post-Abelardian"
world, 55. See Clanchy for a discussion of Abelard's teaching and the twelfth-century
classroom in *Abelard: A Medieval Life*, especially 65–94. On Abelard's pedagogy, see
Jaeger, *Envy of Angels*, 229–36. To cite just a few recent works examining Abelard's
importance in the twelfth century and beyond, see in addition to Clanchy's volume,
Brower and Jaffrey, *The Cambridge Companion to Peter Abelard*, and Ziolkowsi's *Letters
of Peter Abelard*.

[9] The types of letters written and circulated include business and scholarly letters,
religious recruitment letters, and model letters and treatises in letter form, among others.

including in them one's personal experience; Giles Constable observes that this trend was paralleled by a tendency towards formalization in composition.[10] While it might be reasonable to think of a system of elaborate compositional rules as a limit on expression and the exploration of the personal, I argue that it is against the trend toward formalization in letters that important ways of defining the self become legible. The formalization and institutionalization of letter writing actually *produces* the expression of the personal by providing structures that facilitate its expression. The correspondence of Abelard and Heloise demonstrates how the letter-writing genre, with its many rules and conventions, provided tools for articulating and performing new ways of thinking about the self. Their letters blur the boundaries between public and private, formal and personal, and function as transformative vehicles that shape and change their lives. In this chapter, I examine how Abelard and Heloise deploy letters not only for saying, but also for doing – they show how letters can function as discourse as well as action, with the power to reshape the self from the outside in.

Interrupted Epistolary Circuits

The letters of Abelard and Heloise begin with a letter written by Abelard addressed to someone else, commonly known as the *Historia calamitatum* (Story of my misfortunes).[11] It has been called "the best autobiography written in the twelfth century,"[12] and it recounts events in Abelard's life leading up to his abbacy at St Gildas, where, he reports to his unnamed addressee, he suffers daily torment and persecution and lives in fear for his life.[13] This juxtaposition of personal letter and autobi-

---

[10] Constable, "Letters and Letter-Collections," 34, and Mews, "Hugh Metel, Heloise and Peter Abelard," 59–91.

[11] Early editions identify it as *Abaelardi ad amicum suum consolatoria 'epistula'* (Abelard's letter of consolation to his friend; "Abelard's Letter of Consolation to a Friend (*Historia Calamitatum*)," ed. Muckle, 163.

[12] Southern, *Medieval Humanism and Other Studies*, 89. On autobiography in this period and the so-called "discovery of the individual," see Morris, *The Discovery of the Individual 1050–1200* and McLaughlin, "Abelard as Autobiographer"; for a different perspective on the question of the individual, see Bynum, "Did the Twelfth Century Discover the Individual?"

[13] Peter Abelard, *Historia calamitatum*, in *The Letters of Abelard and Heloise*, trans. Radice, 102–6. All subsequent citations and translations to the *Historia calamitatum* and the letters of Abelard and Heloise are from this edition and are noted parenthetically in the text. Abelard's description of his Breton experience might not be a purely rhetorical

ography reveals a gap between modern and medieval literary genres, and alerts us to a key difference regarding letters in particular: in the expectation of privacy. Medieval letters were "quasi-public" documents, often collected and circulated, and probably composed with this in mind.[14] Therefore, while Abelard could well have directed and sent his letter to a particular friend, it is likely that he wrote it with some expectation of its circulation. This does not necessarily render insincere its contents, but it does invest them with several interpretive possibilities. It suggests that Abelard might have written the *Historia calamitatum* to tell his version of by now famous – and perhaps infamous – events; as a demonstration of his current humility; to record for posterity his life story; and to fulfill the purported goal of the letter, to console a suffering friend.[15]

Richard Southern notes that the *Historia calamitatum* is first and foremost an example of an *epistola consolatoria*, or letter of consolation, a variety of letter whose standard arguments were well known to medieval writers. So well known were these arguments that the skill with which a letter was composed could be of greater interest than what it actually said.[16] The rhetorical function of this kind of letter, its demonstration of

embellishment; Tilliette writes: "La littérature du temps est si unanime à présenter les Bretons comme des êtres incultes, brutaux et impies que l'on peut se demander s'il n'y a pas, dans ce lieu commun, un fond de vérité," in *Baudri de Bourgueil: Poèmes*, ed. Tilliette, Introduction, 9; Bond also comments on "contentious Bretons" in Baudri's experience in " 'Iocus amoris,' " 148 and n. 15.

[14] Constable contrasts the modern attribution of "intimacy, spontaneity, and privacy" to letters with epistolary practice in the Middle Ages, in which letters were largely "self-conscious, quasi-public literary documents, often written with an eye to future collection and publication. In view of the way in which letters were written and sent, and also of the standards of literacy in the Middle Ages, it is doubtful whether there were any private letters in the modern sense of the term," "Letters and Letter-Collections," 11. Piron points to the *Epistolae duorum amantium* as a possible counter-example, whose intimacy suggests confidence of privacy in the writers' lifetime, at least; while his nuancing of Constable's claim is worth noting, the fact of and manner of the letters' survival seem to prove Constable's point; 192–3.

[15] Telling his version of events could well have been instrumental, and part of a plan to return to Paris and teaching. See Luscombe, McLaughlin, "Abelard as Autobiographer," and Newman, "Authority, Authenticity, and the Repression of Heloise," 56. Griffiths characterizes it as an "aggressive attempt to sway future public opinion in his favour," "'Men's Duty to Provide for Women's Needs," 11.

[16] Southern summarizes the arguments that could typically be found: "'your misfortunes, however great, have all happened to other and better men'; or 'these troubles will prove to be a blessing in disguise'; or 'your tribulations are a judgment upon sin'; or 'these things are sent to try us'; and so on"; he adds that "the main interest of letters of this kind lay in the skill with which the writer chose and deployed his limited range of arguments," 89–90. In his multi-volume study on *Consolatio*, Moos identifies consolation

argumentative skill, was considered inseparable from its narrative function. However, as I will show, rhetorically "typed" letters can exceed their generic demands, both working in concert with and against conventional expectations. Far more than simply displaying Abelard's skill in deploying familiar epistolary tropes, the *Historica calamitatum* skillfully paints a picture of a subject at once humiliated and proud, persecuted and intellectually vigorous, who desires yet the good opinion of a public inflamed with the details of his story. This letter of consolation carefully, perhaps instrumentally, articulates this subject's worth and humility to this public.

The *Historia calamitatum* begins with a statement of purpose that follows rhetorical type:

> Saepe humanos affectus aut provocant aut mitigant amplius exempla quam verba. Unde post nonnullam sermonis ad praesentem habiti consolationem, de ipsis calamitatum mearum experimentis consolatoriam ad absentem scribere decrevi ut in comparatione mearum tuas aut nullas aut modicas tentationes recognoscas et tolerabilius feras.[17]

> There are times when example is better than precept for stirring or soothing human passions; and so I propose to follow up the words of consolation I gave you in person with the history of my own misfortunes, hoping thereby to give you comfort in absence. In comparison with my trials you will see that your own are nothing, or only slight, and will find them easier to bear (*Historia calamitatum*, 57).

Abelard suggests that his story be read as a negative exemplum to comfort his reader in two ways: through enabling a comparison of his considerable misfortunes with the reader's own, and through following up on "words of consolation in person" with "comfort in absence." This comfort would seem to be provided by Abelard's letter, and that which it metonymically as well as literally represents: his story. This conception of letters as a way of providing absence in presence is a common topos in this period, a comfort that Heloise will boldly claim in her letters.[18] Despite the altruistic claim to provide comfort, however, there is a

---

as a theme throughout the entire dossier, and ties it to the rhetorical principle of *petitio* as an explanation for Heloise's sudden change in tone in her third letter. I thank Sylvie Lefèvre for this reference.

[17] "Abelard's Letter of Consolation to a Friend (*Historia Calamitatum*)," ed. Muckle, 175.

[18] See discussion in introduction, 6–8.

self-serving tone to this epistle. Abelard's misfortunes are considerable, and his exemplarity in misery connotes extreme humility, yet also a certain status. In this letter purporting to comfort a suffering friend, Abelard offers a vivid rehearsal of the miseries he has suffered, in which expressions of stark humility make the rhetorical pretense seem just that, a prop that enables him to claim his version of his life's controversial events.[19] Fifteen years after his rise and fall in Paris, the *Historia calamitatum* could well serve to as an attempt to circulate his autobiography and humility, and perhaps thereby effect his redemption.

It is in response to this anonymously addressed, rhetorically situated work that Heloise writes her first letter to Abelard. She begins with an explanation:

> Missam ad amicum pro consolatione epistolam, dilectissime, vestram ad me forte quidam nuper attulit. Quam ex ipsa statim tituli fronte vestram esse considerans, tanto ardentius eam coepi legere, quanto scriptorem ipsum carius amplector ut, cuius rem perdidi, verbis saltem tamquam eius quadam *imagine recreer.* Erant memini huius epistolae fere omnia felle et absinthio plena quae scilicet nostrae conversionis miserabilem historiam et tuas, unice, cruces assiduas referebant.[20]

> Not long ago, most beloved, by chance someone brought me the letter of consolation you had sent to a friend. I saw at once from the superscription that it was yours, and was all the more eager to read it since the writer is so dear to my heart. I hoped for renewal of strength, at least from the writer's words, which would picture for me the reality I have lost. But nearly every line of this letter was filled, I remember, with gall and wormwood, as it told the pitiful story of our entry into religion and the cross of unending suffering which you, my only one, continue to bear.[21]

Heloise imparts a great deal of information in these opening lines. Acknowledging the rhetorical form of Abelard's letter (*ad amicum pro consolatione epistolam*), she claims him as hers: he is her "dilectissime"

[19] Indeed, as Dalarun observes, "comment croire un seul instant qu'une telle lettre de consolation puisse apporter le moindre soulagement à son destinataire, superbement ignoré?" 50 n. 164.

[20] Ed. Muckle, "The Personal Letters between Abelard and Héloïse," 68, emphasis added. All citations from this edition are identified in the text with letter number and page number. In citing the Latin letters I follow his numbering, in which Heloise's reply to the *Historia calamitatum* is identified as Epistle 1.

[21] Heloise, "Letter 1, Heloise to Abelard," 109. I have modified Radice's translation of "dilectissime" to reflect the superlative force of the adjective, and also her rendering of "unice" as "only love," an interpolation which appears throughout her translation.

(most beloved), her "unice" (only one). In an echo of his "historia calamitatum," she reveals her perspective on her entry into religion, a "miserabilem historiam" (wretched story), and her current situation, one of loss ("perdidi," I have lost). Fifteen years after their entry into monastic life, Heloise is now the respected abbess of the Paraclete, and this epistolary declaration of amorous attachment to Abelard, her teacher and husband before her entry into religious life, dramatically confesses continued longing for the past.

This passage also reflects a prevailing conception of the function of letters in this period: to "imagine recreer" (to recreate in representation) or, as Radice translates, to "picture a reality," to bring to life that which is absent.[22] To a suffering reader, this epistolary recreation is hoped for in a letter, yet it is an expectation which, Heloise laments, is thwarted by the contents of Abelard's missive. Aligning herself with his anonymous addressee, Heloise interrupts the epistolary circuit of the *Historia calamitatum*, explaining that his letter was brought to her "by chance."[23] Epistolary exchange in this correspondence is thus marked from the beginning as situated and dialogic: letters are written as responses (Abelard following up on the sufferings of an anonymous friend), and as interruptions of epistolary circuits (Heloise happening upon Abelard's letter and answering out of turn). This situatedness is in part a function of epistolary convention as promoted through the *ars dictaminis*. The care Heloise takes to justify her epistolary eavesdropping and intrusion acknowledges this, yet it also nods to the "quasi-public" nature of her exchange with her former lover, in which their avowals resonate widely. In this regard, her justification is suggestive of the complicated nature of their relationship: regardless of their turbulent personal history, they now have very visible roles as leaders of their respective religious houses. This opening sets the tone for their current epistolary relation, comprising multiple layers of indebtedness, dependence, and obligation.

---

[22] Ambrose writes on this revivifying function of letters: "Epistolarum genus propterea repertum, ut quidam nobis cum absentibus sermo sit" (The genre of letters was invented for this, that a friend, through speech, might be present to us when absent), Epistle 66, *Patrologia Latina* vol. 16, col. 1225A, cited in Constable, "Letters and Letter-Collections," 113, my translation.

[23] Dronke provocatively suggests that Heloise's procurement of the letter was not "forte" at all, but that it was brought to her by "ung ami," "a friend, your man": that is, perhaps Heloise did not come upon the letter by chance, as she claims – perhaps Abelard sent it to her; "Heloise," *Women Writers of the Middle Ages*, 113 and n. 12. Dalarun corroborates, calling her coming across the letter by chance a fiction, 50.

Despite the emotionally charged and disarmingly revelatory tone of Heloise's letter, it, too, conforms to rhetorical type. Southern identifies it as an example of an *epistola deprecatoria,* a letter of asking or pleading, another well-known epistolary form whose purpose was to convey a request, and whose value was also measured by the writer's rhetorical skill. The necessary elements for this kind of letter were a demonstration of the reasonableness of the request, the ability of the recipient to grant it, and the writer's worthiness to receive it.[24] On the face of it, Heloise's request is simple, and quite reasonable: she wants Abelard to write to her. The reasons he ought to write are varied: because it will benefit him; because it will benefit Heloise and her sisters at the Paraclete; and because it is their due.[25] Abelard granted them the Paraclete property after they were expelled from Argenteuil, and Heloise reminds him that he is the founder of their house: "Quid tuae debeas attende qui sic curam impendis alienae" (70) (you devote your care to another's vineyard; think what you owe to your own) (Letter 1, 112).[26] That is, having written a letter to comfort an anonymous suffering friend, he should also write to comfort his similarly suffering but more deserving spiritual daughters. Finally, having called on his debt to the community, Heloise calls on his personal debt to her:

> Atque ut ceteras omittam, quanto erga me te obligaveris debito pensa ut quod devotis communiter debes feminis unicae tuae devotius solvas. (70)

[24] "The kind of argument to be employed in it was the subject of scholastic instruction. In the first place it was necessary to show that the request was reasonable; then that it was within the power of the recipient to grant it; and finally that the writer deserved to receive what was asked," Southern, 96.

[25] Heloise explains that Abelard will benefit by writing to them, for he will receive consolation in knowing that his sorrow is shared by his addressees (Letter 1, 110). She then explains that she and the sisters will benefit from his writing by knowing that he has them in mind (110); moreover, this benefit is their due (111).

[26] Radice notes that this gift took place ten years after their separation, placing it roughly five years before the correspondence; 97 n. 1. The gift was confirmed by Pope Innocent II in 1131; see Luscombe, 261. The fact that Suger, a known enemy of Abelard, initiated the expulsion might have contributed to Abelard's motivation to deed the land, and corroborates Heloise's articulation of his debt to her and her sisters. Griffiths suggests that their expulsion might even have been welcomed by Abelard, since it offered him an "opportunity to reinvent himself as the founder of a monastic community and the architect of its religious life, " "Men's Duty to Provide for Women's Needs,'" 10. In his updated version of Radice's translation Clanchy renumbers the letters according to convention: the *Historia calamitatum* is Letter 1 and Heloise's first letter is Letter 2. Since I am citing from Radice's original translation and to avoid confusion with Muckle's traditional numbering in which Heloise's first letter is Letter 1, I use Radice's numbering.

> Apart from everything else, consider the close tie by which you have
> bound yourself to me, and repay the debt you owe a whole community
> of women dedicated to God by discharging it the more dutifully to her
> who is yours alone. (112)

Heloise subordinates the communal debt to the personal debt Abelard
owes her, and she suggests an epistolary economy whereby he might
repay both through writing to her alone. She makes this distinction
through direct description and also in pronominal shift, from "me" to
"nobis," providing grammatical accompaniment to her articulation of the
nature of his debt.[27]

This request for a letter and the multiple reasons provided as
supporting arguments might be understood as compliance with the
conventions of an *epistola deprecatoria*, with its requisite arsenal of
reasons brought forth to demonstrate the worthiness of the writer's
request. Yet they are edged with heavy accusation. Reminding Abelard
that it was his bidding alone that brought her to monasticism, Heloise
writes:

> Omnes denique mihi voluptates interdixi ut tuae parerem voluntati.
> Nihil mihi reservavi nisi sic tuam nunc praecipue fieri. Quae vero tua sit
> iniquitas perpende si merenti amplius persolvis minus, immo nihil
> penitus ... Per ipsum itaque cui te obtulisti Deum te obsecro ut quo
> modo potes tuam mihi praesentiam reddas, consolationem videlicet
> mihi aliquam rescribendo, hoc saltem pacto ut sic recreata divino
> alacrior vacem obsequio. (73)

> I have finally denied myself every pleasure in obedience to your will,
> kept nothing for myself except to prove that now, even more, I am yours.
> Consider then your injustice, if when I deserve more you give me less,
> or rather, nothing at all .... And so, in the name of God to whom you
> have dedicated yourself, I beg you to restore your presence to me in the
> way you can – by writing me some word of comfort, so that in this at
> least I may find increased strength and readiness to serve God. (117)

It is injustice, she reasons, for Abelard to neglect his former wife and
spiritual charge, while he attends to the suffering of another whose claim

---

27 The first person plural often stands in for the first person singular in Latin;
however in this correspondence verbal and pronominal shifts from plural first person to
singular first person accompany shifts in the characterization of the debt from a
communal to a personal one. Glenda McLeod suggests that Heloise employs the
first-person singular in her private role as Abelard's wife, and the first-person plural as
public abbess, " 'Wholly Guilty, Wholly Innocent,' " 65.

is lesser. He owes her, and she deserves his help not only because of the claims of their relationship, but also for the sacrifices she made, and at his bidding: despite her famous resistance, he insisted on marriage, and he insisted on monasticism.[28] Now, years into her monastic vocation, Heloise asks for "some word of comfort" – presumably in the form of a letter – indicating that, despite being separated from Abelard for over a decade and a successful abbess in her own right, she still needs his help in pursuing the monasticism that he commanded. Her grievances are many, and her interruption of the epistolary circuit of the *Historia calamitatum* allows her one form of redress.

Abelard's letter elaborates his misfortunes, and Heloise's letter mirrors her teacher's, cataloguing her grievances to her partner in misfortune.[29] And it is clear that she still considers him her partner: she claims him as hers in the opening lines of her letter, and she claims herself as his, that her very monasticism, that is, belonging to God, is, paradoxically, proof that she belongs to Abelard. As many have pointed out, the medieval notion of marital debt is a fleshly one: marriage is an agreement entered into in order to avoid fornication, and husbands and wives owed to each other specifically fleshly debts.[30] This debt would seem no longer to exist between Abelard and Heloise – he has been castrated, they are monastic people.[31] Yet Heloise draws on its notion of mutuality of obligation as another argument in support of her request that Abelard write to her.[32] The often-repeated literal request is for letters from him. Yet this is not so

---

[28] McLaughlin points out that "opposition to marriage and remarriage was far from uncommon among twelfth-century women," "Heloise the Abbess," 3; what is uncommon is the way in which Heloise articulated this opposition.

[29] Newman describes this letter as "a detailed response to the *Historia Calamitatum* – her own autobiography in return for Abelard's – complete with enhancements and corrections of the story he has already told," "Authority, Authenticity, and the Repression of Heloise," 64.

[30] As many scholars have noted, this notion of debt is grounded in Paul's letter to the Corinthians. On canonical formulations of the medieval marriage debt, see Makowski, and Brundage, 66–79.

[31] In medieval canon law, castration furnished grounds for dissolution of the marriage debt only if the castration was a pre-existing condition unknown to the partner before marriage. See Makowski, and Brooke, 78–92.

[32] Newman calls this insistence on continued mutual belonging a "transmogrification" of the marriage debt, that, in accordance with their change in personal and social status, Abelard is no longer merely husband, but must also "take full responsibility for Heloise's emotional and spiritual welfare in the life he has imposed on her," "Authority, Authenticity, and the Repression of Heloise," 56. Kamuf's chapter on "Marriage Contracts" in her *Fictions of Feminine Desire* provides a provocative literal and figurative reading of the marriage debt in their writings.

simple a request as it might seem. Writing to Heloise would mean contending with a relationship begun before their marriage and monasticism, a pre-existing epistolary relation that took place in a decidedly different tenor.[33] In addition to attending to the overt request for spiritual attention to the sisters of the Paraclete, Abelard would also have to address the charge of personal debt and, by extension, the complicated nature and status of his relationship to Heloise. Yet how could he acknowledge his debt without accepting responsibility for and even guilt over her current conflicted state?

So begins the body of writing known as the correspondence of Abelard and Heloise, with an interrupted epistolary circuit, an elaboration of debt, and a demand for writing. Both opening letters demonstrate vividly how rhetorical type, far from hindering, seems to facilitate the communication of complicated desires and interpersonal dynamics. I have briefly examined these passages from the beginning of the correspondence to introduce the major theme I explore in greater detail in this chapter: the uses to which letters were put, not only to describe and contest the terms of their relationship, but to enact and, ultimately, transform it.

Salutations, Or, What's In A Name?

As discussed in the Introduction, letter writing was considered an *ars* in the Middle Ages, and epistolary types and requisite elements were established and promoted through letter-writing manuals. The salutation was a particularly developed and nuanced part of medieval letters, identified as one of two indispensable features marking letters as letters.[34] Following Carol Dana Lanham's distinction, I use the term "salutation" for the composite of parts comprising the opening of a letter: the identification of the addressee, the writer, and the initial greeting.[35] Despite its seemingly straightforward task – to begin a letter – this composite salutation had an instrumental as well as rhetorical function: its correct expression

---

[33] They wrote letters to each other before their marriage and separation: "When in the past you sought me out for sinful pleasures your letters came to me thick and fast ..." ("Letter 1. Heloise to Abelard," 117) ("Cum me ad turpes olim voluntates expetres, crebris me epistolis visitabas ...") (Ep. 2, 73).

[34] These two elements are the salutation and the subscription, containing the greeting and farewell; Constable, "Letters and Letter-Collections," 17.

[35] Lanham identifies the three parts to the full salutation of a Latin letter as "the *intitulatio* (the sender's name, with his attributes, if any), the *inscriptio* (the name of the addressee, with his attributes), and the *salutatio*, the initial greeting," *Salutatio Formulas*, 7.

signaled the social status of the correspondents, and it could also secure the good will of the addressee. By implication, goodwill could be lost with an improper observation of social hierarchy.[36]

The composition of the salutation was governed by very detailed rules. An anonymous twelfth-century epistolary manual describes one aspect of the formation of the salutation:

> Est item in salutationibus notandum, ut recipientium nomina semper mittentium nominibus preponantur, sive dativo casu cum omnibus eorum adiectivis, siue accusativo cum omnibus similiter eorum adiectivis. nisi tunc solummodo cum maior scribit minori. tunc enim mittentis nomen preponendum est, ut eius dignitas ipsa nominum positione monstretur.[37]

> The names of the recipients should always be placed before the names of the senders, whether with all their adjectives in the dative case or, likewise with all their adjectives in the accusative, unless – and only when – a more important man is writing to a less important man. For then the name of the sender should be placed first, so that his distinction is demonstrated by the very position of the names.[38]

The construction of the salutation takes on a sometimes bewildering specificity, perhaps appropriate to the deceptively simple task of observing social distinction. At stake was more than the recording of superiority or humility; letters could also actively claim and perform status with a great deal of nuance. Because they structured modes of address that required an acknowledgment of the relative social status of correspondents, letters required a particular representation of the self in relation to its epistolary others. In the hands of skilled writers, they could be sophisticated tools for self-representation, and also instrumental in self-promotion and humility.

The correspondence of Abelard and Heloise reveals a highly devel-

---

[36] Lanham, *Salutatio Formulas*, 93. In this way a salutation could bolster the next part of the letter, the actual captation of goodwill; this overlapping of epistolary function is corroborated by Anonymous of Bologna's "The Principles of Letter-Writing," in *Three Medieval Rhetorical Arts*, ed. Murphy. Nearly half of the *Rationes dictandi*, or "Principles of Letter Writing," consists of a discussion of salutations – from its definition to pages of examples containing numerous categories of salutations ranging from papal salutations to those from sons to their parents. This copious detail has no doubt in part to do with the fact that the *ars dictandi* served as a manual for practitioners, and the attention given to the salutation suggests its importance for the successful practice of professional letter writing; see "The Principles of Letter-Writing," 1–26.

[37] "Rationes dictandi," in *Briefsteller und formelbücher*, ed. Rockinger, I, 11.

[38] "The Principles of Letter-Writing," 8–9.

oped attention to the salutation.[39] Their salutations do more than represent their relative social status, they trace a shift in the way this relation is articulated:

> Domino suo immo patri, coniugi suo immo fratri, ancilla sua immo filia, ipsius uxor immo soror, Abaelardo Heloisa. (Ep. 1, 68)
>
> To her master, or rather her father, husband, or rather brother; his handmaid, or rather his daughter, wife, or rather sister; to Abelard, Heloise
> (Letter 1, 109).

> Heloisa, dilectissimae sorori suae in Christo, Abaelardus, frater eius in ipso (Ep. 2, 73)
>
> To Heloise, his dearly beloved in Christ, Abelard her brother in Christ
> (Letter 2, 119)

> Unico suo post Christum unica sua in Christo (Ep. 3, 77)
>
> To her only one after Christ, she who is his alone in Christ
> (Letter 3, 127)

> Sponsae Christi servus eiusdem (Ep. 4, 83)
>
> To the bride of Christ, Christ's servant (Letter 4, 137)

> Suo specialiter, sua singulariter (Ep. 5, 94)
>
> God's own in species, his own as individual (Letter 5, 159).[40]

While examining the salutations as a whole removes them from their immediate interpretive context, they serve as signposts for the correspondence because their development corresponds to shifts in the discussion

---

[39] Their letters demonstrate familiarity with epistolary convention in many ways. Dronke writes that Heloise's letters in particular suggest a familiarity with Italian dictamen, especially in their use of *cursus*, or prose rhythm, more marked than in Abelard's letters; "Heloise," in *Women Writers of the Middle Ages*, 110–12. See Janson for a discussion of the importance of *cursus* for the question of the letters' attribution, "Schools of Cursus in the Twelfth Century." Other scholars have remarked on the ways in which Heloise might have been an intellectual and rhetorical influence on her teacher; see for example Dronke, *Women Writers of the Middle Ages*, 111–12; Clanchy, *Abelard: A Medieval Life*, especially 169–70; and Ruys.

[40] The final two letters in the collection, Abelard's letters to Heloise regarding the origin of nuns and a religious rule for women, do not contain formal salutations. Salutations to these letters might well have existed, but then been omitted as the rule was copied for reading in monastic chapters. Dalarun points out that Abelard's last two letters and Epistle 9, "De Studio litterarum", preserved in a manuscript containing the *Problemata* "composent sur le fond un même traité qui, trop long pour répondre au genre épistolaire, se présente scindé en trois lettres"; furthermore, Epistles 8 and 9 do not have addresses; Dalarun, 50 and n. 165, and 47 and n. 151.

and nature of their relationship. Much scholarship has been done on these few lines, as the concern for appropriate names is also a concern to adequately describe their complicated relationship.[41] Taken as a whole, their salutations chart not only the range but also the progression of their varied relationships, distilled by the last letter of the correspondence to possessive adjectives.

In Heloise's first salutation, the litany of nouns that claim Abelard's position is punctuated by a succession of *immo*'s, which Radice translates as "or rather," suggesting a progressive intensifying or improvement of the terms; Dronke similarly renders them as "or better."[42] *Immo*, a corroborative particle generally used in contradiction or denial (no indeed, by no means, on the contrary), strongly implies correction, and secondarily extends or qualifies that which precedes (yes indeed, assuredly, by all means).[43] It is significant that Heloise's first salutation carries the sense of correction as well as affirmation, implying the insufficiency of any one name to adequately describe her complicated relationship with Abelard. This salutation, read in light of her others to Abelard, suggests the insufficiency of names and, and by extension letters and writing, to convey nuanced meanings.[44]

Despite this insufficiency, a name can say a great deal, as revealed in Abelard's and Heloise's escalation of salutatory contestation. In accordance with dictamenal prescription, Heloise places Abelard's name before hers in salutations, indicating that he is her superior. In his replies, Abelard places Heloise's name first. She comments on this breach of epistolary convention in her next letter:[45]

> Miror, unice meus, quod praeter consuetudinem epistolarum, *immo* contra ipsum ordinem naturalem rerum, in ipsa fronte salutationis epistolaris me tibi praeponere praesumpsisti . . . Rectus quippe ordo est

---

[41] For example, Dronke writes that the salutation in Heloise's first letter attempts to "convey the gamut of the relationships that she and Abelard have experienced," *Women Writers of the Middle Ages*, 112; see also Newman's observations in "Authority, Authenticity, and the Repression of Heloise," and Glenda McLeod's comments in " 'Wholly Guilty, Wholly Innocent.' "

[42] Dronke, "Heloise," *Women Writers of the Middle Ages*, 112.

[43] E.C. Woodcock, *A New Latin Syntax*.

[44] Baswell calls this a "metastasis of identity," a "focus on one other person so intense as to populate Heloise's universe. Heloise will repeatedly balance this multiplicity of roles against Abelard's uniqueness: 'solus,' 'unice.' Indeed, her insistence that 'you after God are the sole founder of this place [Tu post deum solus]' approaches – no doubt self-consciously – an almost blasphemous worship of another mortal," 164.

[45] McGuire characterizes this as Heloise's commenting on Abelard's bad form: 308.

et honestus, ut qui superiores vel ad pares scribunt, eorum quibus
scribunt nomina suis anteponant. Sin autem ad inferiores, praecedunt
scriptionis ordine qui praecedunt rerum dignitate.

(Ep. 3, 77, emphasis added)

I am surprised, my only one, that contrary to custom in letter-writing
and, indeed, to the natural order of things, you have thought fit to put
my name before yours in the greeting which heads your letter ... Surely
the right and proper order is for those who write to their superiors or
equals to put their names before their own, but in letters to inferiors,
precedence in order of address follows precedence in rank.

(Letter 3, 127, translation modified)

Referencing the "consuetudinem epistolarum" with which her teacher
ought to have been familiar, she corrects his epistolary etiquette and
failure to observe the "natural order of things," suggesting that letter
writing is more than a set of arbitrary rules – it resonates with dynamics
governing interpersonal relationships. In this elaboration of salutatory
convention, Heloise again favors the use of *immo*, suggesting the usefulness of this extending particle to her writing and thinking.

Abelard defends his practice through repeatedly maintaining a subordinate position in his salutations. He also claims subordination to Heloise
in distinctly courtly terms:[46]

De ipso autem nostrae salutationis, ut dicis, ordine praepostero, iuxta
tuam quoque, si diligenter attendas, actum est sententiam. Id enim quod
omnibus patet, tu ipsa indicasti ut, cum videlicet ad superiores scribitur,
eorum nomina praeponantur. Te vero extunc me superiorem factam
intelligas quo domina mea esse coepisti Domini mei sponsa effecta

(Ep. 4, 83)

What you call the unnatural order of my greeting, if you consider it
carefully, was in accordance with your own view as well as mine. For it
is common knowledge, as you yourself have shown, that in writing to
superiors one puts their name first, and you must realize that you
became my superior from the day when you began to be my lady on
becoming the bride of my Lord (Letter 4, 137).[47]

It is not surprising that Abelard and Heloise openly contest salutatory
practice in their correspondence, since salutations represent relationships,

---

[46] Griffiths draws a connection between this courtliness toward Heloise and the relationship he describes for abbot and deaconess in Letter 8, his Rule for religious women:
" 'Men's Duty to Provide for Women's Needs,' " 13.

[47] In support of his letter-writing practice, Abelard cites Jerome's letter to

and they disagree over the nature of theirs. More than offering a polite gesture of simultaneous and mutual humility and praise, Abelard suggests here a reversal of their social status and roles.[48] This is not simply an honorific reversal. It reverses the dynamic that has structured their relationship from the beginning: he was her teacher and husband, at whose insistence she contracted marriage and later took the veil. In his salutations, fifteen years later, he claims her as his superior, and in doing so insists on the altered nature of their relationship. His letters perform the contradictory nature of his position, at once professing courtly humility to the lady of his lord and reinforcing his right to correct his pupil even as he claims her worldly and spiritual superiority.[49]

Abelard is not alone in his praise and salutatory valuation of Heloise. Peter the Venerable also grants Heloise's name pride of place in his salutations, demonstrating that she was held in high esteem by at least one other respected contemporary aware of the events leading to her entry into monasticism:[50]

Venerabili et in Christo plurimum dilectae sorori Eloysae abbatissae, frater Petrus humilis Cluniacensium abbas, salutem quam promisit deus diligentibus se.[51]

To the venerable and greatly beloved sister in Christ, the abbess

Eustochium, in which Jerome grants Eustochium the honorific "my lady" as she is the bride of his lord. Letter 22, Jerome, *Select Letters*, 56–7.

[48] While the ostensible reason for this reversal is Heloise's taking the veil, another factor could be the personal and professional shame resulting from castration that he details in the *Historia calamitatum*. Wheeler and Irvine describe the *Letters* of Abelard and Heloise as a project of remasculinization for Abelard; see Irvine, "Abelard and (Re)writing the Male Body" and Wheeler; Ruys sees a continuation of this remasculinization in Abelard's first *planctus* for the Paraclete, 6.

[49] This gesture of humility is more than one-upmanship; in claiming inferiority to Heloise, Abelard participates in a broader tradition of exploiting gendered terms to express comparative humility and lowliness. Bynum describes this gendered humility: "male appropriation of the notion of woman as weak sometimes became a claim to superior lowliness ... When male writers took femaleness as an image to describe their renunciation of the world, they sometimes said explicitly that women were too weak to be women. They sometimes implied that their own role reversal – that is, their appropriation of or choice of lowliness – was a superior 'femaleness' to the femaleness of women, which was not chosen," *Fragmentation and Redemption*, 166.

[50] Mews discusses Hugh Metel's letters to Heloise, which also evidence admiration for her and specifically for her learning; this admiration sharply contrasts with his scorn for Abelard; "Hugh Metel, Heloise and Peter Abelard."

[51] Peter the Venerable, *The Letters of Peter the Venerable*, vol. I, Ep. 115, "Ad

Heloise, brother Peter, humble abbot of Cluny: the salvation which God
has promised those who love him.[52]

In another letter, his salutation identifies Heloise's praiseworthy qualities
and addresses her in relation to him, his "sister in Christ," and also in
relation to God and the nuns in her charge:

> Venerabili et carissimae sorori nostrae, deique ancillae, Heloisae
> ancillarum dei ductrici ac magistrae, frater Petrus humilis Clunia-
> censium abbas, salutis a deo, amoris a nobis in Christo pleni-
> tudinem. (Ep. 168 "Rescriptum Domini Abbatis," 401)

> To our venerable and dearest sister in Christ, the handmaid of God,
> Heloise, guide and mistress of the handmaids of God, brother Peter,
> humble abbot of Cluny: the fullness of God's salvation and of our love
> in Christ. ("Peter the Venerable: Letter 168 to Heloise," 286)

As in Heloise's first letter to Abelard, this salutation enumerates the relationships that join writer and addressee. However, Peter the Venerable's
terms are remarkably consistent: in both letters, he claims distinctly spiritual relationships triangulated in relation to the divine. And in both
letters, he places her name first.

Heloise tacitly accepts his salutatory honor, and returns in it kind.[53]
Noticeably, she does not mention his salutatory practice in her reply. This
is perhaps not surprising, given her very different relationships with
Abelard and Peter the Venerable, yet it does reveal meaningful variation
in her epistolary practice.[54] In her letters to Abelard, Heloise identifies
and corrects a breach in her teacher's epistolary practice, through which

---

Eloysam Abbatissam," 303. All citations to the letters of Peter the Venerable and Heloise
are from this edition and are identified parenthetically in the text.

[52] "Peter the Venerable: Letter (115) to Heloise," 277, in *The Letters of Abelard and
Heloise*, trans. Radice. Translations of these letters are from Radice's volume and are
identified parenthetically in the text.

[53] "Petro reverentissimo domino et patri, ac venerabili abbati Cluniacensium, Heloisa
humilis dei et eius ancilla, spiritum gratiae salutaris. (Epistle 167 "Epistola Heloisae
abbatissae ad Dominum abbatem," vol. I, 400) (To Peter, most reverend lord and father
and venerable abbot of Cluny, Heloise, God's and his humble servant: the spirit of grace
and salvation) ("Heloise: Letter 167 to Peter the Venerable," 285). Baswell points out that
this is "perhaps the only text by Heloise whose authenticity has always lain beyond
dispute, and probably the last that survives," "Heloise," 161.

[54] Unlike Heloise's correspondence with Abelard, which abbreviates the *salutatio* to
omit the opening salutation, her letters with Peter the Venerable include all three requisite
parts. This difference in salutation shows how epistolary convention can be modified to
register intimacy, informality, reverence, and humility; Ward and Chiavaroli write:

she engages him dialogue about the nature of their relation to each other. Peter the Venerable places Heloise's name before his, and his position as abbot of Cluny might be considered a position of greater authority than Abelard's at the remote St Gildas, and Heloise accepts his laudatory salutation. Her silence suggests that it is neither her place to correct his authority nor her desire to engage him on epistolary propriety and the nature of their relationship. As Peter the Venerable's correspondent, Heloise skillfully – perhaps obediently – observes letter-writing conventions; as Abelard's, she openly and repeatedly contests them. More than registering a different relationship with her addressee, the differences in Heloise's epistolary practice fashion a distinctly different epistolary persona.

Thanks to dictamenal prescription, the concern to affirm relative social status in salutations is to be expected in medieval letters. The correspondence of Abelard and Heloise is distinct for turning this positioning function into a site of contestation about their relationship, and for engaging this concern with names not only in their salutations, but throughout their letters. As they vividly show, names can be extremely complicated signifiers. In one of the more famous passages of the correspondence, Heloise proclaims:

> Et si uxoris nomen sanctius ac validius videtur, dulcius mihi semper exstitit amicae vocabulum aut, si non indigneris, concubinae vel scorti, ut, quo me videlicet pro te amplius humiliarem, ampliorem apud te consequerer gratiam et sic etiam excellentiae tuae gloriam minus laederem. (Ep. 1, 71)

> The name of wife may seem more sacred or more binding, but sweeter for me will always be the word mistress, or, if you will permit me, that of concubine or whore. I believed that the more I humbled myself on your account, the more gratitude I should win from you, and also the less damage I should do to the brightness of your reputation.
>
> (Letter 1, 113)

Heloise ties her concern with appropriate names and words to concern for Abelard's reputation and reveals her awareness of the very public nature of their relationship, even during its early stages.[55] She calls attention to the disjunction between the social and personal significance of names,

---

"whatever the motivation, such divergence from standard salutatory practice was instantly recognized and noted," 74.

[55] For a discussion of Abelard's attention to reputation in his varied writings, see Ruys, especially 7–8.

and sides dramatically with personal standards of naming, even at – or perhaps because of – the risk of public censure. This boldly declared preference for "the word mistress" demonstrates the instrumental use to which naming can be put: Heloise chooses the publicly shameful name not necessarily because she literally considers herself Abelard's whore but to win gratitude from him, and perhaps limit damage to his reputation. This contrasts starkly with the discussion of reputation in the Baudri–Constance exchange, in which Baudri anxiously guards his good reputation by declaring his verse epistles mere "iocos," and Constance subordinates the question of reputation to that of shame in order to catch her teacher at his playful game.

In perhaps the most extravagant name-claiming gesture in the letters, Heloise declares:

> Deum testem invoco, si me Augustus universo praesidens mundo matrimonii honore dignaretur totumque mihi orbem confirmaret in perpetuo possidendum, carius mihi et dignius videretur tua dici meretrix quam illius imperatrix. (Ep. 1, 71)

> God is my witness that if Augustus, Emperor of the whole world, thought fit to honour me with marriage and conferred all the earth on me to possess for ever, it would be dearer and more honourable to me to be called not his Empress but your whore. (Letter 1, 114)

Couching these statements in a larger discourse on love and marriage, Heloise defends her desire not to marry, forgoing her right to a name honorable in the eyes of others to maintain a position defensible to herself: to love without interest in material gain or worldly honor, and free from the burdens of a shared domestic life.[56] Catherine Brown observes that with these charged nouns Heloise describes a self "defined as spiritual shortfall and as empty center."[57] What emerges from this surplus and shortfall is an important record of one writer's attempts to define and clarify ways of thinking about a self whose worldly valuation contrasts starkly with personal values.[58]

Heloise explores names and social relations not only through salutations, but also the roles she assumes throughout her letters to Abelard. As Barbara Newman points out, literary study provides Heloise with access

---

[56] Ruys analyses Abelard's vocabulary regarding childbearing in the *Historia calamitatum* and his *planctus*, 11.

[57] Brown, "*Muliebriter*: Doing Gender in the Letters of Heloise," 32–4.

[58] See Dronke for a discussion of women and what he terms the "primacy of individual conscience" in "Heloise's Problemata and Letters," especially 64–5.

to models provided by history and mythology, "pious Roman matrons" as well as "passionate women in love, seduced and abandoned yet eternally ardent."[59] Heloise's employment of these literary models is epistolary: she performs these roles in her letters. It is worth pointing out that the epistolary relation is one into which Heloise interpellates Abelard: after more than a decade of separation, she interrupts the *Historia calamitatum* circuit, and devises a specifically epistolary way to compel his engagement with her.[60] Her epistolary performances are a function of what she actively crafts as a writer out of the literary models encountered in her reading and her complicated position as an unrepentant abbess with the best means at her disposal: letters and the conventions for their composition.

Heloise was adept at fashioning different epistolary personas. In contrast to her lengthy and topically rich letters to Abelard, her above-cited letter to Peter the Venerable is brief and to the point. In response to his effusive praise and admiration, her brevity is striking, and perhaps entirely appropriate, for to acknowledge his praise would be hubris, to contradict it, potentially awkward; she does, after all, ask favors of him. However her response is interpreted, it is striking that to his one hundred eighty-four lines she replies in a comparatively spare twenty-three, thanking him for his visit and reminding him of promised favors. Perhaps surprisingly, she avers speechlessness as a response to his visit:

> Norunt alii, quantum eis utilitatis vestrae contulerit praesentia sublimitatis. Ego certe non dicam enarrare dictu, sed nec ipso valeo comprehendere cogitatu, quam utilis, quam iocundus vester michi fuerit adventus. (Ep. 167 "Epistola Heloisae abbatissae ad dominum abbatem," vol. I, 400)

---

59 "Authority, Authenticity, and the Repression of Heloise," 69–70. She connects this role-playing with the increase in Marian piety in this period and with mystics of later centuries, all of which share the "adoption of multiple imaginative roles," 71. Offering consolation in very different tenor, Peter the Venerable also urges Heloise to the adoption of a multitude of roles in his letter: "he encourages her to fashion herself as a mother, teacher, and warrior for her nuns, comparing her to the biblical Deborah and the classical Penthesilea. He offers a letter both of consolation and of heroic religious calling and resolve," Baswell, 163.

60 While the argument could be made that Abelard enabled Heloise to perform these roles in his capacity as correspondent and partner, she is the one who initiates and carries out this performance. And, regardless of whether the *Historia calamitatum* fell into her hands accidentally or by design, it is not addressed to her, and she takes the initiative in entering into actual epistolary exchange with Abelard. Recent scholarship has been very interested to explore how Heloise might have influenced Abelard, at least in the field of rhetoric; see above, n. 39.

Others are well aware of the great benefits conferred on them by the presence of your sublimity but, for my own part, I cannot even formulate my thoughts, much less find words for what a benefit and joy your coming was to me. ("Heloise: Letter 167 to Peter the Venerable," 285)

Heloise's ability to formulate thoughts and find words despite great emotion is amply evidenced in her letters with Abelard. This ineffability might be a shortcut to expedite the letter, an epistolary gracefulness that combines humility with efficacy. She then enumerates the date and events of Peter's visit, as if recording them for posterity, and reminds him of what he has promised: masses to be said on her behalf at Cluny after her death and a sealed letter attesting to this; an absolution of Abelard also set in writing and sealed; and a prebend for Astralabe, her son.[61] Once again, *immo* is indispensable in Heloise's articulation of social position and personal relation:

Quod itaque sorori immo ancillae concessistis, frater immo dominus impleatis. (Ep. 167, 400–1)

Fulfill then, my brother or rather, my lord, what you promised to your sister, or I should say, to your servant.
                    ("Heloise: Letter 167 to Peter the Venerable," 285)

An attention to the use of names and the relationships they signify figures in Heloise's letters to two correspondents who occupy very different positions in her life. The different ways in which she articulates this attention demonstrate her skill in accessing the range of rhetorical meanings available in letters.

These efforts are possible in part because of the highly prescribed nature of medieval letter-writing. When forms are saturated with meaning, omissions and nuances can signify greatly, as the salutations attest. The multiplicity of names and roles Heloise accesses in her letters can be read as a sign of the insufficiency of language and social categories to describe complicated relationships and identities – there is no single name or literary model sufficient to express the range of complicated relationships she and Abelard share. Echoing the citation from the *Epistolae duorum amantium* that opens this chapter, the need for, and

---

[61] In this case, preserving details for posterity is essential, as it concerns Abelard's soul and her son's livelihood. In addition to serving as exemplars for other letter writers, letters could also serve a record-keeping function; according to McLaughlin, this letter was hung above Abelard's tomb, "Heloise the Abbess," 11. For more on the possible uses of preserved letters see Beach.

failure of, names to express their signifieds is a concern that subtends the entire correspondence. It reveals a concern with the relationship of outside to inside, reputation to merit, external performance to inner worth. In an example that highlights the ways in which both Abelard and Heloise recognize the critical significance of names, but to very different ends, Abelard meditates on Heloise's proper name:

> Nam et tuae Dominus non immemor salutis, immo plurimum tui memor, qui etiam sanctio quodam nominis praesagio te praecipue suam fore praesignavit, cum te videlicet Heloissam id est divinam ex proprio nomine suo quod est Heloim insignivit (Ep. 4, 90)

> For the Lord is not unmindful also of your own salvation, indeed, he has you much in mind, for by a kind of holy presage of his name he marked you out to be especially his when he named you Heloise, after his own name, Elohim. (Letter 4, 149)

Abelard also employs *immo*, but in the primary sense, that of correction, "nay rather," and discusses Heloise's proper name in a way that shifts attention from her relationship with him to her relationship with God: her very name bears the mark of her belonging to God, and the claim of this divine relationship supercedes her relationship with any other, including Abelard.

A concern with names and what they signify, explicitly addressed in their epistolary salutations, furnishes a point of dialogue through which Abelard and Heloise negotiate the nature of their relationship. Abelard works to shift the tenor of these names and the relationship they imply toward the religious, and, until her third letter, Heloise resists. The epistolary articulation and negotiation of this conflict demonstrates the flexibility afforded by seemingly fixed epistolary forms. Letters required representing the self in relation to its others in specific ways. However, these relations often resist easy representation, and epistolary structures could be navigated and manipulated to better represent these relations, to discuss and even perform conflicting understandings of them. The correspondence of Abelard and Heloise shows that letters were not simply rhetorical exercises that passively reflected relative social status; they also offered a site for the active creation, contestation, and negotiation of this status. Letters were tools for self-representation, and Abelard and Heloise show how they could be instrumental in critiquing the insufficiency of conventional ways of representing the self. Thus, letters did not merely reflect the self, but were tools in the active creation of new ways of thinking about it.

Seneca and Jerome: Modeling Friendship

Given the unusual personal history of Abelard and Heloise, establishing the terms of their relationship is not merely academic but of critical importance, especially as, at the beginning of the correspondence, they are not at all in agreement as to what this relationship ought to be. Abelard is at this point abbot at the remote and, he reports, unruly St Gildas, and he has made powerful enemies, Bernard of Clairvaux and Abbot Suger not least among them. Because visits between Abelard and Heloise generate suspicions of impropriety, it is imperative that declarations of unrepentant desire in Heloise's letters be countered with correction, and Abelard does so through insistence on an exclusively spiritual relationship.[62] Heloise is abbess of the Paraclete, but her monastic career has not been trouble-free; she and her sisters were expelled from Argenteuil, and they hold the Paraclete as a subsequent gift from Abelard.[63] And, as her letters to Peter the Venerable suggest, she is still dependent on the favors of highly placed authorities. Therefore, avowals of dissatisfaction and longing in her letters to Abelard could potentially jeopardize the achievements each has achieved.

Abelard and Heloise struggle to establish the tenor of their relationship in a specifically *epistolary* way: there is no discussion of visits between them, and they actively contest the nature of their relationship in their letters. Their epistolary discussion of their relationship is accompanied by shifts in tone and register that signify on a more than rhetorical level: while letters offer them a means to describe their differing views on their relationship, they also offer a way to perform these views through the adoption of rhetorical modes that signify particular kinds of relationships. One of the key ways in which they communicate their divergent views on their relationship is in the model of friendship each espouses through their choice of epistolary rhetoric.[64] As Martin Irvine points out, their letters follow, respectively, epistolary models provided by Jerome

---

[62] In frustration, Abelard reminds the reader of his castrated status: "now that I have been freed from such suspicion by God's mercy, and the power to commit this sin is taken from me, how can the suspicion remain? What is the meaning of this latest monstrous accusation?" *Historia calamitatum*, trans. Radice, 97–8.

[63] While the ostensible reason for their expulsion is the discovery of documents identifying Argenteuil as the property of St Denis, it is also possible that there were other reasons having to do with Suger's personal enmity for Abelard. See Luscombe, and Radice's introduction, 22.

[64] McGuire treats the cultivation of friendship in these letters through the lens of *consolatio*.

and Seneca. Alcuin Blamires and Brian McGuire, among others, corroborate Jerome's influence on Abelard, who also conducted didactic correspondence with women.[65]

The pedagogical aspect of their relationship is perhaps the only one that they do not dispute: Abelard was Heloise's teacher. Years after the more scandalous events in their history, this dynamic is still in place in their letters, in which Abelard amplifies his pedagogy in several ways: he offers instruction to Heloise individually and the women of the Paraclete collectively; he sends them liturgical texts, often of his own composition; he offers teaching in his letters, incarnating a Jeromian model of instructive friendship. By the last two letters, he is all teacher: Abelard has fully taken on the role – one imagines with some relief – of spiritual director in his letters describing women's monastic life and vocation.[66] It is important, however, to note that these instructional letters were produced in a specific context. They arise in a sometimes heated dialogue taking place over the course of several letters, and they are the direct result of Heloise's requests, rendering Abelard's pedagogy highly situated and contingent on its immediate epistolary context.

Jerome's letters to Roman women on biblical interpretation and monastic life were well known in the Middle Ages, and Abelard's reply to Heloise's first epistolary overture is, in similar vein, determinedly didactic. He sidesteps the issue of their personal history and excuses his epistolary silence through a backhanded gesture of praise: he hadn't written because he thought her so sensible and capable that she didn't need his comfort or advice. Rather, he claims that, between the two of them, he is in greater need, and he asks that she and her sisters pray for him in his adversity. His response to Heloise's next letter is almost clinically method-

---

[65] Jerome instructed his correspondents on the value of virginity, urged religious steadfastness, encouraged the study of scripture, and asked for their prayers. Like Abelard, he was vulnerable to accusations of impropriety on account of his close friendships with women; within a medieval Christian framework, male–female religious relationships were subject to suspicion in part because women were represented as a pathway to sin, presenting the double danger of women offering, and men giving in to, temptation. Jerome acknowledges this suspicion in his letter to Asella: *Select Letters*, Letter 45 "To Asella/Ad Asellam," 178–9. Bitterly, he writes that his fault lies not in his actions, but in the sole fact of his being a male teacher of female students, 180–1.

[66] These letters are responsible for Abelard's reputation as a monastic reformer, and quite likely a reason for their preservation; Dalarun argues that the focus of the sole manuscript containing the complete correspondence is female spirituality: "[s]on unité thématique ne fait aucun doute: il s'agit d'un dossier sur les normes de la vie religieuse féminine," 28.

ical, beginning with a catalogue of the contents of her letter and purporting to answer her points "singulis," each in turn, almost as a teacher writing in the margins of a student's paper, commenting on her performance. He explains that he does this

> non tam pro excusatione mea quam pro doctrina vel exhortatione tua, ut eo scilicet libentius petitionibus assentias nostris, quo eas rationabilius factas intellexeris, et tanto me amplius exaudias in tuis, quanto reprehensibilem minus invenies in meis, tantoque amplius verearis contemnere, quanto minus videris dignum reprehensione. (Ep. 4, 83)

> not so much in self-justification as for your own enlightenment and encouragement, so that you will more willingly grant my own requests when you understand that they have a basis of reason, listen to me more attentively on the subject of your own pleas as you find me less to blame in my own, and be less ready to refuse me when you see me less deserving of reproach. (Letter 4, 137)

He makes explicit his didactic purpose in writing to Heloise, explaining it lest there be any confusion. He seems confident of the instrumental effect of his didacticism: with this explanation, he hopes to secure future, more ready obedience.

Abelard offers teachings more obliquely, as well, and in the medium he and Heloise knew best: learned citation. As discussed earlier, they were known among their contemporaries for their learning, and their letters are replete with markers of erudition and evidence of vast reading in ancient, scriptural, and patristic texts.[67] However, in his letters to Heloise, Abelard cites directly from classical literature only twice, as if reluctant to risk the erotic resonances in pagan literature, upon which Baudri and Constance played so variously.[68] The first reference occurs in his condemnation of false humility, an interesting choice given his own staged and instrumental humility in these letters.[69] The second reference appears in his

---

[67] Dronke characterizes their citations as occurring so frequently and unexpectedly as to suggest "spontaneous recollection" of texts they studied together, "Heloise," *Women Writers of the Middle Ages*, 112. Swanson suggests that the "to-and-fro citation of identical quotations" in the letters had to do with the twelfth-century equating of Latinity with literacy, 49. In Alberic of Monte Cassino's eleventh-century dictaminal treatise *Flowers of Rhetoric*, citation is a recommended feature of letter-writing. Newman points out the combination of patristic and pagan writers as a key feature of Heloise's citational practice, "Authority, Authentiity, and the Represion of Heloise," 69.

[68] In his second letter Abelard refers openly to the carnal sins they committed, but only in demonstration of the deservedness of their punishment.

[69] He cites Virgil's *Eclogues* 3.65, in which Galatea feigns rejection in order to entice a suitor.

admonition to Heloise to redirect her attention to religion and give up her "old and perpetual complaint"[70] against their manner of entry into religion and cease grieving over their lost amatory relations, lest she be a "weeping Cornelia."[71] This reference to Lucan's *Pharsalia* might well be a nod to, and perhaps censure of, Heloise's citation of Cornelia at the moment at which she takes the veil.[72] The account of this scene appears in the *Historia calamitatum*, indicating the intertextuality of these letters, as well as the importance of classical literature at critical moments in their telling of their story.[73]

In contrast to Abelard's Jeromian didacticism, Heloise's first two letters, as Irvine points out, are distinctly Senecan, accessing a classically informed *amicitia*, in which one of the chief activities was the cultivation of learned discourse through the exchange of letters.[74] The repeated request in Heloise's correspondence is for letters from Abelard, and in her first missive she asks for a letter of consolation like the one addressed to his anonymous friend. In interrupting the epistolary circuit between Abelard and his anonymous addressee and demanding a letter in kind, Heloise positions herself as a correspondent in friendship letters.[75] Countering Abelard's epistolary offer of a pedagogical relationship in spiritual vein, she suggests yet another different relationship they might share: that of classically inflected, learned friendship.

Her first letter is Senecan in reference and tone: its first among many learned citations is from Seneca's *Epistulae ad Lucilium*. She cites its opening passage, in which Seneca writes to Lucilius on the good of letter writing:

> Quod frequenter mihi scribis, gratias ago. Nam quo uno modo potes, te mihi ostendis. Numquam epistulam tuam accipio, ut non protinus una

---

[70] "Antiquam illam ... et assiduam querimoniam" (Ep. 4, 71).

[71] "Maerenti Cornelia" (Ep. 92).

[72] As Abelard tells it, immediately before putting on the veil, Heloise utters the words spoken by Cornelia to Pompey in Lucan's *Pharsalia*, lamenting her role in the downfall of her husband: *Historia calamitatum*, 76.

[73] Irvine comments on the intertextual and intratextual aspects of the correspondence, "Heloise and the Gendering of the Literate Subject," 89.

[74] The primary models for this kind of friendship and discourse were known to medieval readers chiefly through Seneca's *Epistulae* and Cicero's *De amicitia*, and indeed Heloise's first citation in this letter is from Seneca's *Letter to Lucilius*.

[75] Irvine sees this as a crafting of a new identity that resisted the gender categories imposed by grammar. For the purposes of my argument, I am interested in showing how Heloise makes use of available resources to express that which resists easy categorization or even expression – her idea of herself and her position in regard to Abelard.

simus. Si imagines nobis amicorum absentium iucundae sunt, quae
memoriam renovant et desiderium falso atque inani solacio levant,
quanto iucundiores sunt litterae, quae vera amici absentis vestigia,
veras notas adferunt?

That you write to me frequently, I thank you. For in the one way you
can, you show yourself to me. Never do I receive a letter from you, but
that I immediately feel that we are together. If pictures of absent friends
are pleasing to us, which renew memory and lighten longing with false
and empty comfort, how much more pleasing are letters, which bring
the true traces, the true impressions, of absent friends?[76]

Seneca's opening salvo reads almost as the inverse of the beginning of
Heloise's letter. Seneca receives letters often, from which he derives great
comfort; according to Heloise, she receives no word from Abelard, and
his intercepted letter brings only misery. In response to this dissatisfying
experience, Heloise invites Abelard to a Senecan exchange, in which
friends bring solace ("solatio") to one another, as letters are traces, literally footprints ("vestigia") of their authors, and the one way in which they
can show, or offer ("ostendere"), themselves when absent. This absence
in presence brings pleasure, an acknowledged classical epistolary function that endured in medieval France.

As Irvine notes, however, Heloise suppresses a telling part of Seneca's
laudatory description of the function of letters, the very next line of the
passage:

Nam quod in conspectus dulcissimum est, id amici manus epistulae
inpressa praestat, agnoscere. (264)

For that which is sweetest when face to face, the same stands out in the
impress of a friend's hand on his letter – recognizing.[77]

Irvine suggests that, in omitting this section, it is possible that Heloise
"suppresses a too vivid reminder of what she desires."[78] Given their
history, this suppression of the description of the "sweetest" physical
presence afforded by a letter is a calculated and prudent one. As Abelard
attests, actual presence is problematic for them: even after their monasticism, he was reproached for neglect when his visits to the Paraclete were

76 Seneca, "40, Seneca Lucilio suo salutem," *Ad Lucilium epistulae morales*, ed. and
trans. Gummere, vol. I, letter 40. 1, 263–4, cited in Irvine 94, my translation.

77 Irvine's translation.

78 Irvine, "Heloise and the Gendering of the Literate Subject," 95.

infrequent, and of licentiousness when he visited more often.[79] Heloise astutely omits from her citation the section of this passage that might give cause for suspicion of impropriety: the imaginative recognition of the beloved in the letter he wrote – a moment of tactile delight that Baudri draws out. This suggests an acute awareness of audience, be it Abelard or a wider reading public, and an effort to make the strongest case possible for continued epistolary contact with Abelard.

Heloise makes use of Seneca by prudently censoring his celebration of that "sweetest" physical recognition to provide literary support for the good done by letter writing between friends. Through careful editing, she identifies this good as innocent, declaring:

> Deo autem gratias quod hoc saltem modo praesentiam tuam nobis reddere nulla invidia prohiberis, nulla difficultate praepediris, nulla, obsecro, negligentia retarderis. (Ep. 1, 69)

> Thank God that here at least is a way of restoring your presence to us which no malice can prevent, nor any obstacle hinder; then do not, I beseech you, allow any negligence to hold you back. (Letter 1, 110)

Heloise adroitly supports her claims for writing from Abelard. She proffers a classically inflected *amicitia*, cites a learned source on the benefits of letters between friends, and edits this citation to forestall suspicions of impropriety; and, once again, the innocuous plural pronoun figures in her request. Heloise demonstrates how letter writing was not merely a compositional practice, it was a varied textual activity that encompassed careful citation and editing, creating dense and complicated meanings through layers of epistolary discourse.[80]

It is likely that the Senecan ethos has significance for Heloise for other reasons as well. According to Abelard, in her arguments against marriage, she declares the distractions of domesticity to be inconsonant with a philosopher's life. Her anti-matrimonial discourse turns, perhaps not surprisingly, to Seneca's authority, and she cites another of his letters to Lucilius:[81]

---

[79] Radice, *Historia calamitatum*, 97–8. In his analysis of medieval *dictamen*, Camargo discusses the variety of letters written in the Middle Ages and suggests that especially with love letters, the physical letter functioned as a metonym for the absent lover whose words it represents. It is not implausible that Heloise would want to avoid such obvious markers of amorous exchange: "Where's the Brief?," 9.

[80] This editorial practice prefigures Christine de Pizan's varied letter-writing practices, which I examine in the next chapter.

[81] Jerome also enumerates anti-matrimonial arguments in the above-cited letter to

Non cum vacaveris, philosophandum est; omnia alia neglegenda, ut huic adsideamus, cui nullum tempus satis magnum est … Non multum refert, utrum omittas philosophiam an intermittas; non enim, ubi interrupta est, manet … Resistendum est occupationibus, nec explicandae sed submovendae sunt.[82]

Philosophy is not for when you have free time; all things must be neglected, in order that we might attend to it, for which no amount of time is great enough … It matters not much, whether you disregard or suspend philosophy; indeed it will not, when interrupted, remain … Occupying affairs are to be resisted, they are not to be attended to, but put aside.

It has been noted that Heloise might well be referring to her own as well as Abelard's pursuit of philosophy. To the extent that a life of *otium philosophicum*, or leisure for study, would have been considered difficult for men to balance with family life, it would have been much more so for women, not traditionally destined for careers in philosophy, and it is not implausible that Heloise, famed for her training and ability in letters, would want to continue her intellectual pursuits.[83]

In his replies to these Senecan epistolary overtures, Abelard adheres to a Jeromian model, steadfastly dispensing advice and writing of spiritual matters. And, as noted above, he cites Jerome's letter to Eustochium in defense of his own salutatory practice, in which Jerome addresses Eustochium as "my lady." However, Jerome begins his letter with the distinctly paternal "filia," and only several passages later does he introduce the more courtly honorific. Like Heloise's citation of Seneca,

Eustochium in ways that prefigure Abelard's version of Heloise's arguments against matrimony: "nec enumeraturum molestias nuptiarum, quomodo uterus intumescat, infans vagiat, cruciet paelex, domus cura sollicitet, et omnia, quae putantur bona, mors extrema praecidat" (Nor shall I now reckon up the disadvantages of marriage, such as pregnancy, a crying baby, the tortures of jealousy, the cares of household management, and the cutting short by death of all its fancied blessings) (56, 57). I am not suggesting that Heloise did not make the arguments Abelard attributes to her, but rather that it is possible that Abelard's report might be shaped by Jerome's account.

82 Seneca, "72, Seneca Lucilio suo salutem," my translation.

83 Ward and Chiavaroli: "What she may have grieved was the loss of her son and of a life of intellectual, social, and sexual concubinage with a learned and challenging cleric in exciting times; the kind of clerical concubinage Heloise may have aspired to was rapidly becoming out of date in the wake of the Gregorian reform movement, but this is easier to see with hindsight," 62. Newman corroborates: "the classical *otium philosophicum* exerted a strong attraction, and she saw the life of contemplative leisure – which absolutely excluded marriage, though not lovemaking – as a real possibility for herself as well as Abelard," "Authority, Authenticity, and the Repression of Heloise," 69.

Abelard's citation of Jerome's epistolary example is selective and perhaps slightly disingenuous; yet in referencing this letter he also references a relationship of spiritual direction, suggesting a similar relationship for himself and Heloise.

However, just as Abelard refuses a Senecan exchange, Heloise resists, in her first reply at least, a Jeromian one.[84] The different models of friendship they espouse enable each to define the tenor of relationship they desire. This negotiation produces a specifically epistolary kind of relationship, and a specifically epistolary way of thinking about the self. In appealing to a Senecan epistolary ethos, Heloise implicitly claims the role of *amicus*, a learned friend who cultivates friendship through letter writing.[85] Her letters reveal the force of genre: Heloise is not merely citing Seneca, she is also writing in Senecan mode and asking for the same in return.[86] A reply in kind would make both writers participants in the long tradition of friendship correspondence and thus participants in a particular kind of relationship, performed publicly through letters. Abelard's resistance exerts similar force in Jeromian mode, advocating the tenor of relationship acceptable to him. His refusal to reply in kind makes a statement about the ways in which he will and will not communicate with Heloise, which is tantamount to declaring the kinds of relations which he will and will not share with Heloise. In this way, epistolary composition functions as a kind of conduct.

The letters of Abelard and Heloise demonstrate close familiarity and engagement with letter-writing forms and traditions. Just as salutations offered them a specific vocabulary and structure for discussing their relationship, so did established epistolary genres. This demonstration of epistolary mastery is not merely erudite display, it is also instrumental: it allows them to conduct a dialogue on several levels on matters of utmost importance to their personal and professional lives. Their dialogue reveals the range and uses of medieval letters and learning, and it also

[84] Despite her eventual epistolary capitulation, contemporaries viewed this correspondence as Senecan; Monfrin and Irvine discuss a thirteenth-century manuscript containing Seneca's letters to Lucilius and the letters of Abelard and Heloise: Abelard, ed. Monfrin, 20–2; Irvine 95 and n. 32.

[85] For a discussion of the masculine nature of the roles Heloise inhabits in her Senecan letters, *amicus* and *litteratus*, see Irvine,"Heloise and the Gendering of the Literate Subject," 106.

[86] It is worth noting, however, Heloise does not write purely Senecan letters. She also references her unrepentant desires and reminds Abelard of the varied debts he owes her, and this is perhaps another reason why Abelard resists replying in kind.

defines important ways of thinking about the self, whose deepest
concerns are not only communicated but also enacted in writing. This is
a particularly textual idea of the self, one that exists only in letter
writing. For Heloise and Abelard, this provided a powerful position from
which to conduct their conversations and negotiations. More than
furnishing a kind of presence in absence, letter writing could be constitutive of action and, as such, a kind of being. Whichever rhetorical model
it follows, their relationship is now an epistolary one. Letters, because of
their ambiguous status as at once representational and real, bordering on
fiction and non-fiction, become the ideal and only space for these two
writers in which to dispute and, ultimately, inhabit contested subject
positions.[87]

Confession, Obedience, and Bringing the Subjunctive into the Indicative

The first three letters in the collected correspondence – the *Historia
calamitatum*, Heloise's first letter, Abelard's reply – follow established
rhetorical models. Heloise's next letter "can be fitted into no rhetorical
category,"[88] and has been called an exercise in "bitter self-analysis."[89] She
begins it with an expression of surprise at Abelard's breach of epistolary
convention, expanding on the problem of the ability of names to
adequately describe that to which they are applied. As part of a broader
plea to Abelard to cease praising her, since, she claims, she is unde-
serving of it, Heloise decries the duplicitous capacity of outward demon-
strations of penitence to mask inner lack of contrition:

> Quo modo etiam poenitentia peccatorum dicitur, quantacumque sit
> corporis afflictio, si mens adhuc ipsam peccandi retinet voluntatem, et
> pristinis aestuat desideriis? Facile quidem est quemlibet confitendo
> peccata seipsum accusare, aut etiam in exteriori satisfactione corpus
> affligere. Difficillimum vero est a desideriis maximarum voluptatum
> avellere animum. (Ep. 3, 80)

---

[87] Ruys argues that his final *planctus* was an attempt to do just this, that it was his
"attempt to find a way to theorize the concept of friendship for himself and Heloise within
the competing demands of sexual identity, gender, and heterosexuality;" this differs from
the correspondence in being a one-sided textual project; 15.

[88] Southern, 97.

[89] Dronke, *Women Writers in the Middle Ages,* 121. Irvine writes that it is a "hybrid
letter fashioned by merging the *epistola ad amicum* and the vocational letter," "Heloise
and the Gendering of the Literate Subject," 102–3.

How can it be called repentance for sins, however great the mortifica-
tion of the flesh, if the mind still retains the will to sin and is on fire
with its old desires? It is easy enough for anyone to confess his sins, to
accuse himself, or even to mortify his body in outward show of
penance, but it is very difficult to tear the heart away from hankering
after its dearest pleasures. (Letter 3, 132)

Heloise exposes the masquerade offered by false confession, and reveals
as potentially non-parallel the relation between outward action and interiority, hinting that the "heart hankering after its dearest pleasures" might
be hers. Then, unequivocally, she offers her own confession in a stunning
self-condemnation:

[I]llae, quas pariter exercuimus, amantium voluptates dulces mihi
fuerunt ut nec displicere mihi, nec vix a memoria labi possint.
Quocumque loco me vertam, semper se oculis meis cum suis ingerunt
desideriis. Nec etiam dormienti suis illusionibus parcunt. Inter ipsa
missarum solemnia, ubi purior esse debet oratio, obscena earum
voluptatum phantasmata ita sibi penitus miserrimam captivant animam
ut turpitudinibus illis magis quam orationi vacem. Quae cum
ingemiscere debeam de commissis, suspiro potius de amissis. Nec
solum quae egimus, sed loca pariter et tempora in quibus haec egimus,
ita tecum nostro infixa sunt animo, ut in ipsis omnia tecum agam, nec
dormiens etiam ab his quiescam. (Ep. 3, 80–81)

[T]he pleasures of lovers which we shared have been too sweet – they
can never displease me, and can scarcely be banished from my
thoughts. Wherever I turn they are always there before my eyes,
bringing with them awakened longings and fantasies which will not
even let me sleep. Even during the celebration of the Mass, when our
prayers should be purer, lewd visions of those pleasures take such a
hold upon my unhappy soul that my thoughts are on their wantonness
instead of on prayers. I should be groaning over the sins I have
committed, but I can only sigh for what I have lost. Everything we did
and also the times and places are stamped on my heart along with your
image, so that I live through it all again with you. Even in sleep I know
no respite. (Letter 3, 133)

Heloise denounces a confession that professes change when silenced
desire remains unchanged. Her own painful confession performs an
opposite function: it avows continued sinful desire and marked lack of
contrition, even after fifteen years of monastic life.

In this middle ground, Heloise transforms confession, an oral and
ephemeral act between a confessing subject and an absolution-granting,
penance-giving confessor, into a different kind of discursive act. Her
confession takes place in a letter addressed to Abelard, leaving her

suspended between world and God and making Abelard her epistolary confessor – adding yet another dimension to the relationships that bind them: teacher and student; lovers; parents; husband and wife; brother and sister in Christ; and, now, confessor and confessant. This epistolary act of confession could only be made to Abelard, her partner in love and misfortune – she does not confess to obtain forgiveness from God, but sympathy and help from Abelard.

The letter materially enables Heloise's confession of unrepentant desire and its insistence on continued contact between her and Abelard – a distinctly intimate epistolary contact, rooted in their shared history and its continuing effects on their lives. The letter also creates a lasting testament to Heloise's suspension in desire in the form of a material document: her self-condemnation increases in magnitude in light of the "quasi-public" nature of letters in this period. Given the epistolary context, it is very likely that, though the letters were not necessarily written with the aim of circulation in their lifetime, they were written with an awareness that they would probably, at some point, be read by others.[90] Thus, through writing her confession to Abelard in a letter, Heloise performs it in a public way, exposing herself to a plural audience: God and Abelard, in her lifetime, and other readers after. This public element adds a dimension of self-humiliation to Heloise's gesture, and works perhaps to further secure Abelard's response.

Heloise's self-condemnation is explicit; she calls herself a hypocrite:

> Castam me praedicant qui non deprehendunt hypocritam. Munditiam carnis conferunt in virtutem, cum non sit corporis, sed animi virtus. Aliquid laudis apud homines habens, nihil apud Deum mereor, qui cordis et renum probator est, et in abscondito videt. (Ep. 3, 81)

> Men call me chaste; they do not know the hypocrite I am. They consider purity of the flesh a virtue, though virtue belongs not to the body but to the soul. I can win praise in the eyes of men but deserve none before God, who searches our hearts and loins and sees in our darkness.
>
> (Letter 3, 133)

---

[90] While no autograph copy of the letters exists, the manuscript tradition strongly suggests that the letters were carefully preserved and maintained with an eye to just this: a readership beyond Abelard and Heloise, for didactic purposes. Dalarun offers a compelling account of how the letters might have survived and a comprehensive discussion of the manuscript tradition. On the manuscript tradition, see Muckle's discussion in his edition of "Abelard's Letter of Consolation to a Friend"; Monfrin's notes to his edition of the *Historia calamitatum*; and Southern, "The Letters of Abelard and Heloise," in his *Medieval Humanism and Other Studies*.

Praised by the world and exposed as a fraud before God, the confessing subject of Heloise's second letter urges Abelard to withdraw undeserved praise, and places him in a privileged yet delicate position: he is given access to that which no one other than Heloise and God has, knowledge of the lack of contrition and continued sinful desire behind a chaste façade. Invited to witness the serious moral peril in which she exists, in a "quasi-public" fashion, he cannot but respond to this crisis, in the only way that he can: with another letter. In this way, Heloise's epistolary confession *acts* on Abelard, compelling his epistolary response.

Abelard's next missive applauds Heloise for shunning praise. He writes:

> Approbo autem quod reprobas laudem quia in hoc ipso te laudabiliorem ostendis ... Atque utinam sic sit in animo tuo sicut et in scripto!
>
> (Ep. 4, 87)

> I approve of your rejection of praise, for in this very thing you show yourself more praiseworthy ... may your written words be reflected in your heart! (Letter 4, 143–4)

Strictly speaking, this "utinam ... sit" ("may it be," or "would that it were") is an optative subjunctive expression of a wish for the future capable of fulfillment, and, therefore, not actually true.[91] In other words, he wants her humble words to reflect a genuine, felt humility, but even as he praises Heloise for her humility, grammatically, Abelard leaves room to read doubt, employing a verbal mood associated with both desiring and commanding.

He then responds to the crisis exposed by the confessing subject with an unequivocal command:

> Superest tandem ut ad antiquam illam, ut diximus, et assiduam querimoniam tuam veniamus qua videlicet de nostrae conversionis modo Deum potius accusare praesumis quam glorificare, ut iustum est, velis ... Quae cum mihi per omnia placere, sicut profiteris, studeas, hoc saltem uno ut me non crucies, immo ut mihi summopere placeas, hanc depone, cum qua mihi non potes placere neque mecum ad beatitudinem pervenire. Sustinebis illuc me sine te pergere, quem etiam ad Vulcania profiteris te sequi velle? (Ep. 4, 87)

> I come at last to what I have called your old perpetual complaint, in which you presume to blame God for the manner of our entry into

---

91 In his letters with Heloise, Abelard employs "utinam" expressions only twice, to her seven.

religion instead of wishing to glorify him as you justly should ... If you
are anxious to please me in everything, as you claim, and in this at least
would end my torment, or even give me the greatest pleasure, you must
rid yourself of it. If it persists you can neither please me nor attain bliss
with me. Can you bear me to come to this without you – I whom you
declare yourself ready to follow to the very fires of hell? (Letter 4, 145)

Abelard makes use of the blunt force of command in this letter but
couches it conditionally, playing upon Heloise's desire to please him in
everything. If she is sincere in this avowal, then she must give up her "old
perpetual complaint": lamentation over their manner of entry into religion and, by extension, their shared losses and current situation. The
force of the final part of this injunction is powerful: although, as his
references to Heloise as "sister" attest, this is a relationship now mediated
through Christ, it is a binding one.[92] Abelard reinforces their insepara-
bility even after death, with the threatening implication of rupture should
she not comply. In enjoining her renunciation of her "old perpetual
complaint," he retains the right to command her, and although he insists
on a spiritual relationship, he acknowledges their close association and
holds out the promise of its continuation, provided that she obey his
injunction.

Abelard commands Heloise to silence over their past, yet how, exactly,
is she to show her compliance? Her solution is to perform her obedience
in a letter, to make her silenced grief legible through discourse on other
topics, not-writing through writing. In response to Abelard's command,
she writes a third letter in which she does not mention her grief over their
past. Rather, she submits matters of spiritual concern to Abelard's
authority, and turns from Senecan to Jeromian epistolary exchange.
Abelard commands, and Heloise complies, in the way that she can – with
a letter. However, she prefaces her effort with a qualification that has
given rise to considerable debate over her sincerity:

Ne me forte in aliquo de inobedientia causari queas, verbis etiam
immoderati doloris tuae frenum impositum est iussionis ut ab his mihi
saltem in scribendo temperem a quibus in sermone non tam difficile
quam impossibile est providere ... Revocabo itaque manum a scripto in
quibus linguam a verbis temperare non valeo. Utinam sic animus
dolentis parere promptus sit quemadmodum dextra scribentis

(Epist 3, 241).

---

[92] Peter the Venerable also writes of this binding relation to Heloise; "Peter the Venerable: Letter (115) to Heloise," *The Letters of Abelard and Heloise*, 283–4, trans. Radice.

I would not want to give you cause for finding me disobedient in anything, so I have set the bridle of your injunction on the words which issue from my unbounded grief; thus in writing at least I may moderate what it is difficult or rather impossible to forestall in speech ... I will therefore hold my hand from writing words which I cannot restrain my tongue from speaking; would that a grieving heart would be as ready to obey as a writer's hand. (Letter 3, 159)

As if to prove that Abelard is still her teacher, and that she is still his to command, Heloise echoes his "utinam sit" expression: he writes, "may your written words be reflected in your heart," and she returns a parallel expression, that her grieving heart be as ready to obey as her writing hand – that is, that her interior life might correspond to its outward expression. Once again, the subjunctive force of this "utinam sit" expression indicates that, at the writing of this passage, this wished-for state is not yet true.

The rest of her letter, and the rest of their correspondence, steers clear of her "old perpetual complaint" and takes up matters of religion.[93] Setting aside the question of whether Heloise truly "converts," what the text tells us is that Abelard commands her to silence her grief, and she obeys. And yet, she draws attention to her obedience, declaring it a surface act committed by her writing hand and refused by her recalcitrant heart. How do we read this seemingly contradictory act? Heloise must demonstrate her obedience to Abelard, to show him that she is still his to command and to secure more letters from him. But in calling attention to the gap between the performing hand and the resisting heart, she calls into question the very nature of obedience: just as confession without true contrition is a false coin, an obedience performed by the writing hand but resisted by the grieving heart is a deeply troubled gesture. Heloise's epistolary obedience accedes to Abelard's authority to command her, yet it points to a disjunction between outward performance and that which it might be assumed to represent, a corresponding interior state. Thus Heloise signals the possibility of resistance in the performance of obedi-

[93] Some critics view this discursive obedience as a moment of repression, others as a moment of conversion. Georgianna provides an overview of the critical debate over the authenticity of Heloise's conversion, and suggests that to "choose sides" in the debate over her conversion "goes beyond the limits of literary analysis," 229. Moos offers a different reading in *Consolatio*; for him, the change in tone in Heloise's third letter does not mask impenitence or masochism, but rather is part of a broader strategy of *petitio*, in which silence on the past is a literary effect that permits the epistolary conversation to continue.

ence. This suggests a limit to the reach of authority and its dependence on obedience; it also suggests a limit to the force of the discursive performance that enables Heloise's claim of obedience.[94]

Letters allow Heloise to perform a confession to the only one who can hear it: he with whom she sinned. This makes Abelard her epistolary confessor, and implicates him in the recuperation of her monasticism. Letters also enable her performance of an instrumental obedience whose authenticity is questionable, but without which her relationship with Abelard would not be able to continue. Through the literal silencing of her grief, whether or not she has stopped grieving, letter writing allows her to behave as if she has – and perhaps this is the best she can do for now. Functioning here as vehicles for saying as well as doing, letters signal the in-between status of the epistolary, at once writing and action, offering the representation of change and possibly constitutive of actual change.

While her epistolary obedience leaves unresolved the question of the authenticity of her conversion, Heloise is decidedly successful in effecting one type of conversion: that of her discursive self, an instrumental conversion that secures that which has been her goal throughout the correspondence: continued contact with Abelard, through letters. She follows her declaration of obedience with an explanation of the rest of her correspondence:

> Aliquod tamen dolori remedium vales conferre si non hunc omnino possis auferre. Ut enim insertum clavum alius expellit, sic cogitatio nova priorem excludit … Omnes itaque nos Christi ancillae et in Christo filiae tuae duo nunc a tua paternitate supplices postulamus … ut nos instruere velis unde sanctimonialium ordo coeperit, et quae nostrae sit professionis auctoritas … [et] ut aliquam nobis regulam instituas … quae feminarum sit propria. (Ep. 3, 241–2)

> And yet you have it in your power to remedy my grief, even if you cannot entirely remove it. As one nail drives out another hammered in, a new thought expels an old … And so all we handmaids of Christ, who are your daughters in Christ, come as suppliants to demand of your paternal interest two things … that you will teach us how the order of nuns began and what authority there is for our profession … [and] that

---

[94] This limit has, of course, far-reaching implications, as every level of their relationship is predicated on this obedience and her epistolary performance of it. On the erotic component to this submission, see Desmond's "Dominus/Ancilla" in her *Ovid's Art and the Wife of Bath*; Brown's "*Muliebriter*: Doing Gender in the Letters of Heloise;" Irvine's "Heloise and the Gendering of the Literate Subject;" and Nouvet.

you will prescribe some Rule for us ... which shall be suitable for women. (Letter 3, 159–160)

Heloise obeys, and with vigor: she moves from writing of her personal grief to making a collective demand on behalf of all the sisters of the Paraclete, appealing to Abelard's "paternal interest." He is no less obligated than before, but now, instead of grounding her demand in his personal debt to her, Heloise emphasizes Abelard's obligation as founder of their house.

The rest of her letter addresses the inadequacy of the Benedictine Rule for women, because it was written for men and does not address concerns specific to women's lives.[95] She enlists Abelard's assistance in this gender-based critique, asking for a monastic rule suitable for women, and an explanation for and history of female monasticism.[96] And Abelard complies: his last two letters, the longest by far in the correspondence, are replies to these demands, and provide a detailed history of female monasticism and a modification of Benedict's Rule. This modified rule is largely responsible for Abelard's subsequent reputation as a monastic reformer.[97] This attention to spiritual life and its administration continues in the *Problemata Heloissae*, which demonstrates that Abelard and Heloise did continue writing to each other, restoring presence in absence, but on Abelard's terms, in spiritual vein.

Despite Heloise's successful discursive turn toward spirituality, however, the gap between performance and interiority remains problematic, and she invites us to read it: she has been suggesting all along that actions can, and ought, to be read beyond their surface meaning. She writes in her first letter that her taking the veil was not a gesture of monastic vocation so much as proof to Abelard that, in obeying his order, she belonged to him. In her condemnation of false confession, she observes that actions can deceive: confession, accusation, and mortifica-

---

[95] These concerns specific to women include the "humoris superflui menstruae purgationes" (242). Heloise also writes that reform was necessary because the rule was written in a time of greater faith and ability to observe the tenets of monastic rules. McLaughlin observes that Heloise was the "first woman of her time speak to the larger issues of the expanding religious life of women," and to "raise the question of the 'authority' for this life," "Heloise the Abbess," 2. See Griffiths for a discussion of men's responsibility in the *cura monialium*, " 'Men's Duty to Provide for Women's Needs.' "

[96] Ep. 3, 242 (Letter 3, 159–60).

[97] McLaughlin notes that the last letter in the collection (Letter 9) is "originally the last section of *Ep.* 8, which ends abruptly with a passage from which this text follows in unbroken continuity," "Heloise the Abbess," 2 n. 4.

tion of the flesh constitute "outward shows of penance," acts that can dissimulate lack of inner contrition. To read beyond the surface meaning of actions is to ask a question of Heloise's obedience: what is the relation between exterior performance and interiority? How does interior change occur? Put another way, can exterior performance effect interior change?

It is entirely plausible that Heloise wanted change as much as Abelard did, and her third letter witnesses an attempt to effect this change through writing. Whether or not she was successful in effecting interior change, letter writing was the best means at her disposal for describing her obedience, and also for bringing it about. As they both write, "utinam sit": may written words be reflected in the heart, may the heart be as ready to obey as the hand. Heloise's third letter suggests that writing letters is her attempt to align heart with hand, to bring the desired possibility of the subjunctive into the actual indicative. In other words, even as her letters act on Abelard and compel his response, they might also act on her, and effect longed-for change.

The *Problemata Heloissae* and the Practice of Epistolary Pedagogy

In his description of their courtship in the *Historia calamitatum*, Abelard describes Heloise's learning as an attractive feature influencing his decision to woo her. Her love of learning would place him in a favorable light, presumably because of his own considerable learning and writing skills, and because it would enable the exchange of letters between them:

> Tanto autem facilius hanc mihi puellam consensuram credidi, quanto amplius eam litterarum scientiam et habere et diligere noveram, nosque etiam absentes scriptis internuntiis invicem liceret praesentare, et pleraque audacious scribere quam colloqui, et sic semper iocundis interesse colloquiis. (183)

> Knowing the girl's knowledge and love of letters I thought she would be all the more ready to consent, and that even when separated we could enjoy each other's presence by exchange of written messages in which we could speak more openly than in person, and so need never lack the pleasures of conversation. (66)

Abelard describes the ability to communicate in absence as an advantage in an amatory relation, and a reason for choosing an amorous partner. He, too, describes letters as a substitute for physical presence. However, while Seneca describes this as a compensatory comfort inferior to the actual presence of loved ones, for Abelard, letters are a means by which lovers might speak more openly than in person. His ardor and enthusiasm for letters in the early flush of their love affair echo Constance's claim that letters enable the articulation of that which would be too bold to speak in person.

A youthful Abelard describes letters as a space of openness and permission, and, perhaps paradoxically, as superior to direct contact for lovers' discourse; later in his career, letters served a different purpose. After the *Historia calamitatum* and the correspondence it inspired, letters fostered another kind of exchange, neither amatory nor contestatory, but spiritual and collaborative, in the *Problemata Heloissa*, a set of missive writings generally attributed to Abelard and Heloise.[98] These letters emphasize pedagogy as the dominant dynamic in their relationship. When read together with the more widely read correspondence, they show how Abelard and Heloise exploited the missive and dialogic qualities of the epistolary genre in profoundly collaborative exchanges throughout their careers; they also show the perhaps unexpected flexibility of letters in negotiating and performing complicated ways of thinking about the self in relation to its most intimate others.

The *Problemata Heloissae* comprises a set of forty-two "problems" set forth by Heloise and their solutions provided by Abelard.[99] The questions deal largely with matters of scriptural interpretation, and several echo the concerns in Heloise's better-known letters.[100] I focus here on the prefatory letter that introduces the *Problemata*, which shares stylistic similari-

---

[98] For Dronke, "[t]he links between the *Problemata* and the letters ... are so far-reaching that the questions of authenticity concerning the two works can hardly be considered separately." He cites as a working hypothesis the conclusions of Damien Van den Eynde that "the *Problemata* are the 'continuation and complement' of the correspondence," "Chronologie des écrits d'Abélard à Héloïse," cited in Dronke, "Heloise's *Problemata* and *Letters*," 53. Benton has argued that the *Problemata* were "retouched" by Abelard, which Newman has refuted in "Authority, Authenticity, and the Repression of Heloise," 49.

[99] While Isidore of Seville defines *problemata* as "propositions or questions having something to be resolved by disputation," *Etymologiae* 6.8.14, cited in *The Lost Love Letters of Heloise and Abelard*, 346 n. 4, Cain identifies "a genre of Christian literature known as *zetemata* (or *quaestiones*), in which knotty scriptural problems were posed and then briefly solved"; he notes that the genre flourished in the fourth and fifth centuries: 17 and n. 18. Mews observes that Heloise's use of the Greek word "*problemata*," and not the usual Latin "*quaestiones*," "may reflect a deliberate desire on Heloise's part to emulate sophisticated scholastic usage," *The Lost Love Letters of Heloise and Abelard*, 116.

[100] Questions such as, for example, "We inquire whether anyone can sin in doing what the Lord has permitted or even commanded," "The Problemata," trans. McNamer, in her *The Education of Heloise*, 174. Dronke writes that although Abelard's answers are "set down with scarcely a personal note," in them Heloise "would have found many thoughts relating to her preoccupations in the earlier letters: her consent to marrying Abelard, her yielding to his sexual demands, her own sexual cravings, and her own later consent to live continently, again at his command," *Women Writers of the Middle Ages*, 137.

ties with Heloise's earlier letters to Abelard.[101] Heloise opens the letter
with an invocation of Jerome's teachings to Marcella. While her earlier
epistolary overtures proffered a Senecan ethos, her citation here quite
literally declares a Jeromian model, a performance of her continuing
obedience to Abelard's injunctions.[102] She asks, once again, that Abelard
write back, but this time the request is more focused: she wants him to
answer exegetical questions that have arisen for her and her sisters in the
studies he commanded them to pursue. These questions "disturb" their
study and cause them to be "sluggish" in their reading.[103]

Performance is a guiding motif in this prefatory letter: the sisters'
performance of obedience depends on Abelard's direction, and the
Jerome–Marcella citation suggests Abelard and Heloise in these roles.
The parallels are difficult to miss: Jerome was known, and often to his
disadvantage, for his learned relationships with women; Marcella, one of
Jerome's principal female correspondents, was widowed early and spent
the rest of her life in learning, leading a monastery and corresponding
with Jerome on spiritual matters. Heloise describes Jerome's "songs of
praise" for Marcella, inspired by her questions about biblical interpretation; this recalls her description of Abelard's early songs which, she
claims, put her name on everyone's lips. She reports that Jerome claimed
Marcella "not a disciple but rather a judge," perhaps echoing Abelard's
earlier, contested praise of herself.[104] Citing another of Jerome's commendations of Marcella, Heloise asks:

> Quorsum autem ista, dilecte multis, sed dilectissime nobis? Non sunt
> haec documenta, sed monita, ut ex his quid debeas recorderis, et
> debitum solvere non pigriteris.[105]

---

[101] Janson concludes that both Abelard and Heloise practiced *cursus* in the correspondence, and while there does not seem to be deliberate use of it the *Problemata*, "there
seems to be deliberate rhythm in the prefatory letter," "Schools of Cursus in the Twelfth
Century," 192.

[102] While in the matter of epistolary style Heloise's letter are Senecan, Jerome was an
important influence on Heloise's thinking, if not her early inspiration for letter writing;
Newman examines the influence of Jerome – and Ovid – in Heloise's letters; "Authority,
Authenticity, and the Repression of Heloise," 65–9. Irvine observes that Heloise "was
especially adept at combining the seemingly conflicting discourses of Ovidian *amor* and
Christian *amiticia* for both rhetorical effect and new self-definition," "Heloise and the
Gendering of the Literate Subject," 91.

[103] "Perturbatae" and "pigriores," respectively.

[104] "Discipulam," "iudicem," respectively; "The Letter of Heloise to Peter Abelard,"
in McNamer, 111.

[105] Heloise, "Epistola Heloissae ad Petrum Abaelardum," *Problemata Heloissae*, ed.
Migne, vol. 178, col. 677 D-678B.

What purpose do these things serve, O beloved to many, but most beloved to us? These are not examples, but admonitions, so that because of these things you may remember what you should do, and not be sluggish in resolving your debt.[106]

For Heloise, Jerome's praise of Marcella does not so much render Marcella an exemplum for the women of the Paraclete as serve as a goad to Abelard to resolve his debts. This gesture is at once humble and demanding, and suggestive for thinking through exemplarity: Marcella is not an inspiration but rather a warning to the Paraclete women and, by extension, their director.[107] Heloise suggests that Marcella's praiseworthy example is a reminder of how far from the mark they could fall, and cleaving to an example through fear of failure is a difficult business for which the sisters require help from their founder. Much as the *Historia calamitatum* failed to provide comfort, so do Abelard's exempla fail to provide guidance and inspiration.

Heloise's address here is different from that found in her other letters. There is no salutation, and the letter is quite brief. Most notably, Heloise is now exclusively part of "nobis," "us," a plural personal noun representing herself and the women of the Paraclete. Read against the backdrop of the other letters, this "dilectis multis, sed dilectissime nobis" is yet another way for Heloise to demonstrate her obedience to Abelard, however subtly: this is a letter about the communal benefit of the Paraclete women, and makes no personal claims or untoward references. The notion of debt is still present, but innocent: the debt invoked is that of founder to charges.

While there is no reference to their personal scandal, there is an undercurrent of impatience in Heloise's explanation as she urges, "non pigriteris" (pray do not tarry). Moreover, the enunciation of debt is rather heavy-handed. Heloise reports that she and her sisters have taken to heart Abelard's recommendation to study, which they do because they have been called to divine service by him: "congregasti" (you gathered), and more strongly, "mancipasti" (you handed over).[108] Echoing her earlier declaration that she had taken the veil to prove that she belonged to

---

[106] "The Letter of Heloise to Peter Abelard," in McNamer, 112.

[107] Newman describes this sleight of hand: "a topos often used to warn consecrated virgins of their precarious stature – the higher the ascent, the heavier the fall – [that] is also turned on its head in this discourse," "Authority, Authenticity, and the Repression of Heloise," 63.

[108] This recommendation to study is enunciated in his final letter to Heloise which contains his modification of the Benedictine Rule.

Abelard, Heloise reminds him in no uncertain terms that she was his to give. Invoking historical precedent, continuing her performance of obedience, and establishing his continued debt, Heloise makes her *petitio*:

> Proinde quaestiunculas quasdam discipulae doctori, filiae Patri destinantes, supplicando rogamus, rogando supplicamus, quatenus his solvendis intendere non dedigneris, cujus hortatu, imo et jussu hoc praecipue studium aggressae sumus. In quibus profecto quaestionibus, nequaquam ordinem Scripturae tenentes, prout quotidie nobis occurrunt, eas ponimus et solvendas dirigimus.[109]

> Therefore as disciples to our teacher, as daughters to our father we send certain small questions, praying and begging that you will not disdain to turn your attention to solving them at whose exhortation and command we have mainly undertaken this course of study. Not holding to the order of Scripture in these questions, but as they daily occurred to us, we set them down and direct that they be solved.[110]

As in her previous letters, this letter also iterates, albeit in abbreviated fashion, some of the roles they have played. While the enumeration of personal relation is a feature of much medieval correspondence, the particular attention and development it receives marks a continuity of concern in Heloise's letters to Abelard. And in light of their earlier rhetorical wrestling with names, it is difficult not to notice the unimpeachable innocence of the positions enunciated: students to teacher, daughters to father. Even in the possessive pronouns, Heloise writes as a member of the Paraclete community, reinforcing that as Abelard is teacher and father to them, she is one in a group of his students and daughters.[111]

Whether or not her spiritual conversion was real, her rhetorical conversion was lasting, extending beyond the correspondence to the *Problemata*. The *Problemata* emphasizes that the primary relationship that binds them is pedagogical. In this light, their correspondence can be read as a testament to medieval teaching and learning, and shows how letters can be a uniquely privileged medium to conduct it. In contrast with the request for writing in the correspondence, accompanied by alarming and potentially damning confession, Heloise's careful couching of the

---

[109] Heloise, "Epistola Heloissae ad Petrum Abaelardum," in *Problemata Heloissae*, vol. 178, col. 678C-D.

[110] "The Letter of Heloise to Peter Abelard," in McNamer, 112.

[111] Another point of continuity with the monastic correspondence is the reappearance of "imo" ("hortatu imo et jussu," perhaps better translated "by exhortation and indeed even command"), which recalls Heloise's letters to Abelard and to Peter the Venerable, and her discursive delight in improving on a term.

request for writing in this prefatory letter enables both writers to participate with dignity in the *Problemata* project. Once again, this pedagogy is
situated: it arises in response to Heloise's demands and carefully articulated need. In submitting questions to Abelard's authority, she provides
him with the opportunity to teach, demonstrate the soundness of his
scriptural mastery, and perhaps effect his redemption through writing. As
before, Abelard complies with the demand for letters, answering the
numerous exegetical questions Heloise puts to him, at times at considerable length, and developing his role as spiritual director for the Paraclete.
In the *Problemata*, Abelard and Heloise cultivate pedagogy as a specifically epistolary and profoundly collaborative practice that offers a textual
medium for negotiating and performing their shifting roles in relation to
each other.[112]

Between the Representational and the Real

The letter plays a prominent role in the relationship of Abelard and
Heloise from its very beginning, and Heloise contrasts their present and
past through the filter of letters:

> Cum me ad turpes olim voluptates expeteres, crebris me epistolis
> visitabas, frequenti carmine tuam in ore omnium Heloisam ponebas.
> Me plateae omnes, me domus singulae resonabant. Quanto autem
> rectius me nunc in Deum quam tunc in libidinem excitares? Perpende,
> obsecro, quae debes, attende quae postulo, et longam epistolam brevi
> fine concludo: Vale unice. (Ep. 1, 73)

> When in the past you sought me out for sinful pleasures your letters
> came to me thick and fast, and your many songs put your Heloise on
> everyone's lips, so that every street and house echoed with my name. Is
> it not far better now to summon me to God than it was then to satisfy
> our lust? I beg you, think what you owe me, give ear to my pleas, and I
> will finish a long letter with a brief ending: farewell, my only one.
> (Letter 1, 117–18, translation modified)

Heloise reproaches Abelard for frequent letters in sin and scanty letters in
faith, and she couches her plea for restoration of their epistolary practice
in spiritual terms: his letters will "excitare in Deum," summon her to

---

112 This is suggested by the format of the collection: each problem is neatly followed
by its solution. Dronke describes the *Problemata* as a dialogue: "Abelard is not simply
addressing Heloise and her nuns but entering into dialogue with them," *Women Writers of
the Middle Ages*, 134. See McNamer, and Dalarun on the compilation of the *Problemata*.

God. The instrument of their sinning, she suggests, can now be the instrument of her salvation.[113] The rest of their correspondence and the *Problemata* might be considered the fulfillment of this plea.

In 1471, more than three hundred years after their epistolary drama, Johannes de Vepria, a scribe at Clairvaux, completed a manuscript containing a transcription of, among other items, a set of anonymous love letters, cited at the beginning of this chapter.[114] The collection consists of one hundred and thirteen letters, some written in verse, most in prose, exchanged between a man and a woman, who, judging from the content of the letters, were lovers as well as teacher and student.[115] The letters are often quite brief – some survive only in the form of salutations.[116] In the

[113] In describing more fully her anti-matrimonial position which Abelard mentions in the *Historia calamitatum*, she explains that she did not seek marriage or any of its attendant material gains. It was Abelard alone, with his considerable personal attributes, she wanted. She writes:

> Duo autem ... tibi specialiter inerant quibus feminarum quarumlibet animos statim allicere poteras, dictandi videlicet et cantandi gratia quae ceteros minime philosophos assecutos esse novimus ... relinquisti carmina quae prae nimia suavitate tam dictaminis quam cantus saepius frequentata tuum in ore omnium nomen incessanter tenebant ... Atque hinc maxime in amorem tui feminae suspirabant. Et cum horum pars maxima carminum nostros decantaret amores, multis me regionibus brevi tempore nuntiavit et multarum in me feminarum accendit invidiam.
>
> (Ep. 1, 71–2)

> You had ... two special gifts whereby to win at once the heart of any woman – your gifts for composing verse and song, in which we know other philosophers have rarely been successful ... you left many love-songs and verses which won wide popularity for the charm of their words and tunes and kept your name continually on everyone's lips ... And as most of these songs told of our love, they soon made me widely known and roused the envy of many women against me. (Letter 1, 115)

Already known for her learning, being the lover of a famous philosopher who wrote verses celebrating their love added to Heloise's reputation; an attention to reputation and public opinion was thus a feature of their relationship at its very outset, even before scandal and separation. Swanson suggests that these songs might appear, though unattributed, in the *Carmina burana*, 43.

[114] The manuscript is a florilegium of extracts from Cicero's *De officiis* and letter writers from the antique period to the twelfth century; for more on its contents, see Piron, 177–85, and Mews's *The Lost Love Letters of Heloise and Abelard*, 3–27.

[115] The woman writer in the exchange refers to the man as her teacher in the penultimate letter in the collection, addressing him as her "most noble and most learned teacher," Letter 112, in *The Lost Love Letters of Heloise and Abelard*, 286–7.

[116] See Ward and Chiavaroli for a discussion of the use and omission of salutations in the *Epistolae duorum amantium*, especially 74–8. In one letter, the woman claims salutation unnecessary because they are able to see each other so readily: M 109, 284–5, *The Lost Love Letters of Heloise and Abelard*. Baswell also makes the case for authenticity in the woman writer's employment of bodily images, and the letters' "tone of the schoolroom exercise": "One can easily imagine a playful (or even a cynical) flirtation that grew into

course of the letters, they write about their relationship and conceptions of love and friendship, enthusiastically express mutual praise, undergo an unnamed crisis for which the man declares himself guilty of sin and regarding which the woman writes that there is nothing to forgive, and the collection ends with an oddly unbalanced pair of letters, cool on her part, impassioned on his.[117]

While these letters do not survive in any form attributed to Abelard and Heloise, their first modern editor suggestively titled them *Epistolae duorum amantium: Briefe Abaelards und Heloises?*[118] Scholars have made compelling arguments for their being the early love letters Heloise recalls, identifying similarities between these and the monastic letters: the writers allude to a wide range of learned texts, religious and pagan; they discuss in detail *amor* and *amicitia*; they show epistolary sophistication, employing varied and creative salutations and greeting formulations; they each enjoy renown for their learning.[119] Sylvain Piron has identified unusual technical terms and citations that resonate with the monastic correspondence and Abelard's other writings.[120] Perhaps not surprisingly, the authorship of these letters and in particular their attribution to Abelard and Heloise has generated energetic debate, with skeptics

complicated love in the context of epistolary set-pieces," 169. This brevity could also have to do with de Vepria's scribal practice: he began transcribing only the salutations, and gradually copied more of the body of the letters. Jaeger suggests that he deliberately omitted passages that might locate the letters geographically and chronologically; "*Epistolae duorum amantium* and the Ascription to Heloise and Abelard," 126. The sources he worked from are unknown; his transcription survives in the epistolary anthology he compiled, now at the municipal library of Troyes (MS 1452, fols. 159r–167v), transferred from Clairvaux during the French Revolution; for a thorough account of the manuscript and letters, see Mews, *The Lost Love Letters of Heloise and Abelard*, especially Chapter 1, "Discovery of a Manuscript," 3–27.

117 Newman suggests that this might have been caused by a confusion in the manuscript; see her review of *The Lost Love Letters of Heloise and Abelard* in *The Medieval Review*, 6 January 2000. Jaeger details distinguishing characteristics of the correspondence that resonates with the story of Abelard and Heloise, "*Epistolae duorum amantium* and the Ascription to Heloise and Abelard," 126–7.

118 Könsgen first edited the letters and suggested that they were written by a couple "like Abelard and Heloise," 97–103.

119 Based on a close thematic and linguistic analysis of the letters, Mews proposes that these are the "lost" love letters of Abelard and Heloise, to which Heloise herself refers: she mentions in her first letter the early amatory writings they exchanged, *The Lost Love Letters of Heloise and Abelard*, 6; see also Jaeger, "*Epistolae duorum amantium*"; Ward and Chiavaroli; and Piron. For a skeptical view, see Ziolkowski, "Lost and Not Yet Found"; Constable, "The Authorship of the *Epistolae duorum amantium*"; and Moos, "Die *Epistolae duorum amantium*."

120 Piron, 175–218.

pointing to, among other features, the lack of evidence that establishes beyond doubt the identity of the writers – such as biographical references in the letters.[121] While such conclusive attribution might not be possible, proponents of the attribution to Abelard and Heloise point out that there are at the very least strong affinities between the letters, and question the likelihood of there having been another such pair of learned lovers in early twelfth-century France who left no other literary traces.[122]

If we accept that the *Epistola duorum amantium* are indeed the "lost" love letters of Abelard and Heloise, they situate their monastic letters in a distinct literary light, allowing us to trace the stylistic and thematic development of their writing. If they are not, they still shed important light on literary production in the early twelfth century, and they extend the tradition of Latin love letters and literary exchange and the range of the female voice in learned Latin letters in significant ways.[123] Most important, they meditate in sophisticated ways on concerns central to the Abelard–Heloise dossier, such as the nature of love and friendship, the ineffability of love, and the insufficiency of language; and they attest to the possibility of conducting a nuanced and sustained, passionate and intellectual relationship in letters, attesting to the importance of letters as more than simply a means to communicate.[124]

Even to the most skeptical eye, there are remarkable resemblances to the correspondence of Abelard and Heloise. The man and woman discuss the nature of love and its obligations; the woman writes at her teacher's bidding and sends him letters as proof of her obedience to him; the man

[121] At issue seems to be the very methods of medieval studies; see especially the Jaeger–Constable exchange in *Voices in Dialogue*. Piron builds on the work of Mews, and Ward and Chiavaroli, and engages with the arguments skeptical of the letters' attribution to Abelard and Heloise to defend it.

[122] See especially Piron, 209. It would seem difficult to decide definitively for or against the attribution in the absence of irrefutable proof, but Piron claims that leaving the two writers in anonymity is not simply a refusal to pronounce on the question of their identity, it implies that authorship by an anonymous couple is more probable than authorship Abelard and Heloise; 209.

[123] For a broader discussion of women writing poetry in Latin, including anonymous compositions, see Stevenson's *Women Latin Poets*, especially the chapter on "Women and Latin Verse in the High Middle Ages," 108–38.

[124] Constable asks, if they were written by Abelard and Heloise, why they would have written so frequently and at such length when they were presumably living under the same roof and in daily contact; "The authorship of the *Epistolae duorum amantium*: A Reconsideration," 172. There is another possible explanation: writing letters while living under the same roof might underscore the distinct pleasures held by letting writing, and the ways it can advance intimacy and intellection.

declares himself the woman's "servus"; for them, letters take the place of presence.[125] Letter 82 resonates with Heloise's impassioned declaration that she would prefer to be called Abelard's whore than crowned empress of Rome:

> Quam michimet vellem mitti tibi mitto salutem.
> Nescio quod magis hac esse salubre queat.
> Si quicquid Cesar unquam possedit haberem,
> Prodessent tante nil michi divitie.
>
> Gaudia non unquam te nisi dante feram ...[126]
>
> I send you the salutation which I would like sent to me.
> I know of nothing more salutary than this.
> If I could have all that Caesar ever owned,
> Such wealth would be of no use to me.
>
> I will never have joys except those given by you ...

These lines participate in a discourse on love as mutuality, delight in word-play that winks at shared knowledge of epistolary convention, and reject worldly values in favor of the immeasurable value of love. It is difficult not to read this as the writing of a young Heloise, but if it is not, at the very least it suggests a writer as learned and skilled as Heloise, broadening the evidence of women's literary abilities in this period.

Even if we accept this as the early amatory correspondence of Abelard and Heloise, however, it stands to reason that there would be appreciable differences in style and content between the earlier and later exchanges. Among these differences are the employment of metrical verse, and the fact that it is the man who accuses the woman of not writing enough.[127] The letters are joyful; in one instance, joy interrupts the man's reading.[128] The letters also include a discussion of the bodily responses engendered by letters – the woman kisses her letters, the man writes that the letters cause his spirit to be shaken by joyful trembling and his body transformed into a new manner and posture.[129] Both writers repeatedly claim the ineffability of their love, enthusiastically belied by their continued and copious letter writing – de Vepria recorded over one hundred letters. They

---

[125] Letter 30. In letter 36, like Abelard, he explains why he addresses the woman as "lady"; however his reason is a distancing occasioned by a possible altercation, not a drastic change in profession and status.

[126] Letter 82, *The Lost Love Letters of Heloise and Abelard*, 260–1.

[127] 17, 42.

[128] 110.

[129] 49 Mulier, 24 Vir.

delight in their epistolary exchange, and the man understands just how much writing means to the woman, perhaps too much. He regrets having written certain words:

> Aliquanto iam tempore formosa mea de fide dilectissimi tui dubitasti propter quedam verba, que subita impulsus contumelia, in ipso doloris cursu dictavi, et utinam non dictassem, quia tu nimis ea memoriter signasti, que rogo ut a corde deleas, et apud interiora tua radicem non figant, sicut ego ea deo teste nunquam fixi, sed ubi ea a manibus dimisi, statim revocare volui, si vox emissa reverti nosset (Vir 75)

> For some time now, my beautiful one, you have doubted the faith of your beloved because of certain words which I wrote, provoked by an unexpected reproach, while in the very throes of sorrow. Would that I had never written them, for you engraved them into your memory too much. I ask that you erase them from your heart and not let them establish roots inside you; just as, God knows, I never let them, but rather after they had left my hands, I immediately wanted to call them back – if only an uttered remark knew how to return.

This passage plays upon the written and voiced elements of letters, and attests to their lasting effects on readers, often beyond the control of their writers: once sent, a reader can make her own meaning independently of the writer's intent. Most poignant about this passage is its depiction of this meaning as an imprinting on the heart, an anticipation of Heloise's confession of an interior grief she hopes to silence with an exterior, written performance of obedience. He urges his addressee to erase words from her heart, words written under the sway of emotion that is no longer felt; decades later, Heloise echoes this fervent wish for malleable memory, effaceable emotion, a heart obedient to the commanding, writing hand.

These letters contribute to the tradition of epistolary dialogue best exemplified by the writings of Abelard and Heloise, in which correspondents carry on extended conversations through letters, and a complex relationship is conducted through direct topical address and subtly advanced layers of rhetorical meaning. The *Epistolae duorum amantium* and the *Problemata Heloissae*, temporally bracketing the more famous letters of Abelard and Heloise, flesh out the varied uses to which epistles could be put to conduct a complicated pedagogical and amatory relationship that was above all profoundly textual. And while the male writer in the *Epistolae* laments that reading letters leaves marks on the heart that are hard to erase, the woman writer portrays letter writing, in contrast, as easy, even natural:

Montes et nemora, silvarumque omnia respondent umbrosa, et quomodo
michi gloria difficilis esset rescribendi? Fallit enim labor laborantem,
animus dum se voluntarius expedit ad rem. Immo nil difficile quod ex
voluntate.[130]

Mountains and groves and all the shaded woods make answer, so how
could the glory of writing back be difficult for me? When the mind
willingly arranges the matter, work lightens the worker. Indeed nothing
is difficult which proceeds from the will.[131]

Writing back to a lover is as effortless and inevitable as the rustling of
trees. This natural faculty is qualified, however: its necessary condition is
an agreement of will. If this is indeed the writing of a youthful Heloise,
these lines movingly prefigure her later, adult situation and determina-
tion: writing, glorious writing, is not hard, as indeed nothing is hard that
proceeds from the will – but is writing powerful enough to transform
will?

The *Epistolae duorum amantium* also touch on issues similar to those
raised by the Baudri–Constance exchange.[132] Both sets of letters articulate complicated desire and authority, and express diverse emotions
ranging from despair to joy and playfulness. Letters provide opportunities
to engage in discourse that borders on illicit, as the proper subjects of
concern in religious houses – and between a male teacher and his female
student – are not the delights of secular love relations but the rewards of
sacred ones. Through letters, these concerns may safely be addressed:
letters provide an outlet to keep sacred spaces properly sacred, by
providing an outlet for their expression, sending secular concerns out

---

[130] Letter 88, *The Lost Love Letters of Heloise and Abelard*, 270. Notice the use of
"immo": of the eight times it occurs in the "lost" love letters, it is used twice by the
woman writer, the first time to express contradiction (25), and in this passage it is used the
way Heloise likes to use it in the correspondence, as a way of extending meaning. The
man uses it mostly in contradiction.

[131] My translation.

[132] If we accept these as the letters of a youthful Abelard and Heloise, this thematic
similarity could be attributed to their temporal and cultural situation, as these letters
would have been composed more than a decade before their monastic letters. Piron situates the letters in the orbit of the "renaissance angevine" at the close of the eleventh
century and claims "il est en tout cas certain" that Heloise's uncle Fulbert "a été en relation avec Baudri de Bourgueil," *Lettres des deux amants*, 12 and n. 2. Jaeger, along with
Ward and Chiavaroli, identify the letters of the woman writer in particular with the
learning of the humanistic cathedral schools and place this correspondence at the juncture
between the flourishing of the cathedral schools and early scholasticism; Jaeger,
"*Epistolae duorum amantium*," 125–66, and Ward and Chiavaroli, 53–119.

through material correspondence. And yet, despite the cloak of playfulness, once iterated, eros and the interpersonal positions it implies resonate, and require a rescripting for dialogue to continue. In the case of Abelard and Heloise, this was a necessary shift through which their secular love was transformed, discursively, into a spiritual one. I argue that this is more than a rhetorical rescripting: letters invest their discursive performances with the force of action.

All of their epistolary writings articulate a vigorous struggle to establish the terms of their relationship, and the various performances they stage suggest that letters were not merely exercises in writing, they were constitutive of action. On a practical level, letters allowed Abelard and Heloise to be in contact with each other – letters substituted for visits and direct discourse for which they no longer had opportunities. However, letters were more than mere representations of absent friends, they made the presence of absent friends felt. In addition to restoring presence, letters could act on their recipients in tangible ways, giving pleasure, renewing memories, and alleviating the pain of separation. And, just as letters have the power to make absent friends present, they also summon their writers into particular subject positions, claiming epistolary positions and the relationships they imply. By providing ways to describe and perform complicated subject positions, letters provided new ways of thinking about and articulating the self in relation to its others: as loving, learned, resistant, obedient, and textually constituted.

Through the meaning-saturated context of letter-writing practice, Abelard and Heloise describe, contest, and enact the different relative subject positions they wish to occupy. This negotiation occurs in their manipulation of salutatory practice, as they offer in each successive letter different names to describe their relative positions and dispute the placement of these names, through which each claims greater humility. It occurs on a tonal level as well, as they write within recognizable epistolary genres that communicate the kind of relationship each hopes to establish with the other. These negotiations of epistolary convention are more than rhetorical maneuvering, they constitute a kind of conduct: writing in the way each hopes to be responded to, amounts to behaving in the way in which each hopes to be responded to. Composition as conduct is most strikingly demonstrated in Heloise's performance of an instrumental confession and obedience. Her epistolary confession implicates Abelard in the recuperation of her monasticism, and it acts on him in a way that requires action in return: having heard her confession, he must respond and offer assistance. Abelard commands her to cease grieving for the past, and his letter acts on her in turn, requiring proof of obedience. Her epistolary obedience also makes a claim: in recompense, she wants his help in pursuing the new direction he has commanded her to follow.

Having performed confession and obedience through writing letters, Heloise's third letter and *Problemata* perform a conversion of her discursive self. Just as letters act on a reader by making requests, anticipating responses, exerting the force of obligation, and compelling action, they also act on a writer: they allow us to occupy subject positions, to perform postures, to speak from positions that might or might not be "true," but speaking from them might help us to make them true. Heloise shows us how letters can be employed to adequate ourselves to the world from the outside in; whether this adequation was successful for her, we can't know. Performance eludes the grasp of attempts to control it, and this elusiveness can work against the performer as well as those who command their performances. However, in enabling these varied performances, letters provided Heloise with a way to try, at least, to align heart and hand, to bring the commanded and perhaps longed-for subjunctive into the actual indicative.[133] While epistolary conventions provided vocabularies through which Abelard and Heloise negotiated the terms of their relationship, gender was also a powerful force structuring these replies, and scholars have shown us ways to read masculine dominance and feminine repression in these letters.[134] However, if the letters witness the exertion of dominance over another, I argue that they also show how letters might also act on the self. Letters enable Heloise to perform – discursively, at least – conversion as an act of obedience, a performance perhaps undermined by her subjunctive wish that heart and hand might align. The pressing issue here is not whether Heloise "truly" resists, but how her writing reveals the ways in which letters work to enable performances with the force of action, but whose authenticity is always in question because of the nature of performance. Her letters make claims for a

---

[133] This is different from Baudri's ambiguity, in which uncertainty is a poetic delight in itself, as well as a possible screen for impropriety. Heloise's performance of epistolary obedience can be deceptive, leaving interiority to be inferred and interpreted. Feminist critics have shown us how to read this gap as a space for resistance and even transgression; I argue that it can also be read to reveal the problematic nature of obedience and will, and the role of performance in occluding and effecting "actual" obedience.

[134] For example, see Nouvet, and Newman's "Authority, Authenticity, and the Repression of Heloise."

corresponding interior, but these claims are troubled by their slippery status as representations.[135]

These letters attest to the profound possibilities and limits of epistolary discourse through which the terms of Abelard and Heloise's complicated relationship are contested, established, and performed, but Heloise asks the question best in her gesture of an outside-in willed transformation: letter writing might well function as conduct, offering a kind of action and as such a specifically epistolary way of being, but are there limits to its performative, transformative powers? The multiplicity of positions and gestures performed by Heloise and Abelard reveals that social categories and structures can be inadequate to convey the complicated situations in which people find themselves. However, they are all we have, and in these letters Heloise provides a moving example of how discursive tools can be employed to shape ourselves to the world from the outside in. Her epistolary performance hangs suspended between the representational and the real, and yet it shows how letters offer ways of articulating an unconventional idea of the self through writing, and it holds out the tantalizing possibility – whether realized or not – of writing ourselves out of the desired possibility of the subjunctive into the actual indicative.

[135] I do not mean to suggest that the sincerity of Heloise's conversion is unimportant. However for the purposes of this study what imports is how, even as the epistolary performance of obedience might occlude unrepentant desire, it might also be a means to effect its change.

3

"Virilis Femina":
Christine de Pizan and the Gender of Letters

In the opening passages of her 1405 *Le Livre de la Cité des Dames* (*The Book of the City of Ladies*), Christine de Pizan reports that she has been reading the misogynist writings of Matheolus, a late thirteenth-century French writer. She is overwhelmed by his negative opinion of women, which is echoed in the writings of many other male writers. Convinced by these negative portrayals of her sex, she laments her fate in being born a woman. At this moment of despair over her biological destiny, Reason, Justice, and Rectitude appear and announce that she is to be the champion for her sex. Specifically, she is to step in where "nobles hommes" have failed their task:

> pour forclorre du monde la semblable erreur ou tu estoyes encheute, et que les dames et toutes vaillans femmes puissent d'ores en avant avoir aucun retrait et closture de deffence contre tant de divers assaillans ... pour ce nous trois dames ... te sommes venues adnoncier un certain ediffice fait en maniere de la closture d'une cité fort maçonnee et bien ediffiee, qui a toy a ffaire est predestinee et establie par nostre aide et conseil, en laquelle n'abitera fors toutes dames de renommee et femmes dignes de loz.[1]

> to keep the world from the same error into which you have fallen, and so that ladies and all valiant women might henceforth have from it a retreat and a place of defense against such various assailants ... for this we three ladies ... have come to you to herald a certain building made in the manner of an enclosure of a well-built and well-constructed city, which is predestined to be made by you and established with our assistance and advice, in which none will live save women of renown and worthy of praise.

---

[1] "Christine de Pizan, The *Livre de la Cité des dames* of Christine de Pisan: A Critical Edition," ed. Curnow, vol. 2, 629–30. Richards has also prepared a bilingual edition, *La Città delle dame/Le Livre de la Cité des Dame*. Translations, unless otherwise indicated, are mine.

This passage adroitly authorizes Christine's writing project: the personified virtues proclaim her "predestinee," establishing her divinely sanctioned role to correct the written record. Their injunction plays on the project's figurative and literal registers: she is to construct, through her writing, a figurative city where women can shelter from misogynist slander, and where discussion of women's virtues can take place.[2] This imaginary city will be a locus for articulating ideas with very real consequences: they will correct women's misrepresentation and increase women's honor. Thus, writing has a critical role to play in righting social wrongs and countering centuries of misogynist discourse.

Christine is by far the most prolific woman writer of the French Middle Ages and while critics debate the feminist nature of her work, it contains a strong current of anti-misogyny, figured as the categorical denigration of women as a sex.[3] She wrote against misogyny throughout the various stages of her career, and not only in the *Cité des Dames*, her most well-known work. I argue that her anti-misogyny is most visible in her diverse epistolary writings, in prose and verse, fictional and otherwise, addressed to a variety of recipients. These two projects – anti-misogyny and epistolary experimentation – can, I argue, be read together as part of her project of self-authorization: misogyny powerfully impedes her authority as a writer, and she addresses its unjustness repeatedly in her varied experimentations with the letter form. Her choice of genre for developing her anti-misogynist project is strategic. Letters were invested with a particular authority as literary works and documents of practice, governed by elaborate rules of composition and unspoken conventions that had by this point in the Middle Ages accrued several centuries' worth of dictaminal freight.

Many scholars observe a claim to masculine authority in Christine's writings. In this chapter, I examine the importance of the letter to this

---

[2] Boccacio's *De claris mulieribus* (*Concerning Famous Women*), which had recently been translated into French, is a clear influence on this city of women. However, Boccaccio writes about famous women, irrespective of the positive or negative valence of their fame, while Christine includes only virtuous women in her city. For a comparison of similarities and differences between the two works, see Bell; Phillippy; and ed. Willard, *The Writings of Christine de Pizan*, 141.

[3] Scholars have interpreted several of her writings as proto-feminist projects, most notably the *Livre de la Cité des Dames*, although the difficulty of doing so is well attested; Christine's views are often described as prudish and even essentialist by modern standards – though as I will argue this can be to strategic ends. For a cogent summary of the debate over Christine's feminism, see Finke, 17. See also Bell; Brown-Grant's introduction to her translation of *The Book of the City of Ladies*; Delaney; Gottlieb; and Huot.

claim. I argue that Christine actively and strategically experimented with epistolary forms and conventions to challenge gender stereotypes and to craft a particular, situated authority for herself as a writer.[4] In *L'Epistre au dieu d'Amours* (*The Letter of the God of Love*), the *querelle du* Roman de la rose, and her letters to the Queen of France, she cultivates an authoritative, and strategically gendered, epistolary self. The *Cité des Dames* follows these letters by several years, and I consider how its arguments and the ways in which they are made are anticipated and even made possible by what Christine accomplishes in the letters. An important step in the foundation of the literally and figuratively sheltering *Cité* is the construction of an authoritative writing persona, and this is what Christine accomplishes in her letters, in which she makes visible the discursive construction of gender and also the authoritative writing self by demonstrating their constitution through letter writing.

L'Epistre au dieu d'Amours and the Authority of Letters

As a woman writer at the turn of the fifteenth century in France, Christine participated in an almost exclusively male and clerical discourse. Consequently, her writing generates a host of questions: on what authority did a woman of this period write, let alone participate in learned literary debate? When a woman writer intervenes in a masculine literary realm, how does she reconfigure the terms of debate? Christine's works deliberately raise these questions and stage a particular answer to them through her experimentation with the letter form. One of her earliest confrontations with textual authority occurs in the 1399 *Epistre au dieu d'Amours*, which is credited with containing the "first recorded reproach of the highly-regarded" *Roman de la rose*.[5] It takes the form of a letter dictated by the god of love addressed to his "loyaulx servans," and it employs a full, and somewhat elevated, tri-partite dictamenal salutation:

> Cupido, dieu par grace de lui,
> Roy des amans, sans ayde de nullui,
> Regnant en l'air du ciel tres reluisant,

---

[4] One of the most well known of her "hybrid" works is the *Epistre Othea*, an allegorical work of prose and verse written in the form of a letter. This preference for letters marks her as a "forerunner in France of the humanist tradition," Willard, "A New Look," 74.

[5] Fenster and Erler, introduction, *Poems of Cupid, God of Love*, 3. For a discussion of how anti-*Rose* criticism begins with the *querelle*, see Fleming, and McWebb, "The Early Opponents," in her *Debating the* Roman de la Rose.

> Filz de Venus, la deesse poissant,
> Sire d'amours et de tous ses obgez,
> A tous noz vrays loyaulx servans subgez:
> Salut, amour, familiarité.
>
> Cupid, a god by virtue of his grace,
> The king of lovers, his alone that charge,
> Who reigns amid the space of radiant skies;
> The son of Venus, goddess powerful!
> The lord of love and all that he surveys,
> To all our true and loyal servitors:
> Greetings and love and affable respect.[6]

The god of love dictates this letter "de toutes femmes generauement" (line 13) (on behalf of all womankind) who ask for his intervention, complaining of "grans extors, des blames, des diffames,/Des traÿsons, des oultrages tres griefs,/Des faulcetez et de mains autres griefs" (lines 18–20) (damage done, blame and blemished name,/and of betrayals, very grievous wrongs,/Of falsehoods uttered, many other griefs). The letter describes the injustices that women suffer at the hands of men largely as discursive acts – slander, defamation, gossip. It enjoins men to desist from this ignoble behavior and adhere to higher principles in their relations with women.[7] This literal and figurative call to arms to promote courtly conduct is staged in a literary mimicry of a royal edict, striking a balance between playfulness and seriousness in Christine's treatment of "villennie et meffait."

Not all men fall short in adhering to courtly ideals.[8] Cupid identifies several admirable men who serve him steadfastly. However, among the guilty are clerks who teach schoolboys to scorn women.[9] One of the primary parties guilty of this clerical calumny is Jean de Meun, author of the second part of the thirteenth-century *Roman de la rose*.[10] As is well known, the encyclopedic two-part dual-authored allegorical dream vision features a dreamer who falls in love with a rose, suffers a series of

---

[6] Christine de Pizan, *Epistre au dieu d'Amours*, lines 1–7. All citations and translations of this poem, unless otherwise indicated, are from this edition; line numbers are indicated parenthetically in the text.

[7] Lines 75–82.

[8] On the poetics of masculine literary defense of women, see Swift.

[9] Lines 259–80; 291–308.

[10] The other author is Ovid, in his *Remedia amoris* and *Ars amatoria*. Cupid deems the *Ars amatoria* "mau nommez" (misconceived), and he renames it: "Car c'est *Livre d'Art de grant decevance*,/Tel nom lui don, *et de faulce apparence*!" (lines 376–8) (Its subject is The Art of Great Deceit,/Of False Appearances – I dub it that!).

setbacks in obtaining the object of his desire, and receives advice and assistance from various allegorical figures, including a personage alternately referred to as "Amour" and "Dieu d'Amors." The *Rose* also advances a host of often contradictory teachings about women.[11] Its second part, attributed to Jean de Meun, has been described as a "privileged clerkly text," and its wide-ranging discourse characterized as learned, male, and often deeply misogynistic.[12]

The *Epistre* specifically criticizes this "clerkly" part, identifying the *Rose* as one in a long line of ill-reasoned attacks on women.[13] The god of love functions as a "corrected Cupid" who sides squarely with the complainant women against Jean de Meun and false lovers.[14] As he counters arguments of women's inconstancy, he pits royal epistolary authority against clerical authority, which has been abused to misogynist ends.[15] At issue is not only the *Rose*'s didactic program, but also the practice of unworthy teaching. This critique of texts employed in pedagogy at once equates and questions the status of textual and writerly authority – texts teach, and writers teach through them, but they can teach erroneously. The god of love denies the truth value of misogynist writing, and he claims that the written record would read differently if women were equal participants in book writing.[16] This argument recurs in the *Cité des dames* and the *querelle*, which demonstrates a thematic continuity in Christine's writing and suggests a career-long engagement with misogyny and the mistreatment of women.[17] In this critique of textual

---

[11] Gaston Paris remarks: "Amour recommande avant tout, dans le premier poème, de respecter les femmes; elles reçoivent dans le second les plus sanglantes insultes qui leur aient jamais été adressées" *Littérature française au moyen âge*, 165–6, cited in Hicks, "The 'Querelle de la Rose' in the *Roman de la rose*," 158.

[12] Brownlee describes the first part of the *Rose*, written by Guillaume de Lorris, as a "privileged courtly text," and identifies its courtly and clerkly modes as the "two principal vernacular literary discourses of the late fourteenth century," "Discourses of the Self," 234–5. On the authorship of the *Rose*, see Hult, *Self-Fulfilling Prophecies*, and Guynn.

[13] Lines 389–406.

[14] Brownlee, "Discourses of the Self," 236.

[15] This association of clerics with lovers is likely an intentional slight and has a history in satirical debate poems such as the twelfth-century "Concilium Romarici Montis" (Love Council of Remiremont), Andreas Capellanus's *De Amore*, and the songs of the *Carmina burana*. On the origins and development of the association between *curialitas* and the clergy, see Jaeger's *The Origins of Courtliness*, especially 152–61.

[16] Mais se femmes eussent li livre fait,/Je sçay de vray qu'aultrement fust du fait,/Car bien scevent qu'a tort sont encoulpees (If women, though, had written all those books, I know that they would read quite differently, For well do women know the blame is wrong) (417–19).

[17] The language used here to denounce the *Rose* recurs in Christine's later writings,

culture as inadequate because of its predominantly single-sex member-
ship, women's participation would correct and therefore improve the
written record. This critique raises the possibility of women writing, and,
however obliquely, creates a divinely sanctioned, necessary space for
Christine to fill, as a woman writer who sets the record straight.

While it reveals the abuses of textual authority and alleges that texts
and their authors very often deceive, the *Epistre au dieu d'Amours* relies
on its own status as an authoritative text to advance its arguments. The
result is that the *Epistre* is an act of textual ventriloquism, aping the
authority inhering in other texts of its ilk, but winking at the stagedness of
this performance. The letter unfolds following dictaminal convention:
after the formal greeting and introduction comes a *narratio* of circumstances leading to the request, the formal presentation of the request in
the *petitio*, and finally the conclusion. As suggested by the standardization of the *petitio* in dictaminal prescription, letters seek, but supplicant
letter writers are not always subordinates: this letter, coming from the god
of love, is a royal proclamation. And in his *petitio*, the god of love
employs distinctly imperial tones: having described in detail the
wrongdoings of false male lovers against virtuous women, he commands:

> N'il n'est blame si lait ne si nuisant
> Comme tenu estre pour mesdisant.
> Voire, ancor plus especiallement
> De diffamer femmes communement.
> C'est un vice diffamable et villain;
> Je le deffens a homme quant je l'aim (lines 735–40)

> No blame so foul or damaging exists
> As being thought a bearer of false tales,
> And that is more especially the case
> When women as a group are criticized.
> For that's a shameful and a vulgar flaw,
> Which I forbid to any man I love.

The god of love identifies falsehood as the primary crime in his realm,
exceeded only by the distribution of categorical blame from individual
wrongdoing women to women as an entire sex. To slander a woman is

most notably in the *Cité des dames* and the *querelle* letters. Fenster and Erler document
the expression of anti-*Rose* sentiments in Christine's works preceding and following the
querelle, such as the *Debat de deux amants*, the *Enseignements moraux*, the *Livre de la
Mutacion de Fortune, Autres ballades, Cité des Dames*, and *L'Avision-Christine: Poems
of Cupid, God of Love*, 7–8.

"lait" (foul), but to extend blame to the entire sex for the wrongdoing of one or several is worse, and deserves punishment.[18] The crime Cupid denounces is unmistakably gendered – it is a harm done to women by men, and the recipient of the harms enumerated is "elles."[19] This allegorical letter is an account of women who, wronged by men, appeal to a male authority figure for redress of harm; he complies by issuing a condemnation in the form of a letter. The *Epistre* thus mimics the operations of legal authority, in which textual production is inseparable from the exercise of authority: grievances are brought before an authoritative figure who issues judgment in the form of authoritative text.[20] Moreover, this authority is gendered, the prerogative of those who write and punish (men, gods, participants in textual culture) on behalf of those who do not (women): since women have not written books to set the record straight, Cupid does it for them.

A royal decree is a curiously one-way missive that does not anticipate an answering letter, but rather compliance with commands. However, even as it commands, the *Epistre* relies on the operations of textual authority – it is dictated to a scribe and issued in the presence of other gods and goddesses, underscoring how even the exercise of royal authority depends on governing conventions. By drawing attention to these operations, and through its explicit critique of the abuses of textual culture, the *Epistre* paradoxically undermines its own claims even as it accesses the authority granted to a particular kind of authoritative text, the royal proclamation. Thus, texts are presented as powerful authorizing agents, yet their ability to authorize is contingent, and subject to flawed as well as successful constructions. Critics differ in how they evaluate the *Epistre*'s role in instigating the *querelle du* Roman de la rose, a literary debate that takes place a few years later. Some call it a "good-natured attack," others suggest that it "opened the door to the discussion of the *Roman*" and provided "a preliminary to the Debate."[21] Whatever its

---

[18] He declares that deceivers "villenez soient tres laidement,/Injuriez, punis honteusement,/Pris et liez, et justice en soit faite" (lines 785–7) (Be treated contemptuously, fully shamed,/Thoroughly ruined, punished in disgrace/And seized and bound. Justice be done to them!); translation modified.

[19] Line 775.

[20] Smail examines the various social purposes served by litigation in late-medieval southern France in *The Consumption of Justice*.

[21] Willard observes, "[i]f it is indeed an 'attack,' it is relatively good-natured," and claims that in the *Epistre* Christine "was merely intent on showing that a false concept of chivalry was rather ridiculous," "A New Look," 80. Fenster and Erler claim that she "might not have foreseen the Debate when she wrote the *Epistre*, but she clearly hoped to

intent, the passage on the *Rose* in the *Epistre* is at the very least a critique, lighthearted or not, suggesting that texts, even famous ones, can do wrong.

When read in light of Christine's later works, it establishes significant continuity in her themes and argumentation, providing a starting point for her experimentation with epistolary form and her negotiations of textual authority.[22] In criticizing flawed yet authoritative teaching texts as a primary source of the mistreatment of women, the *Epistre au dieu d'Amours* identifies texts as a locus of potential harm, thereby participating in a well-established tradition in medieval thought.[23] Through adroit mimicry of an authoritative epistolary genre, the royal decree, it also explores the ways in which textual authority is a quality that is attributed and created, and not necessarily inherent in the status of a writer or text. In thus making visible the operations of textual authority, the *Epistre* at once demonstrates and deploys the authorizing force of the epistolary genre. It shows that texts, particularly certain kinds of texts, can be authorizing agents, and therefore instrumental in lending authority to a writer. And, while this textual authority is vulnerable to flawed use, the *Epistre*'s reliance on this constructed authority to advance its arguments claims the availability of textual authority to all capable writers, not just male or clerical writers.

La querelle du Roman de la rose: The Uses of Gender in Debate

Christine's most visible epistolary engagement with authority occurs in the *querelle*, or debate, on the *Roman de la rose*, a sometimes polemic exchange that takes place primarily in letters from 1401 to 1403, where

create a climate of opinion in which Meun's work could be reevaluated," *Poems of Cupid, God of Love*, 3, 4. For Enid McLeod, Christine's "full-scale attack on Jean de Meun" was "rather timidly initated" in the *Epistre*; she also discusses Christine as the initiator of the *querelle*, 65 and 71, respectively.

22 The lyric forms Christine composed early in her career, many of which contained *envois*, might arguably be considered a form of missive writing. I examine here lengthier letters that more closely resemble correspondence, for the authority lent by letter-writing rules and structures governed by the *ars dictaminis*. Lefèvre examines the term *envoi* in relation to *ballades* and its intriguing multiple epistolary functions in "Longue demouree fait changier ami," especially 230–3.

23 The use of commentaries in the *accessus ad auctores* and in particular the allegorical interpretations supplied for pagan writings, discussed in Chapter 1, suggests a concern that texts could mislead without proper guidance; interpretations were necessary for pagan texts to be useful in monastic instruction; see Leclercq, "Liberal Studies," in his *The Love of Learning and the Desire for God*.

the central topic is the merit of the *Rose*.[24] Her *querelle* letters offer more than a continuation of the *Epistre*'s arguments, however; they also show how gender can be deployed strategically to polemic ends. Defending the *Rose* in this first literary debate in France is a group of men associated with the royal chancellery, considered as among the first humanists in France: Jean de Montreuil, Gontier Col, and his brother Pierre Col.[25] Criticizing the *Rose* are Christine de Pizan and Jean Gerson, Chancellor of the University of Paris.[26] In this debate, Christine advances her experimentation with the letter, its requisite parts and its governing conventions, to create a particular epistolary authority of her own. A key component of this experimentation is a strategic deployment of gender, in which she makes gendered claims and stakes gendered positions that ultimately leave the debate at an impasse.[27]

Christine was not, initially, part of the debate. She represents the original debate as taking place in an oral context, which Jean de Montreuil continued by writing a letter to an anti-*Rose* friend, following up on arguments made in person.[28] This letter was accompanied by a treatise on the *Rose*, and copies of both were sent to Christine.[29] Her reply to Jean was thus, like Heloise's first missive, a response unsolicited by the letter to which it replied. However, this is an interrupted epistolary circuit with a difference: whereas Heloise mentions vaguely that "by chance" she came across a letter from Abelard to a friend, Christine can and does account for how Jean's letter came into her possession: he sent her a copy himself.

---

[24] The debate also generated treatises, sermons, and poems.

[25] They were, respectively, the Provost of Lille; royal secretary and notary; and royal secretary of Notre Dame and Tournai.

[26] Alma le Duc comments that the *querelle* constitutes a "departure from the theological quarrels indulged in by the men in orders," 152.

[27] Enid McLeod notes that the *querelle* also allowed Christine a "combative enjoyment unlike any she had tasted before," 65. Thus, just as Heloise aspired to the ideals of *otium philosophiae*, so might writing have been more than a vocation for Christine – even a source of pleasure.

[28] She describes their "paroles meues," and while this could refer to written exchange, most critics take it as a reference to conversation and not writing. The fact that no documentation survives suggests that the previous communication was of a less formal nature, whether written or oral, and this letter marks its transition into a more serious discourse. The language in which the letter was written is not known, but according to references made in subsequent correspondence, the treatise was likely composed in French.

[29] This first missive and the treatise it accompanied do not survive. Hicks observes that the "relative autonomy of the several letters has permitted, if not favored, the loss of the treatise inaugurating the epistolary stage of the quarrel," "The 'Querelle de la Rose' in the *Roman de la rose*," 152. See Potansky on the attempt to reconstruct this document based on information in subsequent letters.

She thus actively enters the epistolary exchange as a second-tier epistolary recipient invited to read but not necessarily to write back.

Her experimentation with epistolary form is evident from the start. Her letter modifies strict dictaminal observation, employing a full tripartite salutation but rearranging the order of its parts. She begins with the *inscriptio*, the addressee's name and attributes, and presents the *salutatio*, the initial greeting, before she identifies herself as the writer in the *intitulatio*, performing humility through salutatory position as well as open declaration:

> A moult souffisant et sçavant personne, maistre Jehan Johannez, secretaire du roy nostre sire. Reverence, honneur avec recommandacion, a vous mon seigneur le prevost de Lisle, tres chier sire et maistre, saige en meurs, ameur de science, en clergie fondé et expert de rethorique, de par moy Cristine de Pizan, femme ignorant d'entendement et de sentement legier – pour lesquelles choses vostre sagesce aucunement n'ait en despris la petitesse de mes raisons, ains vueille supploier par la consideracion de ma femmenine foiblece.[30]

> To the very capable and wise person, master John, secretary of the king our lord. Reverence, honor with recommendation, to you my lord the provost of Lille, very dear sir and master, wise in morals, lover of knowledge, well-founded in clerical matters and expert in rhetoric, from me, Christine de Pizan, a woman lacking in learning and of light understanding – for which things may your wisdom in no way hold in scorn the smallness of my reasoning; rather, I wish to entreat consideration for my feminine weakness.

Christine addresses her adversary with an array of honorifics and praise and casts herself as his epistolary opposite, a woman of mean understanding and learning. Of course, humility and unaffectedness are studied postures, and they mollify what follows: her criticism of his praise of the *Rose* and of the *Rose* itself. Further blunting the edge of her critique, she carefully aligns herself with his anonymous addressee, buttressing her criticism with reference to authoritative support.

As the letter progresses, however, it becomes clear that this humility is not so much false as distinctly double-edged. She describes her writing abilities:

---

[30] Ed. Hicks, 11–12. All citations from the *querelle* letters are from this edition and are identified parenthetically and by page number. Translations of the letters in the *querelle*, unless otherwise indicated, are mine. An English translation is available: Baird and Kane; Hult has recently prepared a new edition and translation; Greene has recently completed a translation into modern French.

Et combien que ne soye en science aprise ne stillee de lengage subtil
(dont sache user de belle arenge et mos polis bien ordonnéz qui mes
raisons rendissent luisans), pour tant ne lairay a dire materiellement et
en gros vulgar l'oppinion de mon entente, tout ne la saiche proprement
exprimer en ordre de paroles aournees (12–13).

And although I might not be learned in knowledge or skilled in subtle
language (by which I might be able to avail myself of beautiful arrange-
ments and polished well-ordered words which would make my speech
gleam), nevertheless I will not leave off from saying practically and in
coarse vernacular what I think, although I do not know how to express it
in proper order with decorative words.

These studied claims of humility and inability exploit the positions that
might be expected of their respective social status – the learned Provost
of Lille, the helpless widowed woman – and make her position a privileged place from which to critique the *Rose* and the values of humanist
rhetoric as practiced by her clerical antagonists. The letter, ostensibly a
means to continue their discourse on the *Rose*, becomes a site for challenging intellectual and social hierarchies. This challenge, at least
initially, is subtly couched: Christine elaborates her positions and qualifies her criticisms with gestures of advance and retreat, boldness and
apology. She reads his letter, but with what she claims is a limited ability;
she disagrees with him, but this is not her own opinion, it is one she
shares with his addressee; she expresses what she thinks, but bluntly, inel-
egantly, in "gros vulgar," not the Latin of elevated intellectual engagement.[31] How literally can one take these protestations of humility? The
multiple references to her "petit engin" are belied by her detailed discussion of the *Rose*, and the recurrent "sauve vostre grace," which might
read at the beginning of the letter as a gesture of polite deference, is by its
conclusion roundly sarcastic. This repetition is a key component of Christine's strategy in the *querelle*. She claims defensive postures of humility,
each time with a slightly different emphasis, that, by the letter's end, have
been undermined by force of repetition and roundly contradicted by her
performance as a reader of the *Rose*.

[31] Christine's correspondents write to each other in Latin and to her in French, and, as
Margolis notes, the difference in language is "not merely a lexical difference but one of
discursive register, and therefore of rank and prestige, so important in the polemical
epistle," 44. In her examination of vernacular humanism in this period, Fenster suggests
that Christine's writing in French is part of her activism, which she conducted in a
language suited to reach a wider public, thereby "elevating" the vernacular; by contrast,
her adversaries appear more interested in private, "exclusivizing" literary exchange in
Latin: " 'Perdre son latin.' "

This humility is claimed for strategic purpose: while Christine apologizes for her own unpolished rhetoric, she implies that her unadorned words are valuable for the very reason that they do not attract for their style but for their substance. In contrasting their writing styles, she stages a critical issue in interpreting the *Roman de la rose*, one of the central points of contention in the *querelle*: the relationship between signifier and signified, between things and the language used to describe them.[32] The immediate disagreement is over the sometimes bawdy language of the *Rose*, which its defenders claim must be interpreted in order to arrive at the salutary teachings it contains, and which its detractors criticize as unnecessarily vulgar. Yet this is not merely a matter of rhetorical style, for, as Christine contends, a proper understanding and expression of this relationship are central to writerly authority.

Christine calls the *Rose* a work of "droicte oysiveté" (12) (pure idleness), a rather pointed characterization, as Oiseuse is the *amie* of Deduit (Amorous Diversion) in the *Rose*.[33] This kind of writing contrasts starkly with Christine's own, in which moral edification and the public good are always in sight. Yet, while her critique of the *Rose* is more than aesthetic, she does praise the manner in which the *Rose* is written:

> Bien est vray que mon petit entendement y considere grant joliveté, en aucunes pars, tres sollennellement parler de ce qu'il veult dire – et par moult beaulx termes et vers gracieux bien leonimes: ne mieulx ne pourroit estre dit plus soubtilment ne par plus mesuréz trais de ce que il voult traictier (13).

> It is true that my small understanding considers there to be great prettiness there; in some parts, he expresses very appropriately what he wishes to say – and with very beautiful terms and graceful leonine verse: what he wished to discuss could not have been better said or more subtly or in more measured lines.

Although she professes an inability to produce dazzling language herself, she presents herself as capable to judge it. However, she implies that graceful rhetoric can mask less than desirable content: she follows her acknowledgment of the pleasing presentation of the *Rose* with criticism of its objectionable teachings. Thus she undermines her praise with the

---

[32] For an introduction to this question in medieval literature, see Eugene Vance; as it applies to the *Rose*, see Hult, "Words and Deeds."

[33] Oiseuse is the gatekeeper to Deduit's garden, in which most of the *Rose* takes place.

implication that fine words can mask erroneous thinking. Her care to combine praise with critique provides the appearance of reasoned consideration, and the ability and willingness to praise and censure impartially.[34]

Christine's discussion of aspects of the *Rose* that are not praiseworthy demonstrates her ability to deal critically with texts and contradicts her claimed position of intellectual insufficiency. She singles out for censure Reason's improper vocabulary: Reason employs "plainement" the terms for "secréz membres." Ultimately, her own position on names is one of limited use determined by necessity. The *Rose* is not, in her opinion, soberly written, nor its writing a matter of necessity, sickness, or genuine need. Therefore, its manner of referring to private body parts is more than mere idleness, it is an impropriety.[35] This argument gets to the heart of her perspective on writing, which she casts as an undertaking with moral implications in the *Cité des dames*: writers have an obligation to teach, and to teach with propriety. Her insistence on writing's didactic and moral imperatives underwrites her argument against misogyny. To bolster the authority with which she argues against misogynist parts of the *Rose*, she refers to *L'Epistre au dieu d'Amours*:

Et comme autrefoys ay dit sur ceste matiere en un mien dictié appellé *L'Epistre au Dieu d'amours*: ou sont les contrees ou les royaumes qui par leurs grans iniquitéz sont exilliéz (17–18)?

And as I have at another time expressed on this topic in my work called *The Letter of the God of Love*: where are the lands and kingdoms that have been destroyed by [women's] great sins?

---

[34] Hicks suggests that, as this letter is a response to Jean de Montreuil's, this dialectic method reveals the arguments and structure of his lost letter; *Le Débat sur le Roman de la rose*, xviii–xix. While this might well be the case, I suggest that the structure of Christine's letter might also constitute a deliberate strategy: her primary method of exposition is to describe points raised by her adversary, explain her reasons for disagreement, and provide supporting examples, offering praise and critique to accompany her assessment of merits and flaws. This thoroughness provides the appearance of fairness and reflection and is almost legal in tone, lending credibility through method to her arguments. See Finke for a discussion of Christine's *style clergiale*.

[35] "[L]e nom ne fait la deshonnesteté de la chose, mais la chose fait le nom deshonneste. Pour ce, selon mon foible avis, en doit estre parlé sobrement – et non sans neccessité – pour fin d'aucun cas particulier, comme de maladie ou autre honneste neccessaire (14)" (the name does not make the dishonorable quality of the thing, but the thing makes the name dishonorable. Because of this, according to my feeble opinion, it ought to be spoken of soberly – and not without necessity – in special cases, such as sickness or another genuine necessity).

This reference demonstrates thematic continuity in her writing, and at the same time it reminds the reader that she too is a writer by mentioning as if in passing her authorship of a well-received and well-known literary work.[36] It at once strengthens her argument through citation of an authoritative text, and furthers her own reputation as a writer. The breezy "et comme autrefois ay dit" functions as part of what Brownlee identifies as "explicit auto-citation" in Christine's writings. It claims her privileged status as an *auctor*, and invites the reader to reread and recontextualize her earlier writings through her later ones.[37] While this self-referentiality might well be self-promoting, it also gestures beyond the immediate outcome of the debate to a project of greater significance: countering misogyny, which is, of course, necessary for this authorization to occur.

Christine's project to craft an authorial persona thus works on several levels in the *querelle*: she is a correspondent in a learned debate, in which she is also a source of textual support. She understands how texts authorize each other, their writers, and their users, and this evident knowledge complicates her repeated and increasingly suspect protestations of intellectual inability. She concludes this letter with a return to her opening concern: the way in which her status as a woman affects the reception of her writing. In contrast with her initial apologies for insufficiency, here, she asks for no special consideration, nor does she apologize for her "petit engin":

> Et ne me soit imputé a follie, arrogance ou presompcion d'oser, moy femme, repprendre et redarguer aucteur tant subtil et son euvre admenuisier de louenge, quant lui, seul homme, osa entreprendre a diffamer et blasmer sans excepcion tout un sexe (22).

> And may it not be imputed to me as folly, arrogance or presumption to dare, I, a woman, to reproach and blame so subtle an author and to diminish praise for his work, when he, one man, dared to undertake to defame and blame without exception an entire sex.

---

[36] See Fenster and Erler's introduction for a discussion of the transmission, reception, and influence of the *Epistre au dieu d'Amours*, especially in England.

[37] Brownlee, "Rewriting Romance," especially 182–3. Moreover, as he points out, Christine claims as her own words that are presented in the *Epistre* as issuing from the god of love, "Discourses of the Self," 254–5. Brownlee focuses here on the *Livre du Duc des Vrais Amans* and the *Livre des Trois Vertus*; he observes that both works offer, among other things, a corrective rewriting of the figure of La Vieille of the *Roman de la Rose*. See Parussa on intertextuality in Christine's works, and Hindman on cross-references in the illuminations of Christine's works, which she is known to have supervised, *Christine de Pizan's* Epistre Othéa, 47.

The unqualified "moy, femme" contrasts starkly with the repeated protestations of "petit entendement." She acknowledges that others might interpret her criticism of a respected male writer as folly or arrogance.[38] However, this foolish criticism is distinct from what her letter actually offers – a reasoned and thoughtful, albeit at times heated, discussion of a literary text and its effect on the public. She thus activates stereotypes about women in order to prove those stereotypes wrong through the example of her writing. These defused stereotypes, along with the protestations of humility, are emptied out through repetition. This repetition, along with Christine's other strategies of authorization, carefully crafts an authoritative, gendered, and above all epistolary persona.

It is not entirely true, however, that Jean de Meun defames all women without exception. He does praise one woman in the *Rose*, the woman conspicuously omitted from the *Cité des dames*: Heloise.[39] The story of Heloise and Abelard is translated into French and condensed into seventy-three lines in the *Rose*, appearing in the discourse of the misogynist Le Jaloux. Describing the rarity of honest women and agitating against marriage, Le Jaloux claims Heloise as the sole example he knows of a wise woman. He describes her as "bien entendant et bien lettrée" (very intelligent and learned), and her arguments against marriage are sound,

> Car les livres avoit veüz
> Et estudiez et seüz,
> Et les meurs femenins savoit,
> Car trestouz en soi les avoit.[40]

> For she had seen
> And studied and understood books,
> And she knew feminine ways,
> For she fully possessed them herself.

Le Jaloux describes Heloise's learning and her feminine ways as if in opposition, and her possession of both as noteworthy. To his credit, in describing what Heloise seeks from Abelard, Le Jaloux cites her desire for learning:

---

[38] Indeed, the terms "follie," "presompcion," and "oultrecuidance" that she claims in order to disclaim are echoed in the letters of her adversaries.

[39] Jean de Meun translates into French the Latin letters of Abelard and Heloise in 1290; see Hicks's critical edition, *La vie et les epistres Pierres Abaelart et Heloys sa fame*.

[40] Guillaume de Lorris and Jean de Meun, lines 8777–80. All citations from the *Roman de la rose* are from this edition and identified parenthetically by line number in the text; my translation.

Et requerroit que il l'amast
Mais que nul droit n'i reclamast
Fors que de grace et de franchise,
Sanz seignorie et sanz maistrise
Si qu'il pouist estudier
Tout suens, tous frans, sanz soi lier
Et qu'el rentendist a l'estuide,
Car de science n'ert pas vuide. (lines 8781–88)

She asked him to love her,
But without seeking any good for herself
Beyond favor and kindness,
Being neither her lord nor her master,
So that he might be able to study
For himself, freely, without binding himself
And that she might apply herself to study as well,
For she was not devoid of learning.

The insistence on an unconventional relation, so striking in Abelard's and
Heloise's accounts, echoes differently here, because it is employed in an
anti-matrimonial diatribe to further Le Jaloux's argument about the scar-
city of good women who do not seek to fetter men with marriage.

Although he uses it to advance his own projects, Jean de Meun does
appreciate Heloise's love of learning, and the possibility that a life dedicated to *otium philosophiae* could well have appealed to her as much as to
Abelard. This desire for learning, which might make her appealing for
Christine, is overshadowed by her wish for a non-marital amorous relationship with Abelard. According to the *Rose*, it is Heloise's learning that
enables her to advance this anti-matrimonial position:

Mais je ne croi mie, par m'ame,
C'onques puis fust une tel dame.
Si croi je que la letreüre
La mist a ce que sa nature,
Que des meurs femenins avoit,
Vaintre et donter mieus en savoit.
Ceste, se pierres la creüst,
Ainc espousée ne l'eüst. (lines 8829–36)

But I do not believe, upon my soul,
That since then there has existed such a woman.
And I believe that learning
Placed this in her nature,
That she had feminine ways,
And knew how to vanquish and overcome them.

This woman, if Peter had heeded her,
He would never have married.

In Jean de Meun's account of the story, feminine ways advocate marriage, and Heloise's learning enables her to "vaintre" and "donter" her feminine nature. Learning de-sexes her, and enables her resistance to marriage. While Christine includes a scene of desexualization in the *Livre de la Mutacion de Fortune,* discussed in the final section of this chapter, it is not knowledge that desexualizes; rather, allegorical Fortune transforms a woman into a man so that she can survive in a man's world. Christine's objection to such a portrayal of the relationship between women and learning would probably have been forceful enough to override evidence of Heloise's considerable learning and warrant her exclusion from the city of ladies.[41]

While Christine herself never remarried, she would never advocate the kind of relationship Le Jaloux describes. However she does anticipate the attention inevitably paid to her sex in relation to her writing, and although it is a far cry from Le Jaloux's formulation of learning as masculinization, she preemptively invites consideration of her sex in relation to her writing in the *querelle.* When she opens her letter with an appeal to her addressee's superiority in learning and status, she places him in an epistolary bind: he is churlish if he does not make allowances for her claimed "femmenine foiblece," but what exactly would this entail? That he tolerate her criticism of the *Rose* on the grounds that, coming from a flawed source, her critique does not merit engagement and therefore ought not be challenged? Framing the dialogue in these terms, as between a man of elevated learning and a woman of inferior understanding for whom allowances ought to be made, hopelessly skews the discussion and makes an equal exchange impossible. It demonstrates how unequal claims to authority can damage the possibility of dialogue. It also illustrates how certain dynamics, fraught from the beginning, necessarily engender fraught conclusions – and indeed, the *querelle* ends inconclusively, as is perhaps inevitably the case when parties do not agree and escalating invective renders conciliation impossible. Of greater impor-

---

[41] Newman argues that Heloise is excluded because she has already been "canonized" in the annals of misogynist writing, "Authority, Authenticity, and the Repression of Heloise," 68. In contrast, Brook concludes that because "[t]here is no sympathetic re-evaluation of Heloise by Christine as there was of Medea in the *Livre de la Cité des Dames*," Christine never read the Abelard–Heloise correspondence; "Christine de Pisan, Heloise, and Abelard's Holy Women," n. 5–6, and 558.

tance than the outcome of the debate, however, is how Christine uses letters to establish credibility in a new public role, and to articulate a radical view on gender and genre: that both are constructed and established through practice and, in this case, the practice of writing letters.

Her repeated claims of feminine weakness are strategic: Christine does not so much denigrate her writing as acknowledge that it will never be assessed apart from the fact of her sex. Marilynn Desmond suggests that this self-deprecation is enforced by epistolary rhetoric, within which women have no position, as they do not occupy clerical office.[42] However, Christine knows that her critics will judge her first and foremost as a woman writer, and that her sex will serve as an excuse for flaws in her writing or a reason to reduce its interest to its novelty. She plays upon this certainty: she draws attention to her status as a woman and employs it to gain leverage, claim a questionable humility, silence her detractors, authorize her claims, and stage a specific writing persona.[43] She exploits her exclusion from clerical office to her advantage: she mines epistolary debate for the ways a kind of writer conventionally excluded from its practice – a secular woman – can use it effectively. This opening epistle thus witnesses what might be considered Christine's strategic essentialism, that is, positing a reductive, stereotyped notion of women's abilities which she debunks as she moves from a staged apology for feminine deficiency to a challenge, if not to disregard her sex, then at least to consider the different standards by which men's and women's writing is judged.[44] Moreover, she implicitly claims a gendered authority, whereby her status as a woman not only authorizes her defense of women,

---

[42] Desmond, "The *Querelle de la Rose* and the Ethics of Reading," 168–9.

[43] She asserts that, as a cleric, Jean de Meun could not have had direct experience of married life, and reduces his observations on marriage to speculation. She charges him with inexperience of matrimony and virtuous women, alleging that his contact with "femmes dissolues et de male vie" forms the basis of his information (Hicks, 18). This is all but an accusation of frequenting prostitutes, and the speculative insult is surprising given her care to construct and support her arguments and her disapprobation of dishonorable topics. She might well be attempting to account for the basis of Jean de Meun's information, but accusing him of fabricating lies would be less vicious than accusing him of speaking from direct experience of *luxure*. On the experiential standard in Christine's anti-misogyny, see Case.

[44] Brown also refers to the strategic use of essentialist stereotypes in her discussion of Heloise's letters: "manipulation of authoritative (and 'oppressive') constructs through the artifice of performance – be it strategic theatricality or strategic essentialism – far from constituting surrender, can be an active, nay aggressive, means of rewriting those very constructs to the pragmatic benefit of the (re)writing subject," "*Muliebriter*: Doing Gender in the Letters of Heloise," 42–3.

but constitutes an exclusive rhetorical position that she can exploit to her advantage in this literary debate. Her opening letter in the *querelle*, which is no less representational for being a "real" letter sent to a "real" addressee, reveals the usefulness and unexpected flexibility of the epistolary genre for gendered self-fashioning and authorization.

By Way Of Response: The Efficacy of Letter Collections

As Christine has set it up, the very fact of her interlocutors' response authorizes her incursion into their discursive space. Writing back to her tacitly admits her, and by extension women's, ability to participate in literary culture. However, there are many missed circuits in this correspondence. It is less a traditional epistolary exchange between a writer and an addressee than a witness to an epistolary community assembled under the rubric of debate.[45] Christine's letters in this context evince an active experimentation with the rhetorical and material possibilities of letters in the construction of authority. In 1402, she compiles a dossier of the debate letters. This is not a complete record: Jean de Montreuil's instigatory treatise and letter are excluded, and the *querelle* actually generates documents for another year. Explaining the selective nature of the compilation project, Eric Hicks writes that the opening documents do not appear because this would have been "préjudiciable à sa cause."[46] Moreover, the dossier is not faithful to chronology: while the first surviving letter of the debate is hers, the dossier opens with a missive addressed to her from Gontier Col, thus presenting her as the respondent, and not the initiator, in the debate letters.[47] Thus, in addition to being a correspondent, textual authority, and capable reader in the *querelle*, Christine also fashions a role for herself as an invited interlocutor and editor.[48]

---

[45] Jean de Montreuil does not answer Christine's response; only Gontier and Pierre Col directly address letters to her.

[46] Hicks, *Le débat sur* Le Roman de la rose, xxxvi. Brownlee corroborates that this first letter is "suppressed" in Christine's dossier; "Discourses of the Self," 253.

[47] She does, however, include an introductory statement summarizing the chronology of the *querelle*. This chronology is faithful to the historical order of events and letters, listing the "words exchanged" between Christine and Jean de Montreuil; the lost letter from Jean; the letter from Christine; and the letter from Gontier Col. This chronology, paired with the actual order of appearance of the letters, highlights the deliberately inverted order of Gontier's letter to Christine and her letter to Jean.

[48] Brownlee distinguishes between the "first level" of the debate – the letters exchanged between adversaries – and the "second level," consisting of the dossier of selected pieces of the correspondence compiled and sent to prospective patrons by

She sends copies of this selectively presented debate, with accompanying dedicatory epistles, to two prospective defenders: Isabeau de Bavière, the Queen of France, and Guillaume de Tignonville, the Provost of Paris. The different ways she represents the project to each reveal a strategic assessment of the uses of rhetoric in the best sense of the word: language carefully crafted to produce a desired effect. In this way Christine experiments with the boundaries between genres and even textual media: her compilation and dedication make of the *querelle* letters a book of which she is the author.[49] It presents her version of the quarrel, over which she exerts authority. However, it also preserves the structures of textual authority; the dossier literally mimics the complaint of the wronged women in the *Epistre*, as it offers up a record of wrongs to the proper authority. In a patronage system, the fact of dedicating works is not surprising; what is surprising is the selective nature of the dossier, presented as if complete, sent to two different patrons with such different accompanying rhetoric.

And yet, even as it participates in this textual culture, this project of compilation and dedication underscores the obligations that such a gift imposes.[50] Wealthy individuals often commissioned texts, an exchange with which Christine was certainly familiar. But if offering a text as a gift is implicitly to request patronage and protection, to accept it suggests an obligation to read it and support the point of view it represents. The sources of support in this case are carefully chosen – the Queen of France and the Provost of Paris – and Christine addresses herself to each with gender-based strategies of appeal.

The dedicatory letter to the queen opens with an enumeration of praise and honorifics: Christine writes that she has heard of the queen's "delicte" (delight) in hearing "dittiéz de choses vertueuses et bien dictes" (5) (well-spoken works regarding virtuous matters). Positioning herself as Isabeau's thoughtful subject, she reports that, in the enclosed letters, she defends "l'onneur et louenge des femmes (laquelle pluseurs clercs et autres se sont efforciéz par leurs dittiéz d'amenuisier)" (6) (the honor and praise of women – which several clerks and others have undertaken in

---

Christine; "Discourses of the Self," 250. Holderness discusses compilation as a form of commentary in "Compilation, Commentary, and Conversation in Christine de Pizan."

   [49] Brownlee also makes this point in "Discourses of the Self," especially 201.

   [50] As Finke observes, "[t]he book, in a manuscript culture, is not a means of disseminating knowledge widely; rather it is a means for delivering up control of that knowledge to a patron – or to a series of patrons," 30.

their works to diminish). Although she is of "petit entendement," she is "de verité meue," moved by the truth, to participate in the debate.[51] She professes a by now familiar inability, this time for the purpose of securing the assistance of her royal addressee. This inability is juxtaposed with another gesture of auto-citation in reference to her other works, a reminder of her status as a writer. Christine is thus paradoxically situated: at once "foible" in the face of "soubtilz maistres," and an established writer in her own right, claiming a decidedly qualified weakness along-side a qualified authority.

After this careful positioning, she makes her *petitio* to the queen:

> Si suppli humblement Vostre Digne Haultesce que a mes raisons droicturieres, non obstant que ne les sache conduire et mener par si beau lengage comme autre mieulx le feroit, y vueilliéz adjouster foy et donner faveur de plus dire se plus y sçay (6).

> So I humbly implore your worthy Highness that to my righteous propo-sitions, notwithstanding that I know not how to bring them forward and conduct them in such beautiful language as others are better able to do, you may wish to give credence, and grant me the favor of saying more about it if I am able.

She claims a rhetorical deficiency, but noticeably, she does not here attribute it to her female sex. Brownlee writes that the *querelle* subject matter is "presented in terms of an implicit solidarity between speaker and addressee."[52] This is an unspoken solidarity occasioned by their shared status as women at court, a community they share and from which antifeminist clerics are excluded. One can well imagine how this soli-darity would have been ill-served by apologies for feminine weakness.

Other than appealing to female solidarity, however, what, exactly, is Christine asking of Isabeau? Not that she join in writing, or that she condemn or suppress Christine's opponents; she asks the queen to "adjouster foy" to her writings and "donner faveur" to her to say more – largely intangible matters. While it is clear that she desires the queen's support, what matters is less any specific action requested of Isabeau, but rather her status as a royal addressee. Desmond writes that this royal

---

51 Hicks, 6.
52 Brownlee, "Discourses of the Self," 251. It is worth remarking that Gontier Col and Jean de Montreuil are both in the immediate employ of the king, and Christine does not send the dossier to Charles VI, but to Isabeau. Although Charles's mental condition provides a logical reason for sending the dossier to the queen, the staging of the gift is the critical element, with its address suggesting a specifically female solidarity or alliance.

destination authorizes Christine's "rejection of the subject position [Gontier Col] identifies for her,"[53] a position of inferior ability and judgment. Moreover, she fashions it into a position of privilege: she shares a common, gendered cause with a powerful royal addressee that her *querelle* interlocutors cannot access. This dedicatory epistle to the queen activates the nexus of power relations inherent in patronage relations, and through a manipulation of the material epistle as well as the subject positions it affords, aggressively positions the writer with respect to royal authority.

The letter to the queen offers Christine's "recommendacion." The one to Guillaume de Tignonville offers "recommendacion avec obeissance premise" (7) (recommendation with promised obedience), which subtly signals Christine's different relationships with her two prospective *querelle* patrons, the one slightly more deferential than the other. She describes the *querelle* as "le debat gracieux et non haineux meu par oppinions contraires entre solempneles personnes" (9) (the amiable and not hateful debate motivated by opposite opinions between serious persons). In the letter to the queen, she reductively describes it as a dispute over women's reputation. Here, she does not discuss the content at all, assuming perhaps that the provost will actually read the letters, or that he is already familiar with the dispute.[54]

Christine makes a gender-based appeal for assistance to this male authority figure:

> requier vous, tres sçavant, que par compassion de ma femmenine igno-
> rance, vostre humblece s'encline a joindre a mes dictes vraies oppinions
> par si que vostre saigesce me soit force, ayde, deffense et appuyal
> contre si notables et esleuz maistres (7).

> I pray you, very wise man, that out of compassion for my feminine
> ignorance, your humility will deign to join to my writings true opinions
> so that your wisdom might be to me strength, assistance, defense and
> support against such noteworthy and distinguished masters.

Feminine ignorance requires compassion, not dismissal, Christine argues, again strategically activating gender stereotypes. She writes that his support will enable her to persevere in her "guerre," a term distinctly at

---

[53] Desmond, "The *Querelle de la Rose* and the Ethics of Reading," 169.

[54] Of the subject matter, she writes simply that "vous pourrés oïr les premisses par les epistres envoiees entre nous et par les memoires que de ce feront si aprés mencion" (7) (you will be able to understand the premises by the letters sent between us and by the references which they make to the discourse).

odds with the earlier description of the "debat gracieux et non haineux," and she suggests a concrete form for this assistance to take: she invites him to participate in the debate and join his opinion to hers. She concludes with an apology for her poverty of language, explaining her choice to write in prose:

> Aussi, chier seigneur, ne vous soit a merveille, pour ce que mes autres dictiéz ay acoustuméz a rimoyer, cestui estre en prose. Car comme la matiere ne le requiere autressy, est droit que je suive le stille de mes assaillans, combien que mon petit sçavoir soit pou respondant a leur belle eloquence (8).

> Also, dear lord, may it not be surprising to you, because in my other works I have been accustomed to rhyming, that this one is in prose. For as the matter does not require otherwise, it is right that I follow the style of my assailants, although my small learning might indeed answer poorly to their beautiful eloquence.

To the queen, Christine refers apologetically to her unpolished rhetoric. To the provost, she explains her lack of eloquence as a lack of experience with prose, compared with her strength in another area, verse composition. Despite the apology, she signals her status as a writer and her right to address him as an intellectual peer.

Taken as a whole, these dedicatory epistles and the dossier they introduce now comprise, materially, distinct documents in their own right. The preparation of this dossier is in some ways analogous to the medieval practice of letter collection, in which a general rule for inclusion in a collection is the style or subject matter of the letters, or the status of the correspondents. However, Christine's dossier is distinct from these collections, because it contains the selected letters of several writers, as compared to the collected composed and received correspondence of a single writer. And while generally medieval letter-collections are organized according to chronology or "pleasing variety of subject-matter and style,"[55] hers is clearly organized to create a particular impression of the unfolding of the *querelle*. Most notably, letter collections were gathered by their writers with a view to eventual publication. She initiates this publication process when she sends her collection to illustrious addressees and invites engagement in a way that claims the debate as her

---

[55] Constable, *Letters and Letter-Collections*, 60. Patt writes, "Letters were often composed and collected mainly for the sake of their stylistic qualities, with regard for factual or doctrinal content as a secondary consideration," 135.

project. First she induces her adversaries to respond to her epistolary overtures; she then controls the debate when she selectively compiles and presents it as a gift to prospective patrons.[56] The dossier is thus a complicated arrangement of texts and relationships in which Christine stages her appearance as, variously, a woman appealing to female solidarity, a woman in need of male support, a humble supplicant, a capable reader, a respected writer, and an author, in all the loaded senses of the word.[57]

The "Virilis Femina" and the Exclusions of Genre

In June of 1402, a scant few months after Christine sent the *querelle* dossier to Isabeau de Bavière and Guillaume de Tignonville, she prepared the first edition of her collected works, whose last item is titled *Epistres du débat sus le* Roman de la Rose.[58] Despite these seemingly definitive dates and editions, the debate not only continued to generate documents, it produced in the following year some of its most heated invective, with gender-based arguments offered on both sides of the debate, and a repeated insistence on the superior claims of the male gender to the epistolary genre. In Jean de Montreuil's letter defending the *Rose* he identifies "a certain woman by the name Christine," whom he compares to an audacious Greek whore.[59] He also singles out an unnamed male critic for similarly dubious personal attack: his anti-*Rose* sentiments can be explained by his religious vocation, as he is a man for whom "the continuation of humankind is useless."[60] This other adversary is quite probably Jean Gerson, though he, unlike Christine, is not openly identified.[61] It is likely that solidarity of sex and profession motivate this differential treatment, and Christine's naming, a breach of the rhetorical convention that clerical humanists so prized, can be seen as a closing of ranks against a

[56] As a central identifying feature of letter is its status as a sent communication, the very act of sending makes the dossier itself a kind of letter.

[57] An "author" was not only a person who wrote texts, but also a text containing "authorities." A writer, a text, gained "auctoritas" largely through being read and cited; see discussion in Chapter 1.

[58] According to Laidlaw, "[f]ifty of the extant manuscripts of her works are presentations copies which were planned, copied, decorated, corrected and perhaps also bound under Christine's personal supervision," 297.

[59] Hicks, 42.

[60] Hicks, 44.

[61] This reticence seems a conventional practice; as Hicks observes, there is a "qualité allusive des appellatifs dans toute cette correspondance polémique, où il semble avoir été de règle de ne jamais mentionner les noms des intéressés," *Le débat*, xvi.

female interloper. Jean de Montreuil concludes his post-dossier riposte with an explanation of his use of the second person singular "tu," which could well be another jab at Christine, who employs the polite second person plural "vous."[62] The ostentatious attention to modes of address claims as a clerical and masculine domain the proper observance of epistolary registers of familiarity, friendship, and learning.[63]

Pierre Col's letters initiate the *querelle*'s most extended and heated exchange. He explains how he sought out Christine's letters, in another instance of unsolicited epistolary exchange. In this case, however, a royal secretary and canon seeks out a woman writer, indicating the degree to which her writing is being taken seriously by her addressees and her unaddressed readership. Despite this implicit compliment, he offers serious offense. Her professions of rhetorical insufficiency, however she intends them, are turned against her as a comparative insult: however poor she thinks her rhetoric, it is at least better, he claims, than her flawed reasoning.[64] The debate begins to resemble a shouting match, with largely the same points being raised that, each claims, clearly demonstrate the fallacy of the other's arguments.[65] While the argument does not advance much, the invective fairly explodes off the page. Like Jean de Montreuil, Pierre treats his adversaries unequally. He, too, avoids naming Jean Gerson as an adversary, but identifies Christine explicitly and launches against her an *ad feminam* attack. At one point in the *Rose*, Reason states that it is better to deceive than to be deceived in love, which Christine disputes: to deceive is simply wrong, and cannot be good or better than anything. Pierre derides her interpretation as elementary, even childish.[66] He corrects her reading and insists that the passage does not teach that it is good to deceive. He adds to his assessment an extraneous note:

---

[62] "Et parce quod tibi per 'tu' confidenter sum loquutus. Hoc enim ex lectione antiquorum didisci: singularem personam plurali numero alloqui non deberi" (44) (and forgive that I have spoken to you boldly as "tu." Indeed I learned this from reading the ancients: it is not necessary to speak to one person in plural number).

[63] Gontier Col, who also comments on his use of "tu" in an earlier debate letter, describes it as a mark of friendship; despite the difference in explanation, the attention to "tu" functions in his and Jean de Montreuil's letters as a claim to elite knowledge.

[64] Hicks, 89. He, too, draws attention to his use of "tu," identifying it as proper classical usage, useful instruction, and an indication of amicability, 90.

[65] His letter does not introduce substantively new arguments; his primary defense lies in Jean de Meun's subtlety, and in the inability of faultfinders to correctly read his didactic purpose in contested passages.

[66] Hicks, 99.

En oultre je dy qu'il me vaulroit mieux – c'est a dire qu'il me greveroit moins – faire samblant de toy amer pour moy aasier charnelement de ton corps qu'il ne feroit pour celle meisme fin que j'en fuisse fol amoureux, pour quoy j'en perdisse mon estude, "sans, temps, chastel, corps, ame, los" (come dit est) (99).

Furthermore, I say that it would be better for me – that is, that it would harm me less – to pretend to love you in order to enjoy your body carnally than it would be that, for the same end, I were a foolish lover, for in that state I should lose "my learning, my sense, my time, castle, body, soul, reputation," as it is said.[67]

Ostensibly, this hypothetical situation provides an example of how deception, while harmful, can be preferable to sincere yet foolish behavior. However, in imagining a canon's enjoyment of Christine's body, it could not have been better calculated to insult. Moreover, even as it does hypothetical violence to her body, it does violence to her text: it reduces her to a physical, rather than a textual, body, denying her the *auctoritas* she has been painstakingly cultivating.[68] He then sweeps aside the entire passage with an unsupported claim that the lines in dispute, as well as others, are interpolations.

Pierre justifies his different treatment of Christine and Jean Gerson in the form of another correction. His explanation implies a solidarity of men of letters, who understand the stylized, unspoken rules of literary engagement: one does not crudely pass judgment on another. Christine's "presumpcion oultrageuse" is to judge Jean de Meun, while Jean Gerson, more "preudent et gracieux," leaves the matter unresolved.[69] As with the predilection for not naming names, at issue is a matter of convention, even style and delicacy, but also of gender: Pierre takes issue with judgment of a man issuing from a woman.[70] He excludes her from the rules of epistolary courtesy ostensibly because of this breach, yet the primary reason for her exclusion, as his rhetoric attests, is the fact of her sex. Her

---

[67] He cites here from the discourse of the foolish lover, who claims, citing popular axiom ("come dit est"), that it would be better to be a false lover than "fol amoureux." *Le Bel Inconnu*, a romance surviving in a late thirteenth-century manuscript, offers exactly the opposite advice. The protagonist declares that it is better to be foolish than to be disloyal in love: "Cil qui se font sage d'amor,/Cil en sont faus et traitor./Por ce mius vel faire folie/Que ne soie loiaus m'amie ("Those who make themselves out to be wise in love are false and traitorous. For I prefer to do foolishness than be disloyal to my *amie*"; my translation): Renaut de Beaujeu, 1261–4.

[68] Thanks to Anthony Welch for this observation.

[69] Hicks, 99–100.

[70] Hicks, 103.

judgment of Jean de Meun is not only a breach of etiquette, it is unforgivable because she is a woman, intruding in a masculine domain and criticizing one of its masters as a matter of public, textual record.

Pierre is much gentler with Jean Gerson who, he explains, objected to the *Rose* because he did not read it closely and so did not understand it.[71] He urges that the Court of Christianity pardon him and suggests that he read the *Rose* three times as penance. This might be a humorously partisan way to conclude the matter, were it not for the glaring omission of Christine's pardon and the continued preservation of Jean's anonymity.[72] Pierre calls attention to his mastery of the rules of literary disputation, which Jean observes and Christine doesn't. She remains unexonerated, and her exclusion is marked. Despite her self-authorizing gestures, this partisanship suggests the existence of a coded, gendered epistolary language and conduct for which her work and study avail her little; she is not steeped in clerical culture as her correspondents are.

In response, Christine shows that she is attuned to the subtleties of inclusion and exclusion. She makes use of the woman she will bar from the *Cité des dames* in just a few years' time, Heloise:

> Tu dis que quant a toy, plus desires estre "repris pour prisier et amer son livre que estre des trop subtilz blasmeurs." Tu ressembles Helouye du Paraclit qui dist que mieux ameroit estre *meretrix* appellee de maistre Pierre Abalart que estre royne couronnee; si appert bien que les voulantés qui mieux plaisent ne sont pas toutes raisonnables (146).

> You say that, as for yourself, you wish more to be "understood to prize and love his book than to be among the too subtle critics." You resemble Heloise of the Paraclete who says that she would better love to be called the *meretrix* of Peter Abelard than to be a crowned queen; so it is manifestly clear that the wishes that please most are not all reasonable.[73]

---

[71] In Christine's letter to Jean de Montreuil she admits that she "passed over" parts of the *Rose* that were distasteful to her (ed. Hicks, 13). Jean de Montreuil questions the ability to criticize when a text has been read incompletely in Christine's case, but uses it to excuse Jean Gerson's alleged misunderstanding of the *Rose*; Pierre Col seems to follow suit.

[72] Such delicacy of treatment in regard to Jean Gerson might reflect a concern to avoid charges of defamation. If so, it is also a direct affront to Christine's objection to the defamation of one woman being extended to calumniate the entire female sex. See Solterer's *The Master and Minerva* for an examination of women and injurious speech in medieval French literature.

[73] Heloise corroborates this sentiment about the unreason of desire in her pivotal third letter to Abelard, in her vivid description of the great difficulty in getting the heart to cease "hankering after its dearest wishes"; see Chapter 2.

Jean de Meun's account of the story of Abelard and Heloise, by which it was known to a thirteenth-century audience, does not retain the Latin word Heloise scandalously claimed, "meretrix," but translates it into French, "pute."[74] His translation of their letters similarly translates it into French: "putain."[75] Christine cites the original Latin of the letters of Abelard and Heloise, signaling her familiarity with the French literary tradition in both learned Latin and "gros vulgar."[76] Her vocabulary choice shows her attention to scholarly register and aggressively positions her as a member of the learned elite; not surprisingly, it also avoids the impropriety of such a word as "pute."[77] More daringly, she equates her correspondent's unreasoned loyalty to Jean de Meun with Heloise's unreasoned love for Abelard, turning him into Jean de Meun's "meretrix." This assigns a gendered and pejorative status to his desire to defend his *maître*. She gives lie to the claims of gendered attributes, and turns seemingly fixed positions into epistolary usefulness: Heloise's impassioned love, parallel to Pierre's impassioned loyalty, is not an inevitable function of gender, but of unreason. Christine thus unmoors one of the *Rose*'s most misogynist dialogues from the one-sidedness of its gender assertions, and reveals her interlocutor's position as uncritical, unreasonable, and, by implication, inferior.

Nadia Margolis observes that Christine "had no use for Heloise" and "could not forgive her for having sold out to the misogynistic double standard."[78] In Heloise's defense, having her story appropriated in a misogynist discourse is unfortunate but hardly an act of complicity; however, it is likely that her story in this period was known largely through Jean de

[74] " 'Se li empereres de Romme/Souz cui doivent estre tuit homme/Me daignoit vouloir prendre a fame/Et faire moi du monde dame,/Si voudroie je mieus, dist ele/Et dieu a tesmoing en apele,/Estre ta pute apelée/Qu'empereriz coronnée' " ("If the emperor of Rome, to whom all men should be subject, should deign to take me as his wife and make me mistress of the world, still I would rather," she said, calling God as her witness, "be called your whore than crowned as empress"; my translation) (lines 8821–8).

[75] *La vie et les epistres: Pierres Abaelart et Heloys sa fame*, ed. Eric Hicks, 50. His word choice is telling: "meretrix" means simply prostitute, while "pute" and "putain" mean, more coarsely, whore.

[76] This is not the first time Christine uses this word. It also occurs in her earlier letter to Jean de Montreuil, citing his comment that Jesus used the word "meretrix" when speaking of "pecheresses."

[77] On Christine and Latin, see Mews on "The Latin Learning of Christine de Pizan in the *Livre de paix*."

[78] She continues, "[t]hat Heloise's and Abelard's letters had been translated, and thus appropriated, by none other than Jean de Meun confirms her compliant image in this regard," Margolis, 46.

Meun's account of it in the *Rose*, and that she was thereby associated with him is probable.[79] For Christine, for whom virtue, honor, and moral rectitude are of paramount importance, a woman's preferring worldly dishonor and, by her example, lending authority to Jean de Meun's argument, would certainly be grounds for disapproval. Christine recasts Heloise's positive portrayal in the *Rose* negatively here, to further her criticism of Pierre's approval of the *Rose*. The circulation of Heloise's image in the service of opposing ideologies might seem alarming and even arbitrary. However, Christine can claim the authority of experience for her judgment and condemnation of Heloise. Cupid lamented the lack of women writers who might set the written record straight in the *Epistre au dieu d'Amours* – presumably because they could write from their own experience, which for centuries had been represented by men, and to their disadvantage. Here, finally, is a woman writing, and to prove her lack of unreasoned female bias, she condemns a woman celebrated for her learning in the French Middle Ages and beyond.

Perhaps motivated by the prominent attention given to him in the *querelle*, Jean Gerson also replies to Pierre Col's letter to Christine. This indicates the circulation of these letters, and reinforces epistolary discourse in this period as a profoundly public matter. He writes in Latin to his clerical colleagues, and his tone is firmly corrective as he points out the theological unsoundness of many of Pierre's propositions. Notably, he defends Christine:[80]

> in opusculi mei impugnacione, cum insigni femina miscuisti ... virilis illa femina cui tuus sermo dirigitur ... magno racionis aculeo urgebat te mulier (166–8).

> in attacking my little work, you associated me with a distinguished woman ... this manly woman to whom your discourse is directed ... the woman pressed you with a great sharpness of reason

When he describes her as "virilis femina," he identifies learned literary discourse as a masculine activity, in which her participation is noteworthy and even a success. He calls attention to the temperateness of his own language and criticism in his treatise, a model for courteous literary

---

[79] On Gontier Col's role in the preparation of the manuscript containing the French translation of the letters, see Bozzolo, and Brook, "Christine de Pisan, Heloise, and Abelard's Holy Women," 558.

[80] Richards discusses the textual evidence for points of intellectual contact between Christine and Gerson in "Christine de Pizan and Jean Gerson: An Intellectual Friendship."

comportment which neither Pierre nor Christine observes.[81] He concludes with an exhortation that the jokes cease, and that Pierre devote himself to more wholesome and virtuous studies.[82] Noticeably, he does not identify Christine by name.

For New Year's Day of 1403, Christine prepared a second dossier of the debate letters, with two addressees – Isabeau de Bavière and, it has been suggested, Guillaume de Tignonville.[83] This collection circulates the debate letters yet another time, and cements their status as a literary work beyond their initial epistolary context. She declares that the queen's favor will improve her cause, and invites her to read and judge the matter. To her second dedicatee she addresses a twelve-line rondeau that opens and closes very directly: "Mon chier seigneur, soiez de ma partie!" (My dear lord, may you take my part!).[84] Brownlee describes this compilation as an act to "take final and complete control of the *Débat* as written artifact by means of an additional letter, which both expanded the original dossier and definitively effected its closure."[85] The creation of these "books" through strategic compilation, and their circulation through strategic address, is central to understanding the *querelle*: they demonstrate Christine's multi–layered participation in and negotiation of elite literary discourse through material and rhetorical manipulation of letters.[86] This negotiation amounts to pushing the boundaries of who can say what, and how.

In the *querelle*, Christine operates as both reader and writer. She advertises her reading of the most important work in the medieval French literary tradition, and engages in epistolary debate with clerical authorities on the basis of this reading. Invited to observe this clerical literary debate, but not to write back, she literally inscribes herself into this tradition. She gains the authority to participate in learned male debate through her successful and innovative employment of the epistle, and she bases her criticisms on a classical notion of the public accountability of literary

---

[81] Hicks, 174.

[82] Hicks, 174–5.

[83] Piaget suggests Guillaume de Tignonville as the addressee; Hicks observes that this is plausible but not a proven certainty; see *Martin Le Franc*, 74, cited in Hicks, xlvii n. 97.

[84] Lines 7, 12.

[85] Brownlee, "Discourses of the Self," 257.

[86] Some claim that the *querelle* establishes the groundwork for the later *querelle des femmes*. For example, Kelly writes that Christine "sparked the four-centuries long debate," 5, and Bloch writes that the "'querelle des femmes' and the 'querelle des anciens et modernes' can be seen to constitute continuations of the Quarrel of the *Rose*," *Medieval Misogyny*, 48.

works.[87] Her mastery of formal elements and her intellectual preparation authorize her presence in this male discursive space, and her very participation validates the learned persona she seeks to portray. Her compilation projects demonstrate that her self-authorization occurs both rhetorically and materially, and her epistolary experimentation in the *querelle* testifies to her varied and successful efforts to mine the letter for its authorizing possibilities.

This success is measured not only by the fact of response, but the considerable attention the *querelle* generates. It is also suggested by the fact that Jean de Montreuil literally borrows a page from her book. Sometime in 1403–04, he sends selected letters from the debate to a superior, seeking to bolster support for his side of the argument.[88] This suggestively reveals that the authority Christine so painstakingly constructs in her letters was also a concern for male writers: authority was not immanent but constructed for men, as well. And yet, despite these successes, Jean Gerson's memorable defense of her participation in the *querelle* as a "virilis femina" raises the question of the effects of her interventions: through Christine's epistolary experimentation and rhetorical maneuvers, had the field of literary letters been opened up for women?

Letters to the Queen: Isabeau de Bavière and the Powers of Gender

Two years after the inconclusive end of the *querelle*, France was in considerable political turmoil, racked by decades of often violent conflict with England and internecine strife.[89] In this turbulent climate, Christine addressed a letter to Isabeau de Bavière, the *Epistre a la royne*.[90] Written

---

[87] See Solterer's *The Master and Minerva*, especially the chapter on "Christine's Way: The *Querelle du Roman de la rose* and the Ethics of a Political Response," on how Christine makes the subject of the *querelle* a profoundly public matter affecting the good of the city, 151–75.

[88] He sends a copy of his original defense of the *Rose* to a friend, demonstrating that he, too, knows the value of gaining prestigious readers and intercessors through strategic epistolary address. Hicks provides a thorough chronology the *querelle* and its various documents in his edition, *Le débat*, lii–liv.

[89] At this point, the conflict known as the Hundred Years' War had been ongoing for over half a century, and despite the "second peace" of 1389–1415, France continued to see domestic political instability. Isabeau was acting regent for her young son during Charles VI's periodic bouts of madness, and in uneasy relation with Charles's Burgundian and Orleanist relatives. Most immediately, she had been involved in a failed attempt to remove the dauphin from Burgundian influence; see Green, 264–5.

[90] Isabeau was a frequent addressee of Christine. See Laidlaw for a discussion of her manuscript addressed to the queen and the queen's gifts in return, 298.

in prose, it is primarily an appeal for intervention in the civil war that
arose out of the quarrel between the Dukes of Orléans and Burgundy. The
letter has topical timeliness, and its claims are consistent with Christine's
idea of writing as social advocacy. It also continues her project of epistolary positioning and gendered claims in the service of constructing an
authorial persona. She describes herself humbly as Isabeau's "povre
serve" (lowly servant), and in this letter, her non-royal status is essential
to the epistolary position she claims:

> non obstant que vostre sens soit tout adverti et advisié de ce qu'il
> appartient, touteffoiz est-il vray que vous, seant en vostre trosne royal
> couronné de honneurs, ne povez savoir, fors par autruy rappors, les
> communes besoingnes, tant en parolles comme en faiz, qui queurent
> entre les subjiez.[91]

> although your mind is well aware and told of what it should know,
> nevertheless it is true that you, seated on your royal throne surrounded
> with honors, cannot know, except by someone's report, the common
> problems, in words as well as in facts, which prevail upon your
> subjects.[92]

In her earlier letters to the queen, Christine played upon a solidarity occasioned by their shared status as women. She sought patronage and protection from someone who would, by virtue of her sex, understand the
damage wrought by misogyny. In this letter, she trades upon her status as
one of the Isabeau's "subjiez" who is nevertheless invested with unusual
status, a go-between authorized to communicate with the queen on behalf
of other subjects. She claims that the queen's vulnerability necessitates this
intermediary: those in power are, by virtue of their position, weakened in at
least one regard, knowledge of the daily lives of citizens. This letter positions Isabeau as a monarch in need of counsel, through no fault of her own,
from a citizen who can report on conditions on the ground; it positions
Christine as advisor and moral compass for the queen of France.

In this position, Christine claims the role of champion not just of
women, but also of children and all of France's downtrodden. She thereby
expands the role decreed for her by the allegorized female triumvirate of
the *Cité des dames* and models the intervention she urges of Isabeau.
However, she does exploit the key difference in their positions: Isabeau is
royal, Christine is not. She aggressively develops maternal metaphors and

---

[91] "Epistre a la Royne," in *The Epistle of the Prison of Human Life*, 72. All translations from this text, unless otherwise indicated, are from this edition.
[92] Translation modified.

insists on the queen's maternal role for her immediate family and for France as a nation, thereby elaborating a distinctly maternal model of queenship.[93] This motherhood is invoked in the name of protecting the "natural heritage" of Isabeau's "very noble children," and civil discord is described as a "disagreement between father and son," a "very human and common occurrence" in which mothers must intervene. Christine's metaphors are not only maternal, they are divine. The royal mother is analogous to Mary:

> tout ainsi comme la Royne du ciel, mere de Dieu, est appellee mere de toute christienté, doit estre dicte et appellee toute saige et bonne royne, mere et conffortarresse, et advocate de ses subjiez et de son pueple.

> just as the Queen of Heaven, Mother of God, is called mother of all by all Christendom, so must be said and called any good and wise queen, mother and comforter, advocate of her subjects and her people.[94]

The expansion of Isabeau's responsibility is not merely prescriptive. By means of these metaphors, Christine authorizes and even demands Isabeau's political intervention, justified by gender, maternity, and royal birthright.[95] Her epistolary rhetoric constructs a mutually dependent authority for Isabeau as a sovereign with an inalienable right and obligation to govern, and, equally important, for herself as a subject with an obligation to offer counsel.

Proving her worth as an advisor, her letter offers more than galvanizing rhetoric; she elaborates a cost-benefit analysis of intervention. To stand by passively and allow strife to continue would constitute a breach of maternal duties: it would be "the work of the devil," with injurious results to her literal and figurative progeny – her children and France.[96] Intervening would benefit the queen in three ways: she would acquire merit for her soul; secure the restitution of the "bien" of her children and their subjects; and obtain "perpetuelle memoire" and praise in the chronicles and tales of France.[97] This last benefit is of no small moment in Chris-

---

[93] Green also makes this point, describing it as an "original maternalist image of queenship," 265.

[94] "Epistre a la Royne," 78–9.

[95] See Adams for a discussion of how Christine is not reproaching Isabeau but rather rallying public support for the queen.

[96] "Epistre a la Royne," 72–3.

[97] "Epistre a la Royne," 73–4. This is pithy advice, given Isabeau's ultimate maligning at the hands of chroniclers; see Adams, "Recovering the Queen;" on the disparity between Isabeau's reputation during and after her lifetime, see Adams's forthcoming *The Life and Afterlife of Isabeau of Bavaria*.

tine's universe, as her *Livre de la Cité des dames* sought to provide, among other things, much-needed exempla of worthy women.[98] Extending the natural metaphors, she makes an explicitly sex-based argument for Isabeau's intervention: royal women have an obligation to this kind of action for, to the extent that "pity, charity, clemency and love" are "by nature in the female sex," the presence of these qualities in royal women is magnified.[99] She cites a negative exemplum in Jezebel, a royal woman who has failed her natural duty and as a result is defamed, cursed, and damned.[100]

Christine closes the letter on a cautionary note. She reminds Isabeau of the turns of Fortune that can affect even princes and princesses. She urges her to act generously now, while Fortune favors her, as insurance for public support in a less favorable time.[101] To illustrate, she selects an example more startling than Jezebel. An unwise ruler risks having his actions censured in public and shameful fashion, and

> tout ainsi comme a un chien qui est chacié tous lui queurent sus, et est celli de tous deffoulez, en criant sus lui qu'il est bien employez.

> just like a dog who is chased by those who run after it, this man is trampled by all, shouting at him that he is being deservedly treated.[102]

Offering the examples of the Virgin Mary at one end and Jezebel and hounded curs at the other, Christine pulls out all the rhetorical stops in this letter. Its interpretation is doubtless shaped by the relationship between the two women, on which both contemporary testimony and subsequent scholarship have been divided. However, whatever the tenor of their actual relationship and the valence of this exhortation, it significantly expands Christine's sphere of epistolary influence. Through her letters, she participates in the discourse of monarchy, what constitutes legitimate rule, and what kind of person constitutes a legitimate ruler – and this ruler's counselor.[103]

---

[98] Green points out that among the contemporary women included in the *cité* are women who have helped in governance and acting as regents for their sons; 267.

[99] "Epistre a la Royne," 74–7, translation modified.

[100] "Epistre a la Royne," 76–7. The choice of Jezebel as a negative exemplum is not accidental: a foreign-born queen herself, Isabeau would certainly have been attuned to the implication that, should she meet with public disfavor, her foreign birth would certainly situate her in the history of nefarious non-native queens.

[101] "Epistre a la Royne," 79–80.

[102] "Epistre a la Royne," 80–1, translation modified.

[103] Christine's 1404 *Livre des fais et bonnes meurs du sage roy Charles V* and 1407 *Livre du Corps de Policie* can be considered continuations of this discussion.

The *Epistre a la royne* appears in a major medieval formulary, All Souls College, MS 182.[104] Its inclusion strongly suggests the desirability of its use as a template for other letters. The fame of both addressee and writer probably had something to do with its inclusion as well, and this is key: to be able to write to the queen confers a certain status, a fact of which Christine was no doubt aware in her compilation projects in the *querelle*. It is a letter of entreaty that once again situates Isabeau as a powerful addressee who can grant or refuse requests, and Christine as a supplicant. However, these privileged positions are complicated by the didactic tone of the *Epistre a la royne*, and its articulation of the contingent nature of female rulership. Christine's gambit met with no surviving recorded response from the queen, but her letter clearly circulated and survived, a fact that attests to the afterlife that letters took on outside of their immediate intended epistolary circuit.[105]

Christine's multiply-claimed position as Isabeau's correspondent reveals an astute assessment of resources and a close attention to the uses of gender.[106] For her project of authorization as a writer, Isabeau's role as an addressee suggests that authorization can work by epistolary association, as the relationship of correspondents inherently confers status. This association plays on sameness and difference: Isabeau and Christine share the same status as women, yet their positions in regard to social power and authority diverge widely. Christine reduces this gap, however vivid her expressions of subservience, in claiming her royal correspondent: her epistolary positioning emphasizes gender sameness with the result of reducing difference in social authority. This gender sameness is every bit as strategic as the gender difference she aggressively claims in the *querelle*, and demonstrates her attention to the ways in which gender

[104] This formulary compiled by ecclesiastical judge John Stevens has been described as "one of the most important surviving dictaminal formularies of the late Middle Ages," Richards, *"Seulette a part,"* 162.

[105] "According to the Monk of Saint-Denis, it was immediately after Christine's letter was written that the king of Navarre and Louis of Bourbon, sent as ambassadors to the queen, were finally successful in getting her to heed their prayers. On October 8 she moved to Vincennes and began serious peace negotiations. By October 17 Isabeau and the duke of Berry were publicly thanked for having negotiated the reconciliation of the warring dukes," Green 265–6 and n. 68, citing Bellaquet, ed., *Chronique du religieux de Saint-Denys*, 3:345.

[106] Christine claims Isabeau as an addressee throughout her career for the dedication of a variety of documents including letters, *ballades*, and editions of assembled documents.

figures power relations, and is therefore an important resource for strategic self-positioning.

It is worth noting that Christine was an established writer by 1405, and scholars surmise that she wrote the *Epistre a la royne* at the request of one of the warring dukes.[107] The manuscript containing it, widely held to be an autograph copy, concludes with a brief and incomplete rondeau that suggests that it was composed at the request of a noble patron.[108] It begins on a note of supplication:

> Prenez en gré, s'il vous plaist, cest escript
> De ma main fait aprés mie nuit une heure.
> Noble seigneur, pour qui je l'ay escript
> Prenez en gré. (82)

> Take in good part, if you please, this writing done
> By my hand one hour after midnight.[109]
> Noble Lord, for whom I wrote it
> Take it in good part.

This rondeau complicates the *Epistre a la royne* as a letter written in Christine's voice, for it marks it as having been written at the request of a noble patron. Regardless of its inspiration, however, it demonstrates an evolution in her engagement with gender in her letters. In the *querelle*, Christine makes an epistolary appeal to a powerful patron through their shared status as women, and their implied common cause: shared outrage over misogyny. In the *Epistre a la royne*, Christine is an authority as well, and it is tempting to guess at the reasons for which she was asked to write this letter: she was an established writer of repute, she had an established history as a correspondent of the queen, and she shared with the queen status as a woman. It would seem that the authority and gendered association she had been at pains to construct, largely through her letters, had achieved recognition.

It is, of course, entirely possible that this rondeau speaks not to historical circumstance but to another instance of constructed authority: she could have invented the "noble seigneur" for whom she composes this letter. Even if this were the case, these letters to the queen reveal Christine's canny assessment of authority and gender as constructed and

---

107 See ed. Willard, *The Writings of Christine de Pizan*, 252, and Green, 265.

108 See Laidlaw on the autograph element.

109 Sankovitch examines the trope of the woman writer's nocturnal labor in "The French Woman Writer in the Middle Ages."

contingent, and accessible through careful epistolary positioning. Through her adroit use of the letter form, she plays upon the constructed nature of gender and authority and, through a variety of epistolary strategies including selective compilation and address, she performs in her letters a carefully constructed gender and an equally carefully constructed authority.

Practicing Gender, Practicing Genre

Misogyny and the difficulties women experience form a nexus of concerns prominent in many of Christine's writings. In the *Livre de la Mutacion de Fortune*, in which Christine offers an allegorical account of her struggles with Fortune, a simple solution is offered to women's adversities. The narrator loses her husband during a storm at sea, an autobiographical reference to Christine's widowhood. To save her, Fortune changes her into a man, which enables her to face the challenges and adventures occasioned by the shipwreck. This masculinity has been an enduring condition:

> Com vous ouëz, encor suis homme
> Et ay esté ja bien la somme
> De plus de .XIII. ans tous entiers,
> Mais mieulx me plairoit plus du tiers
> Estre femme, com je souloie[110]

> As you perceive, I am still a man
> And I have been for a period
> Of more than thirteen years,
> But better it would please me by more than a third
> To be a woman, as I was accustomed

This allegorical masculinization coincides with Christine's historical widowhood and the development of her career as a writer.[111] It is hardly the same masculinization Jean de Meun claims for Heloise, although Christine and Heloise were both unmarried women of letters. She

---

[110] Christine de Pizan, *Le Livre de la Mutacion de Fortune*, Tome I: lines 1395–9; my translation.

[111] The *Livre de la Mutacion de Fortune* was completed in November 1403; Etienne de Castel died in an epidemic in 1390 after about a decade of marriage with Christine, leaving her a widow at 25. See Willard, *Christine de Pizan*, 34–9. Many of Christine's works are at least semi-autobiographical; Huot describes the *Avision* as "a sort of autobiographical manifesto," 366. Leslie Altman suggests that the autobiographical element might have been for the benefit of prospective patrons, 8.

describes her coming to letters as necessitated by circumstance, not as a motivation for eschewing honorable marriage. In her case, masculinization is necessary for a woman to function in roles designated as masculine. She casts her participation in her profession as facilitated by a change in sex, and she offers a simple solution to the problem of misogyny: women's adversity is a matter of sex, and if only one were a man, one would be able to salvage a shipwreck, earn a living through writing, write in defense of women, with credibility. Fortune's sleight of hand casts masculinity as a quality that is magically, materially acquired; Christine makes good this fictional transformation through her performance of roles conventionally performed by men.

Fortune's solution in the *Mutacion* is not an isolated one in Christine's writings. The allegorical triumvirate in the *Cité des dames* also enjoins her to step in where men have failed to defend women, to become a figurative, if not literal, chivalric knight. Her storylines draw attention to the privileges and deprivations occasioned by sex status. However, solving the problem of misogyny is not as simple as performing roles reserved for members of the privileged sex – she is, as she pointedly reminds readers in the *querelle*, a woman, for all that she participates in what is up to this point an exclusively male learned literary discourse. Her writings point not to sex, but rather to gender, as the real locus of possibility. They do this through interrogation of another social practice, the practice of genre – specifically, the epistolary genre.

On the issue of gender and genre, Dante, a noted influence on Christine's writing,[112] describes the distinction between tragedy and comedy, observing of comedy in particular:

> Ad modum loquendi, remissus est modus et humilis, quia locutio vulgaris, in qua et mulierculae communicant.[113]

> As for the manner of speaking, the style is light and colloquial, because it is in the common speech, in which even simple women communicate.

---

[112] Christine is often credited with being one of the first readers of Dante in France. On his influence on her writing, see Brownlee, "Literary Genealogy and the Problem of the Father;" Huot; and Willard, *Christine de Pizan*, 5, 89, 91.

[113] "Epistola X: To Can Grande della Scala," *Dantis Alagherii Epistolae*, 175–7. Tragedy and comedy are described as opposites in introduction and conclusion: tragedy begins "admirabilis et quieta" (admirably and peacefully) and ends "foetida et horribilis" (stinking and dreadful), 175; comedy begins with "asperita[s]" (harshness) and ends "prospere" (favorably), 176. Dante references the *Ars poetica*, where Horace describes how comedians sometimes make use of the tragic register and vice versa, lines 93–6.

In this alignment of gender and genre, which Christine's *Rose* interlocutors seem to have shared, Dante taps into the ideological seduction of classification – as like goes with like, so light and easy speech goes with women's discourse, whose mean understanding and speech are suggested by the diminutive "mulierculae." However, the very fact of Christine's writing, the subject matter she treats, and the manner in which she does it, provide a bracing counter-example to the "modus et humilis" style properly reserved for "mulierculae." Is she simply a "virilis femina," as Jean Gerson describes her, or do her epistolary interventions have deeper impact? Critics have pointed out that Christine, embodying a living example of a learned woman writing in an exclusively male writing world, does not urge other women to follow her example.[114] She occupies an awkward middle ground, proving through example that women could be worthy writers, yet stopping short of promoting this as a desirable position. Thirteen years after Fortune's sleight of hand, she still prefers to be a woman.

Christine advocates a complicated program of anti-misogyny coupled with preservation of courtly values, which does not easily lend itself to a modern notion of feminism. However, through her varied epistolary writings she suggests that what is determinative of identity as a writer is the practice of a set of behaviors, not biological accident. She raises the question: what happens when like does not go with like, when a woman does what men do? She could simply be a "virilis femina," or her example could point to a flaw in gender-based classifications of behavior. Through the various stagings of persona that occur in her writings – weak woman, unskilled rhetorician, anti-misogynist, learned reader, established writer, social advocate, humanist – Christine represents far more than the novelty of woman writing. She demonstrates that what is considered "virilis" – in this case, effective reasoning and writing – can by done by a woman, and *muliebriter*, in a womanly way.[115] The literary epistle, whose composition was governed by rules and conventions, is an ideal genre for showing that the ability to write and reason need not be limited by gender, but rather consists in the mastery of skills and practice of forms. In demonstrating that participation in literary discourse is not limited by

---

114 See Bell, 173–84.

115 Brown describes Heloise's "muliebriter" negotiations of gender in "*Muliebriter*: Doing Gender in the Letters of Heloise." Janet Gurkin Altman observes that Christine "effectively invests the nascent humanism in France with a distinctly female voice," "Women's Letters in the Public Sphere," 104.

biology, Christine raises the possibility that it need not be limited by social practice, either.

Christine's broadening of the configurations of the writerly class is parallelled by her expansion of the epistolary genre, and the incorporation of the explicit goal of promoting the public good. In the *Epistre au dieu d'Amours*, Christine explores the letter's authorizing function through an allegorized representation who is in many ways an ultimate authorized speaker – Cupid is male, he is a god, and he has read authoritative texts. His mode of redress is the production of a letter, a royal proclamation addressed to his subjects. However, his defense of women against slanderous men identifies texts and their writers as a primary locus of harm, attributing to them great didactic authority. It also points out the abuse of this authority as a flaw in a textual culture. In thus revealing the ways in which textual authority works – and doesn't – Christine reveals the constructed nature of textual authority, which has the result of making textual authority available to any writer, male or female, clerical or lay, who knows how to employ these operations.

In the *querelle du* Roman de la rose, Christine engages with the textual authority offered by epistles in varied ways. Rhetorically, through gestures of humility and defiance, she stages a kind of strategic essentialism. She asks for protection and consideration for her feminine weakness, while she openly criticizes misogynist views and tacitly demonstrates her logical and linguistic self-sufficiency, thus obviating the need for protection. Moreover, she claims women's experience as a necessary corrective to masculine textual culture. Materially, she positions and repositions herself as an author, editor, and publisher through rearranging and directing the debate correspondence to powerful prospective patrons. Topically, she connects her anti-misogynist arguments to a concern for the public good, aligning her writing with broader humanist projects. In her letters to the queen, Christine explores the constructed nature of both textual authority and gendered authority, and her expanding uses of gender reflect her own increasing authority as a writer.

In all of these letters, she mines the epistle for its possibilities – as a material object, a rhetorically coded set of positions and behaviors, a platform for social advocacy, an authorizing genre. Her ultimate intervention is not simply to demonstrate that women, too, can write, can reason, are worthy of defense. The logical result of exposing the constructed, contingent operations of textual authority as she does is to make them available to writers regardless of sex, and to invite an interrogation of the strategies available to writers, male or female, clerical or otherwise, to authorize their writing projects and personas in a textual culture dominated by an authoritative elite. In her repeated selection of the epistolary genre for the composition of her topically pointed works and in her experimentation with its forms and conventions, Christine provides a model of letter writing as social practice, with implications for both self and society. She agitates for public good and demonstrates that the possibility for change lies in the practice of writing. In her hands, the cultivation of letter writing is the equivalent of cultivating the self, and the self she constructs is learned, authoritative, and above all strategically gendered.

4

The Pursuit of Spiritual Quietude in the Correspondence of Marguerite de Navarre and Guillaume Briçonnet

In the *querelle du* Roman de la rose, Christine de Pizan's primary criticism of the didactic poem turns on the issue of rhetoric: what is most objectionable about the *Rose* is that its teaching is cloaked in such lovely language that readers might misunderstand what should be espoused and what should be eschewed in the romance. In her opinion, all writing has a moral function, and so rhetoric has an important role to play in its teachings. A similar concern with the uses and effects of language subtends the early sixteenth-century writings of Marguerite de Navarre, arguably the most influential French woman writer in this moment of transition from the medieval to the early modern. The last and most well-known of her works, the *Heptaméron*, grapples directly with the powers and even dangers of rhetoric: in the Prologue, the *devisants* decide to exclude "gens de lectres" (people of letters) from their storytelling project, lest their rhetorical skill interfere with the truth value of the tales. However, Marguerite's writings also explore rhetoric's salutary powers, and her letters in particular investigate how rhetoric, and specifically epistolary rhetoric, can be a vehicle for the experience of spirituality.

Like Christine, Marguerite was a skilled practitioner of the epistolary arts, composing letters in verse and in prose, and employing letters in her fictional writings. However, unlike Christine, her epistolary ventures are not guided by an overarching interest in combating misogyny. Rather, spirituality is Marguerite's principal concern, and its relationship to the worldly receives a complex treatment in the thirteenth *nouvelle* of the *Heptaméron*. In this tale, a married captain falls in love with a married woman, professes his love in a letter accompanied by a diamond ring as a pledge of his love, and dies not long after. The virtuous married woman returns the diamond to the captain's wife.[1] She also sends along a forged

---

[1] In an astonishing prefiguring of this gesture, Marguerite sends François I a verse epistle accompanied by a rock, during her pregnancy about thirty years earlier.

letter: she writes under the guise of a nun to whom the captain had confessed his sins before his last mortal adventure – and to whom he professed a desire to make amends with his wife upon his return. The happy *épistolière* preserves her virtue by refusing adulterous love, and she "rights" the wrongs occasioned by the captain's letter, occluding his attempted adultery with the fiction of his marital devotion and returning the precious jewel to the rightful recipient of his amorous *gages*. While this impersonation brings about a happy ending, it is nonetheless a fabrication, and this tale of mischievous, well-intentioned meddling poses an important moral problem: do salutary ends justify dissimulating means?

Rather than address this problem, the *devisants* focus on the diamond, and whether the lady ought to have kept it.[2] In this way, *Heptaméron* 13 portrays letter writing as a primarily material exchange, in which the letter is accompanied by a valuable object that guarantees its contents and that takes on greater interest than the letter itself.[3] The success of the lady's forgery reveals the vulnerability of letters – they are falsifiable, and dependent on material assurances of authenticity. However, the authenticating material object also dissimulates: it was given to the lady as a token of adulterous love, and returned to the wife as a pledge of marital fidelity. This fragile authenticity suggests the fact of exchange as the central value in letter writing. It also establishes the perhaps alarming efficacy of letters: letters can bring about significant changes not only in the emotions of recipients but in the reputation of third parties, regardless of the truth value of their contents. Seen in this light, the *Heptaméron*'s insistence on authenticity betrays an anxiety about the duplicitous capacity of letters, but at the same time testifies to their transformative

---

Middlebrook calls this rock a "gift which Marguerite claims as her portrait at a moment of anguish during her 'exile' in her husband's lands in Navarre," 1129.

[2] It is worth noting that the storyteller, Parlamente, often taken to represent Marguerite, opens the discussion by saying that the lady should not be accused of fraud ("tromperie"), but praised for her good sense, "qui convertist en bien ce qui de soy ne valloit rien," *L'Heptaméron*, 134. This is by no means to be considered a dismissal of the moral content; critics have commented on the intertwining of temporal and spiritual in the *Heptaméron*; Thyssell considers it a profoundly theological work; see *The Pleasures of Discernment*, especially Chapter 1, "Gender and Genre: Marguerite de Navarre and the Tradition of Allegorical Rhetoric." Jacob Vance examines the *Heptaméron* as the site of Marguerite's interrogation of reciprocal love at the juncture of Christian humanism and Renaissance neo-Platonism in "Humanist Polemics, Christian Morals."

[3] In a sense this is a very medieval model of correspondence; Constable writes of letters as placeholders, with the "real" message being transmitted orally by the messenger; see Introduction.

power. These epistolary values, and this model of epistolary exchange, have their roots in Marguerite de Navarre's real-life correspondence with Guillaume Briçonnet, an exchange that precedes the *Heptaméron* by more than thirty-five years.

The collected correspondence of Marguerite de Navarre[4] and Guillaume Briçonnet, Bishop of Meaux, a leading figure in the French evangelical movement and often identified as Marguerite's mentor, guide, and spiritual advisor, begins in 1521 and continues until the end of 1524.[5] While sixteenth-century scholars have often taken these letters to be unique, they continue medieval letter-writing traditions in several recognizable ways. They are part of the centuries-old tradition, discussed in Chapter 1, of male religious authorities writing letters of spiritual advice to noble women.[6] Formally, they bear the marks of the five-part epistolary structure promoted by the medieval *ars dictaminis*; they ostentatiously display their concern with the relative status of the correspondents and develop an increasingly ornate humility with respect to this status; and, like the medieval letter-writers I have examined, these writers, too, navigate layers of scripted epistolary discourse to arrive at a new use of the letter, and a new way of thinking about the self and articulating its needs.

Against the backdrop of this tradition, the innovation of these letters is all the more striking. While medieval epistolary conventions still pertain in this early sixteenth-century correspondence, like their medieval predecessors, these early modern writers continue a centuries-long exploration of the possibilities and limits of missive writings. This exploration is shaped by generic experimentation but also by the shifting concerns and needs of premodern people. Here, the primary concern is spirituality, the practice of which often carried significant consequences beyond the

---

4 At the time of the correspondence, she was married to the duc d'Alençon. Studies treating the correspondence exclusively generally refer to her as Marguerite d'Alençon, and those encompassing her later writings employ her later name, after her marriage to Henri d'Albret, king of Navarre. I follow the convention of identifying members of the royal family by their first name alone.

5 The sole manuscript containing both sides of the correspondence, BNff 11495, does not contain autograph copies of the letters. It records nearly one hundred and thirty letters, and terminates abruptly in the middle of a letter from Briçonnet to Marguerite on the "bonté" of spiritual "maladie" (Letter 123, Briçonnet à Marguerite, 18 novembre 1524, vol. 2, 293). The editors of the correspondence suggest this as evidence for the likelihood of other, uncopied letters; *Guillaume Briçonnet, Marguerite d'Angoulême, Correspondance*, vol. 1, Introduction, 3.

6 Corrie points out another possible model for this relationship: the epistolary direction of Gaius by Pseudo-Dionysius, to which Briçonnet refers in his letters to Marguerite and which he quite likely takes as a model for their correspondence, 37–44.

personal in this prereform period.[7] These letters address Marguerite's spiritual inquietude, and, as I will show, they do not describe but rather enact different responses to this inquietude, demonstrating how reading and writing letters can constitute a kind of spiritual practice. This real-life letter exchange, though in many ways far removed from the fictional epistolary excesses of the *Heptaméron*'s thirteenth tale, suggests a career-long engagement with the uses and abuses of rhetoric, and the limits of what epistolary rhetoric can accomplish. Moreover, it establishes an instrumentality of letters for Marguerite, and a fascination with the power of letters – whether realized or not – to effect results.

Extensive critical efforts have been made to demonstrate Briçonnet's influence on Marguerite as a thinker and a writer. My interrogation of the dynamics of this correspondence considers how Briçonnet responds in increasingly amplified ways to Marguerite's repeated requests, making the primary dynamic in this correspondence not so much one of spiritual direction, but collaboration. In my reading, these letters constitute a collaborative reading and writing project in which each correspondent elaborates a particular approach to and experience of spirituality, showing how the letter is an important tool not only in the discussion of spiritual matters, but also in the cultivation of spiritual practice. I argue that Marguerite's participation in this epistolary collaboration shaped her later writing. It establishes an early attempt to explore letter writing for producing sought-after quietude, and it lays the groundwork for her later work in different literary genres, in which she continues to grapple with spirituality, the effects of rhetoric, and how it might articulate the needs of a prereform self.

Marguerite's First Letter: The Contradictions of Epistolary Entreaty

The much-studied first letter of the correspondence is brief, and the editors of the modern edition of the correspondence summarize it in one

---

[7] Carrington comments on the political climate at the beginning of the correspondence, before a definitive split with Rome and when reform in the Roman church was still a possibility, and before François I joined in the persecution of reformers who threatened his authority. She points out that the correspondence preceded this, "during a period of fluidity and promise when a segment of the French reform party looked to the court as a source of support against their deadly enemies, the conservative theologians of the Sorbonne in Paris," 218. However, this period of "fluidity" was not exactly a consequence-free period of religious permissiveness; see also Thyssell, "Gender and Genre," in her *The Pleasures of Discernment*.

sentence: "Marguerite demande à G. Briçonnet des prières pour son mari partant à l'armée et pour elle-même ainsi que secours spirituel et envoi de Michel (d'Arande)" (Marguerite asks G. Briçonnet for prayers for her husband leaving for the army and for herself, as well as for spiritual aid and the dispatching of Michel (d'Arande)).[8] The letter's requests unfold in this order, but, as I will show, this order is highly significant. In this letter, Marguerite communicates a host of complex and important meanings through ways other than direct entreaty. The letter is so dense in meaning that it is worth reproducing in full:

> Monsieur de Meaulx, congnoissant que ung seul est necessaire, m'adresse à vous pour vous prier envers luy vouloir estre par oraison moien qu'il lui plaise conduire selon la saincte volonté Monsieur d'Alençon qui, par le commandement du Roy, s'en va son lieutenant general en son armée que, je doubte, ne se departira sans guerre. Et, pour ce que la paix et la victoire est en sa main, pensant que, oultre le bien publicque du royaulme, avez bon desir de ce qui touche son salut et le mien, vous emploie en mes affaires et vous demande le secours spirituel. Car il me fault mesler de beaucoup de choses qui me doivent bien donner crainte. Et encores demain s'en va ma tante de Nemours en Savoye. Parquoy, vous faisant les recommandations d'elle et de moy et vous priant que sy congnoissez que le temps fust propre que maistre Michel peult faire ung voiage, ce me seroit consolation que je ne quiers que pour l'honneur de Dieu, le remectant a vostre bonne discretion et la scienne. La toute vostre Marguerite.[9]

> Monsieur of Meaux, knowing that one thing only is necessary, I address myself to you to request that you might wish to be, through your prayers, the means by which it might please him to deliver according to his holy will Monsieur d'Alençon who, at the command of the King, goes forth as his general lieutenant in his army which, I fear, will not leave without war. And, because peace and victory are in his hands, believing that, beyond the public good of the realm, you have good will

---

[8] Michel d'Arande was an Augustinian friar; the dependence of his movements on Briçonnet's permission suggests that he belonged to an Augustinian abbey at Meaux, l'abbaye de Notre-Dame de Chage, of which Briçonnet was a benefactor; see Becker, 398 and n. 4.

[9] Letter 1, Marguerite à Briçonnet, vol. 1, 25. The letter was probably written before June 21, the date of Briçonnet's reply. According to Becker, the fact that Briçonnet's letters are signed and dated and Marguerite's are not suggests that the manuscript was compiled under Marguerite's direction. He points out that "la date mise en tête de certaines lettres de Marguerite est celle de la réponse de Briçonnet qui a servi à les classer," 395. All citations to the correspondence are from this edition and are identified by letter number, volume, and page number.

toward what touches his well-being and my own, I employ you in my affairs and ask of you spiritual help. For it is necessary that I be involved in many things which must give me cause for fear. And also tomorrow my aunt of Nemours departs for Savoy. For which, making to you commendations from her and from me, and asking that you acknowledge that the time is appropriate for master Michel to make a voyage, it would be consolation for me, which I seek only for the honor of God, placing it in your discretion and his own. Wholly yours, Marguerite.[10]

Upon first read, this letter might seem simply to communicate uxorial concern, and indeed this is how the letter is generally taken. By the early sixteenth century, the letter-writing conventions promoted by the medieval *ars dictaminis* had been well established for generations, and, I argue, it is likely that Marguerite was well acquainted with them.[11] That medieval epistolary forms persist in the early sixteenth century is not surprising. However, the interpretive rubric of the *ars dictaminis* – an understanding of the parts of a medieval letter and their ordering – produces a different reading for this letter.

According to the *ars dictaminis*, letters begin with a *salutatio* – an opening salutation that consists of the addressee's name and attributes, an initial greeting, and the sender's name and attributes, in that order. These elements are rendered in this letter as a brief "Monsieur de Meaulx," and the slightly cryptic "congnoissant que un seul est necessaire." This phrase could function as an initial greeting, or as the second requisite element in a letter, the *captatio benevolentiae*, the securing of goodwill. The brevity of the salutation shows a relaxed observance of dictaminal prescription, perhaps a reminder of Marguerite's royal prerogative in writing to a subject of the crown.[12] Indeed, all of her letters to Briçonnet are brief, often less than a page long, while his frequently exceed twenty pages, perhaps signifying in another way their difference in status and privilege.[13]

---

[10] All translations, unless otherwise indicated, are my own.

[11] On Marguerite's education, see Jourda, *Marguerite d'Angoulême,* vol. 1, 19–28, and Blaisdell.

[12] It should be noted that while aspects of the *ars dictaminis* were lasting, certain conventions had shifted with time and in vernacular composition, such as an increasing abbreviation of the salutation; thus this brevity could simply be conventional. For examples of contemporary letters with brief salutations, see the Bibliothèque nationale's *Les plus belles lettres manuscrites de la langue française.* I thank Sylvie Lefèvre for this reference.

[13] While autograph copies of the letters do not survive, the transcription is done in one hand through the end of 1524, assuring some continuity in spacing. The captain's

Despite the abbreviated opening, Marguerite's letter does contain the dictaminally prescribed elements, and it unfolds in accordance with letter-writing conventions: after the opening, the *narratio* of circumstances leads to the *petitio*, the request for which the letter is written. Critics have suggested a marital dutifulness in Marguerite's asking for prayers for her husband before voicing her own requests.[14] However, dictaminally, a letter generally does not lead with its primary request. According to medieval letter-writing convention, the expression of concern for her husband is not so much a privileging of his concerns over her own, but rather establishes the circumstances leading to the central request of her letter, her own "secours spirituel." After expressing concern for her husband, she writes that she wishes to employ Briçonnet in her own affairs, signaling the personal, and not shared, nature of the "affaires" with the first-person singular possessive adjective, "mes."[15] The appearance of a dutiful wife placing her husband's concerns before her own is a function of equating primacy of concern with ordinal placement. However, a dictaminally informed reading suggests a different understanding of the letter's central preoccupation.

When expressing concern for her husband, Marguerite writes "[je] m'adresse à vous pour vous prier ... oraison," not an unusual formulation for asking for prayers. The request for her personal "salut" is more complicated, and differently expressed: "[je] vous demande le secours spirituel," and "[je] vous emploie en mes affaires." Her concern is their "salut," both her husband's and her own, but this distinction in the formulation of the request suggests two very different kinds of need and help at issue. "Salut," of course, signifies well-being as well as salvation, physical well-being and the safety of the soul.[16] Briçonnet's prayers would seem to be enough for her husband's well being, but not for her own; for

letter in *Heptaméron* 13, which the text implies is rather long, is described as "de deux fueilles de pappier escriptes de tous coustez," 123.

[14] For example, Beaulieu writes that Marguerite presents "indirectement ses propres besoins, qui ne sont véritablement exprimés qu'au centre de la lettre, après avoir privilégié les intérêts de son mari," 48.

[15] This first-person singular pronoun is given more weight by the preceding sentence, in which she writes that she is sure that Briçonnet has good will regarding all that touches the well-being of the duke as well as her own ("son salut et le mien").

[16] Cottrell observes that well-being is the primary concern of the letter, and points out that the word "salut" appears at the midpoint of the letter, a technique employed by many and particularly medieval writers to signal thematic importance; *The Grammar of Silence*, 6–7.

this she must also "employer" him in her "affaires."[17] To what situation, spiritual or administrative, could this expression refer? While these "affaires" remain unarticulated, the ambiguity is marked, for it appears alongside very specific information – her husband the Duke is leaving at the king's orders to be lieutenant general of the army, her aunt of Nemours is departing for Savoy tomorrow. Furthermore, "employer" appears in the indicative, couching this request in the form of a declarative statement of fact, more subtle and forceful than a direct imperative command or simple interrogative request. This commanding tone and administrative vocabulary are awkwardly juxtaposed to the nature of the need, spiritual assistance, which Marguerite addresses in other ways in this letter.

Marguerite successfully portrays herself as an anxious female subject in this letter, expressing concerns appropriate for a woman at court: she is worried about the departure of her close relatives, and asks for a visit from Briçonnet's colleague Michel d'Arande for consolation in the absence of her loved ones.[18] However, she also mentions that she must involve herself in unspecified affairs which "doivent bien donner crainte." This recurring ambiguity of expression might have to do with the delicacy of the situation: Marguerite, noted for her learning and her influence at the French court, was seeking spiritual assistance from a leader of the evangelical reform movement at a time when François I's relations with the papacy were unsettled and often strained.[19] A direct admission of spiritual conflict in a letter might be imprudent because of her position and that of the court, and further complicated because of the

---

[17] Cotgrave's 1611 *Dictionarie of the French and English Tongues*, the closest contemporary bilingual English dictionary, defines "employer" as "to imploy, applie; use, occupie, busie; confer, bestow, dispend, distribute, lay out," carrying the same overtones of administration and practicality as today; *A Dictionarie of the French and English Tongues*.

[18] In fact, Michel d'Arande was such a favored visitor to the court that in October 1522, Marguerite writes to Briçonnet explaining that d'Arande has not yet been able to leave to visit him "par le commandement de Madame, à qui il a commancé lyrre quelque chose de la saincte Escriture qu'elle desire qu'il parface," Letter 43, vol. 1, 218. Veissière suggests that "[c]e que maître Michel faisait habituellement c'était d'apporter des compléments, par oral ou par écrit, à ce qu'avait exprimé l'évêque et en accord avec lui," "En echo à 'Marguerite de Navarre aux temps de Briçonnet,'" 193, attesting to the survival of the medieval epistolary practice of entrusting both oral and written messages to a carrier into the early modern period.

[19] The court tolerated and sanctioned evangelical efforts at this date; a definitive break came with the Affair of the Placards in 1534. Heller provides an overview of Franco-papal relations in this period in "The Briçonnet Case Reconsidered."

difficulty of articulating emotional and spiritual need – how does one ask for God?

Whatever Marguerite's reasons for the ambiguities in this letter, they are clearly a function of studied dictaminal strategy. Her spiritual concerns and religious leanings are revealed obliquely, through her epistolary choices: her mode of address and the nature and shape of her requests all signify meanings that are not immediately obvious, particularly when read against letter-writing conventions. This obliqueness is suggestive of a deep spiritual incertitude; it also establishes a dynamic of indirection and hidden meanings in this correspondence. An interpretive key to these meanings, which Briçonnet was not likely to have missed, appears in the opening greeting, "congnoissant que un seul est necessaire," which casts Marguerite's concerns into clearer light.

The phrase is an "archly reformist" reference to Luke 10:38, in which Jesus visits the home of the sisters Mary and Martha.[20] Mary sits at Jesus' feet and listens to his teaching. Martha, serving the guests alone, complains that her sister does not help her: "Sire ne te chault il que ma seur me laisse seule servir? Dis luy doncques que elle me ayde"[21] (Lord, do you not care that my sister leaves me to serve alone? Tell her to help me). To which Jesus replies: "Marthe Marthe: tu es en soucy et es troublee en beaucoup de choses. Mais certes ung seul est necessaire. Marie a esleu la tresbonne partie: laquelle se ne luy sera point ostee"[22] (Martha, Martha, you are worried and troubled about many things. But truly one thing only is necessary. Mary has chosen the best part, and it will not be taken from her). In opening her letter with this allusion, Marguerite foregrounds her familiarity with the gospels, and suggests her direct personal reading of them. Moreover, she translates this important gospel teaching into the French in which she composes her letter.

The translation of the Bible into the vernacular was a particularly pressing concern at this moment, and its first translation into French was completed by Jacques Lefèvre d'Etaples, a close associate of Briçonnet.[23]

---

20 I would like to thank George Hoffmann for this description.

21 John 10:38, *Le Nouveau Testament*, trans. Lefèvre d'Etaples. Lefèvre d'Etaples's close association with Briçonnet is well attested; Screech suggests in the introduction to his edition of the translation that it could have been prepared "sous les yeux de Guillaume Briçonnet," vii. While this translation does not appear until two years after the Marguerite's first letter, the texts are nevertheless close contemporaries, and the likelihood of Briçonnet's influence makes it an apt choice for citation.

22 John 10:38, *Le Nouveau Testament*, trans. Lefèvre d'Etaples.

23 For his influence on Briçonnet, see among others Corrie, " 'Sy excellent pasture,' "

Thus Marguerite's reference and its translated form subtly indicate her religious leanings.[24] Most telling is the circumlocution "ung seul necessaire," a phrase normally completed by its key term: faith. Marguerite withholds this term, signaling in veiled but easily recognizable fashion her familiarity with the central notion of the Reform: justification by faith alone.[25] And, once again, placement is key: the location of this phrase at the beginning of the letter suggests that it is part of the initial greeting or the *captatio*, securing of goodwill. Seen in this light, Marguerite's letter hastens to assure its addressee of shared pro-reform inclination, making reformist ideals a sort of epistolary password for access.

This opening citation is also instrumental in establishing a framework for Marguerite's epistolary role-playing. That is, she does not simply evoke the Mary–Martha passage, she also performs their two roles in her letter. As Cottrell observes, her letter suggests an identification with the Martha figure, preoccupied with worldly concerns, and an aspiration to emulate the Mary figure, undistracted in concentration on Jesus' teachings.[26] I suggest that the letter is not only a place for her to articulate this identification, it provides her a forum in which to enact it. The first word of the letter after "Monsieur de Meaulx" is "congnoissant" (knowing); the letter opens with a declaration of her awareness that one thing only is necessary, that she, like, Mary, has identified "la tresbonne partie." This avowed knowing contrasts with the rest of the letter, which offers an epistolary performance of Martha's role, preoccupied with worldly concerns.

and Nauert, "Marguerite, Lefèvre d'Etaples, and the Growth of Christian Humanism in France."

24 One of the pre-reform centers in France was at Meaux, the seat of Briçonnet's bishopric, and Marguerite has been described as the "undisputed patroness" of this movement; Blaisdell, 40–1. This reputation is confirmed by Marguerite's contemporaries: Pierre de Sibiville writes to Anemond de Coct that "[i]l n'y a point aujourd'hui en France plus évangélique que la Dame d'Alençon," 28 December 1524, in *Correspondance des réformateurs*, ed. Herminjard, vol. I, no. 132, 315, cited in Heller, "The Briçonnet Case Reconsidered," 246.

25 "Ung seul necessaire" has been taken in various ways; Constable traces its many interpretations in the Middle Ages, ranging from "unity, the Trinity, eternal life, the vision of God, the reward of contemplation, and love for and commitment to Him," "faith and love of humanity," " 'to look constantly at the living God' " self-denial, "hearing the divine word" and "the love of neighbour," "The Interpretation of Mary and Martha." Lefèvre points out that syntactically, it reasonably means "God," as suggested by Briçonnet's second letter; while this is a persuasive reading, given Marguerite's reformist sympathies and the tenor of her writings it is plausible that "ung seul necessaire" refers to faith.

26 Cottrell, *The Grammar of Silence*, especially 3–10.

Marguerite, weighed down and troubled like Martha, wishes but is unable to perform Mary's single-minded devotion. Thus, her request for Briçonnet's assistance is couched in layers of meaning: wifely concern and female anxiety, reformist sympathy lodged from a position of royal privilege, and spiritual inquietude desirous of repose. Moreover, it projects reformist concerns: enacting the Mary–Martha tension would be recognizable to a reformist in that it expressed a desire to return to a more apostolic spirituality. Thus, Marguerite's epistolary performance functions as a sort of code, communicating shared sympathy.

The simplicity of her signature takes on heightened significance in light of this citation. Briçonnet is a bishop, and her address, "Monsieur de Meaux," indicates this – from 1500 on, a bishop was addressed as "Monsieur" followed by the name of his diocese.[27] In medieval correspondence, respective social positioning was observed in forms of epistolary address and signature, and particularly in names and titles and their order. The acknowledgement of Briçonnet's ecclesiastic title might be a humble acknowledgment of their difference in spiritual status, particularly since Marguerite signs simply as "Marguerite"; the omission of her own title and social status claims a certain humility for Marguerite as a correspondent.[28] In medieval letters, the names of both the writer and addressee customarily appear at the beginning of a letter; here, Briçonnet's name appears at the letter's beginning, Marguerite's at the end. This is consistent with medieval letter-writing conventions, in which placing an addressee's name first grants them pride of place, acknowledging and performing their superiority. As a member of the "trinité," Marguerite had an undeniable social status, therefore it is likely she claims a spiritual humility in this letter. Thus, both writers perform a

---

[27] It was not until later that "Monsieur" was replaced by "Monseigneur." I thank Sylvie Lefèvre for pointing this out. This observation of status is consistent with Marguerite's broader epistolary practice, in which she often acknowledged the title and rank of her correspondents; see *Lettres de Marguerite d'Angoulême* and *Nouvelles lettres de la reine de Navarre.*

[28] It could be argued that the unadorned signature is an exercise of royal privilege, however given the abject humility Marguerite develops in her letters it is more likely that the signature suggests humility; either way it signals a difference in the way writer and addressee are identified. Beaulieu suggests a Christian reading of this humility: "les multiples protestations de Marguerite lui font adopter une posture qui occulte partiellement son rang social, au profit d'une image de dénuement et de vulnérabilité: celle d'une chrétienne parmi d'autres, voire même l'une des moins méritoires, la 'pauvre indigne de nul bien,' " 49.

sensitivity to status repeatedly through effusive and at times extravagant epistolary expressions of humility.

This aggressive humility, reminiscent of that claimed by Abelard and Heloise in their letters, belies the fact that Marguerite's and Briçonnet's social positions are far from equal. Despite her unadorned signature, Marguerite exercises her royal prerogative in writing commandingly to a subject of the crown, and Briçonnet is not likely to refuse assistance to a potential source of royal support.[29] This commanding request for assistance is undercut by the deep spiritual need evidenced by Marguerite's epistolary petition and performance, as she seeks help with something she is unable to achieve alone. Suspended between desire for spiritual contemplation and demonstrated worldly preoccupation, Marguerite performs, through her letter, the role of distracted Martha, even as she avows that she knows what Mary knows. This epistolary role-playing is instrumental. It allows Marguerite to make her plea for Briçonnet's assistance in a carefully crafted way, mining epistolary ways of meaning to articulate their shared religious feeling while emphasizing the advantages of granting her request. It allows her to perform her complicated position as preoccupied princess and intent worshipper who wishes to shun worldly preoccupations, but cannot. It also reminds Briçonnet of the contingencies of her royal position, her distinct and perhaps incompatible sets of concerns and the limitations on her actions. In performing this in-between position, Marguerite articulates the privileges and even burdens of royal status. The correspondence thus begins on a note of knowing contradiction, hinted-at frustration, and uncertainty of place and role.

In this first letter, Marguerite exploits the letter for the positions of privilege, humility, and supplication encoded in its forms and conventions, to perform the contradictions of her position: a devout woman with reformist leanings, a princess asking a subject for something she cannot accomplish alone, a ruler preoccupied with worldly concerns, a prereform self desirous of spiritual quietude. She establishes, through an adroit deployment of epistolary rhetoric, a complicated nexus of relations and positions, social, royal, ecclesiastical, and spiritual, that extends throughout the correspondence. It is important to note that this corre-

---

[29] Beaulieu observes: "la posture d'humilité de Marguerite investit Briçonnet d'une responsabilité pastorale qu'il ne saurait refuser," 49; Stephenson discusses Marguerite's role as a political actor, examined through the lens of her correspondence with nobles, in *The Power and Patronage of Marguerite de Navarre*; Fèbvre considers their correspondence as an exchange of spiritual direction for political advocacy, 88.

spondence takes place during a moment of religious and also royal uncertainty. François I's claim to the throne was not uncontested, and the royal family was in the midst of an aggressive campaign to establish the legitimacy not only of his rule but also the regency of his mother Louise de Savoie in his absence. Marguerite played an important role in this drama, as the third in this much-touted "trinité."[30] Her correspondence with Briçonnet, and the varied positions she assumes in it, chart the increasing complexities of her royal and public role, and her attempts to negotiate these complexities through writing.

Briçonnet's Response: The Rhetoric of Courtly Submission

Briçonnet's response to Marguerite's opening epistle offers its own complexities and illustrates an important feature of epistolary humility: its postures can be double-edged. In many respects, he responds in a way that might be expected of a royal courtier. Frequently signing his letters as "vostre très-humble et très-obeissant serviteur," he is polite, respectful, and submissive, if perhaps a touch ornate. A distinguishing characteristic of many of his letters is an extended initial greeting. Often buried parenthetically or in a clause, the initial greeting is, at its core, simply "Dieu vueille" (God willing) – and what Briçonnet hopes God might want is Marguerite's spiritual well-being:

> Madame, le doulz et debonnaire Seigneur qui est et seul est, car tout estre avec icelluy conserve et en lui subsiste, et, estant devant tout estre, est l'estre de tout estre qu'il a produit de son excessive bonté, et, par ce, pour estre bien, car de bien ne vient que bien et sont toutes creatures à bien et pour bien crées, selon la qualité de la nature de chacun estre particulier (qui ne peult estre ne se entretenir que en son seul necessaire estre), de tout estre, source (*vueille* par sa grace tellement vostre estre … estre abismé et noié, pour mieulx congnoistre qu'il est ung et, par ce, seul parfaict et necessaire). (Letter 2, vol. 1, 26, emphasis added.)

> Madam, the sweet and good Lord who is and is alone, for every being is kept in him and lives in him, and, being before every being, he is the being of all beings that he has produced in his exceeding goodness, and, by this, to be well, for of goodness comes nothing but good and all beings are created in and for good, according to the quality of the nature of each particular being (who can neither be nor maintain itself save for in his only necessary being), the source of all beings (*may he wish* in his

---

[30] See Middlebrook's cogent discussion of these efforts and in particular in regard to Marguerite's role in the "trinité."

grace that your being ... be ruined and drowned, to better know that he is the one and, by this, only perfect and necessary thing).

Briçonnet's prose bears the marks of rhetorical study: he employs ample wordplay and *figura etymologica*, with "estre"/"estant," "bien"/"bonté," "creature"/"crée"; his sentences tend toward the periodic; and, like Marguerite's letter, his missive incorporates the dictaminally prescribed five epistolary sections. Thematically, his letter is most noticeable for its response to Marguerite's opening phrase "ung seul est necessaire," upon he which elaborates, expanding on its qualities in this and in many of his ensuing letters, and expresses his wish that she be "abismé et noié, pour mieulx congnoistre" that God is the only perfect and necessary thing. Of course, this is not a wish that Marguerite be literally ruined and drowned. Rather, it is part of a mystical spirituality Briçonnet cultivates in his letters, and a specific response to Marguerite's declaration that she is "congnoissant." She knows, but she can know better: spiritual knowing is a central problem in this correspondence, and Briçonnnet proposes a solution in which letters play a central role.

In response to the requests made in Marguerite's letter, Briçonnet does not address her concern for the duc d'Alençon. This omission reinforces her "salut" as the primary concern of her letter, treating the expression of concern for her husband as a matter of form. He approves her acknowledgement of "ung seul necessaire," adding, however, that this has not to do with her own ability but rather with the fact that the divine "makes himself known in you."[31] As for her expressed desire to "emploier" him in her affairs, he protests his unworthiness:

> moult vous esgarez, Madame, de prendre moien pour plus avant parvenir à sa cognoissance et union ailleurs que en luy et de luy et mesmement quant le cuidez avoir de moy qui suis en continuelles tenebres, attendant la grace de la benignité divine, de laquelle par mes demerites suis banny et exillé. Loing est de secours bailler qui l'attend.
> (Letter 2, vol. 1, 27)

> you err greatly, Madame, to take measures to arrive further in knowledge of him and union elsewhere than in him and from him and similarly when you think to have it from me, I who am still in continuous shadows, waiting for the grace of the divine benignity, from which by my faults I am banished and exiled. He who is waiting for help is far from offering it.

---

31 "[I]l se face congnoistre en vous," 26.

This is a familiar gesture of modesty in letters, responding to a request for assistance with a profession of inability. Through varied expressions of personal inadequacy in his letters, Briçonnet retains the humility of servitude; however, humility is sufficiently established as an epistolary trope that he retains the authority to advance spiritual teaching and prereform interests. Moreover, Briçonnet undercuts the force of the humility topos by criticizing Marguerite for seeking and expecting help from sources other than the divine.[32] This correction is at odds with his professed unworthiness, and despite this personal inability and the general futility of "plus avant parvenir à cognoissance," he implicitly grants her demand for "secours" through writing her letters – dozens of them. The contradiction is all the more noteworthy since, by the time of Marguerite's reply, he has not yet complied with the request to send Michel d'Arande.[33] This seems to suggest that the primary way to meet her need is through letters.

In the passage in which Briçonnet responds most directly to Marguerite's charge, he offers her "secours ... pour plus forte guerre avoir," distinctly martial terms compared with her more general request for "secours spirituel." Moreoever, he agrees to assist but in a qualified way, insofar as God gives him grace, embedding his agreement in fulsome protestations of unworthiness. His acquiescence to Marguerite's entreaty insists on his humility, which he then contradicts: he declares the futility of seeking grace from any source other than the divine, and then agrees, however humbly, to provide assistance. Although, as Curtius observes, humility formulas have to do with "conventions of courtly submission,"[34] they are not necessarily exclusive of genuine expressions, of personal inadequacy or indeed even its opposite. In Chapter 1, I discussed the impossibility of determining the sincerity of Baudri's epistolary play; similarly, the sincerity of Briçonnet's epistolary humility is impossible to determine definitively.[35] What does seem clear is that his acceptance

[32] For a discussion of the pre-Christian origins of modesty formulas and their development through Late Antiquity and the Middle Ages, see Curtius, 83–5, 407–12.

[33] Marguerite's next letter indicates that the visit from Michel d'Arande has not occurred: "vous prie avoir pitié me veoir sy seulle et, puis que le temps, le pays et les propos ne sont propres pour la venue de maistre Michel, à quoy je m'accorde, ... au moings je vous prie que par escript vueillez visiter et exciter à l'amour de Dieu mon cueur" Letter 3, Marguerite à Briçonnet, vol. 1, 30.

[34] Curtius, 410–11.

[35] This performance of humility might well have to do with the Briçonnet family's status as courtiers; according to Beaulieu, the family "s'était signalée depuis un siècle dans les emplois de la cour et l'administration des finances"; his father was an archbishop

declaims humility even as it tacitly admits to his ability – though God-given – to assist, a position at once superior and inferior, in ways exactly opposite to Marguerite's temporal authority and spiritual insufficiency. Briçonnet acknowledges that while Marguerite might know that one thing only is needed, she does not yet have it – and he can help.

In a very practical way, letters allows him to establish an equality of status that would be difficult or at least awkward to assert in a face-to-face encounter. This equality of status, and their mutual need, articulates the terms of humility and authority in which the correspondence will take place. It also suggests that at issue will be more than a simple matter of spiritual direction: both writers access positions of supplication, appealing to the power of their correspondent and complicating their respective positions of authority. This acknowledgment of status is more than courtly flattery; it constitutes a careful respective positioning. In a medieval Latin letter, much of this positioning was accomplished in the salutation, in the names of the writer and addressee: their order and inflection signaled relative status. Here, in French, several centuries after the "golden age of epistolography" and in a community of reform-minded sympathists, this courtly submission could not be accomplished in quite the same way. Briçonnet's effusive protestations of unworthiness offer another way to perform this important gesture. Moreover, they signal the continuing usefulness of epistolary recognition of status.

Having examined how Briçonnet accepts his spiritual direction of Marguerite and submits to royal authority, what exactly is the nature of the "secours" he agrees to provide? Of the varied direct and less direct requests and explanations she articulates, he selects one and repeats it back to her, in a gesture of tacit approval: that she is involved in fear-causing things ("choses qui me doivent bien donner crainte"). He explains to her her own request and the very need that prompted it: she asks for help because she is assailed by love of Jesus and wishes to experience this more intensely. He also echoes her opening acknowledgement that "ung seul est necessaire," and implies the contradiction in her following this declaration with a litany of concerns and fears. Notably, his teachings are all responses to her iterations.[36]

---

and two of his brothers also had careers in the church; see Becker, 397. Heller makes the case for Briçonnet's "unswerving loyalty to the monarchy," "The Briçonnet Case Reconsidered," 253.

36 Carrington offers a similar reading, observing that Briçonnet's references to "ung

Upon first impression, it seems that Briçonnet supplies in his letters a sort of teaching by dilation and expansion, which reinforces his deference to Marguerite's position.[37] This occurs not only with "ung seul necessaire," but with many other motifs: in mid-October 1521, Marguerite compares herself to a "brebis errant,"[38] and Briçonnet's next two letters elaborate on the theme of wandering sheep, identifying four categories of wandering sheep corresponding to various states of spiritual development.[39] She writes of her longing for a "robbe des nopces" signaling her invitation to God's "grand convive,"[40] his reply explains the origin and meaning of the wedding dress motif in Matthew, discussing its spiritual and material aspects.[41] This pattern repeats throughout the correspondence, through such topoi as "feu," "manne," "eau," "foiblesse," "vigne" and "vin," and even organs and pipes.[42] Briçonnet's letters gloss Marguerite's, selecting terms of interest and explaining them, teasing them out, mining them for their usefulness in his evangelical teaching.[43] Cottrell claims this "exegesis" as central to Briçonnet's pedagogy, teaching Marguerite a particular reading of the world through a particular reading of the text of their correspondence.[44] Beaulieu suggests that it is a

---

seul necessaire" "show how the very thing [Marguerite] requests is implicit in her own words that she has offered to him. Briçonnet's task as Marguerite's adviser will become that of expanding again and again on the language she offers him, unfolding the spiritual aid that she already has embedded in her words," 220. Where I differ from Carrington is in my focus on the critical role of letters and the attendant dynamics of epistolary exchange in this teaching.

[37] Carrington writes that "this expansiveness on his part is the very substance of his deference to her, as her servant," 223.

[38] Letter 7, vol. 1, 37.

[39] Letter 8, vol. 1, 38–9; and Letter 9, vol. 1, 40–8.

[40] Letter 10, Marguerite à Briçonnet, vol. 1, 49.

[41] Letter 11, Briçonnet à Marguerite, vol. 1, 50–62.

[42] On "la vigne," "le vin," and "le grant vigneron," see vol. 2, Letters 52 and 53. On organs and pipes, see vol. 1, Letter 12, in which Marguerite compares God to a "grand organiste" and herself to one of his "petitz tuyaulx," 63, to which Briçonnet responds commenting on the "inégalité de tuyaulx," and the relation of "vent spirituel" to "orgues materielles" and "orgues spirituelles," Letter 14, 67–8.

[43] This very medieval practice of textual glossing of authoritative texts is distinct from Christian humanist methods of explaining texts; see Nauert, "Humanism as Method."

[44] "Using one of the most venerable and far-reaching metaphors in Christian thought, Briçonnet suggests that the world is a text that, if read properly, reveals only one message: the reign of charity. Christ is inscribed in the world, and it is the duty of the Christian exegete to read and reread the text before him until the meaning that *must* be there is fully revealed. Thus, in a sense, fear results from misreading the world. To dispel her anxiety, Marguerite ... must learn to *read* correctly ... To assist her toward this end, Briçonnet

selective "deconstruction" of Marguerite's letter, focusing on elements that might bolster his teaching.[45] These descriptions both respond to the way Briçonnet's epistolary instruction takes root in Marguerite's writing, reacting to elements in her letters through elaboration and redescription, to specific didactic and homiletic purpose.

Letters do more than facilitate this exchange, they structure it. They make requests and anticipate responses, and in a very basic way set up a structure of call and response. Marguerite sends out the first epistolary "call," setting into motion a cascade of responses that circle back to the terms of her first letter. In sending back elaborations on themes she raises, Briçonnet's primary response to the request for "secours" is to offer advice that consists largely of a combination of courtly flattery and rearticulation of her previously stated positions, in a way that insists on continued reading and writing by providing both clarification and obfuscation. With motifs echoing back and forth between them, this correspondence reinforces that what is urgently sought is already there – "ung seul est necessaire," and indeed is already possessed. All that Marguerite requires, Briconnet's echoing implies, she already has; all that she needs to "mieux congnoistre" that which she already knows is his letters. Briçonnet's role in this so-called spiritual direction is to take his cues from the princess scholars have called the "undisputed patroness" of the early sixteenth-century French evangelical movement.[46] He does so in a way that gives lie to the epistolary posture of courtly submission, showing how rhetoric can be used to finesse situations that require displays of both humility and authority.

Advocacy "Par Adopcion"

Thus far, I have examined how letters are instrumental for Marguerite: they are the vehicle by which she makes a specific, though complicated, request of Briçonnet, and they facilitate her performance of the role of penitent sinner in need of direction while maintaining the flavor of royalty and its prerogatives. Through the positions of humility and

---

provides her with an illustration of exegesis by using her own letters as texts on which he writes exegetical commentary ... Ultimately, Briçonnet's exegesis of Marguerite's letters becomes an interpretive exercise designed to metacommunicate the principles of hermeneutics, which he proposes to Marguerite as a means of consolation," Cottrell, *The Grammar of Silence*, 11–12.

[45] Beaulieu, 49.
[46] Blaisdell, 41.

authority that a letter scripts, Briçonnet could reply in a way that respected both his own authority and Marguerite's. Thus, letters functioned as a staging ground for the performance of important positions for the pursuit of their respective projects of spiritual quietude and prereform support. Having articulated these initial positions, they also adopt increasingly imaginative, and more direct, epistolary positions. Unlike Baudri and Constance, for whom letters gave voice to roles that were forbidden in real life, Marguerite and Briçonnet actively mine another kind of close relationship for the urgency it can lend to their respective pursuits: not that of lovers, but of family.

Familial metaphors abound in these letters, constituting a kind of role-playing distinct from the biblical role-playing Marguerite performs in her first letter. It might also be considered a precursor to the married lady's epistolary impersonation in the thirteenth *nouvelle* of the *Heptaméron*. Most important, it offers metaphors of propriety, intimacy, and filiation that are critical to advancing Marguerite's and Briçonnet's respective projects. The first occurrence of the familial is in a signature: Marguerite signs her second letter as "La toute vostre fille, Marguerite."[47] This elicits Briçonnet's correction:

> je vous supplie qu'il vous plaise ne user plus de semblables parolles que avez faict par voz dernieres. De Dieu seul estes fille et espouze. Aultre pere ne debvez reclamer ... Je vous exhorte et admoneste que luy soiez sinon telle et si bonne fille qu'il vous est bon pere, car ne pourriez y parvenir, par ce que finitude ne peult corespondre à infinitude, que luy suppliez qu'il luy plaise accroistre et unir vostre force, pour, de tout vous, l'aymer et servir. (Letter 4, vol. 1, 32)

> I beg that it please you not to use words similar to those you used in your last letter. Of God alone are you daughter and spouse. Another father you ought not to claim ... I exhort and admonish that you be if not as good a daughter to him as he is to you a good father, for you will never arrive at that, because finitude cannot correspond to infinitude, that you beg him that it please him to grow and to unify your strength, so that you might fully love and serve him.

Briçonnet turns the "vostre fille" signature into an opportunity to expound a teaching. However, he elaborates on the filial theme beyond the terms introduced by Marguerite. He admonishes her for calling herself his daughter when God alone is her father, and adds to this

---

[47] Letter 3, Marguerite à Briçonnet, vol. 1, 30.

admonition that God is also her only spouse.[48] This nuptial metaphor is a curious comment on Marguerite's secular matrimony, especially given Briçonnet's continued silence on her concern for her husband's safety. It also shows us another dimension of the call-and-response dynamic in these letters: Briçonnet does not simply elaborate on Marguerite's words, he also corrects them. While this is a reactive teaching, it nevertheless exercises a corrective, if situated, authority, and reveals another way in which letters facilitate a both-at-once position of authority and dependence.

Several months later, after a visit between Marguerite and Briçonnet,[49] she continues the filial vocabulary and adopts a beseeching tone, appealing to his "charité paternelle," calling him her "père," and, like Heloise, asking for more letters.[50] Here, however, letters are not valued for their ability to reproduce or compensate for presence, but rather for their didactic value: Marguerite asks for letters so that she can study Briçonnet's teaching at greater length. Noticeably, he does not again rebuke her use of familial language; rather, he offers graciously in return that her letters provide consolation, as well, and he thanks her for the "esguilon" they offer.[51] This is an oblique acknowledgement of the opportunity to teach her, and, by extension, further his evangelical project of reform. He signs his next letter "De vostre maison de Meaulx," which an early editor of reform correspondence calls "une simple formule de politesse fréquemment usitée à cette époque."[52] Whether this signature is merely a polite gesture or whether it acknowledges patronage, it establishes a proprietary connection between them, and his silence on her continued use of filial vocabulary seems to

---

[48] Encouraging nuns to consider Jesus their bridegroom is a well-known gesture in their instruction. This nuptial vocabulary recurs throughout Briçonnet's letters to Marguerite. For another reading of filiation in this correspondence, see Corrie.

[49] "En septembre-octobre 1521 Marguerite avait séjourné à Meaux avec sa mère Louise de Savoie." Cf. Bibl. nat. ms. Fr. 2978 (fol. 5–12). Voir aussi Herminjard, *Correspondance des Réformateurs*, I, 76 et note 3," vol. 1, 37 n. 3. Becker observes that with this letter, written after a visit between Marguerite and Briçonnet, "une cordialité plus franche s'établit dans leurs rapports et remplace le ton cérémonieux des premières lettres," 401.

[50] Letter 7, vol. 1, 37.

[51] "[V]oz gratieuses et humbles lettres … m'ont donné ung esguilon de plus grande consolacion que ne pensez" (your gracious and humble letters … have given me an incentive and greater consolation than you think), Letter 8, vol. 1, 39.

[52] Herminjard, *Correspondance des Réformateurs*, I, 81 note 6, cited in *Correspondance* 48 n. 81.

encourage it. Marguerite concludes her next letter as "vostre bonne fille,"[53] and from this point on, periodically refers to herself as Briçonnet's "fille"; he regularly signs his letters "de vostre hermitage," "de vostre maison." These signatures suggest that the value of familial roles is their proprietary, and not necessarily literal, relational value. However, for as prolix and reactive a writer as Briçonnet, the courtly reticence regarding this breach is noteworthy, especially as the familial metaphors continue and even proliferate in both of their letters; it subtly acknowledges their power differential despite the confusion of roles and respective authority at play in the letters.

As the correspondence progresses, so do the familial metaphors. After a silence of nearly two months at a later point in the correspondence, Marguerite writes again in entreaty, this time accusing Briçonnet of "avarice spirituel": "D'avoir et ne distribuer où est la necessité, ne vous peult excuser d'offence contre celluy qui tant vous a donné de tallentz pour les faire prouffiter" (To have and not to distribute where there is need, cannot excuse you of offense against him who gave you such talent for benefiting [those who are separated from you]).[54] This is more than a request for a letter, it is an accusation of neglect, stinginess, and offense against God. Yet, even as she accuses, she offers implicit praise: her vocabulary alludes to the parable of the talents, in which the servant hides the talent entrusted to him by his master.[55] Reinforcing her position as a reader of the gospels, Marguerite then cites the parable of the Canaanite woman, in which a woman talks back to Christ and wins her plea after having been initially refused.[56] Marguerite aligns herself with both the Canaanite woman and the prodigal son, accumulating biblical references and familial roles. She luxuriates in her epistolary humility, asking Briçonnet almost pathetically for scraps of his attention. And yet, in her royal abjection, base qualities are juxtaposed with sublime ones – she refers to "marguerites" with punning effect, and as she asks for crumbs and classes herself with lowly swine, she is still, she writes, also

[53] Letter 10, Marguerite à Briçonnet, vol. 1, 49.

[54] Letter 65, vol. 2, 59.

[55] Matthew 25:14–30; here, of course, "talent" refers to a monetary unit; the servants who spent the talents entrusted to them accrued more and were rewarded by their master with praise and more talents, and the servant who hid his talent was punished and cast out.

[56] Letter 65, vol. 2, 59–60. This is the same parable referenced by the anonymous nun at Admont writing to the Archbishop of Salzburg, discussed in the Introduction. It seems no accident that this parable is cited by women writers seeking to bolster their epistolary pleas addressed to authoritative male correspondents.

his "advocatz."[57] This letter's closing effectively demonstrates the both-at-once, contradictory nature of the subject position she writes for herself in her letters to Briçonnet:

> Toutesfois à mon besoing m'aidere(z), de mon nom vous priant, comme Dieu le vous commande, n'oublier vostre necessiteuze mere. Vostre venue est plus necessaire que ne vous puis dire.

> However, you will meet my need, asking you in my name, as God commands it of you, not to forget your needy mother. Your coming is more necessary than I am able to tell you.[58]

Marguerite claims the position of needy mother, underscoring her authority with the force of a double commandment – she asks him to help her, and God asks too. She ends this letter with another play on the passage from Luke referenced in her first letter, suggesting that more than "ung seul" is "necessaire": Briçonnet's arrival is also "necessaire," more so than she, "necessiteuze," can express.

In his reply, Briçonnet appeals to Marguerite's "charité maternelle," calling her a "bonne mere" who "se nomme veritablement en l'inutilité de ses enfans necessiteuze" (names herself correctly, in the uselessness of her children, "needy").[59] His carefully crafted responses demonstrate an advantage of letter writing that face-to-face conversation does not permit: time for rhetorical craftsmanship, combing over letters for vocabulary and images to develop. Earlier in their correspondence, Briçonnet had reprimanded Marguerite's signatorial claim of kinship: by signing as his daughter, she wrote him into a paternal role. Now, Briçonnet reverses the metaphor: he accepts her claim to the position of mother, which figures him as her child. Acknowledging her metaphorical maternity, he identifies himself, metaphorically, as among her "enfans"; more explicitly, he frequently signs his letters "votre inutile filz." In 1523, Marguerite is thirty-one years old, has been married for fourteen years, and is child-less.[60] By accepting the role of a figurative substitute for a child, Briçonnet provides her with one way to perform, in letters at least, the

---

[57] Heller comments on the "hardening of attitude toward heterodoxy at court in the fall of 1523 [that] also marked a decisive turning point in the history of reform at Meaux," "The Briçonnet Case Reconsidered," 245.

[58] Letter 65, vol. 2, 60.

[59] Letter 66, vol. 2, 60.

[60] Génin notes that Henri is the last duke of Angoulême; Introduction, *Lettres de Marguerite d'Angoulême*, 5. This fact likely made the childlessness of the marriage an even more pressing concern.

maternity expected of aristocratic and royal women in this period.[61] In this way, letters enable Marguerite to inhabit roles unavailable to her in "real" life.

Briçonnet does more than echo and reverse Marguerite's familial metaphors, he complicates them in ways that demonstrate the symbolic value of family in these letters. Thus far, their letters play with the positions of parent and child. However, Briçonnet also invokes a familial relationship in which he is not directly implicated. Referring back to the passage from Luke, he mobilizes the metaphor of sisterhood to encourage Marguerite in her efforts on behalf of church reform. Drawing on such binary descriptions as "noble" and "villaine," he identifies Mary and Martha as, respectively, the daughters of the "nouveau pere" and the "viel pere:"[62]

> Impetrez, s'il vous plaist, du Roy des Roys anoblissement de innovacions de la fille du viel homme par adoption du nouveau, à ce que les deux cooperent et tendent à labourer en l'heritaige paternel, qui est le doulx Jesus, fruict de vie viviffiant ses laboureurs en et par eulx, et plus souvent sans eulx pour eulx.

> Obtain, if it please you, from the King of Kings the ennobling brought by renewal of the daughter of the old man by adoption of the new, so that the two might cooperate and begin to work together in paternal heritage, who is sweet Jesus, fruit of life vivifying his workers in and by them, and more often without them for them.[63]

This "adoption" is a fitting description of what Marguerite has already done in her first letter, in which she adopted the roles of Mary and Martha by writing from Martha's preoccupied position while claiming to know that which is "necessaire," like Mary. Briçonnet suggests a different kind of "adoption," describing a new maternal position for Marguerite: she can be the mother, or supporter, of both daughters, both the old and the new in the church, "par adoption." This implies that the Mary/Martha split she performs is not necessarily oppositional or even contradictory: she can be both spiritually concerned and active in the world. Despite his unfavorable descriptions of the "old" way, Briçonnet advocates for

---

[61] See Middlebrook for Marguerite's complicated relationship to maternity in her verse epistles.

[62] This vocabulary recurs in Briçonnet's letters; the editors observe that it is "[t]oujours le theme paulinien du *vieil homme* et de *l'homme nouveau*. Cf. Rm 6, 6; Ep 4, 22–24; Col 3, 9," Letter 123, vol. 2, 293, n. 1.

[63] Letter 66, vol. 2, 62–3.

conciliation, emphasizing that the two sisters share a goal: "leur ouvraige tendoit à une fin: pour honorer leur bon hoste" (their work shares the same goal: to honor their good host).[64] This is an unmistakable statement of his own evangelical position: one of conciliation, seeking reform but not abolition of the institutions of the Roman Catholic church.[65]

In their letters, both Marguerite and Briçonnet pursue a poetics of seeming contradiction. Both are humble and authoritative and write from positions of supplication and benefaction, and the profusion of familial metaphors underscores this contradiction: both claim the roles of child and parent for themselves and each other. These roles serve as metaphors for the needs articulated in these letters, and they identify positions from which Marguerite and Briçonnet can pursue their respective spiritual goals. This role-playing could only take place in letters: letters were ideally suited for making appeals; they scripted positions of humility and authority that could be manipulated for political maneuvering; they structured a call-and-response dynamic ideal for expounding teaching and demonstrating mastery – or studied incomprehension – of lessons; and they enabled fanciful articulations of need and demonstration of evangelical reading and exegesis that conversation does not allow, at least not at such detailed length. Moreover, in letters, roles could be "adopted" in two ways: as roles performed in epistolary discourse, and, as Briçonnet urges, as positions to be championed. The shape of these metaphors shows how Briçonnet articulates prereform sympathies while rhetorically operating within the parameters established by Marguerite's vocabulary. The kinship rubric they both develop reveals the value of elective affinities, and how they can be as complicated and compelling as the royal ones that authorize Marguerite's literary incursions even as they increasingly come into conflict with her evangelical sympathies.

---

[64] Letter 66, vol. 2, 62.

[65] Heller discusses Briçonnet's reputation as "lâche" and "conservative" in the pre-reform movement; "The Briçonnet Case Reconsidered," 247–8. One example of this conciliation is in his attitude to the censure of Michel d'Arande by the bishop of Bourges; Heller comments that Briçonnet's family loyalty to the monarchy "explains in large measure why Briçonnet did not seriously try to proceed with reform in the face of royal indifference or opposition ... to attempt it would have involved opposition to an authority which he had long been conditioned to believe was the guarantor of social order as well as the only hope of religious reform," 253.

Reading, Writing, and Mysticism: Letter Writing as Spiritual Practice

In previous chapters I explored how letters offer a substitute for material presence in the absence of a correspondent, a presence often invoked in amatory missives. Here, letters were not necessarily valued for this compensatory comfort, for visits did take place between Marguerite and Briçonnet.[66] Rather, Briçonnet's letters are crafted to produce a particular kind of experience. Marguerite asks for "secours," and Briçonnet returns, in addition to expansive meditations on her words, complicated and often convoluted metaphors and language. While Marguerite's letters are brief, Briçonnet's are often lengthy, and his prose, in particular, is quite distinctive, eliciting colorful commentary from the nineteenth century to the present. Critics tend to agree that his writing style and figures of speech are confusing, they comment on the extreme length of his letters and his ample use of Latin, and seem to hold him at best pedantic and at worst foolish.[67] I argue that these obfuscations constitute a deliberate epistolary style that in itself offers a response to Marguerite's ambiguity and epistolary role-playing, and that is as important as the actual content of his letters.[68] As Philippe de Lajarte observes, this writing style is not without its own "logique rigoureuse."[69] Heller claims the cultivation of confused imagery and language as a deliberate evangelical strategy, describing the influence of Pseudo-Dionysius's promotion of the use of rhopographical and rhypological images – that is, insignificant and low or sordid images, respectively, to cultivate spirituality outside of reason.[70] This is important

66 For thorough accounts of the details of the acquaintance and relationship of Marguerite and Briçonnet, see Jourda, *Marguerite d'Angoulême*, and Becker.

67 Heller describes his "pedestrian style" and "contorted and confused language" in "Marguerite of Navarre and the Reformers of Meaux," 277. Beaulieu describes his letters as "épître-traités," a "flot généreux de paroles" that produces a "tourbillon étourdissant," 53. On Briçonnet's Latin, see Guy, "Compte rendu de Marguerite, duchesse d'Alençon et Guillaume Briçonnet, évêque de Meaux," 215; cited in Heller, "Marguerite of Navarre and the Reformers of Meaux," 277–8. Perhaps most scathingly, Génin writes: "On serait tenté de regarder les lettres de l'évêque comme l'oeuvre d'un fou ... Dans le fatras de sa volumineuse correspondance avec la duchesse d'Angoulême, vous chercheriez en vain une lueur de sens commun," Introduction, *Lettres de Marguerite d'Angoulême*, 6.

68 Heller observes this as a deliberate style as well but for him it is specifically Dionysian. Contrasting Briçonnet's letters here with his other writings, in particular his sermons and decrees, he adds that Briçonnet was capable of clarity when he chose; "Marguerite de Navarre," 278.

69 Lajarte, 619.

70 He writes that Briçonnet "in accord with Dionysius was deliberately using nonsense and gibberish as a means of religious expression ... he viewed the pursuit of

for my discussion for two reasons: it suggests that letters were a way for evangelicals to expound their teaching with apostolic flavor, adding another dimension to the complex persona Briçonnet creates in this correspondence.[71] Second, and more important, it shows the importance of letters in the development of a particular kind of evangelical spirituality: one that relies on reading and writing to produce spiritual experience.

The writing style Briçonnet cultivates in his letters produces a particular kind of religious feeling on the part of the addressee in several ways, but all dependent on one key activity, central to evangelical teaching: reading. He broaches the topic of different kinds of reading in his discussion of manna in the desert. In response to Marguerite's request for "eau," "feu," and "manne" as his "affamée fille,"[72] he meditates on the Exodus passage on manna in the desert and discusses St Paul's explanation of it, and the need for interpretive, not literal, reading. This letter is not without its humor; Briçonnet apologizes for his writing, calling it a cold victual compared with transcendent manna. He demonstrates the need for the different kinds of reading: the scriptural manna passage must be read to produce a figurative meaning, and so, too, must his letter be read. His letter is not literally a hunk of uncooked meat, but rather an insufficient – and figurative – viand compared with the sustenance provided by God.[73]

Having established the need for interpretation in reading, Briçonnet laments the limitations of words, and the impossibility of explaining the divine "goust" to those who have not already tasted it:

reason as antithetical to religious understanding," adding that some evangelical preachers employed obfuscating language in their sermons to avoid Inquisitional charges. The use of everyday and sordid imagery served several purposes: "to conceal mysteries from the vulgar, to shock and awaken the spirit into religious awareness, and ... to suggest how far removed man's ordinary understanding was from a genuine comprehension of the essence of a wholly transcendent God," "Marguerite of Navarre and the Reformers of Meaux," especially 271–4.

[71] See Corrie for a discussion of the importance of Pseudo-Dionysius for Briçonnet and his conflation of the fifth-century Pseudo-Dionysius with the third-century French martyr St. Denis and the Dionysius converted by St. Paul in Acts.

[72] Letter 22, vol. 1, 132, written in early 1522.

[73] In a later letter, Briçonnet elaborates at greater length on the difference between figurative and literal reading: "toute l'Escripture Saincte est ou spirituelle seulement, sans intelligence litterale, ou litterale sans la spirituelle (et bien peu), ou litterale et spirituelle ensemble. Moings se trouvera de passaiges qui se puissent seulement entendre litteralement que des aultres deux" (Letter 49, vol. 2, 13) (all of Holy Scripture is either only spiritual, without literal meaning, or literal without spiritual meaning – or very little, or literal and spiritual together. One finds fewer passages that can only be understood literally, than the other two kinds).

Helas! je blasphemeray sy je presume et cuyde exprimer le goust que ne
peult angelicque ne humaine nature comprendre, goust sans goust, car
incomprehensible. Qui gouste il comprend; aussy insensible, qui gouste
sent.[74]

Alas! I blaspheme if I presume and think to explain the taste that neither
angelic nor human nature can comprehend, a taste without taste, for it is
incomprehensible. He who tastes understands; however unfeeling, he
who tastes, feels.

In this passage Briçonnet shows himself capable of writing sparely and
varying his writing style, abundantly figurative and circuitous in demonstrating the need for figurative reading and interpretation, and more
simply articulated when advancing a central, though paradoxical,
teaching. However, even as he teaches Marguerite to read figuratively –
and reading the gospels is a central tenet of evangelical teaching – he
decries the limits of discourse, evangelical or epistolary, to effect comprehension of the divine.[75] Despite this inability to understand the divine
through our limited discourse, Briçonnet nevertheless continues to write
to Marguerite; this letter runs to forty-six pages, and their correspondence is documented for at least another two-and-a-half years. This
suggests that of greater efficacy in this correspondence is less what the
letters might say in the face of our incomprehension, than the fact of
continued exchange.

And indeed, Marguerite insists on more letters: she demands that
Briçonnet "excercer par lettres" the "effect" of his care so that she can
better "estudier" his lesson.[76] This lesson, I argue, is the effect his letters

---

[74] Letter 28, vol. 1, 140.

[75] He writes that human beings are less able to "l'incomprehensibilité divine entendre
que les bestes l'humaine," (Letter 28, vol. 1, 141). See Heller, "Marguerite de Navarre,"
and Cottrell's *The Grammar of Silence*, especially 11–19, and "The Poetics of Transparency" on the philosophical, patristic, and specifically Augustinian influences in
Briçonnet's writing.

[76] Letter 7, vol. 1, 37. Jourda writes that the letters were copied "sur son ordre pour
conserver les avis de son conseiller spirituel," 69. Saulnier suggests that the letters were
compiled in order to serve as a sort of breviary for Marguerite. That the letters were
compiled under Marguerite's direction is undisputed; Becker observes: "Tout porte à
croire que ce n'est pas à Meaux, mais sur les ordres de Marguerite que le recueil a été
préparé. On voit, en effet, que les lettres de Briçonnet sont signées et datées, tandis que
celles de Marguerite ne portent ni lieu d'origine ni indication de jour. On a donc copié les
lettres de Briçonnet telles qu'elles furent expédiées et remises par le courrier, celles de la
princesse d'après les minutes conservées par ses secrétaires. L'exception pour 1524 n'est
qu'apparente; car on constate sans peine que la date mise en tête de certaines lettres de
Marguerite est celle de la réponse de Briçonnet qui a servi à les classer," 395.

produce through content and form. That is, the most useful teaching Briçonnet offers is his cultivation of a spirituality that is felt, bordering on mystical. This mysticism is present even in his first letter, in which he writes of the heart's "navrence."[77] He writes of spiritual knowledge as bodily suffering; as "congnoissance" that remains "incognue": not a rational but an affective spirituality. Declaring his certainty that Marguerite is already wounded, the challenge seems to be maintaining this state, and, as cited earlier, Briçonnet expresses his wish that God

> vueille par sa grace tellement vostre estre par amour unir à sa naissance et fontaine qu'il puisse en son vray estre estre abismé et noié, pour mieulx congnoistre qu'il est ung et, par ce, seul parfaict et necessaire.

> might wish by his grace to so greatly unite your being through love to his birth and source that it might in its true being be ruined and drowned, to better understand that he is the one and, by this, alone perfect and necessary thing.[78]

Returning to the theme of "ung seul necessaire," of which Marguerite has already claimed that she is "congnoissant," Briçonnet writes that she needs to "mieulx congnoistre" this precept from Luke, making "congnoistre" not so much cognitive as a somatic activity.[79] In describing this understanding that is not understood, that is somatic and felt, Briçonnet's teaching might well seem contradictory. And while he never directly says how exactly this "congnoistre" is to occur, the abundance of his letters and his flights of mystical prose suggest that his letters are the key vehicles through whose reading she can "mieux congnoistre," and that Marguerite is to arrive at this knowledge through reading his letters.

In addition to providing teaching through advancing precepts which he illustrates in his writing style, Briçonnet's letters offer another level of spiritual meaning. Through language that is at times obfuscating, and through a privileging of the affective over the cognitive and discursive in religious experience, his letters topically and performatively teach humility. Cottrell suggests that Briçonnet takes Pseudo-Dionysius's teaching further than Pseudo-Dionysius himself in his use of strained language and imagery in the service of evangelism. The "unintelligibility" of the writing is "designed to humiliate the reader" in

---

[77] Letter 2, vol. 1, 27.
[78] Letter 2, vol. 1, 26.
[79] Briçonnet elaborates at length on the privilege of spirit over reason in Letter 46, vol. 1, 223–8.

order to "prepare the soul for experiencing God."[80] Thus, Briçonnet's letters are crafted with attention to linguistic register, mystical imagery, and "unintelligible" and even contradictory effects, to lead the reader to an abandonment of reason in favor of a spirituality expressed and experienced in somatic terms, and whose origin must be humility: human comprehension is insufficient to arrive at this spirituality.[81] To reinforce the limits of human comprehension, Briçonnet employs language in specific ways in order to produce incomprehension, teaching by performative effect.

His letters are thus more than instruments for teaching or even propagating evangelical doctrine: they are performative vehicles, dependent for their meaning on the craft with which he prepares them. The fact that he and Marguerite do not necessarily need to write to communicate – there are recorded visits between them – underscores this epistolary performance of reform. And as performances depend on audiences, his letters also depend on Marguerite's reading of them to produce a particular experience of spirituality. In light of this spiritual humility, Briçonnet and Marguerite's acts of rhetorical submission take on an added dimension. Humility is more than a rhetorical position cultivated in order to make requests; it is a spiritual position, a necessary condition for grace.

Marguerite's response to this humiliation is not frustration and abandonment, or even diligent study, but enthusiastic epistolary engagement. In her first reply to Briçonnet she writes: "je vous prie que par escript vueillez visiter et exciter à l'amour de Dieu mon cueur" (I beg you that by writing you might wish to visit and excite the love of God in my heart).[82] Acknowledging the heart as the locus of activity in this spiritual vocabulary,[83] she writes in her next letter:

> puis qu'il luy plaist avoir ouvert l'oeil (puisque par nature aveugle) et par vostre bon moyen l'avoir tourné du cousté de la lumiere, je vous prie, en l'honneur de luy, que, par faulte de continuer voz tant salutaires

---

[80] Cottrell, *The Grammar of Silence*, 32. His analysis of the letter of 20 January 1522, in which Briçonnet writes of the "abisme" of union with God, might well apply to most of the bishop's letters: "Entrapped in a morass of words that reflect each other, the reader may well abandon any effort to 'understand' the text. And that is the point. The letter is not meant to be 'understood' in the usual sense of the word. It is designed to prepare the soul for experiencing God ... By its opaqueness, its repetitiveness, its 'unintelligibility,' Briçonnet's letter is designed to 'humiliate' the reader."

[81] On humility and negative theology in Briçonnet's thinking, see Jacob Vance.

[82] Letter 3, vol. 1, 30.

[83] Lyons examines the importance of the heart in "The 'Cueur' in the *Heptaméron*."

lettres, ne le laissez en paresse recloure, mais, par coustume de fructueuse leçon, rompre la trop grande ignorance de mon entendement, affin que le pauvre coeur verglacé et mort en froit puisse sentir quelque estincelle de l'amour en quoy je le desire consummer et brusler en cendre. (Letter 5, vol. 1, 33)

because it pleases him to have opened the eye (which is by nature blind) and by your good means to have turned it to the side of the light, I beg you, in God's honor, that, by lack of continuing your very salutary letters you not allow it in laziness to shut again, but, by the custom of fruitful lesson, break the too great ignorance of my understanding, so that the poor heart icy and dead with cold might be able to feel some spark of the love in which I desire it to be consumed and burned to ash.

This is a much more explicit demand than for "secours spirituel," for all that it is couched in mystical language. Marguerite refers to her lamentable spiritual state, represented by her "verglacé" heart. She urges Briçonnet to help her persevere in her pursuit of affective faith, to help her "sentir quelque estincelle de l'amour." While the terms of the metaphor are the same, this expression is a world away from Constance's coy evocations of her bodily suffering, caused by reading Baudri's letters. Here, Marguerite employs bodily metaphors to show how for her, letters are salutary because of their affective effects. The lessons they teach, she hopes, will "rompre" the ignorance of her understanding and revive her. The spirituality she pursues is something that is felt, not interpreted and rationally understood. What Marguerite actually felt is not something that we can know. What is important is that Briçonnet's letters seem calculated to produce certain effects, and Marguerite's repeated requests for letters suggest that she does not receive what she seeks – or perhaps that she does; what she seeks now is letters, for the salutary effect their reading and writing have on her spiritual want.

Briçonnet's lessons in humility would seem to be successful. Repeating her need and unworthiness, Marguerite claims a position of extravagant abjection:

considerant que le pere de lumiere ne retire son ray du fumier pour le donner sur l'or, suis contraincte de prier son serviteur faire le semblable, ou il fauldra penser (après longue actente) dyminution de charité en vous ou trop grande indignité à l'indigne Marguerite.
(Letter 40, vol. 1, 215)

considering that the father of light does not withdraw his ray from manure in order to shine it on gold, I am constrained to beg his servant to do the same, or it will be necessary to conclude (after long waiting) diminution of charity in you or too great indignity of the unworthy Marguerite.

Cottrell observes the recurrence of the "self-effacing, self-annihilating" identification with ordure in Marguerite's poetic writings.[84] This vocabulary recalls Heloise's extravagant epistolary gestures of self-humiliation in claiming shameful names and humble positions; abject humility is a gendered position exploited by these two women writers to very different but nevertheless strategic effect. Marguerite revels in this vocabulary of extreme humility, finding ever more creative ways to express her spiritual need. And yet, even in her abjection, she informs Briçonnet – with perhaps the faintest trace of threat – that his silence will be read as a lack of charity, or as judgment of her unworthiness.[85] Even in need, Marguerite is steeped in the respective positions structured by the court, and their implications for interpersonal relations.

As Briçonnet echoes Marguerite's language and metaphors, she echoes back to him elements of his lessons. In addition to professing an extravagant humility, she claims that reading Scripture is a task too great for her in her spiritual need.[86] Despite this claim to an inability to read the Bible unassisted, however, Marguerite provides ample evidence that she is a capable and close reader of Briçonnet's text. She repeats his motif of divine "viande" and "goust" inaccessible by intellection alone, in the service of her demand for more writing from him. Employing mystical contradiction and the Dionysian quotidian imagery favored by the evangelicals, she writes that she does not ask for anything, not knowing what to ask – and then begs for crumbs of the "viande" to which he has access and she has not, obliquely complimenting his ability to grant the request, and obligating him to grant it.[87] She refers to herself deprecatingly as his

---

[84] For a discussion of "creatural functions" and Marguerite's use of the term "fiens" in self-description, see Cottrell's "The Poetics of Transparency," 41, and *The Grammar of Silence*, 122.

[85] George Hoffmann points out that "foi formée de charité" is a catchphrase of Erasmian evangelism; therefore, in proposing "diminution of charity" Marguerite could well be very subtly accusing Briçonnet of diminution in faith, as well.

[86] Letter 48, vol. 2, 10–11.

[87] Briçonnet's response to this, either humble or impertinent, is to remind Marguerite of the three "pauvres mendians d'esprit qui sont icy en vostre hermitaige" (poor beggars of the spirit who are here in your hermitage), that is, Jacques Lefèvre d'Etaples, François Vatable, and Gérard Roussel, "dont se peuvent esclaircir plusieurs tenebres qui sont par maulvaises translacions en l'Escripture Sainte" (from whom it is possible to clarify the shadows occasioned by bad transactions in the Holy Scripture); "Merciez Dieu de ses graces et plus avant les mendiez" (thank God for his blessings and beg from them first),

"vielle mere," repeating the vocabulary of maternity and filiation that is part of their lexicon, and reminds the bishop that she has not forgotten "ung seul necessaire."

Given the varied purposes, spiritual and practical, for which Briçonnet cultivated a particular register and use of language, and of which Marguerite's letters demonstrate her to be an astute student, his letters are more than documents offering spiritual advice. They are performative vehicles crafted to impart a particular reading experience, and to produce a specific feeling – humility. Ultimately, the "secours" he offers lies in his letters themselves, whose reading produces a spiritual experience closely associated with mystical practice. Reading is a central part of prereform thinking – and direct reading of gospels is valued even in the closest possible translation.[88] The development of a spiritual practice centered on direct, personal experience of reading, in the vernacular, and in letters, indicates the evangelical tenor of their thinking, and also something important about letters in this moment of transition for France, on the cusp of the so-called Renaissance: a medieval literary genre so well-suited to the advancement of administrative, literary, polemic, and social projects was ideally suited for spiritual use too, for its immediacy and its emphasis on individual reading experience.

Begging the Question: Marguerite Asks, and Asks Again

The characterization of Briçonnet as Marguerite's spiritual advisor is reasonable, but it has resulted in a perhaps undue emphasis on the bishop's influence not only on her spiritual life, but also on her writings. The extensive critical effort to demonstrate his direct influence on Marguerite's writing, in their letters as well as in her verse and prose compositions, reduces its interest to its spiritual content and neglects the collaborative nature of their correspondence. To a lesser degree, critics have also assigned to Marguerite the dominant role in their exchange.[89] However, the substance of their correspondence amounts to much more

---

Letter 49, vol. 2, 13 and n. 11. As noted above, Lefèvre d'Etaples completed a translation of the New Testament in 1523, Vatable was appointed by François I to the Collège de France, and Roussel later became Marguerite's confessor and almoner.

[88] For a discussion of the importance of translation to the evangelicals see Corrie, and De la Tour, *Les Origines de la Réforme*, vol. 2.

[89] Beaulieu writes that "les épîtres de Marguerite formulent succinctement des questions et des inquiétudes auxquelles Briçonnet répond, sur un mode qui est celui du développement, de l'amplification," 47.

than the pursuit and dispensing of spiritual advice, and, as I have discussed, unfolds as a result of initiatives both writers undertake. Thus far, I have examined how letters facilitate instrumental role-playing for Marguerite and Briçonnet, and the ways in which they cultivate the letter as a tool for the experience of spirituality. In this section, I examine Marguerite's spiritual poetry, and the connection she forges between missive writings and voiced poetry.

While the correspondence with Briçonnet can be considered Marguerite's earliest body of writing, it precedes by only a few years the composition of her spiritual poems.[90] The earliest of these, the *Dialogue en forme de vision nocturne*, was probably written around 1523–24 – the last years of their correspondence – and it is not surprising that their primary concerns are confluent. Critics have identified one of Briçonnet's letters as a direct source for this poem, and indeed the *Dialogue* reproduces his consolations to Marguerite on the death of her niece Charlotte.[91] However, it is the similarity in concern between the letters and her poetry that reveals the variety in Marguerite's literary approach, and her exploration of the possible overlap between letters and poems: it shows her investigation of how epistolary functions might be translated into other literary genres.

The *Dialogue en forme de vision nocturne* consists of short poems written in the voices of Marguerite and Charlotte.[92] Marguerite laments the death of her young niece, Charlotte consoles her bereaved aunt. In the longest of the poems, they address each other in turn, as if they were characters in a play.[93] Despite its title, the opening *rondeau* reads more like a letter than a conversation: the poem's refrain, written in Margue-

[90] It is worth noting that the writing of the *Dialogue en forme de vision nocture*, Marguerite's first spiritual poem, and the first publication of her spiritual poetry, the *Miroir de l'âme pécheresse* in 1531, were both occasioned by the death of a child. While this strongly suggests the turn to poetry as motivated by grief, it makes an important connection between elegy and voiced writing: fictional dialogues offer one way to continue conversations that otherwise cannot be had.

[91] See Martineau and Grouselle; *Marguerite de Navarre, Poésies chrétiennes*, 289–90; and Jourda, "Sur la date du *Dialogue en forme de vision nocturne*," 150–5.

[92] In the opening *rondeau*, Charlotte speaks to her own soul. This *rondeau* does not appear in all the manuscripts containing the *Dialogue*; *Marguerite de Navarre, Poésies chrétiennes*, 289.

[93] Smarr examines the dialogic nature of this and other poems of Marguerite. The functions that she describes as dialogic are the very ones that suggest to me the influence of the epistolary. We do not so much disagree as examine in different ways the generic creativity and flexibility that marked this moment in early modern French literary production.

rite's voice, is an imploring "répondez-moi." Each *rondeau* responds to the previous one, and in the next poem's refrain, Charlotte commands "contentez-vous." In each of these two poems, the *rondeau*'s distinctive refrain, in which the opening words are echoed at the close of each stanza, is a request. This repetition has the effect of emphasizing the poem's *petitio*, giving each poem the force of a letter, making a request and anticipating a response. In the third *rondeau*, Marguerite's refrain is an appeasing "contente suis." These opening *rondeaux* lead up to the much longer poem which contains the "dialogue" by which the collection of poems is known. In this last poem, Marguerite trades the *rondeau* structure for *terza rima*, employed in perhaps the most well-known medieval poetic colloquy with the dead, Dante's *Divina Commedia*. In this way the *Dialogue* mimics the structure in which a meeting between correspondents might take place: through initial letters establishing the desire for conversation. But, because one of the interlocutors is dead, this conversation does not occur not in person, but in letters.

Marguerite's plaintive refrain "répondez-moi" is not just a rhetorical feature of the opening rondeau; her stance throughout the poem is lamenting, even querulous, and she asks questions throughout the poem. One of the more startling queries she poses is on the experience of death. She wants to know what it feels like: "quelle douleur sentîtes au partir?"[94] Charlotte replies with nine-year-old insouciance: "le départir n'est rien qu'un bref soupir."[95] What is remarkable is that this is information that Marguerite cannot have: she imagines it, and she puts it in the mouth of her dead niece. In this poem, Marguerite scripts her own ignorance (Charlotte calls her "Tante trop ignorante"), a prominent feature in the correspondence with Briçonnet. She also scripts a response to her own question and assigns it to Charlotte. As in her letters with Briçonnet, Marguerite would seem to have the questions and the answers, but she needs an interlocutor.

Despite this conversation with her beloved niece, at the end of the poem, Marguerite is no better off than she was at the beginning. Charlotte reassures Marguerite that she is in paradise and remonstrates that it is an offense to lament her well-being, but Marguerite still mourns. In her last words to her niece, she makes a fantastical request. She asks Charlotte to take her with her:

94 Line 167.
95 Line 177.

Ô mon enfant, vous en faut-il aller?
Et si force est, au moins je vous supplie
Que me tirez avecques vous par l'air. (lines 1246–8)

O my child, must you go?
If it must be, then I beg you
To take me with you as you fly away

Her grief is moving, and the wistful tone of this last request attests to her continued suffering. The nocturnal dream vision and the conversation with her dead niece do not seem to have allayed her suffering, and in this way, the *Dialogue* shares one of the principal dynamics of the correspondence with Briçonnet: Marguerite voices her need, asks for help, and receives consolation – none of which seem to provide relief.

To read these works literally might suggest the futility of asking for assistance – for when it is given, relief does not come to the suffering writer. However, these works also suggest that the pattern of question-and-response established in the correspondence sets up a career-long exploration of the question as a rhetorical and intellectual construct. Marguerite scripts her ignorance but she is neither ignorant nor posing as ignorant; rather, she cultivates ignorance as a stance from which she can deploy the query as an opportunity for reflection. The repeated declarations of ignorance or need, even after an "answer" is given, demonstrates the insufficiency of reason to meet spiritual and emotional need. In the *Dialogue*, the grieving aunt is not so much untouched by her departed niece's lessons from beyond the grave as she is showing us how hard it is to stop grieving. The constancy of her grief does not reveal ignorance but a need so deep that it is unresponsive to reason: all it can do is utter – and repeat – its suffering. This might very well be an incorporation of Briçonnet's Dionysian lessons, but the style and the substance of the queries are Marguerite's own, and the structure, while profoundly dialogic, is markedly epistolary.

The importance of the question-and-answer structure in Marguerite's other writings throws into sharp relief what critics have called the dialogism and even theatricality produced by reading the letters she exchanged with Briçonnet as a whole.[96] These observations of dialogism balance assessments of the correspondence as directed by either

---

[96] For example, Beaulieu writes: "les propos quelque peu autarciques de Briçonnet n'acquièrent-ils une valeur pleinement homilétique que grâce à l'encadrement offert par les lettres de Marguerite, le tout visant le troisième terme de la communication épistolaire qu'est le lecteur," 52. Scholars have commented on the platonic and catechistic nature of the correspondence; for Paré, the dialogic form is "au cœur de la *Correspondance*" and

Briçonnet or Marguerite; they also corroborate this central structure in Marguerite's writings. The letters were probably compiled during Marguerite's lifetime and under her direction, and the compilation has the effect of making the princess and the bishop characters in their own epistolary, evangelical drama.[97] However, considering the expectations of the medieval epistolary tradition and the near-certainty of audience when correspondents occupied positions of social status, the positions assumed in the correspondence are no less "real" for their staged quality – just as court life is no less real for being staged. Marguerite's writing shows the usefulness and flexibility of these positions, which she explores through her exchange with Briçonnet and develops in other literary genres.

This epistolary model proved useful throughout Marguerite's writing career. In the spiritual poems, Marguerite sheds the social positioning and attendant postures of authority and humility but retains the core epistolary function of making a request. Moreover, in consistently writing from the position of postulant, Marguerite writes her correspondent into a placeholder position, whose primary function is to provide her with an interlocutor. This is not to say that the contents of the responses do not matter, but in this model of correspondence, the fact of exchange matters just as much, if not more. This epistolary structure facilitates Marguerite's search for spiritual "secours" and shows how it is rooted in experience and exchange, and not necessarily a search for precepts to be meditated upon. As Marguerite's career progressed, she continued to write poems and letters and expanded her repertoire to include plays, *chansons*, and of course the *Heptaméron*, all of which clearly bear the mark of this fascination with voiced and missive writing and the ways in which it can articulate need: by addressing interlocutors and engaging them in questioning and continued discussion.

---

even "de toute l'œuvre subséquente de Marguerite de Navarre. Or ce dialogue, dont l'importance heuristique remonte sans doute à un certain platonisme, devient, dès ces années 1521–1524, avant même la rédaction des grands textes, un des motifs rhétoriques les plus constants et les plus riches chez Marguerite de Navarre," 50; see also Martineau, "Le platonisme de Marguerite de Navarre." For a study on dialogue and Renaissance women writers, see Smarr, especially Chapter 1, "Dialogue and Spiritual Counsel."

[97] The staged effect of the compilation might for some call its sincerity into question; Beaulieu comments on the "théâtre d'un positionnement qui engage les épistoliers dans des postures complémentaires … dans lesquelles il ne faudrait pas nécessairement voir le reflet des rapports réels entre les correspondants," 43–4.

The Recuperation of Rhetoric

Marguerite's exploration of spiritual concerns did not always meet with a positive response. Jeanne d'Albret recalls her mother's spiritual activities and the disapprobation it inspired in her uncle and her father:

> laquelle Royne induite par defunct son frere Mons[ieu]r le Roy Francois pre[mier] de bonne et glorieuse memoire mon tres honnore Oncle, a ne se mettre en cervelle dogmes nouveaux ne se cuyda onques que de Romans jovials, oultres plus me recordant toujours bien des noyses que loing auparavant le defunct Roy Mons[ieu]r mon tres honnore Pere et seig[neu]r que Dieu tienne en grace me chercha alors que laditte Royne faisant dans sa chambre prieres avecques les ministres Roussel et Farel quy dheur sesquiverent en grand esmoy lui bailla un soufflet sur la jouë dextre et me tansca de verges en deffendant asprem[en]t de ne se mesler de Doctrine.

> The said Queen [was] warned by her late brother the King, François I of good and glorious memory, my much honored Uncle, not to get new doctrines in her head and to confine herself to amusing stories. Besides, I well remember long ago, the late King, my most honored father and lord whom may God hold in grace found me while the said Queen was praying in her rooms with the ministers, Roussel and Farel, and how with great annoyance he slapped her on the right cheek and rebuked me with a stick, fiercely forbidding her to meddle in matters of doctrine.[98]

This account appears in a letter written to the Vicomte de Gourdon on 22 August 1555, shortly after the funeral of Henri d'Albret. While the episodes recounted are not dated, they indicate royal disapproval of Marguerite's spiritual leanings, and it is tempting to read the scene with Henri as occasioning her turn to the composition of the *Heptaméron*. As the most secular of her writings, its composition was perhaps a way of not so much suppressing as sending her evangelical tendencies underground. As *Heptaméron* scholars have consistently pointed out, despite their decidedly worldly tenor, the *nouvelles* are not devoid of spiritual concerns, and as we have seen in the *Dialogue*, the autobiographical resurfaces in Marguerite's writing in unexpected ways. Henri's warning to avoid "se mesler de doctrine" in favor of "Romans jovials" finds its inverse in the dauphin's injunction in the prologue against people of

---

[98] BNff 17.044, fol. 446, Jeanne d'Albret to the Vicomte de Gourdon, 22 August 1555, reproduced in part in *Marguerite d'Angoulême, duchesse d'Alençon*, ed. Jourda, I: 181 n. 62, citing G. Bourgeon, *La Réforme à Nérac*, 81–2; trans. Roelker, *Queen of Navarre, Jeanne d'Albret*, 127; translation modified.

letters, lest "la beaulté de la rethoricque feit tort en quelque partye à la verité de l'histoire." Ironically, the dauphin's rationale resonates with the teachings of Pseudo-Dionysius, cautioning against the distracting effects of rhetoric.[99] No less an evangelical contemporary than Jacques Lefèvre d'Etaples associated rhetoric with " 'theatrical pomp,' with cosmetics, ornament, decoration."[100] With injunctions against rhetoric coming from authoritative male figures in her life, the *Heptaméron*'s insistence on truth at the cost of rhetorical ornament reads as a dutiful application of lessons – or perhaps a sly tongue-in-cheek gesture to these authorities.[101]

As Marguerite's writings attest, she desists neither from pursuing doctrinal matters nor from the studied employment of rhetoric and its effects.[102] The importance of posing questions to an interlocutor in her writings strongly suggests the importance of this model to her spiritual pursuit; thus the worldly, dialogue-driven *Heptaméron* might not be evidence of silenced spirituality, but rather pursuit of the same issues that motivated her epistolary and poetic writings, but in different vein. Her correspondence with Briçonnet demonstrates that a strategic use of language to persuade is instrumental in the pursuit of spiritual meaning. While Briçonnet writes at length about the limits of language, he implicitly demonstrates the need for its skillful use – and commonplace, quotidian language is nevertheless a meditated, studied use of language, constituting a prereform rhetoric and even poetics. His own use of such language seems aimed at the production of a particular, affective experience of spirituality. As the intended recipient of this experience,

---

99 Heller notes that "Dionysius not only advocated using rhypographical and rhopographical images in religious discussions but also expressed serious reservations against the use of words which by their beauty might limit religious understanding," "Marguerite of Navarre," 280.

100 He "rebuked the professional rhetoricians who were his colleagues at the University of Paris" and "associated rhetoric, that is, human eloquence, with what he called 'theatrical pomp,' with cosmetics, ornament, decoration," *The Prefatory Epistles of Jacques Lefèvre d'Étaples and Related Texts*, ed. Rice, xx, cited in Cottrell, "The Poetics of Transparency," 35; see also Heller, "The Evangelicism of Lefèvre d'Etaples."

101 A stronger censuring of her writing occurs in response to her *Miroir de l'âme pécheresse*, published in 1531 and condemned two years later by the Sorbonne on charges of heresy; François I's intervention reversed the charges. On the "privilege du roi" emergent in the sixteenth century that overtakes individual patronage as the dominant means of securing copyright protection and protection from censure, see Freccero, 72–3.

102 Marguerite produced writings interrogating spiritual concerns from 1531 until 1548, the year before her death, and the *Heptaméron* appeared in 1559; "Chronologie," in *Marguerite de Navarre, Poésies Chrétiennes*, 40–5.

Marguerite's writing develops a different engagement with language that is nonetheless firmly rooted in epistolary traditions and conventions.

The abundance of Briçonnet's letters and his flights of mystical vocabulary suggest that Marguerite might better "congnoistre" through reading his letters, offering a teaching that is not based on precepts but grounded in the experience of reading, making reading a locus of felt spirituality. Marguerite does not so much refuse this approach as engage in a way that emphasizes continued exchange, asking for more "secours." By the end of her career, however, the insufficiency of Briconnet's approach is crystallized in the *Heptaméron*'s thirteenth *nouvelle*, in which the letter is eclipsed by its adamantine accompaniment: the diamond ring best represents the love deserved by the lonely widow, and its return to her rights the wrongs attempted by her inconstant husband. The efficacy of the letter has little to do with its truth value, and depends rather on the value of the ring, reinforced by the *devisants'* interest in it. This, too, echoes Briconnet's rhetoric; his letters to Marguerite refer to the "adamantine" constancy of hearts. Marguerite borrows the metaphor and literalizes it to show that for her, letters can indeed be transformative, but their chief value lies not in extended meditation and humility but in an efficacy of rhetoric that lies in the materiality of letters, and the experience of reading, writing, and exchanging them.

The structure of Marguerite's spiritual pursuit in her correspondence with Briçonnet shapes her entire writing career. Letters and the positions they fashion for writers are central to this pursuit: they structures modes of address, positions of entreaty and command, and expectation of response. This correspondence also develops a poetics of contradiction, articulating power and influence alongside a politeness bordering on courtly and a humility both extravagant and spare. In addition to this courtliness, dialogism, and contradiction, the epistolary *petitio* is a model for continued query that can be seen in many of her writings. Far from harming the truth, rhetoric functions as a vehicle for spiritual meaning, and epistolary rhetoric provides a structure through which extended engagement with spirituality can be sustained. Yet, while Marguerite had extensive contact with evangelicals and her correspondence with Briçonnet laid important foundations for her thinking and writing, she developed her own methods for pursuing the spirituality she sought in a life-long project of writing.

In previous chapters, the balance of power between writers was unequal, and along predictably gendered lines: male correspondents possessed authority, of which their female interlocutors worked to achieve a measure through their writing. In some ways, these letters allow us to observe how, if at all, this balance figures differently when one of the correspondents is a supremely authoritative woman. Perhaps not surprisingly, postures of supplication and benefaction still appear, implying the deeply embedded nature of power relations in epistolary as well as in social structures.[103] However, Marguerite and Briçonnet both write from these positions, showing us that these positions are gendered, but they are flexible. Their letters show the value of these rhetorical stances in the negotiation of mutual need and assistance – each stands to gain from the influence and assistance of the other, and they sustain this negotiation through letters.

And yet, Marguerite's first letter declares that she already knows that "ung seul est necessaire," making her request for "secours" a performance of need, and not just a request for assistance. Therefore, letters also provide a vehicle for an exploration of want, spirituality, reason and its limits, through writing. Despite being staged in letters, the spiritual need Marguerite articulates is quite urgent. Epistolary conventions actively facilitate her spiritual pursuit, which she continues in other literary genres. Her correspondence with Briçonnet demonstrates the continuing influence of medieval epistolary conventions in the early sixteenth century, and how letter-writing conventions could be employed to pursue spiritual engagement and even produce spiritual experience, broadening the scope of the possibilities afforded by the epistolary. However, Marguerite's writing also demonstrates the limits of letter writing, and the possibilities, in contrast, of the epistolary: she moves from epistolary engagement with a correspondent to scripted colloquy in other literary genres. This move suggests the importance of framing questions and engaging in dialogue to her pursuit, an approach that bears the imprint of letter writing and the dynamics it scripts. In this way, the legacy of the medieval letter in early sixteenth-century France is two-fold: its forms and conventions continued to be useful to a court culture in which performing humility and authority was necessary for survival and advancement. However, its centuries-long traditions also suggested other ways of pursuing some of its central effects, such as

---

[103] See Middlebrook on Louise de Savoie's efforts to fashion a public, authoritative persona through the idea of the "trinité"; these efforts suggest that royal female authority was not a given but had to be assiduously maintained through iconographic representation.

supplication, benefaction, mutual ennoblement, through an exploration of unexpected uses of language and metaphors in fixed epistolary discourse, and the use of these effects in other literary genres. Marguerite shows us some of these ways in her career-long literary exploration of the epistolary, as she navigates its possibilities for articulating the spiritual needs of a prereform self.

5

The *Foedus Amicitiae* of
Etienne de la Boétie and Michel de Montaigne

The friendship of Michel de Montaigne and Étienne de la Boétie has attracted considerable critical attention, particularly as it is portrayed in Montaigne's writings, and most notably in his essay "De l'Amitié."[1] In this much-studied work, Montaigne declares that, when compared with the few years of his friendship with La Boétie, the rest of his life

n'est que fumée, ce n'est qu'une nuit obscure et ennuyeuse.[2]

is nothing but smoke, nothing but a dark and tedious night.

This is a dramatic statement, but it is reasonable to say that Montaigne's legacy as a writer is irrevocably marked by his friendship with La Boétie. In this chapter, I argue that Montaigne's development of the *Essais* is deeply influenced by this friendship and the epistolary genre. More than being a means to express their friendship, I argue that the letter is a means for its very existence. This foundation is belied by Montaigne's near-mystical rhetoric in describing their friendship, which,

ayant saisi toute ma volonté, l'amena se plonger et se perdre dans la sienne; qui, ayant saisi toute sa volonté, l'amena se plonger et se perdre en la mienne[3]

Having seized my whole will, made it plunge and lose itself in his; which, having seized his whole will, made it plunge and lose itself in mine

Compared with this fervent declaration, the image of their friendship

---

[1] Montaigne also writes at length about their friendship in his letter to his father on the death of La Boétie, "Extrait d'une lettre que Monsieur le Conseiller de Montaigne escrit à Monseigneur de Montaigne son pere," *Œuvres complètes d'Estienne de la Boétie*, ed. Desgraves, vol. 2, 167–80.

[2] "De l'Amitié," Michel de Montaigne, *Les Essais*, 193; my translation. All citations of the *Essais* are from this edition unless otherwise indicated.

[3] "De l'Amitié," 189.

represented by Étienne de La Boétie is somewhat more moderate, and certainly much more mediated. In "De l'Amitié," Montaigne exalts their friendship and offers observations on the nature of friendship in ways that critics have pointed out are not unproblematic: their friendship is perfect, but it is unusually short, for which both writers offer justifications; it is praised in light of classical ideals for friendship, but these terms are complicated by the romantic vocabulary Montaigne uses to describe their relationship.[4] Moreover, the perfection of this union is undermined by its predication on an exaggerated and unmistakable misogyny.[5] The triangulation of this friendship is anticipated by the ways in which friendship is a mediated affair in La Boétie's letters, which precede Montaigne's essays by roughly twenty years. La Boétie writes of their friendship in verse epistles addressed to Montaigne, but through the filters of Horatian satire, the humanist recuperation of the classical practice of *amicitia*, and the civic and moral obligations of this *amicitia*. His verse epistles and Montaigne's answering essays and other writings chart the development of an early modern friendship that has a particularly medieval foundation. Its articulation and, I argue, its very existence are rooted in the epistolary genre. Working with and adapting these medieval letter-writing forms and conventions, these writers define through their writing an early modern friendship, and also the contours of the early modern selves who inhabit it.

La Boétie elaborates a nuanced idea of friendship in two Latin poems addressed "Ad Michaelem Montanum."[6] These two verse epistles articulate a structure of friendship in which the acknowledgment and careful negotiation of heterosexual desire is necessary to the pursuit of virtue,

---

[4] Their friendship is praised in ways that raise questions about the *Essais* project in general: Montaigne claims that the essays are trifles, merely about him, but he is also clearly suggesting a study of man through the study of himself; therefore the personal examples he offers are at once exemplary and unique. Mehlman notes that the uniqueness of their relationship and the singularity of emotion are contradicted by La Boétie's *Sonnets*, which are granted pride of place in "De l'Amitié" and "sing the desperate love of La Boétie, in an eloquent frenzy, to the exclusion of all else," 55. Schachter observes that Montaigne seems to "struggle against the restrictions of the discourse of perfect friendship itself and not only to glorify further his own relationship," 15.

[5] I am not attempting demonstrate a biographical misogyny on the part of either Montaigne or La Boétie; rather I am exploring how misogyny works as a rhetorical structure in their writing. For a discussion of antimatrimonial and antifeminist writing and some of the limits of reading "personal conviction" in misogynist writing in the Renaissance, see Gray.

[6] These are identified as poems 3 and 20 in the collection of his writings Montaigne compiled and had published in 1571, several years after La Boétie's death in 1563.

which La Boétie, like the classical writers he and Montaigne admired, claims as a chief goal of friendship. These verse epistles carry clear echoes of their eleventh- and twelfth-century predecessors, the letter-poems composed by the Loire poets. As I argue in Chapter 1, highly stylized medieval verse epistles could convey contradictory meanings, most notably in regard to what to a modern ear sounds like eros; at times the letter-poems seem to capitalize on this ambiguity, raising a host of questions regarding reading, interpretation, and sincerity. For the Loire poets, the erotic figured as at once playful and dangerous – that is, playful when figurative, dangerous when literal – and it could be argued that much of the interest of their verses lies in this studied ambivalence. I consider the differences in the deployment of eros in La Boétie's sixteenth-century verse epistles, in particular the insistence on the pursuit of virtue, how this emphasis shifts in Montaigne's account of their friendship, and what this suggests about the evolution of epistolary culture in early modern France.[7] For Montaigne and La Boétie, the erotic is deliberately cultivated in missive writings, but to very different ends. It is also pursued in ways that are unequivocally misogynist, excluding women from learned, poetic friendship and revealing the limitations of a friendship predicated on this exclusion.

Formally and topically, these sixteenth-century writings show that the letter continues to offer specific ways to carry out personal and public projects. Its fixed elements, established by the medieval *ars dictaminis* and certainly well-known in the sixteenth century, could be abbreviated, combined, and omitted in ways that signified, offering writers a distinct set of tools with which to communicate meaning, in addition to what they actually "say" in their letters. La Boétie's verse epistles also show how gender, as well, can be deployed strategically to achieve specific ends. Christine de Pizan's epistolary writings also make use of fixed gender positions in this way. In her writings, these positions are deployed in order to gain leverage in a particular project of self-authorization, and their use might thus be considered a kind of strategic essentialism. In La Boétie's verse epistles, gendered positions are invoked in advancing the pursuit of virtue, reifying the fact that these positions are not essential, but social, and therefore created. A close reading of his poetic missives

---

[7] An example of the letter's shifting status in this period might be the varied treatment it receives in Joachim du Bellay's 1549 *Défense et illustration de la langue française*. As Helgerson points out, Du Bellay advises against vernacular practice of the epistle for its insufficient loftiness while indulging in its practice himself, 11.

and Montaigne's response shows how gender positions are in fact defined through epistolary practice. In their writing, the gendered positions of misogynist discourse, aligning men with virtue and strength, women with sin and weakness, become analogous to the fixed positions of epistolary exchange – sender and addressee, teacher and student, humanist friends, correspondents who continue the classical tradition of *amicitia*. Gender is constructed, as are letter-writing rules and conventions, but letter writing makes no claim to immanent meaning, while misogyny does. The conflation of these fixed positions occludes the construction of aspects of identity such as gender, which are in fact produced through epistolary practice.

La Boétie's explicit gendering of friendship and its projects, in particular the pursuit of virtue, recurs in very similar ways in Montaigne's "De l'Amitié," reinforcing in yet another way the great influence of La Boétie on Montaigne's thinking and writing. A similar employment of gender by both writers suggests that the *Essais* offered Montaigne a way to continue his dialogue with La Boétie on this point, to offer homage, to demonstrate the success of his friend's teaching. It also suggests that particular early modern relationships – learned male friendships – were deeply rooted in medieval epistolary culture and rhetorical misogyny. In borrowing the epistolary function of *sermo absentium* – with a difference – I consider how Montaigne's exploration of the *essai* as a literary genre was strongly influenced by the letter, by the possibilities and limitations of the epistolary form for a humanist writer, a distraught friend, a grateful student, a bereaved lover.[8]

Quae Mens? The Figure of Friendship in "Ad Belotium et Montanum"

Etienne de la Boétie is perhaps best known for his treatise against tyranny, the *Discours de la servitude volontaire*,[9] published several years before his friendship with Montaigne.[10] As Montaigne famously reports,

---

[8] For a different view on the origins of the essay in relation to the short narrative form practiced by the medieval *conteurs*, see Perouse, "De Montaigne à Boccace et de Boccace à Montaigne," 15, cited in Losse, *Sampling the Book*, 14 and n. 17.

[9] La Boétie also produced translations, wrote poetry in French and Latin, and completed a commentary on the Edict of January 1562, *Mémoire sur la pacification des troubles*.

[10] In 1557, Montaigne began his thirteen-year career in the Parlement of Bordeaux, where he met La Boétie, also a *conseiller*.

this work was shown to him before he ever met La Boétie, and thus served as the medium of their first acquaintance.[11] La Boétie was a humanist writer and member of the Bordeaux parliament, and he and Montaigne first met by chance, it appears, at a civic function.[12] Much of what we know about their actual friendship is largely based on its description in Montaigne's essays and letters. The image of their friendship painted by Montaigne is striking for many reasons, not least of which is the vocabulary of courtly, romantic love used to describe it. As is well known, this description, found in "De l'Amitié," is first published in 1580, seventeen years after La Boétie's death.

Several years before this immortalization, La Boétie strikes a different note in his depiction of their friendship in his Latin verse epistles addressed "Ad Michaelem Montanum." The verse epistle that opens the collection of his Latin verse writing is addressed "Ad Belotium et Montanum," and it offers, among other things, a meditation on the role of counsel in friendship. Montaigne shares the position of addressee with Jean de Belot, and their friendship is invoked in the service of virtue and civic duty.[13] In keeping with the lofty subject-matter, the letter-poem is written in hexameter, and it begins with a demonstration of the continuing hold of the *ars dictaminis* on sixteenth-century letter writing, with a *salutatio* and a *captatio benevolentiae*:[14]

> Montane, ingenii iudex aequissime nostri
> Tuque ornate quem prisca fides candorque, Beloti,
> O socii, o dulces, gratissima cura, sodales,
> Quae mens, qui vobis animus, quos ira deorum
> Et crudelis in haec servavit tempora Parca?

> Montaigne, most just judge of my character
> And you, Belot, endowed with the faithfulness and frankness of
> > the ancients,

---

[11] "Et si suis obligé particulierement à cette piece, d'autant qu'elle a servy de moyen à nostre premiere accointance," 184. In this way the *Discours* is not unlike a letter, as a text that circulates, generates readership, and inspires response.

[12] "nostre premiere reconcontre ... fut par hazard en une grande feste et compagnie de ville," "De l'Amitié," 188.

[13] For biographical notes on Jean de Belot, see *Œuvres complètes d'Estienne de la Boétie*, ed. Desgraves, vol. 2, 87.

[14] Another example of the continuing influence of medieval letter-writing conventions in this period is the manuscript collection containing the state letters of Petrus de Vineis and Coluccio Salutati, which are preceded by a letter instructing its recipient to study and imitate them – that is, to treat them as a formulary, a medieval collection of model letters; Kristeller, *Studies in Renaissance Thought and Letters*, 565 n. 28.

O companions, dear friends who are my most pleasing concern,
What do you think, what is your disposition, you whom the ire
of the gods
And cruel fate have preserved for these times?[15]

Like his medieval predecessors, La Boétie employs a highly compressed economy of expression, conveying an abundance of meaning in a handful of verses. In accordance with medieval letter-writing convention, his salutation identifies his addressees and their status in relation to himself: they are not only peers, but dear friends. The capturing of goodwill is accomplished through the laudatory description of their personal qualities, and the suggestion that, because of their special qualities, the gods have placed them in these troubled times.[16] This last element serves a double function: it praises the correspondents' elect quality, a complimenting gesture that is an expected element of the *captatio*, and it efficiently does the work of the *narratio*, which explains the circumstances leading to the petition, by invoking contemporary civic unrest in France.[17]

The actual *petitio*, however, is curiously brief, and can be isolated to the first words of the fourth line: "quae mens, qui vobis animus." This is not strictly a request or a demand, but rather a question. As the rest of the verse epistle demonstrates, it is a rhetorical question in the best sense of the term: having asked his friends of what mind they are, presumably with regard to the contemporary political unrest, La Boétie employs the rest of the letter-poem to reveal his own. The remainder of this fifty-line letter-poem details what he intends to do in response to "haec tempora": to leave, abandoning hearth and home.[18] He dramatically describes life in exile as preferable to watching his country's further destruction and collapse. Without explicitly naming the ills afflicting France, La Boétie paints a bleak picture of its demise, suggesting flight as the best option for a loyal citizen. He does not return to the question with which he intro-

---

[15] Etienne de la Boétie, "Ad Belotium et Montanum," in *Poemata*, translation modified. All citations and translations of the *Poemata* are from this edition; modifications to the translation are indicated.

[16] I thank Leah Chang for pointing out the Calvinist undertones of this formulation, which, given the unauthorized circulation of the *Discours de la servitude volontaire* discussed later in this chapter, suggests a thematic continuity in La Boétie's writings that might have been particularly appealing for Protestant projects in this period.

[17] This letter, written during La Boétie's relatively brief lifetime, would probably have been penned in the late 1550s or early 1560s.

[18] "Laribus migrare relictis," line 7.

duces this detailed self-explanation, "quae mens." The closest he comes to asking for advice is indirectly: after stating his plan for flight, he declares that he will carry out this plan unless either of his two friends thinks of something more useful.[19] Coming as early as it does in the verse epistle, and bearing the weight of nearly fifty lines detailing the destruction of their country, the futility of staying, the promise of the New World, the sadness of exile and its superiority to witnessing further degradation, this *petitio* seems slim indeed, and employed not so much to ask, as to tell.

The edifice of friendship with which the letter opens functions as a figure through which the writer offers his views on current events and civic duty. This casts the friendship invoked as primarily useful for its rhetorical value, and the opportunity it affords the writer to offer his views on current political unrest and participate in discourses of the New World.[20] What this suggests about La Boétie's actual friendship with Montaigne and Belot is perhaps little. Rather, this verse epistle, penned in the name of friendship, shows how the role of friend can be claimed for rhetorical purposes, to advance other pursuits. La Boétie identifies Montaigne and Belot as valuable to him for their clarity of judgment, honesty, and loyalty, respectively; whether or not La Boétie actually thought these things of Montaigne and Belot, he identifies them as key qualities to be sought in friends who, in the classical tradition of *amicitia*, are also counselors.

"Ad Montanum et Belotium" demonstrates the public role the verse epistle takes on by the mid-sixteenth century: the fiction of the private letter gives way here to a verse epistle employed to air very public concerns, in which even first-person expressions of despair and plans for flight register less as personal desires, and seem rather to be expedient for communicating the degradation of the polity and the ideal course of action for concerned citizens.[21] The figure of the addressee and the struc-

---

19 "Utilius nisi quid vidistis uterque," line 8.

20 As Cottrell observes, poem 3 deploys "the two main discourses that shaped Renaissance discussions of the New World: a utopian discourse in which the New World is viewed as fundamentally Other; and a colonial discourse in which the New World is perceived as territory ripe for European exploitation," "An Introduction to La Boétie's Three Latin Poems," 7.

21 Moreover, this letter is written in Latin; while early modern humanists actively cultivated Latin composition, with the 1549 publication of Du Bellay's *Défense et illustration de la langue française* writers would certainly have been aware of the politically charged implications of this language choice. For La Boétie, writing in both French and

ture of friendship are deployed to facilitate this quasi-public discourse, in a period in which there were perhaps not many genres available to writers who wished to express with impunity their responses to contemporary social and political turmoil.[22] The letter – for centuries a "quasi-public" document, as I examine in previous chapters – alongside the relationships it scripts, facilitates here a new, public form of communication, in which the personal plays a secondary, almost fictional role: it is a pretext for airing concerns of vital civic interest.[23]

"Ad Michaelem Montanum": Virtue, Gender, and the Obligations of Friendship

In La Boétie's "Ad Belotium et Montanum," friendship offers a rhetorical structure through which to advance views about civic duty, in which friends are assigned the role of counselors.[24] In his verse epistles addressed exclusively "Ad Michaelem Montanum," La Boétie develops the theme of virtue and the duty of friends in exhorting each other to its cultivation. Friendship is not merely a rhetorical pretext in these letter-poems, but a structure charged with obligation. The articulation of this friendship and its obligations relies heavily on the fixed gender positions of misogyny, revealing the importance of gender in the construction of a particular kind of relationship: learned male humanist friendship.

Of the two verse epistles titled "Ad Michaelem Montanum," numbered 3 and 20 in the edition prepared by Desgraves, poem 3 is significantly briefer, offering seventy-two lines to poem 20's three hundred and twenty-two. Composed in alcaic strophes, it opens with a declaration of humility:

Latin in a variety of genres, the choice of Latin for these *Poemata* seems to argue for the more public, elevated tenor of these letters-poems.

[22] This is, after all, the period in which printing began to come under regulation: writers had to have privileges to publish their works, and humanist writers and printers risked punishment for their literary output: in 1546, Etienne Dolet was condemned and burned; Rabelais was hiding in Switzerland; La Boétie's *Discours* was circulated by Protestant sympathizers with the result that Montaigne excised them from the *Essais*, discussed later in this chapter. For more on the privilege system, see Armstrong.

[23] The modern-day analogues to this kind of writing are myriad, ranging from letters to the editor and op-ed pieces to blogs. La Boétie's epistolary cultivation of civic interest seems different from Christine de Pizan's interventions, which seem to be shaped by public and personal concerns in equal measure.

[24] This verse-epistle's dual addressee supports what I suggest as its ultimately more public function.

An te paternis passibus arduos
luctantem honesti vincere tramites,
et ipse fervidus iuventa
Ridiculus monitor, docebo? (1–4)

You, struggling in your father's footsteps
to prevail on the arduous path,
Shall I, myself an impetuous youth
A laughable guide, teach you? (translation modified)

La Boétie begins this verse epistle with a protestation of the inappropri-
ateness of his giving advice to Montaigne on account of his own youth.
This protestation implies, however subtly, a youthful Montaigne's need
for advice, while carefully establishing the humility of the writer in
respect to his addressee. Unwilling to pose as a "viridus magister," literally a "green teacher," La Boétie posits instead Virtue as a proper
instructor for his friend, flatteringly referencing the fable of Hercules at
the crossroads, a young man of great talents choosing the direction of his
life.[25]

Xenophon's version of the fable has Hercules choosing between Ἀρετή
(Excellence) on the one hand, and Κακία (Happiness or Vice) on the
other; La Boétie's Latin retelling has Hercules choosing between Virtue
and *Voluptas*, sensual pleasure.[26] Here I follow Robert Cottrell's reading,
in which the differences in La Boétie's version Christianize the pagan
story, associating vice with sexual sin.[27] His retelling sexualizes vice,
personified in the form of a loose woman on whose body, as Cottrell puts
it, "is inscribed not the signs of pagan happiness, nor even the signs of
pagan vice, but, rather, the wages of Christian Sin, that is to say, Death."[28]
This didactic verse-epistle written to a friend, unlike its medieval predecessors in the letter-poems of the Loire poets, is unequivocal in its
condemnation of fleshly pleasure.

As important as the sexualization of vice in La Boétie's version is its
recasting of excellence, and the attendant implications for his conception
of happiness. Rendering Ἀρετή as Virtue (instead of Excellence) implicitly ascribes a moral character to the good. And of course virtue has as its

---

[25] Line 16.
[26] La Boétie was a translator of Greek and specifically of Xenophon. Hirstein identifies Xenophon's *Memorabilia* 2.1.21–34 as a source for lines 25–72 in "La Boétie's
Neo-Latin Satire," 54. See Desgraves, vol. 1 for more on La Boétie's translations from
ancient Greek into French.
[27] Cottrell, "An Introduction to La Boétie's Three Latin Poems," 8.
[28] Cottrell, "An Introduction to La Boétie's Three Latin Poems," 8.

root "vir," man; the good that must be pursued ardently is cast in moral terms, and has implicitly to do with men and masculine pursuits. Virtue's adversary also shifts in La Boétie's retelling: from Κακία (Happiness or Vice) to *Voluptas*. Though this shift is subtle, it is significant: La Boétie's version of the parable suggests a Virtue that opposed carnal pleasure, but not happiness. And, as he sexualizes Κακία, he privileges Virtue in every way possible, and divorces her from any association with the flesh: Xenophon describes the physical attributes of both allegorical women; La Boétie does not write with any specificity of Virtue's physical attributes, for they are indescribable.[29] In Xenophon's version, Happiness calls out to young Hercules, who enters into dialogue with her, addressing her as "woman"; in La Boétie's version, only lofty Virtue speaks.

La Boétie vividly sets the scene of Hercules's lesson, personifying *Voluptas* as a "shameless old woman, painted with artificial colors" whose ruddy cheeks incite desire that is perhaps all too ready to be enticed.[30] Having described *Voluptas* in terms bordering on derisive, La Boétie stops short of telling us what Virtue says to offset the gaudy enticement proffered by *Voluptas*. Instead, he offers again a gesture of humility: he claims that he is not – nor indeed is any mortal – capable of *memorare*, recounting either Virtue's teaching or her beauty. Instead, he has personified Virtue speak for herself. The remaining third of the poem consists of a direct representation of Virtue's speech, in which she urges Hercules to flee the treacherous favors of the "lewd whore" and to shun indolent leisure.[31] Virtue holds out the promise of reward: she reminds Hercules of the monsters and tyrants he will vanquish with her aid.[32]

However, this direct speech offers merely a fiction of immediacy. Virtue's teaching is highly mediated, *memorata*: Virtue speaks to Montaigne through Hercules; she does so in Latin, in a verse epistle written by La Boétie addressed to Montaigne, and, in this incarnation,

---

[29] "Quis cultus almae, quis fuerit status/Virtuti et ori quis decus aureo,/nec tento mortalis nec ulli/fas fuerit memorare linguae," lines 41–4. (I, a mortal, do not attempt to describe/The teaching, the argument, the grace/Of nurturing Virtue's golden speech;/nor could any tongue describe it).

[30] "Anus impudens ... picta coloribus," lines 37–8, and "purpureo genae/fovent procacem vere Cupidinem," lines 33–4.

[31] "Effuge ... perfida munera," lines 49–50; "obscena paelex," line 49; and "inerti ... otio," line 53, respectively.

[32] "Monstra," line 58, and "tyranni," line 59. The choice of adversaries is not insignificant, given the subject of the *Discours de la servitude volontaire* and its exhortation against tyranny. In this retelling, Virtue is earnest and perhaps purposefully naïve: these are rewards that would be enticing to an adolescent, not necessarily to a grown man.

compiled in a collection of other letters of La Boétie and prefaced with a
dedicatory epistle by Montaigne addressed to Michel de L'Hôpital.[33]
Through multiple layers of ventriloquism, poem 3 couches its pedagogic
claims in gestures of humility and flattery as carefully as it situates its
writer and addressee as friends separated, at this moment, by different
pursuits, one cleaving to Virtue and the other not quite there. La Boétie's
repositionings, offering advice through the rhetorical device of personified, teaching Virtue, suggests the complicated nature of counsel: it must
be offered, but carefully, respecting differences in status and mindful of
authority and to whom it properly belongs. The moral instruction directed
toward Montaigne is never claimed by La Boétie, just as Montaigne is
never explicitly identified as in need of admonition.[34] Rather, the exhortation and gentle chiding take place at a remove, an epistolary distance
further attenuated by layers of allegory and translation. Poem 3 shows
how the verse epistle is ideally calibrated for advancing this kind of
project: its fixed positions allow for the communication of complicated
interpersonal relationships that must respect social status, alongside the
expression of learned friendship between peers. Its expressions of
humility, by now *de rigueur* in epistolary exchange, make possible the
delicate balancing act of offering advice that might not be welcome, while
allowing for vivid expressions of humility and praise between intellectual
peers who are also friends and bear the obligations of this relationship.
Perhaps most important, this verse epistle rehearses the virtuous discourse
between friends that is the hallmark of classical *amicitia*, and had come to
be identified with the ends of friendly exchange.

"Une Satyre Excellent": The Exaggerations of Gender and Genre

Poem 20, also titled "Ad Michaelem Montanum," offers a similarly
careful elaboration of the nature of friendship and counsel, but whereas
poem 3 begins with the writer's modest refusal of the role of teacher and
offer of moral instruction through personified Virtue and *Voluptas*, poem

---

[33] To add to the complications of these various re-positionings, it is worth pointing
out that, just as La Boétie represents Virtue's teaching, so too is her teaching recounted in
Xenophon's version: Virtue speaks through Aristippus, who gives an account of the tale to
Socrates, who also has Virtue and *Ἀρετή* engage in direct discourse with Hercules, reinforcing the truism that teaching operates best through parables.

[34] Montaigne echoes these lessons in "De l'Institution des enfants," in which he, in
turn, discusses how a tutor might lead his pupil to love Virtue; see Clark for a discussion
of how, for a mature Montaigne, "the traditional contest between 'vertu virile' and
'volupté' was something he had put behind him," 123.

20 begins with an unabashedly biographical celebration of the friendship between La Boétie and Montaigne:

> At nos iungit amor paulo magis annuus et qui
> Nil tamen ad summum reliqui sibi fecit amorem.
> Forte inconsulto. Sed nec fas dicere. Nec sit,
> Quamvis morose, sapiens, cum noverit ambos
> Et studia et mores, qui nostri inquirat in annos
> Foederis et tanto gratus non plaudat amori. (4–9)

> But in our case, even though we have been friends for only a
>   little more than a year,
> Our friendship has already reached a rare degree of perfection.
> Perhaps that was rash; but, not recognizing the divine origin of
>   our friendship,
> No perceptive man, however fastidious, knowing us both –
> Our interests and characters – would ever suspect that we have
>   known each other for so short a time;
> Nor would he fail to applaud generously a love as great as ours.

La Boétie dates the composition of this letter-poem to within a year of his meeting Montaigne, and he concedes the precipitancy of extolling exemplarity and even superlativeness on the slim evidence of one year.[35] Yet despite its unlikelihood, their "foedus" would not fail to garner praise, should men "noverit" its nature. *Foedus* is a favorite term of La Boétie's for describing his relationship with Montaigne. It means agreement, alliance, pact; by extension, it can signify treaty, law. La Boétie's use of "foedus" to describe their friendship encompasses these multiple connotations: it is volitional and yet has the compulsory force of law; it is a private matter between two and an entity to be respected by others – and one of the duties of this verse epistle is to make sure that it is.

While this verse epistle extols the virtue of their friendship, its praise is juxtaposed with at times explicit references to unvirtuous love relations between men and women. As preparation for his derisive portrayal of unvirtuous heterosexual coupling, La Boétie borrows a metaphor from the plant world to describe his friendship with Montaigne. He compares their friendship to the grafting of similar kinds of fruit trees, which take successfully when like is grafted onto like, "obeying nature's secret laws" ("occulto naturae foedere").[36] A specific form of vegetal generation is

---

[35] Montaigne also expounds on this worthiness despite youth in his letter to Michel de l'Hôpital, signaling the importance to both friends of establishing credibility on this count.

[36] Line 16. The use of the horticultural metaphor in this hortatory missive echoes

invoked here for its metaphoric value: just as plant grafts take only when stock and scion are compatible, friendship succeeds only when the two grafted parts, that is, friends, are compatible. Significantly, the term "foedus" is used to describe the inevitable force that governs the natural world and also relations between men.

The metaphor of grafting for the creation of friendship, while decidedly physical, is also noticeably non-procreative, thereby avoiding the idea of reproduction and its associative human corollary of sexual activity. This avoidance would seem appropriate and perhaps even expedient for describing close friendship between men in this period; Montaigne takes care to condemn "that ancient Greek vice" in his discussion of (male) friendship. And yet, while the non-procreative nature of this metaphor is useful for avoiding connotations of heterosexual coupling, it does not exclude associations with another kind of non-procreative coupling: that of same-sex sex. Thus even as the grafting metaphor seems to avoid one nexus of potentially unfavorable associations, it cannot avoid another, suggesting a fundamental difficulty in conceptualizing same-sex friendship in a climate hostile to same-sex sexual relations: while it is not procreative, it is propagative. Something new *is* made, a friendship, and yet it must be attempted, at least, to claim it as a licit – that is, non-sexual – relationship.[37] While the complications of a biological metaphor for male friendship are clear, its usefulness seems to lie in its inevitability: the mechanism of grafting is governed by a natural force, an "occulto foedere" that metaphorically describes the "foedus" that governs friendship.[38] And, while the laws governing the success of friendship are, within the logic of the graft metaphor, "occulto," their existence is, as in the plant world, deducible through observation, and La Boétie offers up the specimen of his friendship with Montaigne for this scrutiny.[39]

Seneca's letter to Lucilius, in which the planting of olive trees is something veterans ought to undertake for the benefit of posterity.

[37] See Stone for an examination of the influence of pederastic friendship and procreancy in Plato's *Symposium* on Montaigne.

[38] On the perhaps inevitable speculations about the nature of the relationship between Montaigne and La Boétie, Stone observes: "To be sure, from time to time [De l'Amitié'] has been cited as evidence that Montaigne and La Boétie were homosexual lovers, but this assertion has never won broad support," 25; see also Schachter on speculations about the nature of their relationship.

[39] In a way, La Boétie sets an example for Montaigne's *Essais*, where he offers himself as an object of scrutiny – his own as well as ours. Gray observes that this is not, however, to be mistaken for autobiography: "Montaigne is never the object or the subject

"Foedus," however, can also mean "law," and "alliance, compact, agreement," as it clearly does when La Boétie boasts about the duration of their friendship, "annos foederis."[40] La Boétie explains the basis for a man-made "foedus":

> Te, Montane, mihi casus sociavit in omnes
> et natura potens et amoris gratior illex
> virtus. Illa animum spectata cupidine formae
> ducit inexpletum. Nec vis praesentior ulla
> conciliatque viros et pulchro incendit amore. (23–7)

> You, Montaigne, have been bound to me once and for all
> By natural instinct and a love of virtue, which is the greatest
>   charm
> Of friendship. The sight of virtue arouses in the unfulfilled soul
> A desire for beauty; no other force unites men so effectively,
> Nor kindles in them such a noble love.

"Foedus" does double duty in this poem: it describes the secret workings of nature, and it also describes a pact made between La Boétie and Montaigne. It is driven by a natural force, and a shared love of virtue.[41] In poem 3, the relationship between friendship and virtue is one of obligation: a friend must help his friend cleave to virtue, and if he can't do it alone, he must enlist the aid of rousing rhetoric, classical mythology, and allegorical personifications in carefully couched epistolary discourse. In poem 20, virtue is once more a significant factor in friendship, but in a much more elemental and compelling way: it is a unifying force and perhaps even the source of friendship: shared love of it binds men together. As La Boétie describes it, virtue is the medium of their friendship, whose active cultivation exerts obligations on friends, and whose force ("vis") acts as a mysterious binding compulsion. The metaphor is so compelling that it occludes the fact that *letters*, in fact, are the chief medium of this friendship, for it is in letters that its affections and alliances are declared and its obligations met.

Having established shared love of virtue as the motivating force of their friendship – and, by extension, of all friendships – La Boétie humbly concedes his own inferiority in its pursuit:

of the *Essais*; his presence, resolutely peripheral, is essentially that of a writer positioning and situating himself in relation to the question, quotation, or theme he is in the process of exploring," 15.

[40] He describes his friendship with Montaigne as being a little over a year old ("paulo magis annuus"), line 4.

[41] "Natura potens," line 24.

> Ipse ego virtuti vix ulli affinis et impar
> Officiis, tamen hanc fugientem impensius ultro
> Insequor atque ubivis visam complector amoque (28–30).

> I myself have scarcely any aptitude for virtue, and am unequal
> To her high service; yet I pursue her devotedly as she ever flees,
> And whenever I find her, I embrace her and love her.

Once again, virtue is personified, and this time La Boétie capitalizes on the female gender of virtue: employing a vocabulary of romantic and even courtly love, he writes of his devoted pursuit, and employs a physical register in his praise of virtue: he embraces and loves her. Having modeled devotion to virtue, he then observes guardedly that

> At tibi certamen maius, quem scimus amici
> nobilibus vitiis habilem et virtutibus aeque (37–8).

> But as for you, you are engaged in a loftier struggle. Your friends
>   know that
> Your errors as well as your strengths spring from greatness.

Risking seeming to criticize his friend, his younger by three years, La Boétie then appeasingly praises Montaigne's qualities and situates himself among his supporters. Moreover, he assures that

> … At virtus cum se firmaverit aevo,
> Tum poteris (nec fallit amor) contendere summis (41–2).

> … but once your virtue is matured and strengthened by age,
> Then – and my love does not blind me – you will be able to vie
>   with the greatest.

La Boétie is careful to identify the virtue Montaigne already possesses, and his potential to ultimately triumph over youthful weakness.[42] As an additional mollifying element, he writes of his great love for Montaigne, which is strong enough to risk clouding judgment. Noticeably, La Boétie never directly admonishes his friend as in need of instruction. Rather, he implies it through following these ambiguous statements with invocations of the teacher-student relationship, and, as he does in poem 3, offering instruction through the words of another.

   In this poem, as in poem 3, La Boétie again offers a scene of youth faced with a life-determining moral choice. He presents Socrates describ-

---

[42] This is praise that Montaigne will echo of La Boétie: that his writing held the promise of greatness to come with maturity and age.

ing Alcibiades in the Hercules position, at the junction between good and
evil and in need of guidance.[43] He then offers a dialogue between an
anonymous advice-giver and a youth cleaving to pleasure:

> ... Acerbus
> si iurgem ut patruus, frustra hunc fortassis et ipsum
> me cruciem: ludam vacuus blandisque ferocem
> aggrediar melius. Quod si nihil maius, at illum
> tantisper potero pronum ad peiora morari. (71–5)

> ... If I reprove him
> With severity, it would probably just upset both of us,
> And do no good anyway. I'll just mention it jokingly, for a casual
>   remark
> Is more likely to disarm the headstrong boy. If nothing else,
> I'll succeed, at least temporarily, in preventing him from slipping
> further into vice.

As a first-person narrator apostrophizes to an imaginary third interlocutor or perhaps aloud to himself, La Boétie again offers words that are
literally addressed to Montaigne, but seemingly directed at another, as if
to mollify the positions of relative inequality suggested by pedagogy.
What follows is a sometimes explicit exploration of various vices –
chiefly, physical love with women, and more specifically, with married
women and prostitutes.[44] The narrator focuses on that which most interests the youth: illicit and carnal relations, and their always deleterious and
even disastrous consequences. He explores these consequences in detail,
including descriptions of entanglements with crafty serving-girls; competition with "muscular stableboys" and house slaves "filthy with horse
manure from the stables"; and having to hide from jealous husbands in
baskets, terrified and crouching on all fours.[45] There is even a reference
to "purulent ulcers" and "the notorious plague the Italians call the French
disease."[46] La Boétie spends nearly half of this verse epistle in the vivid

---

[43] "Pravique bonique," line 49; "pravus" carries a perverse charge, and the narrator
takes the boy to task for cleaving to unseemly pleasures: "Quisuis erit, dubium virtuti
adducere conor" (At present he is vacillating between the two, and I am trying to guide
him to virtue), line 50.

[44] "Meretrici," line 87; "moechae," line 227.

[45] "Servae," line 94; "durus agaso," line 162, "verna ... increvit stabulis et pulvere
sordet equino," lines 152–3; "cumera aut pavidum et spirare timentem/quadrupedem
angusta componet fervida capsa," lines 181–2.

[46] "Ulcere putri," line 257; "nota lues, Italis si credis, Gallica," line 253; he adds,
humorously, "et nomenque et rem Italiae concedimus aequi" (We can just as fairly
concede both the name and the disease to Italy), line 254.

and at times graphic exploration of the pleasures and swiftly following harms of sexual contact with women. The examples he raises are ridiculous, bawdy, explicit, and deeply misogynist.

Having enumerated in some detail the various amorous and sexual temptations that lead men to ruin, La Boétie draws this didactic verse epistle to a close with a series of rhetorical questions:

> Unde igitur miseris iucunde vivere? Quidve
> constanter pureque dabit gaudere? Nihilne est
> tristia quod vitae permixtum condiat? (301–3)

> How then can wretched humans live happily? Can anything
> provide them with a joy that is constant and pure? Is there
>   nothing
> That can be mixed with life's sorrows to mitigate them?

With these questions, La Boétie universalizes the youth's attraction to harmful vices and, rhetorically at least, identifies with them. He makes the search for satisfaction in vice not so much a result of personal moral failure, as a function of humanity's lack of access to pure and constant joys. He then provides a rhetorically equivocal answer to these questions:

> Aut nihil est felix usquam aut praestare beatum
> sola potest virtus ... (308–9)

> Either there is no such thing as happiness, or virtue alone is able
> To make us happy ...

The teacher-friend-interlocutor returns to the terms with which he began this entertaining lesson. Having opened his verse epistle praising the shared love of virtue that bound him to Montaigne in friendship, he concludes with praise for the virtue that will alone bring happiness to human beings. Thus, friendship between these correspondents is triangulated through the figure of Virtue, suggesting an intimacy that is necessarily mediated.

There is another figure through which this friendship is mediated: woman. Montaigne describes this verse epistle as "une Satyre Latine excellente" in his dedicatory letter to Michel de l'Hôpital, and it certainly relies on the operations of satire and its exaggerated positions in its ridiculing of vices and follies.[47] However, despite the vividness of this

---

[47] Montaigne calls it "une Satyre Latine excellente, qui est publiée, par laquelle il excuse et explique la precipitation de nostre intelligence, si promptement parvenue a sa perfection" (an excellent Latin satire, which is published, in which he excuses and

ridicule, virtue and vice are abstractions; La Boétie makes the lesson concrete with reference to women. His injunctions to virtue, while replete with allusions to well-known classical texts and figures, are noticeably dependent on the invocation of eros and the operations of misogyny. Knowing the youth's interest in the carnal, his interlocutor indulges its discussion – not all the passages discuss purulent ulcers. There is a pleasure in hearing – and in recounting – titillating tales, making this a perhaps problematic pedagogy. However, he is careful to immediately counteract the arousing effects inspired by talk of sex and seduction. For example, one passage vividly imagines the youth in the carnal act:

> Tandem magnanimus thalamum expugnabis adulter
> et iunges niveo lateri latus ... (149–50)

> At last, you, the brave adulterer, will take the master bedroom by
> storm.
> You will press your flesh to her snow-white body ...

This visualization is immediately followed by a taunt:

> ... Hoc quoties et
> quanto commodius fecit nulloque periclo
> Verna prior? (150–2)

> ... But how much more often,
> And with greater ease and safety, has not a house slave
> Done the same thing?

In the very same line, the visualization of the scene of sexual enjoyment is chased by a taunt, in which the narrator raises both the specter of amorous competition and the unworthiness of competing with social inferiors.[48] He rhetorically fans the flames of youthful ardor and casts cold water on amorous projects with detailed and often caustic depictions of things that go wrong in love affairs.

His narrative technique, however skilled at offering negative exempla

---

explains the rapid nature of our understanding, so quickly arrived at its perfection), 188. In his introduction to the *Essais*, Villey describes satire as a "sorte de discours familier"; Hirstein expands, identifying among the elements that qualify Poem 20 as satire its "relaxed structure, abrupt transitions, dialogues spoken by imaginary interlocutors" and "diatribe," whose goal is ridicule in order to provoke change; he also discusses the poem's classical references: 48–50.

[48] Hoffmann observes that "La Boétie's Horatian satire ... analyzes, over-solicitously, Montaigne's promiscuity by borrowing political terms of 'servitude' from the *Discours*" in "Montaigne's Nudes," 130.

in amusing, attention-grabbing juxtapositions, is predicated on a deeply ingrained misogyny. The sexually suggestive injunctions against *voluptas* operate at the cost of licit, non-harmful sexual relations with women – every woman is crafty, a tease, out to get something; prostitutes are merely better at it than other women.[49] This focus is, presumably, the result of the narrator's professed choice to write only about illicit relations, as these are the ones that most interest the youth. However, just as eros invoked resonates, so too does misogyny, regardless of the uses to which each is ostensibly put. In the imaginative universe evoked by this letter-poem, the only virtuous relationship is same-sex, sexless friendship.

There *is* a brief mention of the one relationship with women that is not pernicious: marriage. It is discussed in four lines; its "most pleasant pledge is children,"[50] and the closest the narrator comes to describing physical love in marriage is in decorously hushed tones:

> te iura vocent ad iusti foedera lecti,
> invitet natura (212–13)

> laws call you, nature urges you,
> to the bonds of a lawful bridal bed (translation modified)[51]

---

[49] One passage details the comparative skills of prostitutes and adulteresses; the prostitute

> ... est doctior. Usus
> plus habet et locat insidias instructius. Angit
> callidius curasque ciet mollitque calentem
> et regit et multa veteratrix temperat arte. (234–7)

> ... is more skilled; she has had more
> Experience and sets her traps more expertly; she is better
> At riveting the yoke; she causes turmoil and assuages desire;
> The crafty girl commands and governs with consummate art.

[50] "Gratissima pignora," 215.

[51] The narrator briefly praises marriage as sanctioned by both nature and society:

> Cum te iura vocent ad iusti foedera lecti,
> invitet natura parens et praemia ponat
> libera – cum primis et duri pura laboris
> gaudia, tum dulces, gratissima pignora, natos –
> tu tamen his demens quaeris peccare relictis,
> Legibus infensus naturae disque tibique (212–17)

> Although the laws encourage you to accept the solemn bond of a
>   legitimate marriage bed,
> As does mother nature, whose greater rewards
> Are free (foremost among them being the pure joys of hard
> Work and then, better yet, loving children, the most pleasant pledge
>   of marriage),
> You, nevertheless, are mad enough to abandon all that and to offend
> The laws of nature, the gods, and yourself.

The irresistible call of *foedus* recurs here, and recalls the "foedus" used to describe the one relationship that *is* unequivocally lauded in the text: the friendship between Montaigne and La Boétie. In both cases, the operations of the "foedus" are occluded but its force is undeniable and, moreover, authorized by nature. By contrast, the marital relationship is, of all the relationships described in the letter-poem, governed not only by nature but also society: "iura vocent." Moreover, it is the relationship that redeems women from their association with lewd Κακία. This makes it all the more noticeable that it is also the relationship that gets short shrift, sketched in a cursory four lines.[52]

While the text maintains reticence about the "foedus" of the marriage bed, it is also silent about how, exactly, to pursue Virtue and resist *Voluptas*, despite describing at length the importance of avoiding it. What it does offer is a model of what friends can do to encourage this pursuit and resistance: offer negative exempla, take up extreme rhetorical positions, and indulge in ribald imagery – at the expense of women – all in a literary genre that celebrates mutual facility with and love of letters. La Boétie thus participates in a long tradition of learned friendship cultivated through letters, which saw a flowering in France in the twelfth century in the monastic tradition and expanded through several centuries to thoroughly permeate literary production. As a good humanist, he would have been familiar with letter-writing conventions advanced by the medieval *ars dictaminis*, the discipline of letter writing, in which the five-part structure seems to have been one of its most enduring teachings. Here, La Boétie collapses the petition and the conclusion into a mutual exhortation. Having proclaimed that virtue "alone possesses what is necessary for happiness,"[53] he closes the verse epistle on an urgent note:

> O mihi si liceat tantos decerpere fructus,
> Si liceat, Montane, tibi! Experiamur uterque.
> Quod ni habitis potiemur, at immoriamur habendis! (320–2)

> O that I may gather such fruit,
> And may you also, Montaigne! Let both of us try.
> If we are not able to reach it now, may we at least die in the
>   attempt.

---

[52] The argument could be made that this reticence is decorous, but since women receive a nearly total calumniation in this poem in the tradition of most virulent medieval misogynists, their oblique recuperation in four lines seems perfunctory at best.

[53] "Sola haec quo gaudeat in se/semper habet," lines 309–10.

Swiftly shifting register from ridiculing satire to earnest mutual exhortation, La Boétie explicitly identifies with his addressee and declares the pursuit of virtue a mutual goal, rhetorically rolling over the objections posed by the figure of the desiring youth, and leveling the positions of inequality implied by pedagogy. This verse epistle claims love of virtue as a force that binds individuals together in friendship, posits the cultivation of virtue as its shared goal, and suggests succor in achieving this goal as its most compelling obligation.

Dutifully carrying out his obligation to friendship, La Boétie offers assistance to Montaigne through writing. His choice of the learned Latin verse epistle reinforces their shared love of letters, and situates himself and his addressee as educated humanists who cultivate friendship through letters. His careful counsel is couched in a medium calculated to bring pleasure: this is not a treatise, or a discourse, on virtue. It is a letter written to a friend, composed in verse, referencing figures of pagan mythology, and evoking bawdy images certain to provoke amusement. Moreover, it is written in Latin, the language of high-minded intellectual endeavors. La Boétie proves the point that there can be pleasure in the pursuit of virtue. Noticeably, however, virtue is cultivated here through the careful discursive exploration of that which threatens it: *Voluptas*, figured explicitly as heterosexual sexual enjoyment.

To refer back to the medieval traditions that inform these sixteenth-century writings, it is striking that the learned Latin verse epistle, and a very studied deployment of eros, both figure in medieval and early modern articulations of male friendship. This demonstrates one way in which early modern literary culture was quite medieval. Yet La Boétie's employment of eros differs from that of Baudri and his correspondents in important ways. In writing of the pedagogy of the Loire poets, Stephen Jaeger observes that eros invoked in the teacher-student relationship circulates but never comes to fruition. In La Boétie's hands, eros is deliberately and even explicitly invoked, and is carefully corralled into an explicit teaching: fleshly pleasure is indeed titillating, and it is also disastrous. It leads to illness, ridicule, and distraction from loftier pursuits. It even poisons the mind.[54]

La Boétie's Latin verse epistles addressed to Montaigne articulate a friendship in which offering counsel is an obligation, whether the virtue threatened is that of the polity or of individual men risking sexual folly.

---

[54] Love is described as a "furor" throwing everything into confusion that can even lead to madness; lines 109–20.

This counsel is offered in ways that carefully avoid claims of superiority and the inequalities of position often suggested by pedagogy. Moreover, it employs misogyny as a tool in cultivating friendship: misogyny is deployed to describe threats to virtue that friendship must seek to dissolve. In poem 3, misogyny takes the form of sexualizing and gendering vice, appropriating the tale of Hercules at the crossroads and recasting Virtue and Happiness/Vice as Virtue and *Voluptas*, personifying *Voluptas* as a "decrepit whore." Poem 20 describes the threats to virtue, and, by extension, friendship, as sexual dangers presented by mortal women. Women's wiles are figured as the common enemy that binds them in a common pursuit: the pursuit of virtue.

These verse epistles articulate a structure of friendship in which the invocation and appropriate management of desire – through suggestive and explicit invocations of sex, highly stylized and learned ridicule, and unqualified misogyny – is a necessary bond of friendship. How exactly individuals are drawn together in friendship might well be a "foedus occultus," but not all of the operations of friendship need be hidden: in poem 20, La Boétie offers a model for how friendship might manage the threats posed to its existence: through explicit, rhetorical exploration of these threats that seemingly defuses them of their force through ridicule. That male friendship is predicated on the exclusion of women, expressed in a sometimes heated misogynist rhetoric, is not a surprise. What is perhaps unexpected is the critical role played by letters in articulating this relationship: letters structure its amical and misogynist expression. They provide the established vocabulary and interpersonal positions of epistolary convention with its requisite observation of respective social status, and the dynamics of learned *amicitia* with its attendant obligation to cultivate virtue. Misogynist positions are easily and convincingly voiced through these positions, and become conflated with them. Thus La Boétie's letter-poems define friendship as learned, humanist, necessarily gendered, misogynist, and above all, epistolary.

Sermo Absentium: Montaigne, La Boétie, and Life After Death

As Montaigne famously reports in "De l'Amitié," his friendship with La Boétie begins with an act of textual circulation. Before their first meeting, and before Montaigne had even heard of La Boétie, he was shown a copy of the *Discours de la servitude volontaire*:

> Et si suis obligé particulierement à cette piece, d'autant qu'elle a servy
> de moyen à nostre premiere accointance. Car elle me fut montrée

longue piece avant que je l'eusse veu, et me donna la premiere connoissance de son nom, acheminant ainsi cette amitié que nous avons nourrie, tant que Dieu a voulu, entre nous, si entiere et si parfaite que certainement il ne s'en lit guiere de pareilles, et, entre nos hommes, il ne s'en voit aucune trace en usage. Il faut tant de rencontres à la bastir, que c'est beaucoup si la fortune y arrive une fois en trois siècles (184)

And I am particularly obliged to this work, as it served as the medium of our first acquaintance. For it was shown to me long before I had seen him, and it gave me my first knowledge of his name, leading thus to this friendship that we have nourished, for as long as God was willing, between us, so whole and so perfect that certainly one hardly reads of its like, and, between us, one hardly sees any trace of it in practice. So many encounters are needed to build it, that it is a lot if Fortune manages to do so once in three centuries.

This autobiographical description of a rather ordinary event – Montaigne's being shown a piece of writing – swiftly takes on tones bordering on courtly, reminiscent of medieval romances in which love is inspired from afar by images and reputations. In Montaigne's case, love between friends is inspired by a book: the circulation of La Boétie's book is a catalyst, and is directly responsible for starting this perfect friendship. Throughout the rest of his career, Montaigne continues this textual circulation of La Boétie's writing, with each act of circulation reinforcing this originary act, and his privileged position as La Boétie's friend. However, each successive circulation set into motion by Montaigne is, significantly, accompanied by an epistolary text of Montaigne's own, creating a missive-writing practice reminiscent of Christine de Pizan's work with the *querelle* letters, but to distinctly different purpose.[55]

Montaigne's textualization and circulation of his friendship with La Boétie has an established history by 1580, the date of the first publication of "De l'Amitié" in his *Essais*. It is inspired by La Boétie's *Discours*, which moves Montaigne to seek friendship with him; La Boétie writes his verse epistles addressed to Montaigne a little over a year after they actually meet and become friends; several years after La Boétie's death, Montaigne dedicates La Boétie's *Poemata* to Michel de l'Hôpital and publishes his French and Latin verse; and within the decade Montaigne publishes "De l'Amitié" in the first edition of his *Essais*. Their friendship

---

[55] As Schaeffer remarks, "the author of the dedication necessarily presented himself as well," 216. However, Montaigne does more than present himself while he presents La Boétie; he blurs the distinction between his two roles – friend and publisher.

thus undergoes several stages of textual representation, instigated by La
Boétie's youthful writings, and strategically deployed by Montaigne,
beginning with the dedication and circulation of the *Poemata* in 1571.[56]

As Christine de Pizan compiled, sent, and resent the *querelle* letters,
Montaigne also circulates the letters addressed to him from La Boétie,
sending them to other readers. However, while Pizan's missive projects
formed part of a strategy to garner authority and support, Montaigne's
resending of the letters La Boétie wrote to him – as well as letters he
writes to various others – operates on a different register, and the treatment of friendship in the verse-epistles, their recirculation, and
Montaigne's writing heralds the development of a new means of personal
expression: the essay. I am not suggesting that the epistle directly leads to
the invention of the essay; rather, my reading of the La Boétie–Montaigne
exchange shows how, by the sixteenth century, the letter, carrying the
weight of centuries of prescription and convention developed throughout
the Middle Ages, continues to offer ways to express and enact complicated and at times seemingly contradictory interpersonal dynamics.
However, the letter also has its limits; and, within the structure of friendship articulated by these two friends, generic innovation can be seen as a
response to the ossification of medieval epistolary forms, producing new
forms of writing that have at their heart the missive and performative
functions of medieval letters.[57]

Dedicating La Boétie I: The Power of the Friend

In 1570, several years after La Boétie's death, Montaigne addressed some
of his friend's verses, along with a dedicatory letter, to Michel de
l'Hôpital, the Chancellor of Paris. Whereas the addressees of La Boétie's

---

[56] In fact, Montaigne had a quite developed publication plan for La Boétie's writings.
He intended to publish La Boétie's more well-known *Discours de la servitude volontaire*
at the center of his *Essais*, but decided against it because of "those who seek to disturb the
state of our government without worry whether they will improve it" ("De l'Amitié").
Instead, he published twenty-nine love sonnets by La Boétie. His intention to grant his
friend's writing a central place of honor in his own text was thwarted by the seditious
activities of reformists circulating unauthorized and perhaps altered versions of the
Discours to further their cause. It is curious that Montaigne did not choose to set the
record straight with a corrected version, as so many of the letter writers examined in this
book have attempted to do. Rather, his decision seems protectionist: of the fragile state of
France, and of the reputation of his friend's work.

[57] As did the essay; Hoffmann argues in *Montaigne's Career* that material constraints
in publishing might have affected the third edition of the *Essais*, which was the first to
offer the essays in the three-volume form in which we know them today.

"Ad Belotium et Montanum" create a tripartite friendship of concerned citizens, Montaigne's dedicatee is identified in the very first line as someone who does not merely respond to civic unrest, he has an important role to play in its rectification: he is among those "à qui la fortune et la raison ont mis en main le gouvernement des affaires du monde" (in whose hands fortune and reason have placed the governing of the affairs of the world).[58] Neatly collapsing the *salutatio* and *captatio benevolentiae* by thus identifying his addressee, Montaigne proceeds to enumerate what might be considered the varied reasons for which L'Hôpital has been singled out for receipt of La Boétie's Latin verses. The first of these is that men who govern seek to understand the nature of those in their charge, and, presumably, La Boétie's writings will give L'Hôpital a better understanding of human nature. Perhaps contradictorily, Montaigne follows this justification with a description of La Boétie's many merits and the superlativity of his personal qualities: La Boétie was no common man, but an exemplary one.

In extolling La Boétie's virtues, Montaigne emphasizes his modesty: "il a esté si nonchalant de se pousser soy mesme en lumiere, comme de malheur la vertu et l'ambition ne logent gueres ensemble" (he was so careless of pushing himself into the light, as, unfortunately, virtue and ambition seldom lodge together) (54). This praise of La Boétie justifies Montaigne's recirculating his friend's writing. In fact this circulation is his obligation as friend:

> ie souhaitte merveilleusement que, au moins apres luy, sa memoire, à qui seule meshuy ie dois les offices de nostre amitié, recoive le loyer de sa valeur, et qu'elle se loge en la recommandation des personnes d'honneur et de vertu (54)

> I wish particularly that, at least after him his memory, to which alone now I owe the obligations of our friendship, receive the praise of his virtue, and that it be lodged in the recommendation of persons of honor and virtue.

Having dispensed with the perhaps perfunctory invocation of civic duty, Montaigne arrives at the heart of the matter: to garner praise for La Boétie, a duty he owes to his departed friend.[59] While it was not

---

[58] *Œuvres completes d'Estienne de la Boétie*, ed. Desgraves, vol. 2, 53. All citations to this letter are from this edition.

[59] Montaigne reports that, in one of his last lucid moments, La Boétie reproached him: "My brother, my brother, do *you* refuse me a place?" Much has been made of this

uncommon that dedicatory epistles introduced works of humanistic contemporaries, Montaigne introduces the work of a recently dead author, and his desire for this dedication is motivated as much by personal obligation as by the merit of the author and his writing.[60]

The choice of L'Hôpital as the dedicatee of "ce peu de Vers Latin qui nous restent de luy" is not accidental. As Desgraves points out, Montaigne considered him among the best Latin poets of the day.[61] L'Hôpital was no stranger to missive writings; like many humanists, he participated in the culture of dedicating poems.[62] Neither was L'Hôpital a stranger to La Boétie; La Boétie reported advice given by L'Hôpital to the Bordeaux Parliament on the handling of religious strife.[63] And, pressing the advantage of his first-hand knowledge of La Boétie, Montaigne suggests that La Boétie admired L'Hôpital and desired his friendship. Urging L'Hôpital to read his friend's verse, Montaigne suggests that he might "monter par ce sien ouvrage à la cognoissance de luy mesme, et en aymer et embrasser par consequent le nom et la memoire" (arrive by this work of his at an understanding of him and for it to love in consequence his name and his memory) (54–5). That is, by reading his writing, L'Hôpital will come to love La Boétie. Not only will he approve and admire these writings and by extension La Boétie, he will also achieve after death that which he did not accomplish during La Boétie's lifetime, for by reading and admiring La Boétie,

> vous ne ferez que rendre la pareille à l'opinion tresresoluë qu'il avoit de votre vertu, et si accomplirez ce qu'il a infiniment souhaité pendant sa

deathbed request; see Greenblatt for an interpretation of this demand and Montaigne's response.

[60] Schaeffer discusses the generic criteria for dedicated works: "The work itself, a literary production within that very broad definition of literature employed in the early sixteenth century ... might have been a classic of antiquity or a work of the Latin Middle Ages, a new discovery or at least a new edition or perhaps a translation within the practice of rendering Greek works and those originally written in the various vernaculars into Latin. It could also have been the work of a humanistic contemporary, previously known or even introduced for the first time, or even the author's own work presented by himself," 216–17. Although his study treats early sixteenth-century Germany, the general principles he outlines are relevant for an understanding of dedicatory epistles in France in this period, given the nature of humanist enterprises that often transcended national boundaries.

[61] Desgraves asserts that Montaigne "rendait hommage à celui qu'il regardait comme un des meilleurs poètes latins de son temps," vol. 1, 87 n. 1.

[62] Most notably to Pierre du Chastel; see Michel de L'Hôpital, Œuvres complètes, ed. Dufey, 3: 99–109, 517, cited in Smith, 35 n. 15.

[63] Smith, 39 n. 25; citing La Boétie, Œuvres complètes, ed. Bonnefon, xxiii–xxiv.

vie: car il n'estoit homme du monde en la cognoissance et amitié
duquel il se fust plus volontiers veu logé que en la vostre (55)

you will but render the same to the very firm opinion that he had of
your virtue, and so you will accomplish that which he infinitely wished
during his life: for there was not a man in the world in whose acquaintance and friendship he would not have been more willingly lodged than
in yours.

In short, Montaigne claims that L'Hôpital can become friends with La
Boétie by reading his works. A nexus of Montaigne's concerns is
reinforced in this dedicatory epistle: the relationship between writing and
the self; the importance of virtue in the seeking of friends; and the
accomplishment of friendship through the written word: friendship that
can be gained through reading and writing.[64] And, once again, this is a
triangulated friendship: it is effected through Montaigne's dedicatory
letter, making Montaigne at once a friend promising exclusive access,
and a middleman, broker to a friendship with an esteemed, though dead,
writer.

This dedicatory epistle addressed to L'Hôpital performs a positioning
function in its observation of social status that is central to medieval and
early modern letters. Medieval letters, as we have seen, take pains to
recognize the respective social status of sender and addressee. Here, the
positioning is triangulated: La Boétie is a man who merits greater celebration than he received in his lifetime. His writing is sent to L'Hôpital,
situating the addressee as a man of authority and learning and an arbiter
of taste, and therefore an appropriate reader of La Boétie's writing. And
the dedicatee stands in, of course, for a wider reading public.[65]
Montaigne's role is thus that of sender, but also negotiator, one who
brings together great minds. He is privileged to do so because of his
access to the addressee and, most important, because of his close friendship with the man whose writings are addressed. Montaigne thus manipu-
lates the very medieval expectation of social positioning through letters,
offering new ways to position writers and readers, and creating new kinds
of epistolary relationships.

---

[64] He also repeats the plant imagery initiated by La Boétie: "le vray suc et moëlle de
sa valeur l'ont suivi, et ne nous en est demeuré que l'escorce et les feuilles" (the true sap
and marrow of his worth followed him, and we have left only the bark and the leaves), 54.

[65] Schaeffer corroborates: "it was always the writer of the dedication who acted as
intermediary between the work and its destined recipient, simultaneously the addressee of
the dedication and the reading public at large," 217.

Although it receives slight mention in this letter, it is nonetheless significant that Montaigne represents as an obligation of friendship the rendering of due renown, an element lacking from La Boétie's portrait of friendship. In La Boétie's verse epistles, the obligation of friendship is moral: friends help friends cleave to virtue. For Montaigne, perhaps as a function of circumstance – his friend is no longer alive – the obligation to garner praise for his friend serves a way to continue practicing this friendship, textually. Montaigne suggests that L'Hôpital, too, can accomplish friendship with La Boétie textually – simply by reading his writing. He demonstrates his own continued practice of this kind of friendship through circulating his friend's writing, with each act of circulation increasing his friend's readership and acclaim, and affirming his own privileged role as friend and promoter.[66]

Montaigne seems aware, however, of the potential awkwardness of his position as promoter of a dead man's reputation and writing.[67] He explains,

> Mais si quelqu'un se scandalise de quoy si hardiment i'use des choses d'autruy, ie l'advise qu'il ne fut jamais rien plus exactement dict ne escript aux escholes des Philosophes du droit et des devoirs de la saincte amitié que ce que ce personnage et moy en avons prattiqué ensemble. (55)

> But if someone is scandalized that I so boldly use the things of another, I advise them that there was never anything more exactly said nor written in schools of Philosophers of law and duty and holy friendship than that which this person and I practiced together.

He acknowledges that the posthumous circulation of La Boétie's writings, in some cases perhaps not intended for wider readership, might be taken amiss as a bold gesture.[68] However, this license is justified not only because of their friendship, but also because it is superlative. They were exemplary friends, who embodied the best ideals of friendship. Here we

---

[66] Rigolot considers this circulation as a response to La Boétie's impassioned plea that Montaigne render him his "place" in the world.

[67] On the politics of literary legacies, see Descimon.

[68] Montaigne laments that there remains nothing of the fruit of his friend's studies – perhaps conveniently forgetting the *Discours* and the *Memoire sur la pacification des troubles*; given L'Hôpital's status as "fallen statesman," he dedicated to him lighter works, "ce que, par maniere de passetemps, il escrivoit quelquefois" (that which, by way of past-time, he wrote sometimes), *Œuvres completes d'Estienne de la Boétie*, ed. Desgraves, vol. 1, 54.

see a shift, however subtle, from praise of La Boétie, to praise of his friendship with Montaigne. Moreover, this defense occludes what might seem the greater license: the fact that the circulation of La Boétie's texts after his death is always accompanied by Montaigne's texts, and his framing of their friendship.

As discussed in earlier chapters, the primary functions of medieval letters are often considered to be the salutation, registering relative social status, and the petition, containing the request the letter was written to make. The petition in a dedicatory letter is in some ways merely phatic: that the addressee receive the accompanying materials is a request as purely rhetorical as it gets, since reception of the letter would usually imply reception of the accompanying materials. Of course, a dedicatory letter can be more than a cover letter accompanying other materials, as I examined in my discussion of Christine de Pizan's dedicatory missives. In addition to announcing the arrival of enclosed writings, it can also entreat that the addressee read it and fashion a judgment of it in the way desired by the writer: that is, it can position the addressee's reading. Montaigne's dedicatory letter claims La Boétie as his friend, and it also claims L'Hôpital as his reader – a reader of La Boétie's writing, certainly, but also of Montaigne's dedication and his presentation of La Boétie's writing. The positioning of these three men (writer, dedicatee, dedicated author) seems to be the chief function of this letter. And, despite the identification of L'Hôpital as an important player in governing the affairs of the word, by this date he had already fallen out of royal and public favor and was living in seclusion. To take the dedicatory letter at its word is to read it as an appeal to a powerful prospective friend. Considering it in context suggests a different reading: it implicitly criticizes L'Hôpital for not having recognized La Boétie's worth and promoted him to a position of greater responsibility when he was at the peak of his influence, and it suggests that L'Hôpital's appearance as a dedicatee is primarily symbolic. Most important, it reinforces that the relationship that is most privileged in this dedicatory epistle is the friendship between La Boétie and Montaigne.

Dedicating La Boétie II: The Difference of Gender

The accompaniment of the *Poemata* by a dedicatory letter to Michel de L'Hôpital throws into sharp relief Montaigne's and La Boétie's compositional choices. Montaigne wrote of their friendship in French and in prose; La Boétie, adept in both prose and verse, chose Latin poetry for his varied but thematically consistent treatment of friendship.[69] Against the backdrop of deeply signifying linguistic choices and generic differences is a shared, consistent, and misogynist perspective on women. This misogyny is unmistakable when we compare Montaigne's dedicatory epistle to Michel de L'Hôpital with the one addressed to Madame de Grammont, the Comtesse de Guissen. Montaigne dedicated La Boétie's writings to both; however, he did not dedicate the same writings, and he did not explain his dedication in the same way. He sent to the chancellor poems written in Latin on a variety of subjects, including civic duty and the obligations of friendship; to the countess, he sent love sonnets written in French. The differences in the dedication and choice of dedicated texts reveal the difference gender makes in Montaigne's literary, epistolary, and friendship projects.

Montaigne explains the reasons for which he has chosen the countess as dedicatee of La Boétie's twenty-nine love sonnets: he would like that these verses "portassent vostre nom en teste, pour l'honneur que ce leur sera d'avoir pour guide cette grande Corisande d'Andoins" (carry your name at their head, for the honor that this will bring them, to have as a guide this great Corisandra of Andouins).[70] Acknowledging her self-styled mythical honorific, he praises her other qualities and "beautés," and offers the implied compliment that the poems will fare better with her support.[71] In the letter to the chancellor, the emphasis is on La Boétie's worth; here, it is the countess's merit, and Montaigne does not miss a well-worn opportunity to praise her as unusual among her sex.[72] She is an appropriate choice of dedicatee and for the role of "Corisande" because there are few women in France who "jugent mieux

[69] La Boétie also wrote French poetry and translated Greek literary works; Montaigne appears only to have written in French. These are not insignificant choices, given the contemporary efforts by Pléiade poets to bring glory to French language and literature. See note above on the *Defense et illustration de la langue française* penned by Du Bellay, with whom La Boétie certainly had contact.

[70] "A Madame de Grammont, Comtesse de Guissen," *Essais*, vol. 1, 196. "Corisande" is a role with which Diane d'Andouins had already publicly identified herself. Ritter explains the Corisandra reference as an allusion to the medieval Spanish romance Amadis de Gaule, 69. For more on Montaigne and Diane d'Andouins, see Balsamo.

[71] This might not have been strictly untrue; Diane D'Andouins is generally held to have had an affair with Henri IV at about this period. However, to the extent that any dedicated work stands to gain from the support of powerful readers patrons, openly pointing it out might seem superfluous and grasping, and perhaps even hubristic.

[72] Praising a woman's worth for its comparative rarity, rather than on its own terms, is a familiar gesture in the Renaissance and the Middle Ages; recall that Heloise, too, was "unusual for her sex"; see Chapter 2.

et se servent plus à propos que vous de la poësie" (judge better, and make better use of, poetry than you). Notably, this compliment to the countess comes at the cost of the literary judgment of other women. His fulsome praise has a calculated purpose: he links the value of the poems to their dedicatee's worth: "Madame, ces vers meritent que vous les cherissez" (My lady, these verses merit your cherishing them). Montaigne then anticipates the countess's jealousy that he had some of the verses printed "sous le nom de monsieur de Foix" (196), and as if placating a child, he assures her that the verses he sends to her are "plus vif et de plus bouillant" (more vivid and ardent) than the others.

These verses dedicated to the countess are more ardent because, Montaigne confides, they were penned by La Boétie in "sa plus verte jeunesse, et eschauffé d'une belle et noble ardeur" (his most green youth, and heated by a beautiful and noble ardor). Somewhat flirtatiously and even salaciously, Montaigne promises to tell the countess of this youthful ardor one day, "à l'oreille," in her ear. Further reassuring her of the quality of "her" verses, the verses dedicated to Foix, he writes, were penned later, when La Boétie "estoit à la poursuite de son mariage, en faveur de sa femme, et sentent desjà je ne sçay quelle froideur maritale" (was in pursuit of his marriage, in favor of his wife, and they smack of a certain marital coldness).[73] Montaigne closes this letter with the astonishing declaration that poetry laughs only when it treats a subject "folatre et des-reglé" (foolish and disordered). He implies a host of perhaps surprising positions: that marital coldness produces tepid poetry while youthful, unmarried ardor produces poetry that is exciting to read; that his friend's early French language poetry treats foolish subjects; and, perhaps most serious given his devotion to his friendship with La Boétie and advancing his "place" in the world, that potentially titillating biographical details regarding the author's youth are an incentive to read, and can be hinted at in writing and exposed in person. Montaigne implicitly relegates the interest of these elements to the female realm: women are interested in love, flirtation, secrets, and categorically not inclined to the same subjects as men: virtue, friendship, and civic duty.

While it might be an exaggeration to read a studied project of misogyny on the basis of this dedicatory epistle, nevertheless this letter, when read against the dedicatory letter to Michel de l'Hôpital, suggests

---

[73] 196. In Poem 20, La Boétie's discussion of marriage is certainly brief, but it lacks this "froideur" Montaigne ascribes, suggesting another way in which Montaigne might be seen to take liberties with his friend's writings.

an approach to gender difference that is consistent with Montaigne's avowed and much-studied views on women: namely, that women are excluded from masculine *amicitia* by reason of their natural insufficiency.[74] The letter to Madame de Grammont displays a humility and flattery that might be considered courtly, perhaps exaggeratedly so, and that are conspicuously absent from the letter to L'Hôpital.[75] This is suggestive of Montaigne's views on men and women in regard to the appreciation of literature, and demonstrates his attentiveness to the uses of genre to reflect this attitude toward gender. However, as in the letter to L'Hôpital, this dedicatory epistle demonstrates an attention to the importance of social positioning and praise to obtain desired ends: in this case, a powerful woman's reading of what is becoming a joint textual entity: the writing of Montaigne and La Boétie.

"De l'Amitié": The Limits of Epistolary Friendship

The desired ends of dedicating and circulating La Boétie's writing are, as I have been suggesting, multiple: to fulfill a last request of a dying friend; to continue a friendship; to advance Montaigne's position not only as friend but also as promoter and, as such, arbiter of taste and wielder of influence. These poetic writings appear in public thanks to Montaigne's direct intervention, and his access to them as La Boétie's privileged intimate is carefully constructed in his various writing and publishing projects. In his letter to Madame de Grammont, Montaigne declares that it would be an honor to have her name at the head of La Boétie's verses. And, in fact, this letter appears in the *Essais*, ostensibly preceding La Boétie's love sonnets which Montaigne had planned to grant pride of place at about the midpoint of volume I.[76] These twenty-nine sonnets would have comprised Chapter 29 of the *Essais*. While the verses appeared in every version of the *Essais* published during Montaigne's

---

[74] On the fascinating question of Montaigne and women, see the issue of *Montaigne Studies* on "Woman's Place: Within and Without the *Essais*," eds. Dora E. Polachek and Marcel Tetel.

[75] For example, his letter begins with an equivocating humility formula: "Madame, je ne vous offre rien du mien, ou par ce qu'il est deja vostre, ou pour ce que je n'y trouve rien digne de vous" (Madame, I do not offer you anything of mine, either because it is already yours, or because I find nothing there worthy of you), 196.

[76] Referencing La Boétie's work at the midpoint of his own writing is something Montaigne does more than once; as Rigolot points out, in the letter to his father recounting La Boétie's death, Montaigne places at the midpoint of the letter the description of La Boétie's leaving him his "literary legacy": his library and books, 150.

lifetime, in the famous 1588 Bordeaux copy and the posthumous 1595 edition this work is famously removed and replaced with the cryptic "ces vers se voient ailleurs" (these verses appear elsewhere).[77]

These publication plans demonstrate the ways in which Montaigne pushes at the boundaries of missive writing. While the dedicatory letter might well have been previously sent to Madame to Grammont, encasing it in the *Essais* constitutes another method of exposition. It has the effect of making its publication and circulation in this form a kind of speech act, performing the dedication to her at the same time that it articulates it on the printed page.[78] Yet, in the 1588 copy and the 1595 edition, the dedicatory function of the letter is voided, for that which it purports to dedicate – the verses – has been removed. The letter's presence at the figurative and literal heart of volume I of the *Essais* draws conspicuous attention to its placement, an attention that is disappointed by its coy, very nearly banal, and, when read against Montaigne's other dedicatory letters, gender-determined contents. This disappointment is, in the Bordeaux copy and the 1595 edition, heightened by the ostentatious omission of the love sonnets. The reader, to whom Montaigne addresses the *Essais*, is made an eavesdropper, a reader of missives addressed to others, and most important, a witness to the friendship of La Boétie and Montaigne, which, in its carefully constructed, textual nature, requires an audience.

It is no accident that this literally and figuratively central chapter is the celebrated essay "De l'Amitié."[79] Montaigne begins this essay with an anecdote about watching a painter at work. He admires his ability to place and center his paintings, while filling the marginal space surrounding the painting with "grotesques."[80] Comparing his own writing to such grotesques and declaring himself incapable of producing a "tableau riche, poly et formé selon l'art," he borrows one from La Boétie – the *Discours*

---

[77] 196. The Bordeaux copy, on which Montaigne worked during his lifetime but which was never published, contains numerous emendations and commentaries. For an intriguing hypothesis about "ces vers se voient ailleurs," see Simonin.

[78] Publishing letters after the historical situation in which they might have been "really" sent is another recurrent strategy in Montaigne's writing: after La Boétie's death and the death of his father, Montaigne published La Boétie's *Œuvres*, appending to them the letter written to his father recounting the death-scene; for more on this letter and its composition, see Desan's "Lettre sur la mort de La Boétie," in his *Dictionnaire de Michel de Montaigne*, 579.

[79] Desan considers "De l'Amitié" the real center of volume 1 of the *Essais* in "La place de La Boétie dans les *Essais*."

[80] "Crotesques," vol. 1, 183. Hoffmann's "Montaigne's Nudes" discusses the relationship between the paintings in Montaigne's study and his *Essais*.

de la Servitude Volontaire.[81] Most of the rest of the essay performs the lack polishedness of which Montaigne accuses himself, in the form of a digressive discussion of the rarity and perfection of their friendship.[82] This departure from the topic of artistic production serves as a preamble to La Boétie's writing, and instructs the reader on how to read this borrowed text.[83]

Their affection, Montaigne reports, began by means of reputation: the two young men heard of each other, "qui faisoient en nostre affection plus d'effort que ne porte la raison des rapports" (which had more effect on our affection than such reports would reasonably have); "nous nous embrassions par noz noms" (we embraced each other by our names). And, as Montaigne reports, he responded not only to La Boétie's reputation, but also to his *Discours*, a copy of which he was given before ever meeting its author. Their first meeting sounds like a *coup de foudre*: "Nous nous trouvasmes si prins, si cognus, si obligez entre nous, que rien des lors ne nous fut si proche que l'un à l'autre" (we found ourselves so taken with each other, so well acquainted, so bound together, that from that time on nothing was so close to us as each other) (188). While La Boétie's verse epistles seem acutely aware of the different positions implied by the counsel-giving obligations of friendship, Montaigne's essay emphasizes the mutuality of their friendship:

> Je ne sçay quelle quinte essence de tout ce meslange, qui, ayant saisi toute ma volonté, l'amena se plonger et se perdre dans la sienne; qui, ayant saisi toute sa volonté, l'amena se plonger et se perdre en la mienne, d'une faim, d'une concurrence pareille. Je dis perdre, à la verité, ne nous reservant rien qui nous fut propre, ny qui fut ou sien ou mien. (189)

> I know not what quintessence of all this mixture, which, having seized my whole will, led it to plunge and lose itself in his, which, having seized his whole will, led it to plunge and lose itself in mine, with equal

---

[81] Suggesting a more nuanced reading of this claim in his discussion of Montaigne's treatment of art, Rigolot points out that describing the *Discours* in this way is "hardly a compliment," 153.

[82] And yet the "centering" of this chapter praising his friendship with La Boétie and showcasing his writing might well demonstrate this very skill of placement Montaigne claims to lack.

[83] Gray writes that Montaigne is "all digression," and the "indeterminacy" of his writing style "constrains the reader to turn back on the words just read and to consider them in their *contexture*, that is to say in their relation to one another in the projection and expression of meaning," 18, 19.

hunger, equal rivalry. I say lose, in truth, for neither of us reserved anything for himself, nor was anything either his or mine.

This vocabulary of total loss has more in common with mysticism and spiritual transport than with the neo-stoic tendency throughout the *Essais* to survey the events of his life with dispassion. Moreover, Montaigne's emphasis on mutuality is decidedly lacking in La Boétie's verse epistles, which describe their affection sparingly.

Montaigne's vocabulary is noticeably more affective than La Boétie's. He rhapsodizes over the emotional aspect of their friendship:

> Nos ames ont charrié si uniement ensemble, elles se sont considérées d'une si ardante affection, et de pareil affection descouvertes jusques au fin fond des entrailles l'une à l'autre, que, non seulement je connoissoy la sienne comme la mienne, mais je me fusse certainement plus volontiers fié à luy de moy qu'à moy. (189–90)

> Our souls pulled together in such unison, they regarded each other with such ardent affection, and with a like affection revealed themselves to each other to the very depths of our hearts, that not only did I know his soul as well as mine, but I should certainly have trusted my self to him more readily than to myself.

His account of their friendship emphasizes affection, and the joining of souls. La Boétie also invokes the idea of union in friendship, but his metaphor, while not unproblematic, is direct, clear, and almost scientific: that of plant grafting. In contrast, Montaigne's description resonates not only with the language of spiritual mysticism, but even of romantic love, liberally mixing metaphors. The terms in which he describes their friendship could easily describe an amorous relationship:

> En l'amitié dequoy je parle, elles se meslent et confondent l'une en l'autre, d'un melange si universel, qu'elles effacent et ne retrouvent plus la couture qui les a jointes. Si on me presse de dire pourquoy je l'aymois, je sens que cela ne se peut exprimer, qu'en respondant: Par ce que c'estoit luy; par ce que c'estoit moy. (188)

> In the friendship I speak of, our souls mingle and blend with each other so completely that they efface the seam that joined them, and cannot find it again. If you press me to tell you why I loved him, I feel that this cannot be expressed, except by answering: Because it was he, because it was I.

La Boétie's "foedus," governed by nature in occluded fashion, finds an answering echo here. However, La Boétie's metaphor is rooted in the natural world, while Montaigne's transcends metaphor and even expression: for all his effusive description, their affection is, he claims, ineffable. For La Boétie, love of virtue joins men together in friendship; Montaigne's friendship is rooted in the particularity of himself and his friend. Despite his insistence on singularity, however, this language of union evokes the relationship that Montaigne deems incompatible with friendship: marriage.

The friendship Montaigne describes is rare, singular, and perfect, and it categorically excludes women. The one elective relationship with women that is acceptable, marriage, is disparaged. In extolling the various kinds of relationships inferior to friendship, Montaigne writes of it with a marked lack of enthusiasm.[84] However, while marriage seems to be a burden because of the nature of the relationship,[85] friendship with women is not possible because of the nature of women:

> La suffisance ordinaire des femmes n'est pas pour respondre à cette conference et communication, nourrisse de cette saincte couture; ny leur ame ne semble assez ferme pour soustenir l'estreinte d'un neud si pressé et si durable. (186)

> the ordinary capacity of women is inadequate for that communion and fellowship which is the nurse of this sacred bond; nor does their soul seem firm enough to endure the strain of so tight and durable a knot.

The fault, it seems, is female nature, essential and disqualifying.[86] However, Montaigne writes that were women capable of friendship, this would be the best kind of friendship, for in a relationship

> où, non seulement les ames eussent cette entiere jouyssance, mais encores où les corps eussent part à l'alliance, ou l'homme fust engagé tout entier: il est certain que l'amitié en seroit plus pleine et plus comble. (186–7)

---

[84] "C'est un marché qui n'a que l'entrée libre (sa durée estant contrainte et forcée, dependant d'ailleurs que de nostre vouloir), et marché qui ordinairement se fait à autres fins" (It is a bargain to which only the entrance is free – its continuance being strained and forced, depending otherwise than on our will – and a bargain made ordinarily for other ends, trans. Frame), 186.

[85] This is a point on which Heloise and Montaigne are, perhaps surprisingly, in concert: they seem to share the point of view that married life is not compatible with a mutual pursuit of intellection.

[86] Like La Boétie's articulation of the "foedus" of friendship, Montaigne's friendship, as well, relies on the claims of nature, to support his exclusion of an entire sex. In support of this idea, he cites the "escholes anciennes," which are, however, not identified; for an examination of this evocation of the ancients, see Stone.

in which not only would the souls have this complete enjoyment, but the bodies would also share in this alliance, so that the entire man would be engaged, it is certain that the resulting friendship would be fuller and more complex.[87]

Having praised a relationship permitting the union, or "alliance," of body and soul as the most full and complex, Montaigne passes immediately to a condemnation of "cet'autre license Grecque" (that other, licentious Greek love), "justement abhorrée par nos meurs" (rightly abhorred by our morality).[88] Categorically, women are excluded from the best kind of relationship, which permits of the union of the body and the soul, because of their insufficient nature. Men, however, are excluded from this kind of perfect friendship not because of their nature, but because of convention – religious, social, moral – that forbids physical love between men.[89] What they are left with, by implication, is a less than perfect friendship.

The exclusion of women from friendship comes at the cost of the exclusion of the body from friendship.[90] This formulation demonstrates the usefulness but also the vexed nature of gendered positions for Montaigne's construction of friendship. His barring of women from friendship is grounded in a difference a modern reader might be comfortable calling gendered, and not biological. The exclusion of women, like that of male sexual relations, is predicated on positions that are not essential, as Montaigne's description would have us believe, but rather constructed. Put in other terms, the exclusion of women and the body from friendship are not necessary exclusions, but grounded in socially

[87] This disqualification of women casts Montaigne's relationship with Marie de Gournay, his self-styled "fille d'alliance," as one of filiation more than alliance; see Chang's chapter "The Hand of Gournay" on the relationship between Montaigne and Marie de Gournay in *Into Print*, 175–209.

[88] Montaigne raises this moral objection but does not explore it; he reports the other grounds on which this abhorrent love might be considered flawed: in the disparity of age between lovers and its foundation on physical beauty.

[89] Reeser examines how same-sex sexual relationships between men were painted as immoderate in order to recuperate heterosexual masculinity as moderate and draw attention away from the dangers male-male friendship might run of the same immoderacy; Introduction and "Une Ardeur immodérée," *Moderating Masculinity*.

[90] In "Sur des vers de Virgile," Montaigne paints a slightly different view of marriage, explaining the reasons for which reticence regarding conjugal happiness is desirable. This makes the absence of this discussion all the more striking in *De l'Amitié*. Rather than "proving" or "disproving" Montaigne as a pro- or anti-marriage, a historical misogynist or not, what I examine is how this position on women and marriage is articulated in the service of promoting his friendship with La Boétie.

constructed perceptions of gender-based limitations and what constitutes appropriate relations between men.

With these exclusions, Montaigne paves the way for a different kind of union, one in which his friendship with La Boétie might conceivably include a physical component: in the realm of texts. What Montaigne achieves through his varied writing and publishing projects is a textual, instead of a sexual, "alliance" with his friend.[91] The text becomes a surrogate for the beloved's male body denied to men, and for the dead friend who no longer has any physicality. Montaigne's dedication and successive publications of La Boétie's work produce this union, for not only is La Boétie's reputation preserved and Montaigne's status and reputation increased in turn, the two friends become textually linked in each of Montaigne's successive textual endeavors. Montaigne claims La Boétie as a friend, and he joins his name to his friend's for the ages.

This project of textual joining, or alliance, is evident in the dedicatory epistles, and especially in "De l'Amitié." At the end of Chapter 28 of the *Essais*, Montaigne enjoins the reader to lend an ear to La Boétie: "Mais oyons un peu parler ce garson de seize ans" (now let us hear this boy of sixteen speak a little).[92] His intention is to have readers "hear" a youthful La Boétie's words, invoking the vivifying effects of the printed word and demonstrating that, just as an epistle can bring presence in absence, by extension, so too might carefully situated writing produce a sort of authorial presence. Instead of providing La Boétie's writing, however, Montaigne explains the reasons for which he has excised the prose he had intended to include:

> Parce que j'ay trouvé que cet ouvrage a esté depuis mis en lumiere, et à mauvaise fin, par ceux qui cherchent à troubler et changer l'estat de notre police, sans se soucier s'ils l'amenderont, qu'ils ont meslé à d'autres escris de leur farine, je me suis dédit de le loger icy. (194)

> Because I found that this work has been since brought to light, and to ill ends, by those who seek to trouble and change the state of our polity, with no concern for whether they improve it, and that they have mixed it along with other works of their fashioning, I disavowed my intention to house it here.

---

[91] On Montaigne's view of sexuality and its relationship to his writing, see Cottrell's *Sexuality/Textuality*.

[92] The intimacy of the body, and specifically the ear, is multivalent in Montaigne's hands, suggestive and titillating in his letter to Madame de Grammont, and earnest here, when enjoining readers to appreciate La Boétie's writing. On the "oreille" and "oyez" imagery that unites I.28 with I.29, see Ferguson.

It appears that Montaigne had intended to include here, at the end of his essay on friendship, La Boétie's *Discours de la servitude volontaire*. What prevented its inclusion is probably the fact that the *Discours* had been published in 1576 in the *Mémoires de l'Estat de France sous Charles IX*, and circulated along with "pamphlets virulents."[93] Rather than simply supplying another text, Montaigne charts the steps that lead to the suppression of the *Discours* and its replacement with another – the love sonnets discussed earlier, which are in turn excised in subsequent editions. This is consistent with Montaigne's practice with the successive editions of the *Essais* of revising and emending while at times leaving contradictions in place; it also reveals the pains he takes to create a certain profile and reputation for his friend's work.

In the dedicatory epistles, Montaigne's concern is, ostensibly, to perpetuate his friend's memory, advance his honor, and garner his due praise in the world. In this explanation of the excision of the *Discours*, Montaigne is more concerned to protect La Boétie's reputation and counteract negative associations with anti-monarchical factions.[94] And, because the purloined text was to appear in his *Essais*, Montaigne must surely have been anxious to protect his own reputation from seditious taint as well.[95] Not only does Montaigne suppress the work from his *Essais*, he anticipates possible objections to the *Discours* and excuses them on account of La Boétie's youth at the time of its composition, and on account of its genre.[96] Despite being an intellectual exercise, Montaigne asserts, La Boétie did not, however, misrepresent his views or lie.[97] Finally, Montaigne proclaims the superlativeness of La Boétie's

---

[93] Rigolot observes: "[a]fter Protestant activists had used this attack against tyranny for their propaganda, it would have been extremely dangerous for any writer to refer to it positively in his works," 154.

[94] Tournon considers how the conspicuous absence of the *Discours* in I.28 might be a pointed political statement.

[95] As Mehlman describes it, "La Boétie's text, then, had been unduly exploited, inscribed in a political circuit Montaigne would extricate both his friend's memory and his *Essais* from," 47.

[96] "Ce subject fut traicté par luy en son enfance, par maniere d'exercitation seulement, comme subjet vulgaire et tracassé en mille endroits des livres" (This subject was treated by him in his early youth, as an exercise only, as a subject common and handled in thousands of works), 194.

[97] "Je ne fay nul doubte qu'il ne creust ce qu'il escrivoit, car il estoit assez conscientieux pour ne mentir pas mesmes en se jouant." (I have no doubt that but he that believed what he wrote, for he was sufficiently conscientious to never lie even when in jest), 194.

loyalty as a citizen.[98] This confusion of assurances at once dismisses the *Discours* as a compositional exercise, perhaps in order to assuage concerns raised by the work's association with anti-monarchists, and insists on the qualities of the writer that are to be admired.

After providing these assurances and qualifications, in place of this work whose content and recent unauthorized associations might render it suitable for Montaigne's multiple projects in publishing La Boétie's work, he offers instead his friend's youthful twenty-nine love sonnets:[99]

> Or, en eschange de cet ouvrage serieux, j'en substitueray un autre, produit en cette mesme saison de son aage, plus gaillard et plus enjoué.

> Now, in exchange for this serious work, I will substitute for it another, produced in this same season of his age, more playful and more cheerful.

This description of the poetry is distinct from the slightly salacious one he gives to Madame de Grammont, "eschaufé d'ardeur," and accompanied by promises of revelations better made in person, revealing Montaigne's attention to gender and adjusting the tenor of his writing accordingly.[100]

This convoluted history of a text's intended honoring, its suppression and replacement, and the ultimate suppression of this replacement while leaving in place its dedicatory letter, leaves a reader in some confusion, caught in the role of witness to a complexity of projects that seem at times to be at cross-purposes. These various projects work to increase honor and reputation not just for La Boétie, but also for Montaigne, and

---

[98] "Il ne fut jamais un meilleur citoyen, ny plus affectionné au repos de son païs, ny plus ennemy des remuements et nouvelletez de son temps." (There was never a better citizen, nor more concerned by the peace of his country, nor a greater enemy of the unrest and changes of his time), 194.

[99] In fact, Villey informs us, in earlier editions, this essay ended with a passage which Montaigne ultimately suppressed along with the sonnets: "Ce sont 29 sonnets que le sieur de Poiferré, homme d'affaires et d'entendement, qui les connoissoit long temps avant moy, a retrouvé par fortune chez luy, parmi quelques autres papiers, et me les vient d'envoyer; dequoy je luy suis tres-obligé, et souhaiterois que d'autres qui detiennent plusieurs lopins de ses escris, par cy, par là, en fissent de mesmes," 195 n. 1.

[100] The replacement of the *Discours* with the sonnets is remarkable for several reasons. Mehlman discusses La Boétie's enactment in the sonnets of the voluntary servitude he decries in a political context in the *Discours*. This would seem to suggest a thematic connection between these two seemingly disparate texts. Hoffmann describes amorous subjugation as "the ground of an on-going match" between the two friends; he suggests the replacement of the *Discours* with the sonnets as "projecting the role of the smitten lover back upon La Boétie," "Montaigne's Nudes," 130.

the role of the reader is critical in achieving this increase. Whether or not an actual reader exists, the missive and publicizing functions of these various maneuvers in the dedicatory letters and the *Essais* depend on the figure of a reader to make good the promise of giving La Boétie a "place," and establish in turn Montaigne's own place as his friend. This demonstrates the instrumental use Montaigne makes of the text in his performance of his friendship with La Boétie, a performance that is, repeatedly, dependent on the figure of a third person.

Letters, Essays, and the Uses of Genre

As their writings demonstrate, the celebrated friendship of Montaigne and La Boétie is a relationship that is first and foremost textual: not just because they were learned humanists cultivating a classical and episto-lary *amicitia*, but also because the various writing projects in which they engaged offered a way to practice their friendship and, for Montaigne, to claim and further refine it. It is not insignificant that there are no surviving letters actually exchanged between them. Whether they were destroyed, lost, suppressed, or never existed, the only evidence we have of exchange, dialogue, and *friendship* between these two celebrated friends is produced by reading La Boétie's verse epistles and Montaigne's dedicatory letters and essays.

Montaigne claims rather plaintively that he would have written letters, "si j'eusse eu à qui parler," painting the *Essais* as a literary project that is a response to loneliness.[101] For Montaigne, as for so many letter writers, letter writing constitutes a kind of conversation, a discourse with friends, albeit within certain rhetorical and formal parameters. Essays are in many ways similar to letters, occupying a murky middle ground between fiction and non-fiction. Like letters, essays are at once personal and private; they suggest intimacy, and they require an immediate audience while suggesting a broader, more public one. The writings I examine in this chapter all rely on several triangulations: the relationship of writer–addressee–reader; Montaigne–La Boétie–Virtue, and its opposite, Montaigne–La Boétie–woman; and Montaigne–La Boétie–addressee/reader.[102] Epis-

---

[101] "Et eusse prins plus volontiers ceste forme à publier mes verves, si j'eusse eu à qui parler" (and I would gladly have taken this form for publishing my words, if I had had someone to talk to) (I.40, 252). Montaigne's use of the verb "parler" suggests the spoken, informal nature of letters and, by extension, the *Essais*.

[102] Sedgwick explores male relationships triangulated through women in *Between Men*. Although Sedgwick's focus is on the mid-eighteenth to mid-nineteenth century

tolary culture and misogyny both offer La Boétie ways to articulate a friendship that is triangulated through a third figure: it is grounded in a shared pursuit of virtue, it requires an oppositional relationship to women and common defense against their wiles, and it requires an audience. For Montaigne, the third figure of the woman unites men in perhaps more complicated ways than for La Boétie: Montaigne deploys gender to bend the tenor of his writing and his publication efforts, and also to articulate an exclusive friendship between men and, more specifically, between La Boétie and himself.

The dedicatory epistle is instrumental in Montaigne's fashioning of himself as La Boétie's intimate and as promoter of his friend's writing and reputation. And while he claims the essay as a compensatory literary exercise that presumably takes the place of the conversations that would have occurred had La Boétie lived, the essay is necessarily one-sided, representing address but not reply; and, unlike a letter, it does not antici- pate response.[103] So, even as we might understand them to be written with La Boétie in mind as an absent interlocutor, the *Essais* and "De l'Amitié" in particular offer Montaigne the opportunity to make claims as extravagant and as modest as he would like for the nature of friendship and the nature of his specific friendship with La Boétie. The essay both claims and performs his role as La Boétie's intimate, and, most impor- tant, this position cannot be contradicted. Montaigne has total license in the selection of La Boétie's works to present or suppress, and in his description of their degree of intimacy and the very bonds that joined them in friendship.

Montaigne's writing projects push at the boundaries of what constitutes missive writing, and the kinds of relationships that can be expressed through them. With the *Essais*, he no longer needs the fixed positions of writer and addressee to enact complicated interpersonal relationships or to advance varied public projects through epistolary rhetoric. New kinds of relationships are possible: between writer, compiler, publisher, and editor, through which filiation, kinship, friendship, and love are expressed.[104]

novel, the way she articulates the structure of male relationships resonates with how Montaigne and La Boétie construct their friendship. Here, I am concerned with the ways in which triangulated relationships, inherent in epistolary writing, coincide with misogy- nist rhetoric between men, requiring not only the third figure of the woman, but also the third figure of the reader who is not necessarily the addressee, that is, the "audience."

[103] Rigolot discusses the primacy of the conversational letter over the second-best essay form for Montaigne.

[104] I have been concerned with Montaigne's varied writing projects, and the project of

Montaigne's projects aggressively perform this relationality: all of La Boétie's works published by Montaigne are accompanied by Montaigne's writing; the first publication of La Boétie's *Œuvres* is accompanied by excerpted parts of Montaigne's letter to his father describing La Boétie's death. The result of this editorial intervention is that, as Stephen Greenblatt observes, "dying had become the last and perhaps best part of La Boétie's works."[105] Indeed, some critics interpret Montaigne's publication of La Boétie's works as an attempt to fulfill his dying friend's anguished demand for a "place," according to Montaigne's account of his death.[106] Whether or not this is the case, the successive publications and versions of La Boétie's writings, always in association with Montaigne's, play a critical role in producing their friendship, which, I have argued, is a textual affair. The evidence of the *Essais* suggests that this textual friendship constituted the best part of their work.

The friendship of La Boétie and Montaigne charts a shift from letters to the essay that, while motivated by biographical loss, nevertheless has broader implications. Montaigne's dedicatory epistles, and his experimentation with the *essai*, suggest how the fixed positions of epistolary discourse can be pushed to yield new positions, while preserving many of the same dynamics enabled by letters. The shift reveals the importance of the missive function of letters, and how this function can be imported to other, new literary genres. And indeed the *Essais* are haunted by letters: by the obligations of friendship claimed by La Boétie's verse epistles and the triangulated relationship of friend–woman–friend they represent; by the presence of numerous letters in the *Essais*; and by the fact that they are, in a way, a long letter addressed perhaps to La Boétie but quite literally "Au Lecteur." Like the medieval letters that inform them, the *Essais* deploy the figure of writer and addressee, as well as varied rhetorical registers determined by an acute awareness of social position. However, the *Essais* actively refigure these features in ways to suit their purposes, demonstrating this new sixteenth-century literary form's fidelity to, and departures from, the medieval letter, and in the process revealing how this sixteenth-century writer conceived of the ostensible subject of his writing: his very self, its love, bereavement, and friendship, and its humanist and very human concerns.

making them public through La Boétie's writing and their friendship; on Montaigne as editor of La Boétie see Chang's "The Hand of Gournay."

[105] Greenblatt, 223.

[106] See Greenblatt 223–4, 227; and Mehlman.

Conclusion
Conducting Oneself Through Letters

In Rohinton Mistry's 2002 novel *Family Matters*, Vilas Rane, salesman at
the Jai Hind Book Mart in Bombay, has a sideline business as a reader
and writer of letters for the illiterate. Despite the practical, mercantile
nature of his enterprise, he has a romantic view of the capacity of letters
to represent humanity:

> Vilas, writing and reading the ongoing drama of family matters, the
> endless tragedy and comedy, realized that collectively, the letters
> formed a pattern only he was privileged to see. He let the mail flow
> through his consciousness, allowing the episodes to fall into place of
> their own accord, like bits of coloured glass in a kaleidoscope … If it
> were possible to read letters for all of humanity, compose an infinity of
> responses on their behalf, he would have a God's-eye view of the world,
> and be able to understand it.[1]

Vilas is a modern-day scribe, playing a role similar to that of the medieval
notarius: a professional letter writer, who shaped oral accounts into epistolary form.[2] He also performs the job that medieval messengers did
upon delivery of letters, reading aloud to customers letters addressed to
them that they cannot read themselves. As his business grows, he fantasizes that letters provide an unmediated access to humanity, an elusive
goal that unites the medieval and the contemporary: understanding of our
human condition. However, as his example shows, this unmediated access
is just that, a fiction. His dream of unfettered access to humanity is highly
dependent on scribal interventions: his customers report their news to
him, he crafts their accounts into written messages, and he reports the
contents of the responses these letters engender, no doubt shaped on the
other end by a scribe like himself who reads letters and crafts responses
in turn. By the time news arrives at its destination, it has been mediated

---

[1] Mistry, 122.
[2] For more on the notarial profession see Murphy, *Rhetoric in the Middle Ages*, especially 263–4.

by multiple stages of representation and separated by several degrees from its "original version": the events, thoughts, or ideas to be told.

As I have examined, premodern letters were, much like Vilas's letters, deeply mediated documents. Far from providing a transparent portrayal of events or sentiments, letters offered a complicated conjunction of meanings shaped by compositional forms and conventions and the conditions of their expedition and reception. The goal of this study has been to interrogate some of the structures shaping the composition of letters – language, rhetoric, genre, and the conventions of epistolary practice – and how they are used to express what for lack of a better term might be called a self. However, the aim of this examination is not to seek an unmediated glimpse of this self. Vilas's fantasy of a god's-eye view of humanity through reading its accumulated letters is not a project available to literary analysis. A close, context-informed reading of letters provides, rather, access to the discursive choices made by the writing self. These choices show how letter writers negotiated established ways of representing personal identity, and, by extension, how they thought about and represented themselves. In the letters I have examined, this amounts to calling into question and redefining ways of thinking about the self: as gendered, spiritual, learned, loving, given to playfulness and earnestness, partisanship and antagonism, and deeply invested in the possibility of letter writing for expressing these ideas of the self.

One of the conceptual difficulties of such a project is avoiding the assumption that contemporary ways of thinking about the self are necessarily the same as premodern ones. It seems an obvious claim that people in the past inhabited a world in many ways radically different from our own, and that this difference is mirrored in different ways of thinking about the self and its contexts. It would be rash, however, to argue the opposite: that there was no such thing as a premodern self, or that it was necessarily so different as to be unrecognizable in modern terms. My approach has been to examine texts that represent personal identity in a particular way, and that have this representation as a stated goal: premodern letters necessarily identified correspondents in specific ways. By examining the rhetorical and compositional choices writers made in writing letters, we might not catch a god's-eye view of the self, but we can better understand some of the ways it described itself in relation to its others and, in some cases, found new ways to describe the self and its relations.

Epistolary Performances

Another way to think of the choices letter writers made in negotiating these conventions is performance, an underlying thread in my analysis of letters. In the Baudri–Constance exchange, the staged quality of their letters is explicit. This has in part to do with the genre of the verse epistle and the evocation of recognizable tropes in their use of imagery, vocabulary, and reference to mythological figures. It is this staged quality that allows these two monastic writers to engage playfully in their letters in a relationship that would be impossible, even sinful, if lived outside of letters. Raising the question of whether play is ever merely play, however, Constance replies to Baudri in kind but also refuses his ambiguous game. While her response might well constitute role-playing at a more heated pitch, it rejects Baudri's proffered gesture of light, "iocosa" epistolary exchange, and shows how scripted epistolary positions can be manipulated to produce unexpected discourse that shatters the tone of the game.

In the correspondence of Abelard and Heloise, performance is neither playful nor dissimulating, but a means of effecting change. Abelard and Heloise employ epistolary elements and genres in a high-stakes battle to establish the tenor of their relationship. Letter-writing structures provide them the means to describe this relationship to each other and also to enact it, in the epistolary vein each deems appropriate to their relation. Letters have performative force in this correspondence, as they act on their recipients and perhaps on their writers as well. The epistolary writings of Christine de Pizan engage the performative possibilities of letters in a different way. Christine simultaneously explores two social practices of kind in her project of self-authorization and public advocacy: she repeatedly engages with the structures and conventions of gender and the epistolary genre, suggesting writing as a space of social change as well as what scholars of a later period might call "self-fashioning." Her letters perform the very possibility she is at pains to describe: that women, too, are capable of learned, reasoned discourse.

This capacity of letters to facilitate nuanced, complex performances with the force of action is evident in the sixteenth-century letters of two of France's most celebrated humanists. In the correspondence of Marguerite de Navarre and Guillaume Briçonnet, letters functioned as vehicles for producing an affective spirituality. Much as Heloise might hope that, through writing her new role, her written words might be reflected in her heart, the efficacy of Briçonnet's letters seems to lie in their performative effect, as missives crafted to produce a particular effect on their reader.

Their failure in this regard is suggested by Marguerite's continued pleas for "secours" throughout their correspondence. However, despite this failure, letters facilitated the articulation of spiritual need and pursuit of spiritual concerns, and the development of a collaborative reading and writing project constitutive of a spiritual community. For Montaigne, letters allowed him to perform his friendship with La Boétie in ways that are perdurable, claiming the superlativity of their love beyond the death of the friend and even the death of the writer. The friendship Montaigne performs is indistinguishable from his function as La Boétie's editor and his role as a writer in his own right, reinforcing the profoundly textual nature of the exemplary relationship he boasts.

In this project I have approached epistolary performance in several ways. Because of the highly codified prescriptions governing letter writing, every letter was a demonstration of the writer's ability to observe these conventions, and thus an opportunity to display skill and erudition. I have also considered the ways in which letters, because of their highly troped forms of petition and humility, could stage gendered positions of authority and power to instrumental ends. Finally, I have examined how letters offered a way to enact dynamics otherwise unavailable to these writers in ways that resonated on a wider, public register and yet were invested with highly nuanced personal significance. Letters were a uniquely privileged space for engaging in these performances because of their highly saturated rhetorical context, in which generic choices, such as omission and inclusion of prescribed epistolary elements, could communicate a wealth of meaning. However, letters enabled these performances in other ways as well.

According to various classical and medieval sources, letters provided a compensatory presence that bridged spatial distance between interlocutors, a material presence inferior to actually being in the presence of an interlocutor, but nevertheless revivifying. The letters I have examined suggest that, for all that letters might be inferior substitutes for absent friends, they are superior vehicles for representing the self. Through letters, one loses the immediacy of direct contact with an interlocutor, but gains the space of representation. Letters might well bridge physical distance to bring correspondents into contact with each other, but, by serving as physical reminders of the absence of interlocutors, they reinforce distance. This distance allows for representation – of the self, and its resistance, compliance, authority, desire, and need. Yet, because of the letter's unique status as document of practice as well as representation, this distance invests the epistolary with more than descriptive force. A letter is addressed to a recipient, it makes demands, it compels response; it interpellates writer and addressee into generically typed positions of supplication and benefaction, humility and authority. From these epistolary positions, concerns are articulated and relationships are activated in ways that are not merely descriptive, but embodied, constitutive, active, making letters vehicles for doing as well as saying. As my examination of epistolary performances suggests, these representations are more than descriptive. Voiced from positions within particular structures of authority, they constitute a kind of action, and can be read as exercises of real, if limited, agency.

Both Constance and Abelard describe letters as a means by which lovers might communicate more openly than in person. My project suggests that letters also allow interlocutors to *behave* in ways inaccessible in person. Some of these epistolary performances are successful, others, perhaps less so. Christine de Pizan unquestionably gains a measure of writerly authority through her letter-writing activities, while Marguerite de Navarre does not seem to have achieved the spiritual quietude she sought; whether Heloise's epistolary performance was successful in effecting spiritual change at Abelard's behest is a question for the ages. These correspondences show how, through several centuries of French literature and culture, letters communicated through form as well as content, and epistolary composition functioned as a kind of conduct.

Letters and their Public

This idea of performance implicitly posits the notion of audience. As discussed in the introduction, there was often little guarantee of the privacy of a letter, even in the case of a singular addressee. This possibility of plural audience shaped the composition of premodern letters, in some cases leading to increased circumspection, in others to quite flagrant declarations. Regardless of whether there actually were plural readers, audience served as a figure that influenced not only the nature of the communications entrusted to writing but the very positions in which writers imagined themselves and their addressees. Thus, the figure of the audience shaped epistolary performance by making the ostensibly private letter a space for airing concerns with broader resonance and making claims on a larger scale, and positioning the self not only in relation to an epistolary other, but to many others.

By the eighteenth century, this complex relationship between writer, reader, and audience was framed as an issue of public and private concerns. Dena Goodman details the epistolary theory of Michel de Servan, *avocat-général* of France, who elaborated a notion of the letter as shared private property threatened by the danger of publication.[3] While print technologies created a different landscape for the circulation of numerous new kinds of writing, the continuing influence of the letter was felt in the fact that some of the most important of these new print media, newspapers, journals, and pamphlets, took on epistolary forms and functions.[4] In this moment of textual circulation and even proliferation, Servan claimed the letter as private property, and subject to joint ownership: it belonged both to writer and addressee, since it expressed the ideas of both, and should only be published with the permission of both parties.[5] This implication of both writer and addressee demonstrates the letter's critical role in creating binding relationships that claimed public and even legal acknowledgement. These relationships were, in turn, critical to the articulation of private, as opposed to public, concerns and spheres of action. Thus the letter had a vital role to play in making visible the emerging social and political relationships in pre-Revolutionary France.

With this articulation of distinct, competing, but also intersecting spheres of concern, women became through a complex process relegated to the private sphere. Elizabeth Goldsmith argues how by the eighteenth century the publication and circulation of women's writing was characterized as an immodesty, even a violation; the circulation of male-authored writings was not subject to the same kind of moral charge.[6] One of the unspoken goals of *Lettering the Self* has been to demonstrate women's participation in premodern literary letters and specifically in Latin literary culture. Women could and did write letters, although not in great numbers, and they were vitally important to the development of literary

---

[3] Goodman, "Epistolary Property and the Plight of Letters on the Eve of the French Revolution."

[4] Goodman, "Epistolary Property," 344–5.

[5] That is, even if only one side of a correspondence were published, sufficient information about the letter it responded to or invited could be deduced that, in effect, the identities and views of both writers could be known.

[6] Goldsmith, *Writing the Female Voice*. Michel de Servan literalizes the comparison: an intercepted letter is like a ravished woman; cited in Goodman, 355–6. The history of this shift is of course quite complicated; see also Goldsmith and Goodman's volume *Going Public: Women and Publishing in Early Modern France*.

culture both as writers and as figures. The premodern letters in this study charted a space of possibility for women, and for literary production. Letters were flexible enough to encompass composition in Latin and the vernacular, prose and verse, between men and women, secular and lay, to address concerns that were public and deeply personal. Thus perhaps unexpectedly the premodern offered greater possibilities for women than later periods, at least in the realm of literary composition.

Despite this critical difference, one very important epistolary function that survived beyond the Middle Ages was the capacity of the letter to observe and promulgate social norms and relations. This was a feature of letters in French that continued uninterrupted and reached a culmination in later centuries' interest in letter-writing manuals. Alphonse Fresse-Montval's 1858 letter-writing manual *Nouveau manuel complet et gradué de l'art épistolaire* was printed in five editions within a span of thirty years, and its two volumes featured model letters and an epistolary novel set at a boarding school.[7] In his discussion of these letters, Fresse-Montval focuses on the social relations communicated through letter writing. For example, the margins of the paper on which the letter is written should be proportional to the gap in social status of the correspondents.[8] This might seem at first glance to be a correlate to the dictaminal concern to accurately reflect relative social status in salutations.[9] However, paper margins offer far less precise calibrations of meaning than inflected language, and seem a rather loose way to communicate status. While the general relation of status might seem clear, it is communicated to a far less nuanced degree. Thomas Beebe observes that Fresse-Montval's manual "does not try to teach letter writing as a form of communication ... rather, the letter is meant to cement relations of dominance and subjugation by expressing them as unambiguously as possible."[10] The teaching of letter writing, in Beebe's analysis, has

---

[7] This represents a notable shift from the medieval *ars dictaminis*, whose manuals consisted of an elaboration of rules followed by a collection of model letters. For a discussion of Montval's career and an analysis of his didactic works see Beebe, 79.

[8] "Cet espace doit être d'autant plus large qu'on doit plus de respect à celui auquel on s'addresse," *Nouveau manuel complet et gradué de l'art épistolaire*, Henri-François-Marcel-Alphonse Fresse-Montval, cited in Beebe, 87.

[9] Spacing and placement in letters continued to signify well past the "golden age" of medieval letter writing; Autrand examines two diplomatic manuals preserving documents from the late fourteenth to early fifteenth centuries that pay close attention to the "mise en page" of epistolary protocols and their communication of social status.

[10] Beebe, 87.

become by the nineteenth century a means of social control, where texts of instruction mimic the authoritative structures of French classrooms, particularly those of French boarding schools.[11] The social relations communicated by letters are no longer solely those between writers, but also between writers and institutions.

Letter-writing manuals such as Fresse-Montval's correspond to an increase in correspondence at all levels – between friends and family, to transact business or personal affairs, written by adults as well as children. They also attest to the great flexibility of letters to be deployed as tools in a range of projects, from representing the self in relation to its others to representing these selves in relation to the institutions that organize their lives. What later letters retain from the medieval *arts dictaminis* and their premodern forebears is the notion that epistolary composition operates through observing and negotiating established rules, and through this observation and negotiation it could also function as a kind of conduct – whether through performing relationships of social status through margin width or inflected salutations, or performing ideal, literate citizenship – or rejecting them. This performative capacity of letters is established by centuries' worth of epistolary practice that identified the letter as a document with a peculiar status, at once a practical, administrative document and a nuanced means of representation and self-representation. Necessitated by distance, letters enabled the representation and performance of positions and relationships that might not be possible outside of the space of letters. However, these relationships are, in some ways, superior to those pursued outside of letters. As a writer in the space of letters, one has time to reflect before acting, and employ an arsenal of rhetorical devices to present oneself as one wishes to be perceived, and even as one wishes to be. These positions and relationships are structured by epistolary prescription and convention, but their performance is nevertheless constitutive of action, often with very tangible consequences. While letters might not afford a god's-eye view of the self, letter-writing forms and conventions provide concrete ways for this self to write and to act, to conduct itself through letters.

---

[11] Janet Gurkin Altman corroborates this view in "Teaching the 'People' to Write."

Bibliography

Editions and Translations

Abelard, Peter. "Abelard's Letter of Consolation to a Friend." Ed. J.T. Muckle, C.S.B. *Mediaeval Studies* 12 (1950): 163–213.

———. "Abelard's Rule for Religious Women." Ed. T.P. McLaughlin, *Mediaeval Studies* 18 (1956): 241–92.

———. *Abélard. Historia calamitatum. Texte critique avec une introduction.* Ed. Jacques Monfrin. Bibliothèque des textes philosophiques: Textes et commentaires. Paris: J. Vrin, 1959.

———. *Letters IX–XIV. An edition with an introduction.* Ed. Edmé Renno Smits. Groningen, 1983.

Abelard, Peter and Heloise. "The Letter of Héloïse on the Religious Life and Abelard's First Reply." Ed. J.T. Muckle, C.S.B. *Mediaeval Studies* 17 (1955): 240–81.

———. *The Letters of Abelard and Heloise.* Trans. Betty Radice. New York: Penguin, 1974; revised translation M.T. Clanchy, 2003.

———. *The Lost Love Letters of Heloise and Abelard: Perceptions of Dialogue in Twelfth-Century France.* Ed. and trans. Constant J. Mews and Neville Chiavaroli. New York: St. Martin's Press, 1999.

———. "The Personal Letters between Abelard and Héloïse." Ed. J.T. Muckle, C.S.B. *Mediaeval Studies* 15 (1953): 47–94.

———. *Problemata Heloissae.* Ed. Jacques-Paul Migne: *Patrologia Latina*, vol. 178, Paris, 1855.

———. *La vie et les epistres Pierres Abaelart et Heloys sa fame, Traduction du XIIIe siècle attribuée à Jean de Meun, avec une nouvelle édition des textes latins d'après le ms. Troyes Bibl. mun. 802.* Ed. Eric Hicks. Paris: Honoré Champion, 1991.

Alberic of Monte Cassino. *Flowers of Rhetoric.* Trans. Joseph L Miller, in *Readings in Medieval Rhetoric.* Eds. Joseph L. Miller, Michael H. Prosser, Thomas W. Benson, 131–61. Bloomington, IN: Indiana University Press, 1973.

Augustine. *Against the Academicians* and *The Teacher.* Trans. Peter King. Indianapolis: Hackett, 1995.

———. *On Christian Doctrine.* Trans. D.W. Robertson, Jr., Upper Saddle River, New Jersey: Prentice Hall, 1958, Book 3, chapter 10.

Baudri de Bourgueil. *Baldricus Burgulianus Carmina*. Ed. Karlheinz Hilbert. Heidelberg: Carl Winter Universitätsverlag, 1979.

———. *Baudri de Bourgeuil: Poèmes*. Ed. Jean-Yves Tilliette. 2 vols. Paris: Les Belles Lettres, 1998, 2002.

———. *Les Œuvres poétiques de Baudri de Bourgueil (1046–1130): Edition critique publiée d'après le manuscrit du Vatican*. Ed. Phyllis Abrahams. Paris: Champion, 1926.

Bellaquet, M.L. ed. and trans. *Chronique du religieux de Saint-Denys*. 5 vols, Paris: 1839, 1840–42, 1844.

Bellay, Joachim du. *Joachim Du Bellay, "The Regrets," with "The Antiquities of Rome," "Three Latin Elegies," and "The Defense and Enrichment of the French Language."* Ed. and trans. Richard Helgerson. Philadelphia: University of Pennsylvania Press, 2006.

C. Julius Victor. "Ars rhetorica." *Rhetores Latini minores*. Ed. Karl Halm, 371–448. Leipzig: Teubner: 1863.

Christine de Pizan. *The Book of the City of Ladies*. Trans. Rosalind Brown-Grant. London: Penguin, 1999.

———. *La Città delle Dame/Le Livre de la Cité des Dames*. Ed. Earl Jeffrey Richards, trans. Patricia Caraffi. Milan: Luni Editrice, 1997.

———. *The Epistle of the Prison of Human Life with an Epistle to the Queen of France and Lament on the Evils of the Civil War*. Ed. and trans. Josette A. Wisman. New York and London: Garland, 1984.

———. "Epistre a la royne." *Anglo-Norman Letters and Petitions from All Souls MS 182*. Ed. M. Dominica Legge. Oxford: Basil Blackwell, 1941.

———. "The *Livre de la Cité des dames* of Christine de Pisan: A Critical Edition." 2 vols. Ed. Maureen Cheney Curnow. Ph.D. diss., Vanderbilt University, 1975.

———. *Le Livre de la Mutacion de Fortune*. Ed. Suzanne Solente. Paris: Picard, 1959, vol. 1.

———. *Œuvres poétiques de Christine de Pisan*. 3 vols. Ed. Maurice Roy. Paris: Firmin Didot, 1894; repr. New York, Johnson Reprint Corporation, 1965.

———. *Poems of Cupid, God of Love: Christine de Pizan's* Epistre au dieu d'Amours *and* Dit de la Rose *and Thomas Hoccleve's* The Letter of Cupid. Ed. and trans. Thelma S. Fenster and Mary Carpenter Erler. Leiden: E.J. Brill, 1990.

———. *The Writings of Christine de Pizan*. Ed. Charity Cannon Willard. New York: Persea, 1994.

Christine de Pisan, Jean Gerson, Jean de Montreuil, Gontier and Pierre Col. *Le Débat sur le* Roman de la rose. Trans. Virginie Greene. Paris: Honoré Champion, 2006.

———. *Le Débat sur le* Roman de la rose. Ed. and trans. Eric Hicks. Paris: Éditions Honoré Champion, 1977.

————. *Debate of the Romance of the Rose*. Ed. and trans. David Hult. Chicago: University of Chicago Press, 2010.

————. *La Querelle de la rose: Letters and Documents*. Eds. Joseph L. Baird and John R. Kane. North Carolina Studies in Romance Languages and Literatures, no. 199, 1978.

M. Tullius Ciceronis. *De Re Publica, De Legibus, Cato Maior de Senectute, Laelius de Amicitia*. Eds. J.F.G. Powell. Oxford: Oxford University Press, 2006.

Cotgrave, Randle. *A Dictionarie of the French and English Tongues*. London: Adam Islip, 1611.

Dante Alighieri. "Epistola X: To Can Grande della Scala." In *Dantis Alagherii Epistolae: The Letters of Dante*. Ed. Paget Toynbee, 175–7. Oxford: Clarendon Press, 1966, second edition.

Ferrante, Joan, with the Columbia Center for New Media Teaching and Learning. *Epistolæ: Medieval Women's Letters*. <http://epistolae.ccnmtl. columbia.edu/>.

Fresse-Montval, Henri-François-Marcel-Alphonse. *Nouveau Manuel complet et gradué de l'art épistolaire*. Paris: A. Poilleux, 1848, third edition.

Guillaume Briçonnet, Marguerite d'Angoulême. *Correspondance (1521– 1524)*, 2 vols. Ed. Christine Martineau, Michel Veissière and H. Heller. Geneva: Droz, 1975, 1979.

Guillaume de Lorris and Jean de Meun. *Le Roman de la rose*. Ed. Armand Strubel. Paris: Librairie Générale Française, 1992.

Halm, Karl, ed. *Rhetores Latini minores*. Leipzig: Teubner: 1863.

Herminjard, Aimé Louis, ed. *Correspondance des réformateurs dans les pays de langue française vol. I: 1512–1526*. Geneva, 1866.

Hildebert of Lavardin. *Hildebertus Carmina minora*. Ed. A.B. Scott. Leipzig: Teubner, 1969.

L'Hôpital, Michel de. *Œuvres complètes, précédés d'un essai sur sa vie et ses ouvrages*. 5 vols. Ed. P.J.S. Dufey. Geneva: Slatkine, 1968.

Horace. *Epistles Book II and Epistle to the Pisones ('Ars Poetica')*. Ed. Niall Rudd, 1989. Cambridge: Cambridge University Press, 1999.

Jean de Meun. *La vie et les epistres Pierres Abaelart et Heloys sa fame*. Ed. Eric Hicks. Paris: Honoré Champion, 1991.

Jerome. *Select Letters*. Trans. F.A. Wright. Cambridge: Harvard University Press, 1999 [1933].

Könsgen, Ewald, ed. *Epistolae duorum amantium: Briefe Abaelards und Heloises?* Mittellateinische Studien und Texte 8. Leiden: E.J. Brill, 1974.

La Boétie, Etienne. *Œuvres complètes d'Estienne de la Boétie*. Ed. Paul Bonnefon. Geneva: Slatkine, 1967.

————. *Œuvres completes d'Estienne de la Boétie*. Ed. Louis Desgraves. 2 vols. Bordeaux: William Blake & Co., 1991.

————. *Poemata*. Ed. James S. Hirstein, trans. Robert D. Cottrell. *Montaigne Studies* 3.1 (1991): 15–47.

Lawrence of Acquilegia. " 'La Practica dictaminis' de Llorens de Aquileia, en un codex de Tarragona." *Analecta Sacra Tarraconensia* 6 (1930): 207–29.

Lefèvre d'Étaples, Jacques. *The Prefatory Epistles of Jacques Lefèvre d'Étaples and Related Texts*. Ed. Eugene F. Rice, Jr. New York: Columbia University Press, 1972.

Marbod of Rennes. "Liebesbriefgedichte Marbods." Ed. Walther Bulst. In *Liber Floridus: Mittellateinische Studien, Paul Lehmann zum 65*, ed. Bernhard Bischoff, 287–301. St. Ottilien: Eos Verlag der Erzabtei, 1950.

————. *Liber decem capitulorum*, I. Ed. Rosario Leotta. Rome: Herder, 1984.

Marguerite d'Angoulême. *Lettres de Marguerite d'Angoulême, soeur de François premier, reine de Navarre. Publiées d'après les manuscrits de la bibliothèque du roi*. Ed. François Génin. Paris: J. Renouard et Cie, 1841.

————. *Nouvelles lettres de la reine de Navarre, adressées au roi François Ie, son frère. Publiées d'après le manuscrit de la bibliothèque du roi*. Ed. François Génin. Paris: Jules Renouard et cie, 1842.

————. *Théatre profane*. Ed. Verdun L. Saulnier. Paris: Droz, 1946.

Marguerite de Navarre. *L'Heptaméron*. Ed. Renja Salminen. Geneva : Droz, 1999.

————. *"Dialogue en forme de vision nocturne."* Ed. Pierre Jourda. *Revue du seizième siècle* 13 (1926): 1–49.

————. *Marguerite de Navarre, Poésies chrétiennes*. Ed. Nicole Cazauran. Paris: Les Éditions du Cerf, 1996.

Montaigne, Michel de. *Les Essais*. Ed. Pierre Villey, 3 vols. Paris: Presses Universitaires de France, 1999 [1924].

————. *The Complete Essays of Michel de Montaigne*. Trans. Donald M. Frame. Stanford: Stanford University Press, 1958.

Le Nouveau Testament [traduit par] Jacques Lefèvre d'Etaples, Fac-simile de la première édition Simon de Colines, ed. M.A. Screech. 2 vols., New York: Johnson Reprint Corporation, 1970 [1523].

Peter the Venerable. *The Letters of Peter the Venerable*. Ed. Giles Constable, 2 vols. Cambridge: Harvard University Press, 1967.

Piron, Sylvain, trans. *Lettres des deux amants attribuées à Héloïse et Abélard*. Paris: Gallimard, 2005.

Renaut de Beaujeu. *Le Bel Inconnu*. Ed. G. Perrie Williams. Paris: Champion, 1929.

Seneca. *Ad Lucilium epistulae morales*. Ed. and trans. Richard M. Gummere. Cambridge: Harvard University Press, 1934 [1917 and 1925].

Stehling, Thomas, trans. *Medieval Latin Poems of Male Love and Friendship*. New York: Garland, 1984.

Venantius Fortunatus. *Venanti Honori Clementiani Fortunati presbyteri Italici. Opera poetica*. Ed. Friedrich Leo, Monumenta Germaniae Historica. Auctorum Antiquissimorum 4.1. Berlin: Weidmann, 1981 [1881].

Studies

Adams, Tracy. *The Life and Afterlife of Isabeau of Bavaria*. Baltimore, MD: Johns Hopkins University Press (forthcoming).
———. "Recovering Queen Isabeau of France (c.1370–1435): A Re-Reading of Christine de Pizan's Letters to the Queen." *Fifteenth-Century Studies* 22 (2008): 35–54.
Altman, Janet Gurkin. *Epistolarity: Approaches to a Form*. Columbus: Ohio State University Press, 1982.
———. "Teaching the 'People' to Write: The Formation of a Popular Civic Identity in the French Letter Manual." *Studies in Eighteenth Century Culture* 22 (1992): 147–80.
———. "Women's Letters in the Public Sphere." In *Going Public: Women and Publishing in Early Modern France*, eds. Elizabeth C. Goldsmith and Dena Goodman, 99–115. Ithaca: Cornell University Press, 1995.
Altman, Leslie. "Christine de Pisan: First Professional Woman of Letters (1364–1430?)." In *Female Scholars: A Tradition of Learned Women Before 1800*, ed. J.R. Brink, 7–23. Montreal: Eden Press Women's Publications, 1980.
Altmann, Barbara K., and Deborah L. McGrady, eds. *Christine de Pizan: A Casebook*. New York: Routledge, 2003.
Armstrong, Elizabeth A. *Before Copyright: The French Book-Privilege System, 1498–1526*. Cambridge: Cambridge University Press, 1990.
Astell, Ann W. "On the Usefulness and Use-Value of Books: A Medieval and Modern Inquiry." In *Medieval Rhetoric: A Casebook*, ed. Scott D. Troyan, 41–62. New York: Routledge, 2004.
Autrand, Françoise. "L'enfance de l'art diplomatique: la rédaction des documents diplomatiques en France XIVe–XVe siècles." In *L'Invention de la diplomatie: Moyen Age-temps modernes*, eds. Lucien Bély, Isabelle Richefort, 207–24. Paris: Presses Universitaires de France, 1998.
Bainton, Roland H. *Women of the Reformation in France and England*. Minneapolis: Augsburg Publishing House, 1973.
Baldwin, John W. "L'*ars amatoria* au XIIe siecle en France : Ovide, Abelard, André le Chapelain et Pierre le chantre." In *Le Couple, l'ami et le prochain: Melanges offertes à Georges Duby*, ed. Charles M. de la Ronciere, vol. 1, 19–29. Aix-en Provence: Presses Universitaires de Provence, 1992.
Balsamo, Jean. "Montaigne, le 'sieur de Poiferré' et la comtesse de Guiche: documents nouveaux." *Montaigne Studies* 16 (2004): 75–91.

Bannet, Eve Tavor. *Empire of Letters: Letter Manuals and Transatlantic Correspondence, 1688–1820.* Cambridge: Cambridge University Press, 2005.

Baswell, Christopher. "Heloise." In *The Cambridge Companion to Medieval Women's Writing*, eds. Carolyn Dinshaw, David Wallace, 161–71. Cambridge: Cambridge University Press, 2003.

Beach, Alison I. "Voices from a Distant Land: Fragments of a Twelfth-Century Nuns' Letter Collection." *Speculum* 77.1 (2002): 34–54.

Beaulieu, Jean-Philippe. "Postures épistolaires et effets de *dispositio* dans la correspondance entre Marguerite d'Angoulême et Guillaume Briçonnet." *Études françaises* 38.3 (2002): 43–54.

Becker, Philippe-Auguste. "Marguerite, Duchesse d'Alençon et Guillaume Briçonnet, Évêque de Meaux, d'après leur correspondance manuscrite 1521–1524." *Société de l'histoire du Protestantisme* 49 (1900): 393–476.

Beebe, Thomas O. "Writing Lessons: Representation Versus Rhetoric in the *Ars Dictaminis*." In *The Ideology of Genre*, ed. Thomas O. Beebe, 66–111. University Park, PA: Penn State University Press, 1994.

Bell, Susan Groag. "Christine de Pizan (1364–1430): Humanism and the Problem of a Studious Woman." *Feminist Studies* 3.3–4 Spring/Summer (1976): 173–84.

Benton, John F., and Giles Constable, Carol D. Lanham, eds. *Renaissance and Renewal in the Twelfth Century.* Toronto: University of Toronto Press, 1991.

Beuton, John F. "The Correspondence of Abelard and Heloise." In *Falschungen im Mittelatter*, vol. 5:96–120. Hannover: Hahnsche Buchhandlung, 1988.

Bibliothèque nationale. *Les plus belles lettres manuscrites de la langue française.* Paris: Robert Laffont, 1992.

Blaisdell, C.J. "Marguerite de Navarre and her Circle." In *Female Scholars: A Tradition of Learned Women before 1800*, ed. J.R. Brink, 36–53. Montreal: Eden Press Women's Publications, 1980.

Blanchard, Joël. "Compilation et légitimation au XVe siècle." *Poétique* 74 (April 1988): 139–57.

Bloch, R. Howard Bloch. *A Needle in the Right Hand of God: The Norman Conquest of 1066 and the Making and Meaning of the Bayeux Tapestry.* New York: Random House, 2006.

―――. *Medieval Misogyny and the Invention of Western Romantic Love.* Chicago: The University of Chicago Press, 1991.

Blumenfeld-Kosinski, Renate. *Reading Myth: Classical Mythology and Its Interpretations in Medieval French Literature.* Stanford: Stanford University Press, 1997.

Bolduc, Michelle. *The Medieval Poetics of Contraries.* Gainesville, FL: University Press of Florida, 2006.

Bond, Gerald A. "Composing Yourself: Ovid's *Heroides*, Baudri of Bourgueil and the Problem of Persona." *Medievalia* 13 (1987): 83–118.

―――. " 'Iocus amoris': The Poetry of Baudri of Bourgueil and the Formation of the Ovidian Subculture." *Traditio: Studies in Ancient and Medieval History, Thought and Religion* 42 (1986): 143–93.

―――. *The Loving Subject: Desire, Eloquence, and Power in Romanesque France.* Philadelphia: University of Pennsylvania Press, 1995.

―――. "Origins." In *A Handbook of the Troubadours*, eds. F.R.P. Akehurst and Judith M. Davis, 237–54. Berkeley and Los Angeles: University of California Press, 1995.

Boswell, John. *Christianity, Social Tolerance, and Homosexuality: Gay People in Western Europe from the Beginning of the Christian Era to the Fourteenth Century.* Chicago: University of Chicago Press, 1980.

Bouchard, Constance Brittain. *'Every Valley Shall be Exalted': The Discourse of Opposites in Twelfth-Century Thought.* Ithaca: Cornell University Press, 2003.

Bourgeon, G. *La Réforme à Nérac: Les origines (1530–1560).* Toulouse: Chauvin et fils, 1880.

Boutemy, André. "Muriel, Note sur deux poèmes de Baudri de Bourgueil et de Serlon de Bayeux." *Le Moyen Age, revue d'histoire et de philologie* 4 (1935): 241–51.

Bozzolo, Carla. "L'Humaniste Gontier Col et la traduction française des *Lettres* d'Abélard et Héloïse." *Romania* 75 (1974): 199–215.

Brinkmann, Hennig. *Mittelalterliche Hermeneutik.* Tubingen: Niemeyer, 1980.

Brook, Leslie C. "Christine de Pisan, Heloise, and Abelard's Holy Women." *Zeitschrift für Romanische Philologie* 109 (1993): 556–63.

Brook, Leslie C., ed. *Two Late Medieval Love Treatises: Heloise's Art d'Amour and a Collection of Demandes d'amour.* Oxford: The Society for the Study of Mediaeval Languages and Literatures, 1993.

Brooke, Christopher N.L. *The Medieval Ideal of Marriage.* Oxford: Oxford University Press, 1989.

Brower, Jeffrey and Kevin Guilfoy, eds. *The Cambridge Companion to Peter Abelard.* Cambridge: Cambridge University Press, 2004.

Brown, Catherine. *Contrary Things: Exegesis, Dialectic, and the Poetics of Didacticism.* Stanford: Stanford University Press, 1998.

―――. "*Muliebriter*: Doing Gender in the Letters of Heloise." In *Gender and Text in the Later Middle Ages*, ed. Jane Chance, 25–51. Gainesville, FL: University Press of Florida, 1996.

Brown-Grant, Rosalind. "A New Context for Reading the 'Querelle de la Rose:' Christine de Pizan and Medieval Literary Theory." In *Au champ des escriptures. IIIe colloque international sur Christine de Pizan,*

Lausanne 18–22 juillet 1998, eds. Eric Hicks, Diego Gonzalez, Philippe Simon, 581–95. Paris: Honoré Champion, 2000.

Brownlee, Kevin. "Discourses of the Self: Christine de Pizan and the *Romance of the Rose*." In *Rethinking the Romance of the Rose: Text, Image, Reception*, eds. Kevin Brownlee, Sylvia Huot, 234–61. Philadelphia: University of Pennsylvania Press, 1992.

———. "Literary Geneaology and the Problem of the Father: Christine de Pizan and Dante." *Journal of Medieval and Renaissance Studies* 23.3 (Fall 1993): 365–87.

———. "Rewriting Romance: Courtly Discourse and Auto-Citation in Christine de Pizan." In *Gender and Text in the Later Middle Ages*, ed. Jane Chance, 172–94. Gainesville: University of Florida Press, 1996.

Brundage, James A. "Sexual Equality in Medieval Canon Law." In *Medieval Women and the Sources of Medieval History*, ed. Joel T. Rosenthal, 66–79. Athens & London: University of Georgia Press, 1990.

Burns, E. Jane. *Bodytalk: When Women Speak in Old French Literature*. Philadelphia: University of Pennsylvania Press, 1993.

Bynum, Caroline Walker. "Did the Twelfth Century Discover the Individual?" In *Jesus as Mother: Studies in the Spirituality of the High Middle Ages*, 82–109. Berkeley: University of California Press, 1982.

———. *Docere verbo et exemplo: An Aspect of Twelfth-Century Spirituality*. Missoula, MT: Scholars Press, 1979.

———. *Fragmentation and Redemption: Essays on Gender and the Human Body in Medieval Religion*. New York: Zone Books, 1991.

Cain, Andrew. "Defending Hedibia and Detecting Eusebius: Jerome's Correspondence with Two Gallic Women (*Epist.* 20–21)," *Medieval Prosopography* 24 (2003): 15–34.

Calabrese, Michael. "Ovid and the Female Voice in the *De Amore* and the *Letters* of Abelard and Heloise." *Modern Philology* 95 (1997): 1–26.

Camargo, Martin. *Ars Dictaminis Ars Dictandi*. Typologie des sources du moyen âge occidental 60. Turnhout: Brepols, 1991.

———. "The Verse Love Epistle: An Unrecognized Genre." *Genre* 3 (1980): 397–405.

———. "Where's the Brief?: The *Ars Dictaminis* and Reading/Writing Between the Lines." In *Disputatio: An International Transdisciplinary Journal of the Late Middle Ages Volume I: The Late Medieval Epistle*, eds. Carol Poster and Richard Utz, 1–18. Evanston, IL: Northwestern Press, 1996.

Camargo, Martin, ed. *The Waning of the Medieval* Ars Dictaminis, Spec. issue of *Rhetorica: A Journal of the History of Rhetoric* 19.2, Spring 2001.

Carrington, Laurel. "Women, Rhetoric, & Letter Writing: Marguerite d'Alençon's Correspondence with Bishop Briçonnet of Meaux: 1521–

24." In *Listening to their Voices: The Rhetorical Activities of Historical Women*, ed. Molly Meijer Wertheimer, 215–32. Columbia: University of South Carolina Press, 1997.

Carruthers, Mary. *The Book of Memory: A Study of Memory in Medieval Culture*. Cambridge: Cambridge University Press, 1990.

Case, Mary Anne C. "Christine de Pizan and the Authority of Experience." In *Christine de Pizan and the Categories of Difference*, ed. Marilynn Desmond, 71–87. Minneapolis: University of Minnesota Press, 1998.

Chang, Leah L. "The Hand of Gournay." In *Into Print: The Production of Female Authorship in Early Modern France*, 175–209. Newark: University of Delaware Press, 2009.

Charrier, Charlotte. *Héloïse dans l'histoire et dans la légende*. Paris: Champion, 1933.

Cherewatuk, Karen. "Radegund and the Epistolary Tradition." In *Dear Sister: Medieval Women and the Epistolary Genre*, eds. Cherewatuk and Ulrike Wiethaus, 20–45. Philadelphia: University of Pennsylvania Press, 1993.

Clanchy, M.T. *Abelard: A Medieval Life*. Oxford and Cambridge: Blackwell, 1997.

———. *From Memory to Written Record: England 1066–1307*. Cambridge: Harvard University Press, 1990.

Clark, Carol. "Bradamante, Angelica and the Eroticizing of Virtue in Montaigne's Late Writing." *Montaigne Studies* 8.1–2 (1996): 109–24.

Classen, Albrecht. "Female Epistolary Literature from Antiquity to the Present: An Introduction." *Studia Neophilologica* 60 (1988): 3–13.

Cohen, Jerome Jeffrey, and Bonnie Wheeler, ed. *Becoming Male in the Middle Ages*. New York: Garland 2000 [1997].

Colish, Marcia. "The Renaissance of the Twelfth Century." In *Medieval Foundations of the Western Intellectual Tradition 400–1400*, 175–82. New Haven, CT: Yale University Press, 1997 [2002].

Constable, Giles. "The Authorship of the *Epistolae duorum amantium*: A Reconsideration." In *Voices in Dialogue: Reading Women in the Middle Ages*, eds. Linda Olson and Kathryn Kerby-Fulton, 167–78. Notre Dame, Ind.: University of Notre Dame Press, 2005.

———. "The Interpretation of Mary and Martha." In *Three Studies in Medieval Religious and Social Thought*, 1–142. Cambridge: Cambridge University Press, 1998 [1995].

———. *Letters and Letter-Collections*. Typologie des sources du moyen âge occidental, 17. Turnhout: Brepols, 1976.

———. "The Structure of Medieval Society According to the *Dictatores* of the Twelfth Century." In *Law, Church, and Society: Essays in Honor of Stephan Kuttner*, eds. Kenneth Pennington, and Robert Somerville, 23–67. Philadelphia: University of Pennsylvania Press, 1977.

Corrie, Cathleen Eva Corrie. "'Sy excellent pasture': Guillaume Briçonnet's Mysticism and the Pseudo-Dionysius." *Renaissance Studies* 20.1 (2006): 35–50.

Cottrell, Robert. *The Grammar of Silence: A Reading of Marguerite de Navarre's Poetry.* Washington, D.C.: The Catholic University of America Press, 1986.

———. "An Introduction to La Boétie's Three Latin Poems Dedicated to Montaigne." *Montaigne Studies* 3 (1991): 3–14.

———. "The Poetics of Transparency in Evangelical Discourse: Marot, Briçonnet, Marguerite de Navarre, Héroët." In *Lapidary Inscriptions: Renaissance Essays for Donald A. Stone, Jr.*, eds. Barbara C. Bowen and Jerry C. Nash, 33–44. Lexington, KY: French Forum Publishers, 1991.

———. *Sexuality/Textuality: A Study of the Fabric of Montaigne's Essais.* Columbus: Ohio State University Press, 1981.

Couchman, Jane, and Ann M. Crabb, eds. *Women's Letters Across Europe, 1400–1700: Form and Persuasion.* Aldershot: Ashgate, 2005.

Curtius, Ernst Robert. *European Literature and the Latin Middle Ages.* Trans. Willard R. Trask. New York: Bollingen, 1953.

Dagens, Jean. "Le 'Miroir des simples ames' et Marguerite de Navarre." In *La Mystique rhénane. Colloque de Strasbourg 16–19 mai 1961*, 281–89. Paris: Presses Universitaires de France, 1963.

Dalarun, Jacques. "Nouveaux aperçus sur Abélard, Héloïse et le Paraclet." *Francia* 32 (2005): 19–66.

Delaney, Sheila. "Mothers to Think Back Through: Who Are They? The Ambiguous Example of Christine de Pizan." In *The Selected Writings of Christine de Pizan*, eds. Renate Blumenfeld-Kosinksi and Kevin Brownlee, 312–28. New York: Norton, 1997.

Desan, Philippe, ed. *Dictionnaire de Michel de Montaigne.* Paris: Honoré Champion, 2004.

———. "La place de La Boétie dans les *Essais* ou l'espace problématique du chapitre 29." In *Montaigne dans tous ses états*, 37–68. Fasano: Schena 2001.

Descimon, Robert. "Guillaume Du Vair: Les enseignements d'une biographie sociale. La construction symbolique d'un grand home et l'échec d'un lignage." In *Guillaume Du Vair, Parlementaire et écrivain (1556–1621)*, eds. Bruno Petey-Girard and Alexandre Tarrête, 17–77. Geneva: Droz, 2005.

Desmond, Marilynn, ed. *Christine de Pizan and the Categories of Difference.* Minneapolis: University of Minnesota Press, 1998.

———. "Dominus/Ancilla: Epistolary Rhetoric and Erotic Violence in the Letters of Abelard and Heloise." In *Ovid's Art and the Wife of Bath: The Ethics of Erotic Violence*, 55–72. Ithaca: Cornell University Press, 2006.

———. "The *Querelle de la Rose* and the Ethics of Reading." In *Christine de Pizan: A Casebook*, eds. Barbara K. Altmann, Deborah C. McGrady, 167–80. New York: Routledge, 2003.

Dronke, Peter. *Abelard and Heloise in Medieval Testimonies*. Glasgow: The University of Glasgow Press, 1976.

———. "Francesca and Héloïse." *Comparative Literature* 27 (1975): 113–35.

———. "Heloise's Problemata and Letters: Some Questions of Form and Content." In *Petrus Abaelardus, 1079–1142. Person, Werk, und Wirkung*, eds. Rudolf Thomas et al., 59. Trier: Paulinus-Verlag, 1980.

———. *Medieval Latin and the Rise of European Love-Lyric*. 2 vols. Oxford: Clarendon Press, 1965.

———. *Poetic Individuality in the Middle Ages: New Departures in Poetry 1000–1150*. London: Committee for Medieval Studies, Westfield College, University of London, 1986.

———. *Women Writers of the Middle Ages: A Critical Study of Texts from Perpetua to Marguerite Porete*. Cambridge: Cambridge University Press, 1984.

Duval, Edwin. " 'Et puis, quelles nouvelles?': The Project of Marguerite's Unfinished Decameron." In *Critical Tales: New Studies of the "Heptaméron" and Early Modern Culture*, eds. John D. Lyons and Mary B. McKinley, 241–62. Philadelphia: University of Pennsylvania Press, 1993.

Elliott, Alison Goddard. "Ovid and the Critics." *Helios* 12 (1985): 9–20.

Elliott, Dyan. "Sex in Holy Places: An Exploration of a Medieval Anxiety." *Journal of Women's History* 6.3 (1994): 6–34.

Eynde, Damien van den. "Chronologie des écrits d'Abélard à Héloïse," *Antonianum* 37 (1962): 337–49.

Faulhaber, Charles. *Latin Rhetorical Theory in Thirteenth and Fourteenth Century Castile*. Berkeley and Los Angeles: University of California Press, 1972.

———. "Rhetoric in Medieval Catalonia: The Evidence of the Library Catalogs." In *Studies in Honor of Gustavo Correa*, eds. Charles B. Faulhaber, Richard P. Kinkade, T. Anthony Perry, 92–126. Potomac, MD: Scripta Humanistica, 1986.

Fenster, Thelma. " 'Perdre son latin:' Christine de Pizan and Vernacular Humanism." In *Christine de Pizan and the Categories of Difference*, ed. Marilynn Desmond, 91–107. Minneapolis: University of Minnesota Press, 1998.

Fenster, Thelma and Daniel Lord Smail, eds. *Fama: The Politics of Talk and Reputation in Medieval Europe*. Ithaca: Cornell University Press, 2003.

Ferguson, Gary. "Perfecting Friendship: Montaigne's Itch." *Montaigne Studies* 9 (1997): 105–20.

Ferguson, Margaret W., Maureen Quilligan, and Nancy J. Vickers, ed. *Rewriting the Renaissance: The Discourses of Sexual Difference in Early Modern Europe*. Chicago: University of Chicago Press, 1986.

Ferrante, Joan. *To The Glory of Her Sex: Women's Roles in the Composition of Medieval Texts*. Bloomington: Indiana University Press: 1997.

Fèvbre, Lucien. *Autour de l'Heptaméron. Amour sacré, amour profane*. Paris: Gallimard, 1944.

Finke, Laurie A. "The Politics of the Canon: Christine de Pizan and the Fifteenth-Century Chaucerians." *Exemplaria* 19.1 (Spring 2007): 16–38.

Fiske, Adele. "Alcuin and Mystical Friendship." *Studi Medievali* 3, serie 2 (1961): 551–75.

———. *Friends and Friendship in the Monastic Tradition*. Cuernavaca: Centro Intercultural de Documentacion, 1970.

———. "Paradisus homo amicus." *Speculum* 40 (1965): 436–59.

Fleming, John V. "The Moral Reputation of the *Roman de la Rose* before 1400." *Romance Philology* 18.4 (May 1965): 430–35.

Frame, Donald M. *Montaigne: A Biography*. New York: Harcourt, Brace & World, Inc, 1965.

Freccero, Carla. "Gender Ideologies, Women Writers, and the Problem of Patronage in Early Modern Italy and France: Issues and Frameworks." In *Reading the Renaissance: Culture, Poetics, and Drama*, ed. Jonathan Hart, 65–74. New York: Garland, 1996.

Fulkerson, Laurel. *The Ovidian Heroine as Author: Reading, Writing, and Community in the Heroides*. Cambridge: Cambridge University Press, 2005.

Georgianna, Linda. "Any Corner of Heaven: Heloise's Critique of Monasticism." *Mediaeval Studies* 49 (1987): 221–53.

Gilson, Etienne. *Héloise et Abélard*. Paris: Librairie Philosophique J. Vrin, 1997.

Goldsmith, Elizabeth C. *Writing the Female Voice: Essays on Epistolary Literature*. Boston, MA: Northeastern University Press, 1989.

Goldsmith, Elizabeth C., and Dena Goodman, eds. *Going Public: Women and Publishing in Early Modern France*. Ithaca: Cornell University Press, 1995.

Goodman, Dena. "Epistolary Property and the Plight of Letters on the Eve of the French Revolution." In *Early Modern Conceptions of Property: Consumption & Culture in the Seventeenth and Eighteenth Centuries*, eds. John Brewer, Susan Staves, 339–64. New York: Routledge, 1996.

Gottlieb, Beatrice. "The Problem of Feminism in the Fifteenth Century." In *Women of the Medieval World: Essays in Honor of John H. Mundy*, eds. Julius Kirschner and Suzanne F. Wemple, 337–64. London: Basil Blackwell, 1985.

Gray, Floyd. "The Women in Montaigne's Life: Autobiography and the Rhetoric of Misogyny." *Montaigne Studies* 8.1–2 (1996): 9–22.

Green, Karen. "Isabeau de Bavière and the Political Philosophy of Christine de Pizan." *Historical Reflections/Reflexions historiques*, 32.2 (2006): 247–72.

Greenblatt, Stephen. "1563, 18 August: Anti-Dictator, Montaigne Witnesses the Death of his Friend Etienne de La Boétie." In *A New History of French Literature*, ed. Denis Hollier, 223–28. Cambridge: Harvard University Press, 1989.

Griffiths, Fiona J. "The Cross and the *Cura monialium*: Robert of Arbrissel, John the Evangelist, and the Pastoral Care of Women in the Age of Reform." *Speculum* 83 (2008): 303–30.

———. " 'Men's Duty to Provide for Women's Needs': Abelard, Heloise, and their Negotiation of the *Cura Monialium*." *Journal of Medieval History*, 30 (2004): 1–24.

Guy, Henri. "Compte rendu de Marguerite, duchesse d'Alençon et Guillaume Briçonnet, évêque de Meaux, d'après leur correspondance manuscrite (1521–1524), par Ph.-Aug. Becker." *Annales du Midi* 14 (1902), 215.

Guynn, Noah D. *Allegory and Sexual Ethics in the High Middle Ages*. New York: Palgrave MacMillan, 2007.

Haskins, Charles Homer. "The Life of Mediaeval Students as Illustrated by Their Letters." In *Studies in Mediaeval Culture*, 1–35. Oxford: Oxford University Press, 1929.

———. *The Renaissance of the Twelfth Century*. Cambridge: Harvard University Press, 1927.

Heller, Henry. "The Briçonnet Case Reconsidered." *The Journal of Medieval and Renaissance Studies* 2.2 (Fall 1972): 223–58.

———. "The Evangelicism of Lefèvre d'Etaples: 1524." *Studies in the Renaissance* 19 (1972): 42–77.

———. "Marguerite of Navarre and the Reformers of Meaux." *Bibliothèque d'Humanisme et Renaissance* 33.2 (1972): 271–310.

Henderson, Judith Rice. "Valla's *Elegantiae* and the Humanist Attack on the *Ars dictaminis*," *Rhetorica* 19.2 (Spring 2001): 249–68.

Hexter, Ralph J. *Ovid and Medieval Schooling. Studies in Medieval School Commentaries on Ovid's Ars Amatoria, Epistulae ex Ponto, and Epistulae Heroidum*. Munich: Bei der Arbeo-Gelleschaft, 1986.

Hicks, Eric C. "The 'Querelle de la Rose' in the *Roman de la rose*." *Les Bonnes feuilles*, 3.2 (1974): 152–69.

Hindman, Sandra L. *Christine de Pizan's* Epistre Othéa*: Painting and Politics at the Court of Charles VI*. Toronto: Pontifical Institute of Medieval Studies, 1986.

————. "With Ink and Mortar: Christine de Pizan's *Cité des dames (An Art Essay)*." *Feminist Studies* 10.3 Fall (1984): 457–83.

Hirstein, James S. "La Boétie's Neo-Latin Satire." *Montaigne Studies: An Interdisciplinary Forum* 3.1–2 (1991): 48–67.

Hoffmann, George. *Montaigne's Career.* Oxford: Clarendon Press, 1999.

————. "Montaigne's Nudes: The Lost Tower Paintings Rediscovered." *Yale French Studies* 110 (Winter 2006): 122–33.

Holderness, Julia Simms. "Compilation, Commentary, and Conversation in Christine de Pizan." *Essays in Medieval Studies* 20 (2003): 47–55.

Holsinger, Bruce. *Music, Body, and Desire in Medieval Culture: Hildegard of Bingen to Chaucer.* Stanford, CA: Stanford University Press, 2001.

Holsinger, Bruce and David Townsend. "Ovidian Homoerotics in Twelfth-Century Paris: The Letters of Leoninus, Poet and Polyphone." *The GLQ Archive* 8:3 (2002): 389–423.

Hoven, René. *Lexique de la prose latine de la Renaissance.* Leiden: E.J. Brill, 1994.

Huizinga, Johan. *Homo Ludens: A Study of the Play-Element in Culture.* New York: Routledge, 1998 [1955, 1937].

Hult, David. *Self-Fulfilling Prophecies: Readership and Authority in the First* Roman de la Rose. Cambridge: Cambridge University Press, 1986.

————. "Words and Deeds: Jean de Meun's *Romance of the Rose* and the Hermeneutics of Censorship." *New Literary History: A Journal of Theory and Interpretation* 28.2 (Spring 1997): 345–66.

Hunt, Richard William. "The Introductions to the '*Artes*' in the Twelfth Century." In *Studia mediaevalia in honorem admodum Reverendi Patris Raymundi Josephi Martin*, 85–112. Bruges: De Tempel, 1948.

Huot, Sylvia. "Seduction and Sublimation: Christine de Pizan, Jean de Meun, and Dante." *Romance Notes*, 25.3 Spring (1985): 361–73.

Irvine, Martin. "Abelard and (Re)writing the Male Body." In *Becoming Male in the Middle Ages*, eds. Jerome Jeffrey Cohen, Bonnie Wheeler, 87–106. New York: Garland 2000 [1997].

————. "Heloise and the Gendering of the Literate Subject." In *Criticism and Dissent in the Middle Ages*, ed. Rita Copeland, 87–114. Cambridge and New York: Cambridge University Press, 1996.

Jaeger, C. Stephen. *Ennobling Love: In Search of a Lost Sensibility.* Philadelphia: University of Pennsylvania Press, 1999.

————. *Envy of Angels: Cathedral Schools and Social Ideals in Medieval Europe. 950–1200.* Philadelphia: University of Pennsylvania Press, 1994.

————. "*Epistolae duorum amantium* and the Ascription to Heloise and Abelard." In *Voices in Dialogue: Reading Women in the Middle Ages*, eds. Linda Olson and Kathryn Kerby-Fulton, 125–66. Notre Dame, IN: University of Notre Dame Press, 2005.

————. *The Origins of Courtliness: Civilizing Trends and the Formation of Courtly Ideals, 939–1210*. Philadelphia: University of Pennsylvania Press, 2000.

————. "A Reply to Giles Constable." In *Voices in Dialogue: Reading Women in the Middle Ages*, eds. Linda Olson and Kathryn Kerby-Fulton, 179–86. Notre Dame, IN: University of Notre Dame Press, 2005.

Janson, Tore. *Prose Rhythm in Medieval Latin from the Ninth to the Thirteenth Century*. Stockholm: Almquist and Wiksell International, 1975.

————. "Schools of Cursus in the Twelfth Century and the Letters of Abelard and Heloise." In *Retorica e poetica tra i secoli XII e XIV. Atti del secondi Convegno internazionale di studi dell'Associazione per il Medioevo e l'Umanesimo latini in onore e memoria di Ezio Francheschini, Trento e Rovereto 3–5 ottobre 1985*, eds. Claudio Leonardi and E. Menesto, 171–200. Florence: Centro per il Collegamento degli Studi Medievali e Umanestici nell'Università di Perugia, 1988.

Johnson, Penelope D. *Equal in Monastic Profession: Religious Women in Medieval France*. Chicago: University of Chicago Press, 1991.

Jourda, Pierre. *Marguerite d'Angoulême, Duchesse d'Alençon, Reine de Navarre (1492–1549). Étude Biographique et Littéraire*. 2 vols. Paris: Librairie Ancienne Honoré Champion, 1930.

————. *Repère analytique et chronologique de la Correspondance de Marguerite d'Angoulême Duchesse d'Alençon, Reine de Navarre (1492–1549)*. Paris: Champion, 1930.

————. "Sur la date du *Dialogue en forme de vision nocturne*." *Revue du seizième siècle* 16 (1927): 150–61.

Kamuf, Peggy. *Fictions of Feminine Desire: Disclosures of Heloise*. Lincoln and London: University of Nebraska Press, 1982.

————. "Writing Like A Woman." In *Women and Language in Literature and Society*, eds. Sally McConnell-Ginet, Ruth Borker, Nelly Furman, 284–99. New York: Praeger Publishers, 1980.

Kauffman, Linda. *Discourses of Desire: Gender, Genre, and Epistolary Fictions*. Ithaca: Cornell University Press, 1986.

Kay, Sarah. *Courtly Contradictions: The Emergence of the Literary Object in the Twelfth Century*. Stanford: Stanford University Press, 2001.

————. *The Place of Thought: The Complexity of One in Late Medieval French Didactic Poetry*. Philadelphia: University of Pennsylvania Press, 2007.

Kearney, Eileen. "Heloise: Inquiry and the *Sacra Pagina*." In *Ambiguous Realities: Women in the Middle Ages and Renaissance*, eds. Carole Levin and Jeanie Watson, 66–81. Detroit: Wayne State University Press, 1987.

————."*Scientia* and *Sapientia*: Reading Sacred Scripture at the Paraclete." In *From Cloister to Classroom, Monastic and Scholastic Approaches to*

Truth, ed. Rozanne P. Elder, 111–29. Kalamazoo, MI: Cistercian Publications, 1986.

Kelly, Joan. "Early Feminist Theory and the *Querelle des Femmes*, 1400–1789." *Signs* 8.1 (Autumn 1982): 4–28.

Kettering, Sharon. "The Patronage Power of Early Modern French Noblewomen." *The Historical Journal*, 32.4 (1989): 817–41.

Knowles, David. "The Renaissance of the Eleventh and Twelfth Centuries." In *The Evolution of Medieval Thought*, 71–149. New York: Vintage Books, 1962.

Kristeller, Paul Oskar. "Rhetoric in Medieval and Renaissance Culture." In *Renaissance Eloquence: Studies in the Theory and Practice of Renaissance Rhetoric*, ed. James J. Murphy, 1–19. Berkeley: University of California Press, 1983.

———. *Studies in Renaissance Thought and Letters*. Rome: Edizioni di Storia e Letteratura, 1956.

Kuefler, Mathew. "Male Friendship and the Suspicion of Sodomy in Twelfth-Century France." In *The Boswell Thesis: Essays on Christianity, Social Tolerance and Homosexuality*, 179–212. Chicago: University of Chicago Press, 2006.

Laennec, Christine Moneera. "Unladylike Polemics: Christine de Pizan's Strategies of Attack and Defense." *Tulsa Studies in Women's Literature* 12.1 Spring (1993): 47–53.

Laidlaw, James. "Christine de Pizan: The Making of the Queen's Manuscript (London, British Library, Harley 4431)." In *Patrons, Authors and Workshops: Books and Book Production in Paris around 1400*, eds. Godfried Croenen, Peter Ainsworth, 297–310. Louvain and Dudley, MA: Peeters, 2006.

Lajarte, Philippe de. "Autour d'un paradoxe: les nouvelles de Marguerite de Navarre et sa correspondance avec Briçonnet." In *Marguerite de Navarre 1492–1992. Actes du Colloque internationale de Pau (1992)*, eds. Nicole Cazauran, James Dauphiné, 565–634. Mont-de-Marsan: Éditions Inter-Universitaires, 1995.

Lanham, Carol Dana. *Salutatio Formulas in Latin Letters to 1200: Syntax, Style, and Theory*. Münchener Beiträge zur Mediävistik und Renaissance-Forschung 22. Munich: Bei der Arbeo-Gesellschaft, 1975.

Larsen, Anne R. and Colette H. Winn, eds. *Renaissance Women Writers: French Texts/American Contexts*. Detroit: Wayne State University Press, 1994.

Le Duc, Alma. "Gontier Col and the French Pre-Renaissance." *Romanic Review* 7.4 (Oct.–Dec. 1916): 414–57; 8.2 (April–June 1917): 145–65; 8.3 (July–Sept. 1917): 290–306.

LeBlanc, Yvonne. *Va Lettre Va: The French Verse Epistle (1400–1550)*. Birmingham: Summa Publications, 1995.

Leclercq, Jean. "L'Amitié dans les lettres au moyen âge, autour d'un manuscrit de la bibliothèque de Pétrarque." *Revue du moyen âge latin* 1 (1945): 391–410.

———. "Le genre épistolaire au moyen âge." *Revue du moyen âge latin* 2 (1946): 63–70.

———. *The Love of Learning and the Desire for God, A Study of Monastic Culture*. Trans. Catharine Misrahi. New York: Fordham University Press, 1982 [1961].

———. "Modern Psychology and the Interpretation of Medieval Texts." *Speculum* (1973): 476–90.

———. *Monks and Love in Twelfth-Century France. Psycho-Historical Essays*. Oxford: Oxford University Press, 1979.

Lefèvre, Sylvie. "Longue demouree fait changier ami. De la lettre close à la lyrique dans le *Voir Dit* de Guillaume de Machaut." *Romania* 120.1–2 (2002): 226–34.

Lestringant, Frank. "Introduction: V.L. Saulnier lecteur des lettres de Guillaume Budé et de Marguerite de Navarre." In *L'épistolaire au XVIe siècle, Cahiers V.L. Saulnier, 18*, 9–14. Paris: Éditions rue d'Ulm/Presses de l'École Normale Supérieure, 2001.

Losse, Deborah N. *Sampling the Book: Renaissance Prologues and the French Conteurs*. Cranbury, NJ: Associated University Presses, 1994.

Louis, René and Jean Jolivet, eds. *Pierre Abélard Pierre le Vénérable: les courants philosophiques, littéraires et artistiques en occident au milieu de XIIe siècle*. Paris: Éditions du Centre National de la Recherche Scientifique, 1972.

Luscombe, David. "From Paris to the Paraclete: The Correspondence of Abelard and Heloise." *Proceedings of the British Academy* 74 (1988): 247–83.

Lyons, John D. "The 'Cueur' in the *Heptaméron*: The Ideology of Concealment." In *Les visages et les voix de Marguerite de Navarre: Actes du colloque international sur Marguerite de Navarre 10–11 avril 1992*, ed. Marcel Tetel, 107–21. Paris: Lincksieck, 1995.

Makowski, Elizabeth. "The Conjugal Debt and Medieval Canon Law." In *Equally in God's Image: Women in the Middle Ages*, eds. Julia Bolton Holloway, Constance S. Wright, Joan Bechtold, 129–43. New York: Peter Lang, 1990.

Marenbon, John. "Authenticity Revisited." In *Listening to Heloise: The Voice of a Twelfth-Century Woman*, ed. Bonnie Wheeler, 19–33. New York: St. Martin's Press, 2000.

Margolis, Nadia. " 'The Cry of the Chameleon': Evolving Voices in the Epistles of Christine de Pizan." In *Disputatio: An International Transdisicplinary Journal of the Late Middle Ages, Vol. I: The Late Medieval*

Epistle, eds. Carol and Richard Utz, 37–70. Evanston, IL: Northwestern University Press, 1996.

Martineau, Christine. "Le platonisme de Marguerite de Navarre." *Revue d'Humanisme et Renaissance,* 4 (1976): 12–35.

Martineau, Christine and Christian Grouselle. "La source première et directe du *Dialogue en forme de vision nocturne:* La lettre de Guillaume Briçonnet à Marguerite de Navarre, du 15 septembre 1524." *Bibliothèque d'Humanisme et Renaissance* 32.3 (1970): 559–77.

McGuire, Brian Patrick. "Heloise and the Consolation of Friendship." In *Listening to the Voice of Heloise: The Voice of a Twelfth-Century Woman,* ed. Bonnie T. Wheeler, 303–21. New York: St. Martin's Press, 2000.

McLaughlin, Mary. "Abelard as Autobiographer: The Motives and Meaning of his *Story of Calamities.*" *Speculum* 42 (1967): 463–88.

———. "Heloise the Abbess: The Expansion of the Paraclete." In *Listening to Heloise: The Voice of a Twelfth-Century Woman,* ed. Bonnie Wheeler, 1–17. New York: St. Martin's Press, 2000.

McLeod, Enid. "The Debate on the *Roman de la Rose.*" In *The Order of the Rose: The Life and Ideas of Christine de Pizan,* ed. McLeod, 62–72. London: Chatto & Windus, 1976.

McLeod, Glenda. "A Case of Faulx Semblans: *L'Epistre au Dieu d'Amours* and *The Letter of Cupid.*" In *The Reception of Christine de Pizan From the Fifteenth Through the Nineteenth Centuries: Visitors to the City,* ed. Glenda K. McLeod, 11–24. Lewiston, NY: The Edwin Mellen Press, 1991.

———. " 'Wholly Guilty, Wholly Innocent': Heloise to Abelard." In *Dear Sister: Medieval Women and the Epistolary Genre,* eds. Karen Cherewatuk and Ulrike Wiethaus, 64–86. Philadelphia: University of Pennsylvania Press, 1993.

McNamer, Elizabeth Mary. *The Education of Heloise: Methods, Content, and Purpose of Learning in the Twelfth-Century.* Lewiston, NY: The Edward Mellen Press, 1990.

McWebb, Christine, ed. *Debating the* Roman de la Rose*: A Critical Anthology.* New York: Routledge, 2007.

Mehlman, Jeffrey. "La Boétie's Montaigne." *Oxford Literary Review* 4.1 (1979): 45–61.

Mellinghoff-Bourgerie, Viviane. "L'Échange épistolaire entre Marguerite d'Angoulême et Guillaume Briçonnet: discours mystiques ou direction spirituelle?" In *Marguerite de Navarre: 1492–1992. Actes du Colloque international de Pau (1992),* eds. Nicole Cazauran et James Dauphiné, 137–57. Mont-de-Marsan: Éditions InterUniversitaires, 1995.

Mews, Constant J. *Abelard and Heloise.* Oxford: Oxford University Press: 2005.

———. "Hugh Metel, Heloise, and Peter Abelard: The Letters of an Augustinian Canon and the Challenge of Innovation in Twelfth-Century Lorraine." *Viator* 32 (2001): 59–91.

———. "The Latin Learning of Christine de Pizan in the *Livre de Paix*." In *Healing the Body Politic: The Political Thought of Christine de Pizan*, eds. Karen Green and Constant J. Mews, 61–80. Turnhout: Brepols, 2005.

———. *The Lost Love Letters of Heloise and Abelard: Perceptions of Dialogue in Twelfth-Century France*. Translation by Neville Chiavaroli and Constant J. Mews. New York: St. Martin's Press 1999, Palgrave 2001.

Middlebrook, Leah. " 'Tout mon office:' Body Politics and Family Dynamics in the Verse Epîtres of Marguerite de Navarre." *Renaissance Quarterly* 54 (2001): 1108–41.

Miller, Joseph M., Michael H. Prosser, Thomas W. Benson, eds. *Readings in Medieval Rhetoric*. Bloomington: Indiana University Press, 1973.

Minnis, A.J., and A.B. Scott, ed., with the assistance of David Wallace. *Medieval Literary Theory and Criticism, c.1100–c.1375: The Commentary-Tradition*. Oxford: Clarendon Press, 1988.

———. *Medieval Theory of Authorship: Scholastic Literary Attitudes in the Later Middle Ages*. Philadelphia: University of Pennsylvania Press, 1988.

Mistry, Rohinton. *Family Matters*. New York: Alfred A. Knopf, 2002.

Moos, Peter von. *Consolatio: Studien zur mittellateinischen Trostliteratur über dem Tod und zum Problem der Christlichen Trauer*. Münstersche Mittelalter-Schriften 3, 4 vols. Munich 1971–1972.

———. "Die *Epistolae duorum amantium* und die 'säkulare Religion der Liebe': Methodenkritische Vorüberlegungen zu einem einmaligen Werk mittellateinischer Briefliteratur." *Studi Medievali* 44 (2003): 1–115.

Morris, Colin. *The Discovery of the Individual 1050–1200*. London, S.P.C.K. for the Church Historical Society, 1972.

Murphy, James J. *Medieval Rhetoric: A Select Bibliography*. 2nd ed. Toronto: University of Toronto Press, 1989.

———. *Rhetoric in the Middle Ages: A History of the Rhetorical Theory from Saint Augustine to the Renaissance*. University of California Press, 1974; repr. Arizona Center for Medieval and Renaissance Studies, 2001.

Murphy, James J., ed. *Three Medieval Rhetorical Arts*. University of California Press, 1971; repr. Arizona Center for Medieval and Renaissance Studies, 2001.

Murray, Jacqueline. "Sexual Mutilation and Castration Anxiety: A Medieval Perspective." In *The Boswell Thesis: Essays on Christianity, Social Tolerance, and Homosexuality*, ed. Mathew Kuefler, 254–72. Chicago: University of Chicago Press, 2005.

Nauert, Charles G. "Humanism as Method: Roots of Conflict with the Scholastics." *Sixteenth Century Journal*, 29.2 (1998): 427–38.

————. "Marguerite, Lefèvre d'Etaples, and the Growth of Christian Humanism in France." In *Approaches to Teaching Marguerite de Navarre's* Heptaméron, ed. Colette H. Winn, 38–43. New York: MLA, 2007.

Newman, Barbara. "Authority, Authenticity, and the Repression of Heloise." *From Virile Woman to WomanChrist: Studies in Medieval Religion and Literature*, 46–75. Philadelphia: University of Pennsylvania Press, 1995.

————. Rev. of *The Love Letters of Heloise and Abelard: Perceptions of Dialogue*, by Constant J. Mews. *The Medieval Review*. 6 Jan. 2000 <http://hdl.handle.net/2027/spo.baj9928.0001.006>

Nitze, William A. "The So-Called Twelfth Century Renaissance." *Speculum* 23.3 (July 1948) 464–71.

Nouvet, Claire. "The Discourse of the 'Whore': An Economy of Sacrifice." *Modern Language Notes* 105.4 (1990): 750–73.

Obermeier, Anita. *The History and Anatomy of Auctorial Self-Criticism in the European Middle Ages*. Amsterdam: Rodopi, 1999.

Olson, Glending. "The Profits of Pleasure." In *Cambridge History of Literary Criticism: The Middle Ages*, eds. Alastair J. Minnis and Ian Johnson, 275–87. Cambridge and New York: Cambridge University Press, 2005.

Otter, Monika. "Baudri of Bourgueil, 'To Countess Adela.' " *Journal of Medieval Latin*, 11 (2001): 60–142.

————. "Entrances and Exits: Performing the Psalms in Goselin's *Liber confortarius*." *Speculum* 83.2 (April 2008): 283–302.

Paré, François. "L'écrit théologique féminin au XVIe siècle: la correspondance Marguerite Angoulême/Guillaume Briçonnet." *Atlantis* 19.1 (Fall–Winter/Autômne–Hiver 1993): 47–52.

Paris, Gaston. *La Littérature française au moyen âge* (XIe–XIVe siècle). Paris: Hachette, 1909.

Partner, Nancy. "No Sex, No Gender." *Studying Medieval Women: Sex, Gender, Feminism. Speculum* (1993): 117–41.

Parussa, Gabrielle. "Le concept d'intertextualité comme hypothèse interpretative d'une œuvre." *Studi Francesi* 110 (1993): 471–93.

Pasquier, Henri. *Un poète latin du XIème siècle: Baudri, Abbé de Bourgueil, Archevêque de Dol, 1046–1130*. Paris: E. Thorin, 1878.

Patt, William. "The Early 'Ars Dictaminis' as Response to a Changing Society." *Viator* 9 (1978): 133–55.

Payen, Jean Charles. "La 'mise en roman' du mariage." In *Love and Marriage in the Twelfth Century*, eds. Willy Van Hoecke and Andrès Welkenhuysen, 219–35. Leuven: Leuven University Press 1981.

Perouse, Gabriel-André. "De Montaigne à Boccace et de Boccace à Montaigne." In *La nouvelle française à la Renaissance*, ed. Lionello Sozzi, 13–40, Geneva: Slatkine, 1981, cited in Deborah N. Losse,

Sampling the Book: Renaissance Prologues and the French Conteurs, Cranbury, NJ: Associated University Press, 1994.

Petigny, J. de. "Lettre Inédite de Robert d'Arbrissel à la comtesse Ermengarde." *Bibliothèque de l'Ecole des Chartes* 15 (1853–34), 209–35.

Phillippy, Patricia A. "Establishing Authority: Boccacio's *De Claris Mulieribus* and Christine de Pizan's *Le Livre de la cité des dames.*" *Romanic Review* 77.3 May (1986): 167–94.

Piaget, Arthur. *Martin Le Franc, prévot de Lausanne.* Lausanne: Payot, 1888.

Polachek, Dora E., and Marcel Tetel, eds. "Woman's Place: Within and Without the *Essais.*" *Montaigne Studies* 8.1–2, 1–2, 1996.

Polak, Emil J. *Medieval and Renaissance Letter Treatises and Form Letters: A Census of Manuscripts Found in Eastern Europe and the Former USSR.* Leiden: Brill, 1993.

Poster, Carol, and Linda Mitchell. *Letter-Writing Manuals and Instruction From Antiquity to the Present.* Columbia, SC: The University of South Carolina Press, 2007.

Poster, Carol and Richard Utz. "A Bibliography of Medieval Latin Dicamen." In *Letter-Writing Manuals and Instruction from Antiquity to the Present,* eds. Carol Poster and Linda C Mitchell, 285–300. Columbia, SC: The University of South Carolina Press, 2007.

Potansky, Peter. *Der Streit um den Rosenroman. Münchener Romanistische Arbeiten 33.* Munich: Fink, 1972.

Quilligan, Maureen. *The Allegory of Female Authority. Christine de Pizan's* Cité des Dames. Ithaca: Cornell University Press, 1991.

Raby, F.J.E. *A History of Christian-Latin Poetry from the Beginnings to the Close of the Middle Ages.* Oxford: Clarendon Press, 1953 [1927].

———. *A History of Secular Latin Poetry.* 2 vols. Oxford: Clarendon Press, 1934.

Reeser, Todd W. *Moderating Masculinity in Early Modern Culture.* Chapel Hill: University of North Carolina Press, 2006.

Richards, Earl Jeffrey. "Christine de Pizan and Jean Gerson: An Intellectual Friendship." In *Christine de Pizan 2000: Studies on Christine de Pizan in Honor of Angus J. Kennedy,* eds. John Campbell, Nadia Margolis, 197–208. Amsterdam: Rodopi, 2000.

———. *Christine de Pizan and Medieval French Lyric.* Gainesville: University Press of Florida, 1998.

———. *"Seulette a part* – The 'Little Woman on the Sidelines' Takes Up Her Pen: The Letters of Christine de Pizan." In *Dear Sister: Medieval Women and the Epistolary Genre,* eds. Karen Cherewatuk, Ulrike Wiethaus, 139–70. Philadelphia: University of Pennsylvania Press, 1993.

Richardson, Malcolm. "The *Ars dictaminis,* the Formulary, and Medieval Practice." In *Letter-Writing Manuals and Instruction From Antiquity to the Present*, eds. Carol Poster and Linda Mitchell, 56–8. Columbia, SC: The University of South Carolina Press, 2007.

Rigolot, François. "Montaigne's Purloined Letters." *Yale French Studies* 64 (1983): 145–66.

Ritter, Raymond. *Cette grande Corisande*. Paris: Editions Albin Michel, 1942.

Rockinger, Ludwig, ed. *Briefsteller und Formelbücher des eilften bis vierzehnten Jahrhunderts*. Quellen und Erorterungen zur bayerischen und deutschen Geschichte 9. Munich: G. Franz, 1863; repr. New York: Burt Franklin, 1961.

Roelker, Nancy Lyman. *Queen of Navarre, Jeanne d'Albret 1528–1572*. Cambridge: Harvard University Press, 1968.

Rouse, Richard H. and Mary A. "The Vocabulary of Wax Tablets." In *Vocabulaire du livre et de l'écriture au moyen âge, Actes de la table ronde Paris 24–26 septembre 1987*, ed. Olga Weijers, 220–30. Turnhout: Brepols, 1989.

Ruys, Juanita Feros. " 'Ut Sexu Sic Animo:' The Resolution of Sex and Gender in the *Planctus* of Abelard." *Medium Aevum* 75.1 (2006): 1–17.

Sankovitch. Tilde. "The French Woman Writer in the Middle Ages: Staying Up Late." *Essays in Medieval Studies* 7 (1990): 1–12.

Saulnier, Verdun L. "Marguerite de Navarre aux temps de Briçonnet. Étude de la correspondance générale (1521–1522). *Bibliothèque d'Humanisme et Renaissance*, 39.3 (1977): 437–78; 40.1 (1978): 4–47; 40.2 (1978): 193–237.

Schachter, Marc. " 'That Friendship Which Possesses the Soul': Montaigne Loves La Boétie." *Journal of Homosexuality* 41.3–4 (2001): 5–21.

Schaeffer, Peter. "Humanism on Display: The Epistles Dedicatory of Georg von Logau." *The Sixteenth Century Journal* 17.2 (Summer 1986): 215–23.

Sedgewick, Eve Kosovsky. *Between Men: English Literature and Male Homosocial Desire*. New York: Columbia University Press, 1985.

Shanzer, Danuta. "Some Treatments of Sexual Scandal in (Primarily) Later Latin Epistolography." In *In Pursuit of Wissenschaft: Festschrift für William M. Calder III zum 75 Geburtstag*, eds. S. Heilen, R. Kirstein, et al., 393–414. Spudasmata vol. 119, Hildesheim: Olms, 2008.

Simonin, Michel. "Les papiers de La Boétie, Thomas de Montaigne et l'édition de la chorographie du Médoc." In *L'Encre et la Lumière*, 457–88. Geneva: Droz, 2004.

Smail, Daniel Lord. *The Consumption of Justice: Emotions, Publicity, and Legal Culture in Marseille 1264–1423*. Ithaca: Cornell University Press, 2003.

Smarr, Janet Levarie. *Joining the Conversation: Dialogues by Renaissance Women*. Ann Arbor: University of Michigan Press, 2005.

Smith, Malcolm C. "Early French Advocates of Religious Freedom." *Sixteenth Century Journal* 25.1 (Spring 1994): 29–51.

Solterer, Helen. *The Master and Minerva: Disputing Women in French Medieval Culture*. Berkeley and Los Angeles: University of California Press, 1995.

Sommers, Paula, "Marguerite de Navarre as Reader of Christine de Pizan." In *The Reception of Christine de Pizan from the Fifteenth through the Nineteenth Centuries*, ed. Glenda McLeod, 71–82. Lewiston, NY: Edward Mellen Press, 1991.

Southern, Richard William. *Medieval Humanism and Other Studies*. Oxford: Basil Blackwell, 1970.

Steedman, Carolyn. "A Woman Writing A Letter." In *Epistolary Selves: Letters and Letter Writers, 1600–1945*, ed. Rebecca Earle, 111–33. Aldershot: Ashgate, 1999.

Stehling, Thomas. "To Love a Medieval Boy." *Journal of Homosexuality* 8 (1983): 151–70.

Stephenson, Barbara. *The Power and Patronage of Marguerite de Navarre*. Aldershot: Ashgate: 2004.

Stevenson, Jane. "Women and Latin Verse in the High Middle Ages." In *Women Latin Poets: Language, Gender and Authority from Antiquity to the Eighteenth Century*, 108–38. Oxford: Oxford University Press, 2005.

Stone, Donald. "Women and Friendship." *Montaigne Studies* 8.1–2 (1996): 23–34.

Sullivan, Karen. "At the Limit of Feminist Theory: An Architechtonics of the Querelle de la Rose." *Exemplaria* 3.2 (October 1991): 435–66.

Swanson, R.A. *The Twelfth Century Renaissance*. Manchester, UK: Manchester University Press, 1999.

Swift, Helen. *Gender, Writing, and Performance: Men Defending Women in Late Medieval France (1440–1538)*. Oxford: Oxford University Press, 2008.

Symes, Carol. *A Common Stage: Theater and Public Life in Medieval Arras*. Ithaca: Cornell University Press, 2007.

Thyssell, Carol. "Gender and Genre: Marguerite de Navarre and the Tradition of Allegorical Rhetoric." In *The Pleasure of Discernment: Marguerite de Navarre as Theologian*, 3–18. Oxford: Oxford University Press, 2000.

Tilliette, Jean-Yves. "Culture classique et humanisme monastique: les poèmes de Baudri de Bourgueil." In *La Littérature angevine médiévale, Actes du Colloque du samedi 22 mars 1980*, 77–88. Maulévrier: Hérault, 1981.

———. "Hermès amoureux, ou les métamorphoses de la chimère, réflexions sur les *Carmina* 200 et 201 de Baudri de Bourgueil." *Mélanges de l'école française de Rome: Moyen Age* 104.1 (1992): 121–61.

————. "Note sur le manuscrit des poèmes de Baudri de Bourgueil." *Scriptorium* 37.2 (1983): 241–45.

————. "Une lettre inédite sur le mépris du monde et la componction du cœur adressée par Baudri de Bourgueil à Pièrre de Jumièges." *Révue des Études Augustiniennes* 28.3–4 (1982): 257–79.

Tour, Pierre Imbart de la. *Les Origines de la Réforme*, Vol. 2. Geneva: Slatkine Reprints, 1978.

Tournon, André. "Notre liberté volontaire: le *Contre Un* en marge des *Essais.*" *Europe* 68: 729–30 (1990), 72–82.

Vaillé, Eugène. *Histoire générale des postes françaises*. Paris: Presses Universitaires de France, 1947, 6 vols.

Van Houdt, Toon, Jan Papy, Gilbert Tournoy and Constant Matheeussen, eds. *Self-Presentation and Social Identification: The Rhetoric and Pragmatics of Letter Writing in Early Modern Times*. Supplementa Humanistica Lovaniensia, 18. Leuven: Leuven University Press, 2002.

Van Vleck, Amelia. *Memory and Re-Creation in Troubadour Lyric*. Berkeley: University of California Press, 1991.

Vance, Eugene. *Mervelous Signals: Poetics and Sign Theory in the Middle Ages*. Lincoln, NE: University of Nebraska Press: 1986.

Vance, Jacob. "Humanist Polemics, Christian Morals: A Hypothesis on Marguerite de Navarre's *Heptaméron* and the Problem of Self-Love." *Modern Language Notes* 120 Supplement (2005): S181–95.

Veissière, Michel. "En echo à 'Marguerite de Navarre aux temps de Briçonnet.' " In *Mélanges sur la littérature de la renaissance à la mémoire de V.-L. Saulnier*, 189–95. Geneva: Droz, 1984.

Vulliez, Charles. "L'*ars dictaminis*, survivances et déclin, dans la moitié nord de l'espace français dans le Moyen Age tardif (mil. XIIIe–mil. XVe siecles)." *Rhetorica* 19.2 (Spring 2001): 141–53.

Wagenvoort, Hendrik. "Ludus Poeticus." In *Studies in Roman Literature, Culture and Religion*, 30–42. Leiden: E.J. Brill, 1956.

Ward, John O. "Rhetorical Theory and the Rise and Decline of *Dictamen* in the Middle Ages and Early Renaissance." *Rhetorica* 19.2 (Spring 2001): 175–223.

Ward, John O. and Neville Chiavaroli. "The Young Heloise and Latin Rhetoric: Some Preliminary Comments on the 'Lost' Love Letters and their Significance." In *Listening to the Voice of Heloise: The Voice of a Twelfth-Century Woman*, ed. Bonnie Wheeler, 53–119. New York: St. Martin's Press, 2000.

Wheeler, Bonnie. "Origenary Fantasies: Abelard's Castration and Confession." In *Becoming Male in the Middle Ages*, eds. Jerome Jeffrey Cohen, Bonnie Wheeler, 107–28. New York: Garland 2000 [1997].

Wiesen, David S. *Saint Jerome as a Satirist: A Study in Christian Latin Thought and Letters*. New York: Cornell University Press, 1964.

Willard, Charity Cannon. "An Autograph Manuscript of Christine de Pizan?" *Studi francesi* 27 (settembre-dicembre 1965): 452–57.

———. *Christine de Pizan: Her Life and Works.* New York: Persea, 1984.

———. "The Manuscript Tradition of the *Livre des trois vertus* and Christine de Pizan's Audience." *Journal of the History of Ideas*, 27.3 July-Sept. (1966): 433–44.

———. "A New Look at Christine de Pizan's *Epistre au dieu d'amours.*" In *Seconda miscellanea di studi e ricerche sul quattrocento francese*, eds. Jonathan Beck, Franco Simone, Gianni Mombello, 73–92. Chambéry: Centre d'Etudes Franco-Italien, 1981.

Witt, Ronald G. "The Arts of Letter-Writing." In *The Cambridge History of Literary Criticism*, eds. Alastair Minnis, Ian Johnson, 68–83. Vol. 2, The Middle Ages. Cambridge: Cambridge University Press, 2005.

Wolff, Étienne. *La lettre d'amour au Moyen Age.* Paris: NiL éditions, 1996.

Woodcock, E.C. *A New Latin Syntax.* Oak Park, IL: Bolchazy-Carducci Publishers, 1987 [1959].

Wright, Constance S. " 'Vehementer Amo': The Amorous Verse Epistles of Baudry of Bourgueil and Constance of Angers." In *The Influence of the Classical World on Medieval Literature, Architecture, Music and Culture. A Collection of Interdisciplinary Studies*, ed. Fidel Fajardo-Acosta, 154–66. Lewiston, NY: The Edward Mellen Press, 1992.

Yenal, Edith. *Christine de Pizan: A Bibliography.* 2nd ed. Methuen, New Jersey: The Scarecrow Press, 1989.

Ziolkowski, Jan. *Letters of Peter Abelard: Beyond the Personal.* Washington, D.C.: Catholic University of America Press, 2008.

———. "Lost and Not Yet Found: Heloise, Abelard, and the *Epistolae duorum amantium.*" *Journal of Medieval Latin* 14 (2004): 171–202.

Index

Already Published